FEARS AND SYMBOLS

Northwest Vista College
Learning Resource Center
3535 North Ellison Drive
San Antonio, Texas 78251

FEARS AND SYMBOLS

An Introduction to the Study of Western Civilization

by

Elemér Hankiss

Central European University Press
Budapest

First published in Hungarian as „Az emberi kaland" by Helikon Kiadó, Budapest in 1999

English edition published in 2001 by

Central European University Press

An imprint of the
Central European University Share Company

Nádor utca 11
H-1015 Budapest
Hungary

400 West 59th Street
New York NY 10019
USA

©2001 by Elemér Hankiss

Distributed in the United Kingdom and Western Europe by
Plymbridge Distributors Ltd., Estover Road,
Plymouth PL6 7PZ, United Kingdom

All rights reserved. No part of this publication may be reproduced, stored in a retrieval system, or transmitted, in any form or by any means, without the permission of the Publisher.

ISBN 963 9241 06 7 Cloth
ISBN 963 9241 07 5 PB

Library of Congress Cataloging in Publication Data
A CIP catalog record for this book is available upon request

*Printed in Hungary by
Akadémiai Nyomda, Martonvásár*

To Lili

CONTENTS

Acknowledgements	xv
INTRODUCTION	1
Note	4
Chapter One. **FEAR AND THE SOCIAL SCIENCES**	5
Fear	5
The Paradox of Fear	6
Sociology	8
The Devil in the Indexes	8
Durkheim	10
Weber	11
Parsons	12
'Situational' versus 'Existential' Fear	15
Anthropology	16
Theories of Culture	16
The Genesis of Culture	19
'Existential Problems'	24
Psychology	26
About Indexes Again	26

Experimental Psychology	28
Civilization and Fear	29
Terror Management Theory	32
Fear and Civilization	34
Notes	37

Chapter Two. THE WORLD OF SYMBOLS — 47

Strategies	47
The Promethean Strategy	47
The Apollonian Strategy	48
301,665,722 Angels	50
Symbols, Myths, Civilizations	53
'The Symbolic Animal'	54
Defense Mechanisms	55
'The Premature Animal'	57
The Angel of Death	58
The Social Enterprise of World Building	60
Collapse and Regeneration	61
The Copernican Shock	61
Freedom and Anxiety	63
The Loss of Symbols	64
Notes	66

Chapter Three. AN ALIEN WORLD? — 69

The World	69
And What about Us, Sir?	69
Is This Our World?	71
Incompatibilities	73
Killing Fields	76
Human Beings	77
Dead-Ends	77
Will Butterflies Survive Us?	78
Do We Need Space Suits in New York or Rome?	79
Pain and Suffering	80

The Four Jungles	81
The Physical Jungle	82
The Social Jungle	82
The Jungle in Our Souls	83
The Metaphysical Jungle	84
The Experience of the Alien World	85
Notes	87
Chapter Four. THE GARDEN OF EDEN	**91**
The Myth of the Center	91
On the Periphery	91
A Revolution in Reverse	93
Where Is the Center, If There Is One?	94
God or Satan?	95
Consecration	96
Paradise	98
The Fortress of Innocence	99
Sacred Mountains	100
From the Garden to the City	101
The Cross of Christ and the Skull of Adam	102
The Garden	103
The Enchanted Garden	105
Notes	108
Chapter Five. THE IMAGE OF THE WORLD	**113**
The House	113
Imago mundi	114
The City	116
The City and the Wilderness	116
The City and Its Archetypes	117
The Temple and the Cathedral	119
The Gate of Hell	119
The Gate of Heaven	121
Arabesque	123
Light	124

Chaos and Cosmos Today	124
The World of Light and Shadow	124
The Automobile	125
The Shopping Mall	127
Transcendental Carnival	129
The Realm of the Devil	131
The Negative Myth	132
Notes	134
Chapter Six. THE MORAL UNIVERSE	**137**
Amulets and Sacraments	137
Exorcism	138
Defilement and Purification	138
Rationalization	140
The Origins of Evil	140
Pandora's Box	140
Evil in the Bible	142
Evil Does Not Exist	143
Satan	146
Evil Condensed	147
God's Devil	149
The Apocalypse	150
The Transformation of Evil	151
The Moral Universe	151
Why Have We Forgotten the Victims?	152
Notes	154
Chapter Seven. THE WORLD OF GUILT	**157**
Guilt	157
The Great Reversal	157
The Price of Guilt	159
The Religion of Guilt	161
The Machinery of Guilt	161
'A Pilgrim on Earth'	162

The Philosophy of Guilt	164
Guilt and the Human Condition	164
The Politics of Guilt	165
Show Trials	166
Stigma	166
Hidden Values	167
Double Bind	169
A Negative Social Contract	169
The Psychology of Guilt	171
Freud and Human Unhappiness	171
Eros and Ananké	172
Eros and Thanatos	173
The 'Boiling Cauldron' of Guilt	175
'Guilt without Culture'	176
An Innocent Society?	177
Notes	179
Chapter Eight. THE RATIONAL WORLD	181
Two Faces of Rationality	181
War and Celestial Harmony	181
Prometheus versus Apollo	183
Reason and Meaning	185
The Loss of Meaning	185
'The Kingdom and the Darkness'	187
The Meaning of Life	189
Reason and Morality	192
Reason and Uncertainty	195
Discovery or Invention?	195
'The Wisdom of Uncertainty'	198
'The World Does Not Speak'	199
Notes	201

Chapter Nine. THE WORLD OF BEAUTY — 205

- Art — 205
  - Music — 205
  - Horror and Beauty — 207
- Tragedy — 209
  - Why Did Oedipus Blind Himself? — 209
  - Romeo and Juliet and the Happy Ending — 211
  - Desdemona's Handkerchief — 212
  - Catharsis — 213
- Notes — 216

Chapter Ten. THE WORLD OF PLAY — 219

- Homo ludens — 219
  - In a Strange Land — 219
  - 'Under the Sign of Play' — 220
  - Not All Is Play — 221
  - 'Don't Kiss the Engine, Daddy…' — 222
  - A World of Innocence — 224
  - Chance and Cherries — 225
  - The Paradox of Freedom — 227
- Soccer — 228
  - Sacred Rules — 228
  - The Ball — 229
  - Dionysus versus Apollo — 230
  - American Football — 232
- Play as World Symbol — 233
  - The Cosmic Ball Game — 233
  - God at Play — 233
  - Creation through Play — 235
  - The Loss of Play — 237
  - Frivolity and Ecstasy — 239
- Appendix — 240
- Notes — 242

Chapter Eleven. THE WORLD OF JOKES	245
Jokes and Laughter	245
Did Moses or Christ Ever Laugh?	245
Are Jokes Trivial?	246
Freud and Jokes	248
The Comic Destruction of Reality	250
The Destruction of Logic	251
The Destruction of Causality	253
A Clown's Leap into Freedom	255
Flirting with the Alien World	256
Laughter and Terror	258
Notes	259
Chapter Twelve. THE WORLD OF TRIVIALITIES	261
Perfumes and the Holy Grail	261
Creation and Plenitude	263
Icarian Symbolism	264
Transcendence	264
Spirituality and Sensuality	265
Sensuality and Love	266
Escape from Time and Mortality	267
Escape from Everyday Life	268
The Epiphany of Personality	269
Delusion or Creation?	270
Notes	271
Chapter Thirteen. SYMBOLS AND CIVILIZATION	275
Can Symbols Protect Us?	276
Constructs	277
Civilization: A Brilliant Construct?	279
Notes	281
BIBLIOGRAPHY	283
INDEX	299

ACKNOWLEDGEMENTS

I would like to express my sincere gratitude first of all to three institutions: the Center for Advanced Study in the Behavioral Sciences at Stanford; the Institute for Human Sciences in Vienna; and the Center for German and European Studies at Georgetown University. I doubt that I could have found a more hospitable and congenial environment for this work anywhere else. I am particularly grateful to Neil J. Smelser and Robert A. Scott, director and associate director of the Center in Stanford, to Krysztof Michalski, director of the Institute in Vienna, and to Samuel Barnes, director of the Center at Georgetown. Without their help and advice I could never have completed this project.

I am indebted also to the Hungarian Academy of Sciences, and to its Institute of Sociology, where I have worked for many years.

I have received helpful comments from friends and colleagues who took the time to read all or part of the manuscript: from Richard Sennett, Stephen Graubard, Alan M. Olson, Saul Morson, Philippe C. Schmitter, Charles Rupnik, Alexander Smolar, Zaki Laidi, Daniel Wagner, David L. Kirp, Gianfranco Poggi, Egon Matzner, George Schöpflin, Csaba Pléh, Robert Manchin Szakolczai, László Bruszt, György Bencze, Ferenc Miszlivetz, and others.

Special thanks are due to my students at Stanford University, Georgetown University, and the Central European University. They witnessed the birth of many of the ideas discussed in this book; they were tough and, at the same time, extremely helpful critics.

My thanks go also to the staff of the Central European University Press for their editorial assistance, and to James Patterson for the careful copy-editing of the manuscript.

I would also like to thank my wife, Lili, who serenely tolerated my 'creative' whims and frenzies, not to mention my long hours in libraries and at my PC. I also thank the irreverent, kind, and insightful comments of my daughter and son, who encouraged me not to take my work, and myself, too seriously.

INTRODUCTION

I shall argue that fear and anxiety have played a major role in the generation of human civilizations. This is a futile exercise, one might say. The role is obvious, few people would question it. Why spend time discussing something that is self-evident?

I see two reasons for doing so. First, despite the obvious importance of fear and anxiety in the generation of human civilizations, their role has been, if not ignored, at least much neglected in the social sciences, even in current theories of civilization and culture (the two terms are used interchangeably in this book).[1] Second, as I proceeded to work on this hypothesis, I became more and more amazed by its explanatory force and by the way it put our civilization in a new light. Finally, I decided to check whether this hypothesis about the role of fear and anxiety could be developed into a systematic theory of civilization. The present book is the product of this exercise.

According to my working hypothesis our existential insecurity has played a leading role in the generation of human civilization. It may have been a more important factor than the Kantian or Herderian forces of human betterment, the Durkheimian necessities of social coexistence, the Freudian mechanisms of sublimation, the Foucauldian strategies of domination, or any of the other motive forces so often alluded to in mainstream theories of culture.

In order to mitigate this fear, human beings and communities have surrounded themselves—not only with the walls of their houses and cities, with instruments and weapons, laws and institutions, but also—with protective spheres of symbols: myths and religions, values and belief systems, hypotheses and theories, the shining constellation of works of art. In a word, with a brilliant construct: civilization.

Starting from the ideas of Max Scheler, Ernst Cassirer, Géza Roheim, Mircea Eliade, Clifford Geertz, Ernest Becker, Eric Voegelin, Franz Borkenau, Peter Berger, and others, the book studies the ways in which these symbols and symbolic systems have been generated and have fulfilled their protective role. It pays particular attention to the role of symbols and symbolic systems in contemporary societies.

The book focuses rigorously on its central hypothesis, but, in order to test the general validity of that hypothesis, the examples adduced have been chosen from a wide range of fields and disciplines—from philosophical theories as well as myths and religions, tragedies as well as jokes, from the symbolic world of cathedrals as well as from that of contemporary shopping malls.

Chapter One discusses the relative insignificance of the concepts of (existential) fear and anxiety in the social sciences—they rarely become major explanatory factors in social-science analyses. A brief survey of current theories of culture shows that there are relatively few cases in which fear and anxiety are considered to be among the main motive forces underlying the generation and maintenance of human civilization. The reasons for this surprising absence are discussed and a theory of civilization, based on the primary role of fear and anxiety, is proposed.

Chapter Two develops the main hypothesis of the book and studies the ways in which human communities have surrounded themselves with spheres of symbols, under the protective shield of which they have created for themselves a world of freedom and safety, dignity and meaning. It also discusses the social and human consequences of the impairment or collapse of these symbolic spheres in periods of great historical transition.

Chapter Three argues that it has been extremely difficult for human beings to survive in this world, not only physically, but also spiritually. It has been difficult to defeat not only the dangers of an 'alien world' with which they are only partly compatible, but also the fears and anxieties of their own souls. They have had to struggle for, and protect, their freedom, safety, and dignity from the very beginning of their history, at every moment of their existence. This struggle against external threats and internal anxieties may have played a decisive role in the generation of the symbolic structures of human civilizations.

The following chapters study, based on a wide range of concrete examples, the ways in which people's existential insecurity—and their efforts to overcome this insecurity—generate the patterns, structures, and dynamics of civilization.

Chapters Four and Five describe people's attempts to control their anxiety in the world by generating the hope, the belief, the conviction, or the illusion that they are at the center—perhaps even that they are the very center and purpose—of the universe. These attempts have played a major role in shaping the myths, religions, belief systems, arts, and ways of thinking of all human communities we know and they are still important motive forces in forming contemporary civilization.

Chapters Six and Seven study another important generative force of (Western) civilization: people's need to believe that they live in a 'moral universe'—that is, that there is a kind of moral law functioning in the universe; that justice is being done in the world. These chapters also examine the ways in which human beings have tried to defeat evil or to argue it out of the world. They study the experience and mythology of sin and guilt, and their role in building the symbolic structures and attitudinal patterns of Western civilization.

Chapter Eight deals with the fact—or fiction—of a 'rational universe', which has been especially important for human beings in their efforts to reduce their anxiety in an unknown universe. It also discusses the contradictions and ambiguities inherent in human reason—how it may not only create but also destroy 'meaning'; how it may turn against morality; how it may turn into unreason, that is, into a force that, instead of building, destroys civilization.

Chapter Nine maintains that art plays a vital role in protecting people against their existential fears and anxieties. It surrounds them with its symbolic structures and creates for them a world of beauty and harmony (though without concealing the terror underlying beauty and harmony, as Rilke and others remind us). These structures mesh with other symbolic structures constituting civilization.

Chapter Ten studies the role of play in Western civilization and the ways in which play and games create their own symbolic space, an enclave within civilization which offers especially strong protection against fear and anxiety and is brimful with freedom and meaning.

Chapter Eleven argues that even such seemingly trivial things as jokes are indispensable factors in civilization. They flirt with people's existential anxieties and with the 'alien world': they break through the protective shields of civilization, but, after a moment of hilarity or terror or freedom, they let people escape back to the safety of their everyday lives. By this exercise they renew and reinforce the normative and symbolic structures of civilization.

Chapter Twelve discusses a contemporary mythology, the mythology of perfumes, a system of feelings and beliefs, ideas and symbols, created by the advertising industry. In the course of this analysis it turns out that even trivialities may be indispensable building blocks of civilization.

A short conclusion—Chapter Thirteen—raises two questions. One: Have we managed to prove that people's existential fears and anxieties play a decisive role in the generation of human civilization? Two: How, and how far, can civilizations, with their symbolic structures, protect people against the dangers of an 'alien world' and the fears and anxieties of their own hearts?

In this book I focus my attention—with a few exceptions—on Western civilization. For the validation of my hypothesis it will be crucial to see whether existential fear and anxiety were primary factors in the generation of other civilizations as well, and, if they were, what particular role they played in building the symbolic structures of these civilizations. To explore this field will be the task of further studies.

The present book has been written for both academics and the general public. It is a systematic theory of culture. It discusses its topic on a scholarly level, but people with a high-school education should have no difficulty in following the argument. Its style, and the way it approaches its subject, is a little unusual.

After a rather dry and long introductory chapter, which provides a framework for the argument, the discussion becomes more relaxed and so, I hope, more enjoyable.

NOTE

[1] The relationship of the two concepts has been at the center of controversies for more than a century. Selecting from a multitude of important works see, for instance, Kroeber and Kluckhohn (1952); Geertz (1973); Febvre (1973); Williams (1976; 1981); and Elias (1994).

CHAPTER ONE

FEAR AND THE SOCIAL SCIENCES

> Is it a tautology to say that fear is one of the primary experiences of animal and human life? The evidence is contradictory, at least as far as human beings are concerned.

THIS chapter discusses the relative insignificance of the concepts of (existential) fear and anxiety in the social sciences: they are not absent, but they seldom become major explanatory factors in analyses. A brief survey of current theories of culture will show that there are relatively few cases in which fear and anxiety are considered to be among the main motive forces underlying the generation and maintenance of human civilization. The reasons for this surprising absence will be discussed and a theory of civilization, based on the primary role of fear and anxiety, will be proposed.

FEAR

I shall argue in this chapter that fear and anxiety play a greater role in the generation of human civilization than has generally been recognized in mainstream social science.[1] It may be that they have played a more important role than the Herderian or Kantian striving for perfection, the economic and social forces of Marx, the Darwinian, Wilsonian, or Dawkinsian forces of selection and reproduction, the Durkheimian forces of social integration, the Freudian forces of sublimation and guilt-reduction, the Foucauldian forces of domination, or any of the other factors mentioned in various theories of culture.

However, as we shall shortly see, it is risky to build a hypothesis or a theory of civilization on the concepts of fear and anxiety.

The Paradox of Fear

Fear seems to play a lesser role in human lives than in those of most (other) animal species. Birds, mice, and deer live in a state of continuous alertness and fear—they are all ears, they keep looking around nervously and are startled by any unexpected noise—while we humans calmly walk around in our meadows and cities, feel more or less safe in our homes and shopping malls, and read our newspapers and books, relaxed, sitting in our cozy armchairs, and forget about the world around us.

However, one cannot rule out the hypothesis that just the opposite is true, namely, that *Homo sapiens* is more anxious and fear-ridden than even the most timorous animals. *Homo sapiens* may have been aptly called the "hyperanxious animal, who constantly invents reasons for anxiety even where there are none".[2]

Beyond doubt, fear existed as far back as we can trace human history. Anthropologists have encountered it in every culture and community. As one of them (Aldrich, 1931, 98) says, "primitive society always and invariably feels itself to be in danger. The peril of witchcraft, of taboos broken by oneself or by another that result in bringing disaster upon the whole group, the were-animals that penetrate even into stockaded villages, and legions of ghosts, half-men, demons, and all manner of dark powers, can hardly be over-emphasized".[3]

Later, in the course of the 'civilizing process', nature slowly ceased to be a 'danger zone', but the gradual disappearance of 'external fears' may have been offset by a proportionate increase in "internal fears and anxieties", as Norbert Elias (1982, 297–98) argues in his book on the 'civilizing process'.

> Only now [in the courtly societies of the seventeenth and eighteenth centuries] do forests, meadows and mountains gradually cease to be danger zones of the first order, from which anxiety and fear constantly intrude into individual life ... forest and field cease to be the scene of unbridled passion, of the savage pursuit of man and beast, wild joy and wild fear ... Now, inner fears grow in proportion to the decrease of outer ones ... Social life ... becomes a different kind of danger zone if the individual cannot sufficiently restrain himself, if he touches sensitive spots, his own shame-frontier or the embarrassment-threshold of others. In a sense, the danger zone now passes through the self of every individual.[4]

Although their content and extent may have been different in various ages and places, fears and anxieties have accompanied men and women throughout the millennia and across the borders of civilizations.[5] They have existed in the hearts of people threatened by poverty and distress, war and genocide, flood and starvation, crime and brutality, sickness and death, or by loss of status, loved ones, or the meaning of their lives. They have been present in our nightmares, paranoias, and neuroses.[6] They have been reflected by the overwhelming presence of fearful demons and monsters, gods and devils of various folklores and myths all over the world. In Judeo–Christianity, and other religions, they emerge as the fear of God, temptation, sin, damnation. They have painted black the background of works of art since the Greek tragedies and Seneca's horror plays, through Elizabethan and Jacobean tragedies, to the novels of Dostoyevsky and Joseph Conrad, Kafka, Camus, and others. They stare at us from the pictures of Bosch and Grünewald, the dilated eyes of Michelangelo's figures (May, 1950, 161)[7] and the *danse macabre* of Toulouse-Lautrec's heavenly-hellish pictures. They invade our lives every night in the shape of the monsters, evil spirits, serial killers, and cataclysms, which dominate our television screens.

Fear and anxiety have been present in philosophy since the Stoics' courageous struggle with fear; through Spinoza's *Nec spe, nec metu!* (neither hope nor fear!) and Schelling's famous statement that "the horrendous is the real raw material of all life and existence",[8] to the fear of nothingness or the anxiety of Being central to the thought of Kierkegaard, Heidegger, Sartre, and Paul Tillich.

And here we return to what we called earlier the 'paradox of fear', that is, to the strange fact that fear seems to be—and, at the same time, not to be—a fundamental human experience.

If fear is such a universal human experience as we outlined above, if the human being is a timorous or even 'hyperanxious' animal, then how can we account for the relative absence of fear in our everyday lives; for the relative relaxedness of humans as compared to the permanent alarm of most animals?[9] The best answer seems to be that human beings have succeeded in developing ways and means—belief systems, behavioral patterns and institutions—which have protected them, with more or less success, against their anxieties and fears. They have done even more: they have tamed raw and destructive fear and transformed it into a positive energy, a force that has played a major role in building human civilizations.

SOCIOLOGY
The Devil in the Indexes

If anxiety and fear play—in spite of, or partly as a consequence of, our efforts to suppress them—such an important role in our lives, it would seem justified (to those who did not know otherwise) to assume that they have been at the center of attention and research in the social and human sciences—in sociology, anthropology, and psychology, for instance—or at least that they are among the most important topics researched by scholars in these fields.

Surprisingly, this is not the case. Or at least I have the impression—I may be mistaken—that the role fear and anxiety have played in the lives of people and their communities has not received the attention it deserves and requires.[10] Which is not to say that there are no important works on fear and anxiety by social scientists or that there has not been ongoing research in this field,[11] only that, compared to their evident importance, they seem to be relatively neglected and under-researched, sometimes even ignored. They have received serious attention in philosophy, theology, and psychiatry, some in comparative religion and experimental psychology, less in anthropology and social psychology, and least of all in sociology.[12] This uneven distribution of scholarly attention may represent a reasonable and natural division of labor—but it may have other reasons as well.

It would be difficult, of course, or even impossible, to systematically prove that the two concepts in question have not received the attention they deserve. How could one determine the amount and proportion of attention these and other concepts would deserve on the part of scholars working in these fields? What could be the norm, the measure, of such an assessment? All I can do is to point out some facts which make me think that such a disproportion does exist. I shall start with sociology and continue with cultural anthropology and psychology.

As a first, very superficial and unreliable approach I checked the last 23 years of *Sociological Abstracts*, now published in machine-readable form.[13] Under the heading 'Fear' I found 2,894 citations. This is a substantial number. But if we divide this number by the number of all citations, the result is more discouraging: only about 0.7 per cent of all citations refer to the concept of fear.[14] Is this a lot, a little, or just enough? Does it reflect the real importance of fear in our societies and civilization?

In the same 23 years there were 2,084 citations under the heading of 'Anxiety'. Since citations of 'Fear' and 'Anxiety' overlap significantly, we cannot simply add the two figures together. A fair estimate would be that the citations of 'Anxiety' and 'Fear' together amount to about 1.0 to 1.2 per cent of all citations.[15]

I also checked the indexes of a number of important books in the social sciences. My hypothesis was that if fear and anxiety are important elements of human and social life, they must be dealt with in the main works of the field and, as a consequence, the two concepts should appear also in the indexes of the relevant books. Again, my research has been unforgivably superficial. I consulted only two or three dozen important books in sociology, social psychology, and anthropology.[16] However, after a time I felt discouraged. The fact is that I hardly found any references to these two concepts. Various factors may account for this absence.

First, I may be mistaken: fear and anxiety may not be important factors in human life. Secondly, they may be important, but—for particular reasons—the authors of these books did not realize it. Thirdly, fear and anxiety could be hidden under the headings of other concepts, such as panic, terror, paranoia, stress, distress, social pathology, alienation, life crisis, and so on. (I did the necessary crosschecking, with little result.) Fourthly, fear and anxiety may have received their due share of attention in the texts themselves, but—for particular reasons—their occurrences were not indexed. In the latter case, the question is 'Why not?'

To prepare the index of a book, we know, is a nuisance, and indexes are frequently botched. It is also possible that the indexers did not perceive the presence of fear and anxiety in the texts since the experience of fear and anxiety is as obvious and ubiquitous as air or water. Indexers may also suffer from a kind of myopia characteristic of our age. Twentieth-century Western civilization has done everything in its power to overlook, ignore, or repress disturbing human experiences such as anxiety, fear, human distress, and death.[17] This cultural myopia, this Freudian or non-Freudian repression, or Heideggerian oblivion may, to a certain extent, explain the absence of these disturbing concepts. Since the time of the Victorians, it may have been politically correct not to mention the obvious but disturbing fact that our mortality plays an important role in our lives and human history.

Durkheim

Let me now proceed more cautiously. It would be unjust and foolish to judge the social sciences on the basis of a couple of general introductions and handbooks, so let us look at the works of three great sociologists, Emile Durkheim, Max Weber, and Talcott Parsons.

For Durkheim, the 'social fact' was all-important. Responding to earlier 'naturist' and subjectivist theories—in anthropology and comparative religion—he considered it to be his main goal and mission to prove that everything in human life and history was 'social'; that the key to understanding human beings was to study them as determined by, and as the co-creators of, their social contexts. He stated again and again that to try to explain them from the angle of their subjectivity, affects, or personalities would be misguided.

Two of his works, by their very subject matter, may have forced the author to face the problem of fear and anxiety. The first is his book on suicide, published in Paris in 1897. The subject index of the American edition (Durkheim, 1951) does not refer at all to the concepts of 'Anxiety' and 'Fear', but the text itself, and two of its basic concepts, *anomie* and the isolation of the individual—these are Durkheim's main variables in explaining the increase in the number of suicides in modern European societies—inevitably imply fear and anxiety, even if Durkheim was not interested in this affective, or existential, dimension of human life (at least as far as this book was concerned).

In his seminal work *The Elementary Forms of Religious Life* (1965), he also focused on the questions of social integration and identity formation rather than on the individual experience of the religious person. One of his main goals was to prove that religion was not, in its genesis and function, an individual experience.

Analyzing totemism as one of the major forms of early religion, he stresses that "religious force is nothing other than the collective and anonymous force of the clan" (1965, 253), and argues that even what are apparently the most personal feelings and forms of behavior—for instance, mourning—are socially imposed on the individual: "One initial fact is constant: mourning is not the spontaneous expression of individual emotions ... Mourning is not a natural movement of private feelings wounded by a cruel loss; it is a duty imposed by the group" (1965, 442–43).[18]

He does not ignore the existence of fear and anxiety in human life but—from a positivist, or perhaps Stoic, platform—he seriously questions their importance in generating religions: "The first religious conceptions have often been attributed to feelings of weakness and dependence, of fear and anguish which seized men when they came into contact with the world. We have now shown that the first religions were of a wholly different origin. The famous formula *Primus in orbe deos fecit timor* is in no way justified by the facts" (1965, 255).[19] Religion is not a response to fear and anxiety but "a system of ideas with which the individuals represent to themselves the society of which they are members, and the obscure but intimate relations which they have with it ... god is only a figurative expression of the society" (1965, 257–58).

This famous thesis has been an important source of inspiration for further research ever since.[20] On the other hand, the fact remains that he practically ignored the role religion plays in answering the 'existential' questions and anxieties of people within a broader, if not cosmic, framework of meaning.[21] He hid this disturbing dimension behind the screen of neutral and indifferent "*faits sociaux*".[22]

Weber

Max Weber was an exception to the rule. Far ahead of his time, he was one of the first to realize, and to study systematically, the role—the positive role—fear and anxiety have played in the generation and shaping of human civilizations. It is true that he was interested mainly in the social implications of religions. He devoted most of his attention to the question of how the needs of various societies and social groups, orders, and classes— the peasants, the chivalrous warrior class, the business classes, the intellectuals, and so on—generated various religious creeds, rituals, and institutions. But he did not forget the fact that human suffering, uncertainty, and anxiety were among the main sources of religious feelings. In his famous introduction to a series of studies written in the 1910s on the "economic ethic of the world religions" (1958), the redemption of people from suffering by religion occupied a central place. Religions had always had the function of redeeming people "from distress, hunger, drought, sickness, and ultimately from suffering and death". And also from "political and social servitude ... from being defiled by ritual impurity ... the senseless play of human passions ... from radical evil and the servitude of sin ... from the barriers of the finite ... the threatening punishment of hell", from the lack of moral justice in the universe and the "senselessness of the universe" (280–81).[23]

In his earlier masterpiece, *The Protestant Ethic and the Spirit of Capitalism* (1930), he went even farther when he showed—to put it in a very rudimentary way—how out of a deep and unbearable existential anxiety and isolation the spirit of a new age and a new civilization was born. Calvinism, with the "extreme inhumanity" of its doctrine of predestination, thrusting its followers into an "unprecedented inner loneliness", an almost unbearable "spiritual isolation", an "anxious fear of death", and the "fear for the salvation of their souls", ultimately played a major and positive role in generating a new civilization, the spirit, practice, and culture of capitalist societies.[24]

Parsons

Talcott Parsons was a disciple of Weber. In his systematic theory of societal values belief systems and meanings played a major role. He, too, turned to the problem of death again and again, but—perhaps because he lived in the strictly pragmatic and positivist climate and discipline of mid-twentieth-century social science—his approach to the question of death was more cautious and ambivalent than that of Weber. Let me illustrate this perplexity by quoting some passages from three of his essays dealing with religion. I shall dwell on these texts slightly longer than the pace of the present argument would allow, but I think his example is paradigmatic and worth closer scrutiny.

The first essay was written in 1944 and was entitled 'Religious Perspectives in Sociology and Social Psychology' (Parsons, 1972). Throughout this piece—but mainly in the concluding three or four paragraphs—we can witness a fascinating and moving struggle between, on the one hand, Durkheimian institutionalism and pragmatism (which think only in terms of functions, institutions, and collectivities), and on the other, the Weberian or post-Weberian vision of the existential situation of the human being in search of meaning and deliverance from suffering and the fear of death. As the preeminent example of situations of frustration and uncertainty, he mentions "the occurrence of *premature* death". This is a real shock and the community has to "adjust" itself to it, he says. "*Death must be only a temporary interruption*, the important thing ... is to 'get over it' and to go on living" (1972, 91).[25]

To attribute to death such an important role was an act of courage on the part of a serious and disciplined twentieth-century scientist (who was not supposed to flirt with any kind of existentialist foolishness). Parsons must have felt the risk since he defused the issue *ab ovo* by speaking only of "*premature* death", implying thereby that death in general—'normal' death—was not a shocking or disturbing human experience. As a second line of defense, he did not speak of death as the final and tragic event of a human life, but only as a "temporary interruption" in the activities of the community and claimed—à la Durkheim and Radcliffe-Brown—that funeral ceremonies (although they "support ... the bereaved"), had the essential function of helping the community to "get over" the whole thing as quickly as possible.

He then turns to human suffering and, in the last three paragraphs of the article, returns to the question of death.[26] Throughout these three paragraphs, he courageously maintains that there is an inevitable discrepancy between people's wishes and the fact that they have to suffer and die, and he adds that there is no moral justice in the universe. But he mitigates the impact of these dramatic and gloomy statements in various ways. He starts each paragraph, for instance, with an unusually complicated, abstract, and circuitous sentence ("This complex of circumstances constitutes from a certain sociological point of view the primary focus of the differential significance of ..."). The next moment he corrects himself and describes the human ordeal in straightforward and clear terms ("men must endure deprivation and pain ..."), and even stresses the depth and the unacceptability of this ordeal ("indeed, at all", "always", "inevitable")—yet again, as if frightened by his own boldness, he suddenly retreats and restricts the validity of what he has said ("to some extent", "though it varies greatly in degree").

In the last paragraph, the same drama repeats itself but then, suddenly, he concludes the paper in an almost Pascalian, Kierkegaardian, or Heideggerian tone: "Almost another way of putting the essential point is to say that tragedy is of the essence of the human situation." Here, too, he takes some precautionary measures, however. First, instead of saying directly that tragedy *is* the essence of the human situation, he says only that "tragedy is *of* the essence" of the human situation. And—for safety's sake, or out of a penchant for scholarly understatement—he begins the whole sentence with "*Almost ...*".

Three decades later, in 1972, he returned to the subject of fear and death, stating with satisfaction that "there has been in recent years a significant increase in both medical and popular concern with the 'existential' aspects of death and also suffering" (Parsons, Fox and Lidz 1978, 265).[27] Despite emphasizing the importance of the existential dimension of death, the whole article is a brilliant attempt to argue away the anxiety and fear almost inevitably implied by death. It is a kind of secular theodicy in which God is replaced by nature or by the world as it exists and is studied by the natural sciences. He rejects Peter Berger's thesis about the "denial of death" on the part of the American population, that is, the hypothesis that Americans are unable to face and accept the fact and terror of mortality and death. He describes the American attitude rather as a kind of "apathy", combined with Puritan stoicism. In other words, he says that one does not have to suffer from existential anxiety since one can control it by desensitizing oneself (apathy) or by boosting one's moral courage (Stoic *fortitudo*). Secondly, he again makes the distinction between "normal" death coming after "the completion of a full 'life course'", and "adventitious" death, that is, "premature death" by disease, accident, or violence (1972, 264). He describes a "normal" and "completed" life as one which covers the whole life span warranted by modern medicine (1978, 265), and evokes the authority of science, stating that "it is biologically normal for all individual organisms to die" (1978, 265). He also develops an almost Hegelian or even a neo-Darwinian theory of death, endowing it with the majestic role of contributing to the evolution of the human species and culture.

> Death is now understood to be an important mechanism enhancing the adaptive flexibility of the species through the sacrifice of individuals ... Death may be even more critically important in contributing to cultural growth and flexibility ... Thus we may regard death as a major contributor to the evolutionary enhancement of life. (1978, 265)

Death is transubstantiated here, with stunning virtuosity, from a negative and fearful experience into a positive and glorious one. It is not the final destroyer, but an important instrument of the "enhancement" of life (1978, 265–66).

To complete this apotheosis of death, it is integrated into a grand vision of a just world—described in the scientific terminology of Maussian reciprocity—in which the human being receives its life from God as a "gift", which is then given back, at the end of human life, in the gift of death, to God (1978, 266).[28]

In a paper written five years later, Parsons (1978) became more personal. And he seems to be even more in need of being able to say: Fear, where is thy power? Death, where is thy sting? As if wanting to convince himself, he repeats the anti-fear arguments of the former papers with even greater emphasis. He states again that "the mortality of the individual ... is completely normal. Indeed, mortality could not have evolved [!] if it did not have positive survival value *for the species*, unless evolutionary theory is completely wrong" (1978, 332). He repeats that increased life expectancy (72 years in the United States in 1975) "means that a greatly increased proportion of modern humans live out a full life course" (1978, 384).[29] He gains strength from the fact that he may feel himself to belong to the lineage of such great thinkers as Kant and Marx: their lives were "profoundly meaningful", and so their successors' lives may also be meaningful, in spite of the fact that they are "limited in their temporal duration" (1978, 341), a fine example of euphemism! He takes heart from Kant's ideas on human freedom and the "purposiveness of nature", which means that human life, too, may have purpose and meaning (1978, 339–45). And then, in an almost Nietzschean dash, he calls life "a challenging undertaking ... an adventure" (1978, 345).[30]

Finally, he stresses that the knowledge of these facts about human mortality and death may help us face and "accept" death and he ends the paper by expressing a moving *credo* in the moral courage and cognitive power and honesty of man which are "of paramount significance" (1978, 250).[31]

I willingly subscribe to this *credo*, and I admire him for his courageous fight with the fear of death and the anxieties of the existential dimension of our lives. But if his objective was to study this dimension of human life with the tools of the social sciences and to include it in the complex system of social actions and institutions—and, as a sociologist, this may have been his primary goal—then he failed. Instead of including it in the social system as an important factor and motive force, he excluded it from the system by proving that this dimension, and the human emotions surrounding it, can be controlled—and most Americans do control it—so that it could be dismissed as an important agenda for social research and an important factor in the generation of human civilization.[32]

'Situational' versus 'Existential' Fear

Let me conclude then—tentatively, since I have not yet adduced enough evidence to prove my point—that fear and anxiety have not been major explanatory variables in twentieth-century sociology. I do not claim that there have not been several books and hundreds of papers published every year discussing, or also discussing, the problems of fear and anxiety in human life, but I think that—with some important exceptions, which I shall discuss in Chapter Three—these books and papers studied these problems as secondary phenomena, as side effects or corollaries of other phenomena, such as wars, crime, disease, family life, childhood experience, the learning process, human failure, drug addiction, urban conflicts, riots, and so on.[33]

All these are, of course, important issues that have to be studied, discussed, and dealt with. It is also true that fear and anxiety usually emerge in concrete life situations. The problem is only that, in these contexts, fear and anxiety have been treated only as symptoms, or products, of other 'social facts', and mainly as those of various kinds of social pathology, not as primary and major factors in generating patterns of behavior, social structures, and institutions, and, in general—human civilizations.

Again, this does not mean that these—let me call them 'situational'—fears and anxieties have not contributed to the creation of various social institutions. The fear of crime, for example, has certainly contributed to the development of legal and other institutions—or to that of the art of the locksmith. In the same way, the fear of pain and disease has certainly played a major role in the development of the art and institutions of healing. And so on and so forth.

Beneath these situational fears, there may be a deeper, more universal anxiety, the fear of being threatened in one's very existence, the fear for one's life, the fear of death and of 'nonbeing'.[34] I shall argue in Chapter Three that this underlying fear or anxiety has played a major role—directly and not only through the intermediary of situational fears—in the generation of human civilization.

ANTHROPOLOGY

Theories of Culture

Do cultural anthropologists share the myopia of their colleagues in sociology? At first sight, they seem less reluctant to perceive and study fear and anxiety as important factors in the lives of human communities. There are innumerable studies on fear of ghosts, spirits, spells, totems, taboos, and on rites in which fear and anxiety play an important role (rites of initiation, purification, and the disposal of the dead, for instance). Several writers have considered people's fears, desires, and interests to be the main sources of their cultural responses,[35] but later, in the wake of Durkheim's seminal contribution, mainstream anthropology has tried to avoid this "psychological bias".[36]

In Kroeber and Kluckhohn's (1952) famous review of the main definitions of culture, the concepts of fear and anxiety hardly occur.[37] They classify the various definitions in the following way:

> Group A. Descriptive. Broad definitions with emphasis on enumeration of content: usually influenced by Tylor (1877).[38]
> Group B. Historical. Emphasis on social heritage and tradition.
> Group C. Normative. Emphasis on rule or way. Emphasis on ideals or values plus behavior.[39]
> Group D. Psychological. Emphasis on adjustment; on culture as a problem-solving device. Emphasis on learning. Emphasis on habit. Purely psychological definitions.[40]
> Group E. Structural. Emphasis on the patterning or organization of culture.[41]
> Group F. Genetic. Emphasis on culture as a product or artifact. Emphasis on ideas. Emphasis on symbols.[42]

Fear and anxiety as forces that might play a role in the generation of culture are practically absent from the 164 definitions cited by Kroeber and Kluckhohn. This may be due to various factors.

Mainstream research in cultural anthropology as reviewed by Kroeber and Kluckhohn was mainly positivist in character: scholars were interested in facts, in the detailed description of various cultures, and devoted less attention to the genesis and function of these cultures and of culture in general. Fear and anxiety may thus have had little chance of being seriously studied since, if they are important at all, they play a role only in the genesis of culture—on the other hand, it may be that one of the main functions of culture is to help people cope with their fears and anxieties.[43]

It is also possible that Kroeber and Kluckhohn are responsible for this apparent lack of interest in the genealogical and functional dimensions of human culture. They may have looked at this field through phenomenological spectacles and, as a consequence, could perceive only—or mainly—the descriptive elements of the picture. They failed to notice those genetic and functional elements which were perhaps inherent in the definitions themselves.

None of these hypotheses is entirely correct, since definitions quoted in Groups C and D refer to functional characteristics. Group C definitions state the normative role culture plays in societies, while Group D definitions describe culture as a device for problem solving, social adjustment, and the social curbing or sublimation of individual instincts. The dimension, which is almost completely missing is the genealogical one. The factors and forces that may have generated culture—and which, consequently, should be present in the various definitions of the concept of culture—are absent.

It is true, however, that the need for social integration, which may be one of the most powerful needs that generate culture, is implied in some of the definitions ("social adjustment", the "social curbing of human instincts", and so on). But other human and social needs and forces that may play an equally important role in this field are ignored. How can we explain this?

In part three of their book Kroeber and Kluckhohn list a few more detailed "statements about culture" and also quote passages from several functionalist and psychoanalytic definitions of culture. They even quote the Freudian and Roheimian comparisons of culture to neurosis, in which the emphasis on infantile trauma as a major factor in generating culture obviously involves anxiety and fear as well. In one of the definitions quoted, there is even a direct reference to "anxiety" (p. 207).

Kroeber and Kluckhohn do not deny the role of psychological factors in the generation of culture, or the usefulness of the comparison between culture and personality developed by psychologists and psychoanalysts (1952, 212–23). But they think that it is "arguable" how "helpful the suggestions of Freud, Roheim, and Kardiner are" (p. 214). Their position is understandable. They went beyond the age-old controversy concerning the roles of the individual and of society in the generation of culture and opted for a 'systemic' or 'formal' conception of culture. They acknowledged the contribution of psychologists and sociologists, but warned against the "psychologization" or "sociologization" of anthropology.

> The efficient causes of cultural phenomena are unquestionably human beings, individual personalities who are in interpersonal and social relations. This cannot be denied, and there is neither use nor honesty in trying to whittle any of it away. But the manifestations of culture characteristically come in particular forms, patterns, or configurations. While persons undoubtedly make and produce these cultural forms, our knowledge of persons—and very largely also our knowledge of societies—has conspicuously failed to explain the cultural *forms*: to derive specific cultural effects from specific psychic or social causes. All the characterized qualities of culture, all its variations and specificities remain essentially unexplained by dynamic psychic mechanisms (Kroeber and Kluckhohn, 1952, 371–72).[44]

Since fear and anxiety are likely to belong to these "dynamic psychic mechanisms", this statement may explain their absence from the definitions quoted by Kroeber and Kluckhohn.

If we turn to the works themselves from which Kroeber and Kluckhohn extracted the definitions, we soon realize that, despite the usual descriptive and phenomenological approach, their authors are not unaware of the role played by needs and emotions in the generation of culture, or of the role culture plays in offering relevant answers to the ultimate, existential questions. To give only one example, in one of his papers Kluckhohn (1962, 149) himself refers to such a general and basic function of culture. Having described the conceptions of death among Southwestern Indians, he concludes that culture has always had the function of helping people cope with the fearful experience of death.

> Every culture, as Max Weber showed, must provide orientations for such inescapable problems as death. The answers which the cultures of the Southwestern Indians give to this question may seem to imply the philosophy of Stevenson's phrase, "Take everything as it comes in a forlorn stupidity". I personally prefer Malinowski's verdict: "In short, religion here assures the victory of tradition and culture over the mere negative response of thwarted instincts" (Kluckhohn, 1962, 149).[45]

The Genesis of Culture

If we widen our range of vision beyond the borders of empirical cultural anthropology and check what a wider range of scholars—cultural anthropologists with a penchant for theory building, social scientists, historians, philosophers—may have to say about the genesis and major functions of culture and civilization, the picture instantly becomes much more animated and colorful. Dozens of hypotheses and theories have been proposed to explain their emergence and survival. I shall list some of the generative 'forces' mentioned by the different authors and briefly outline what the role of these forces may have been in generating human civilization.

Theories may be ranked into four categories according to which factor they consider to be the main motive force of culture and civilization: (i) the inherent, automotive force of culture; (ii) an external factor; (iii) society; and (iv) human beings.

Kroeber and Kluckhohn forcefully state the **autogenesis of culture** hypothesis. They acknowledge the importance of community, traditions, environmental factors, accidents, catastrophes, unusually endowed individuals, and even genetic mutations in the generation of culture, but stress the fact that culture is an "autonomous system" of "forms, patterns, or configurations", and state that, at least at present, anthropologists must focus their attention on these products or "consequences" of the cultural process, on these "significant freezings", and not on the presumed motive forces of the cultural process that may reside in individuals, societies, or elsewhere (Kroeber and Kluckhohn, 1952, 365–76). In recent decades, the fact that culture is relatively autonomous and has its own laws of development has been accepted by most anthropologists, whether Durkheimians, Weberians, Marxists, functionalists, structuralists, or poststructuralists.[46]

As far as **external motive forces** are concerned, a great many have been proposed by various authors. Let me give a few examples.

Life Forces

For Bergson (1911), a mystical "*élan vital*" or "life momentum" is the basic motive force underlying "*l'évolution créatrice*" which brings about, in an incessant process, things and people, the forms of life, history, and human civilization. Another example might be Oswald Spengler (1926), who thought that a mysterious life force underlay the cyclical process of the birth, flowering, and decay of human civilizations.

In a much more pragmatic fashion, Georg Simmel (1978; 1980) described culture as the outcome of the interaction of the "energies of life" and an inherent disposition of life to crystallize these energies in a wide variety of "forms". "From its own material, life constitutes or creates forms or structures—cognitive as well as religious, artistic as well as social, technical as well as normative—which represent a surplus or excess of the actual life process and the instruments that perpetuate this process" (Simmel, 1980, 29). According to Simmel, culture, as the product of this dynamic interaction, is inevitably and ontologically "tragic", since the contradiction and struggle between life and form is irresolvable. Life energies need forms but, at the same time, they are choked and annihilated by forms. They create forms in order to express and perpetuate themselves, but they are also caught, encapsulated, frozen, ossified by them. There may be moments of equilibrium and harmony in this struggle—these are the golden ages of culture—but most of the time there is a destructive lack of equilibrium between them. If life energies prevail, people get lost in the flux of a formless and chaotic life. If forms subdue life energies, people suffer in a lifeless and sclerotic civilization.[47]

Spiritual Forces

Since St Augustine (1966–72), there have been innumerable attempts to locate the ultimate motive force of history and the generation of human civilization in God's creative power and will. After the rather naive and pious attempts of Bossuet and his followers, some of the outstanding thinkers of the twentieth century—Jacques Maritain (1957), Reinhold Niebuhr (1951), Paul Tillich (1936), and Rudolf Bultmann (1962) among them—developed brilliant arguments along these lines.[48]

Several other twentieth-century theologians warned against the involvement of God and the church in the generation of human history and culture and the responsibilities which go with it.[49] They criticized the nineteenth-century liberal tradition of identifying Christianity with European civilization in the concept of *"Kulturreligion"* and argued that the church had to distance itself from the secular history of human civilization, which was full of crime and suffering. According to Karl Barth (1926, 365–84), for instance, contemporary culture has become the "accomplice of 'unculture'" and "barbarism". Culture is essentially a secular phenomenon; it has no divine character at all.[50]

Cosmic Forces

According to Hegel (1975), it was the intention of the "Absolute Spirit" to wholly actualize itself that triggered off the dialectical process of universal history, in the course of which the successive phases and forms of human civilization have emerged.

Teilhard de Chardin (1959; 1964) perceived in the history of the universe an uninterrupted cosmic process of "spiritualization" and "hominization", in the course of which not only human civilizations, but also the whole universe was becoming more and more spiritualized.

Ontological Factors

Several brilliant thinkers have argued that in the human being—or the human spirit—there is an inherent striving after freedom and perfection (mainly moral perfection), and that this aspiration is the basic driving force which has created human culture and civilization. Kant (1991a, b), Herder

(1784–91), and Fichte (1964) were the most important proponents of this view, though Kant and Herder believed in the uninterrupted progress of human happiness and morality much less than most of the philosophers of the Age of Enlightenment.[51]

Another group of thinkers derived culture from another basic ontological characteristic of *Homo sapiens*, an essential deficiency inherent in the human species. According to this view, the human being is a premature, deficient creature who could not survive as a mere biological being, as animals do. This genetic or ontological deficiency has forced humans to develop tools, institutions, and symbolic systems: a "second nature", culture, within which they were able to survive and thrive.[52] The question whether this deficiency was due to evolutionary contingencies or was somehow encoded in the blueprint of the universe was left open by most of these thinkers.

Laws of Nature

There are scholars who think that the generation of culture is governed by the laws of nature. According to the organistic view (Vico, Herder, Spengler) cultures grow and decline, irresistibly, like living organisms.

In developing his socioeconomic theory, Marx (1985 [1844]) argued that the progress of the "forces of production" (in dialectical interaction with the "relations of production") had the force of natural laws and pushed human history and social evolution "with iron necessity towards an inexorable destination".

According to the technologists (for instance, Comte, 1830–42), it was technical–technological development that propelled the glorious evolution of human civilization. To give a contemporary example, let me refer to Leslie A. White's (1949) interesting scenario for "culturology". He describes culture as a "dynamic system" which works against the second law of thermodynamics: instead of dispersing energy, as physical and biological processes do, culture concentrates energy, and in so doing makes the life of human beings and communities possible.

> Culture is therefore a thermodynamic system in a mechanical sense. Culture grows in all its aspects—ideological, sociological, and technological—when and as the amount of energy harnessed per capita per year is increased, and as the means of expending this energy is improved. Culture is thus a dynamic system capable of growth ... The history of civilization is the story of the control over the forces of nature by cultural means. (White, 1949, 166 and 362)

Outstanding contemporary cultural anthropologists—Thomas G. Harding, David Kaplan, Elman R. Service, and Marshall D. Sahlins (1960), for instance—have expressed similar views.[53]

Sociobiologists offer another explanation of the genesis and functioning of culture. According to them *Homo sapiens* is one of the species of social animals. Its evolution is governed, like that of any other animal species, by neo-Darwinian genetic chance and environmental necessity. The behavior of its members is governed by the laws of survival and reproduction, need, the competitive environment within the group, and, above all, by the imperatives of group survival.[54]

Some scholars have even gone so far as to posit a "gene-culture coevolution" (Lumsden and Wilson, 1981; see also Durham, 1991). They argue that there is a close interaction between cultural and genetic evolution. Those able to skillfully handle the basic patterns of their culture ("culturgens") have a greater chance of surviving and transmitting their genes to the next generation; and, vice versa, particular genetic patterns help people use the existing cultural patterns and thereby increase their survival chances.

A third group of scholars speak of the **social genesis of culture**, emphasizing the importance of social factors and opting for one version or another of the Durkheimian interpretation of society and culture.[55] Human beings can survive only in communities and the imperatives of social coexistence generate those rules, norms, values, belief systems, attitudes, routines, relationships, and institutions which constitute the culture of a given community. Culture increases the survival chances of the members of the community, helps them adjust to the changing environment,[56] makes coexistence possible by curbing and sublimating instincts,[57] and so on. The existence of these important functions may explain the continuous generation and re-generation of culture and civilization.

Contemporary anthropologists would qualify this statement—which in this form would be too radically functionalist—by emphasizing the importance of the transmission of cultural patterns (leading even to the survival of anachronistic, non-functional elements) or the importance of the autogenesis of culture already mentioned. However, the necessity of social coexistence would remain for them the major underlying motive force in the generation and maintenance of culture. Others would, in a Gramscian or Foucauldian fashion, put the emphasis on the concept of hegemony or domination, arguing that the ruling classes impose on society cultural patterns which best enable them to dominate and exploit people.

Norbert Elias (1994) combined the sociological and historical approach. Instead of studying civilization as a static concept, he spoke of a "civilizing process" and of the "fundamental law of sociogenesis and psychogenesis" controlling this process (p. 105). He described in great detail the historical process in the course of which the medieval knight was transformed into the courtier of the eighteenth century, a process that radically altered the basic "habitus", manners, and "civilization" of the European ruling class. This process was propelled by the transformation of social patterns, institutions, and relationships; the gradual concentration of power and the "monopoly of violence"; the development of means of communication and social control; the increasing division of social roles and functions and the intensifying need for cooperation; the lengthening of the "chains of interdependence"; and so on. To these changes in their social environment people responded—were forced to respond—gradually, unconsciously, or semi-consciously, with a growing sense of shame and embarrassment, by changing their attitudes and conduct, their behavior in public spaces, at table, in the company of other people, in their sexual relationships. This was a spontaneous, non-teleological, 'blind' process, which led, step by step, to a more civilized pattern of human interactions, to a new stage in the history of Western civilization.

There is a fourth category of scholars who focus on the **human being** as the ultimate source of culture and civilization. They do not contest the importance of social factors or of the autonomous and systemic aspects of cultural development, but they claim that the needs and aspirations, drives and emotions of the human being are the primary factors in the genesis of human civilization.[58] Within this framework I shall argue that people's anxieties and fears play a major—if not the most important—role in this process.

'Existential Problems'

We have already shown that fear and anxiety have not been important explanatory variables in mainstream social and anthropological research. Yet, on closer scrutiny, it turns out that anxiety and fear underlie, or are connected with, several of the motive forces we have been considering.

The anxiety-reducing power of cyclical conceptions of history and culture, for instance, is well known by scholars.[59] The salvation histories of contemporary theologians (Tillich [1936], Niebuhr [1951], Bultmann

[1962], and others) portray the drama of sin, anxiety, and redemption. *Homo sapiens* as described by Scheler (1961) or Gehlen (1988) with its ontological deficiency is prompted by anxiety to create a safe environment—human civilization. The anxious efforts of the Wilsonian, sociobiological creature to prevail in the competitive struggle within the community obviously play an important role in shaping and reinforcing cultural patterns and institutions.

Even scholars of the Durkheimian tradition posit a certain interaction between fear and civilization, though according to them it is culture which primarily generates fear and not vice versa. Fear is not a personal emotion but a "social construction" by which societies force their members to observe the rules of social coexistence. Anxiety is "culturally induced"; "cultures produce, communicate, and manage fear". But, as Scruton (1986, 3, 4, 2) admits, the opposite is also true: fear and anxiety also play a role in developing cultural patterns and structures. "Fearing, as a cultural mode, is shown to serve important social functions which may lead to the confirmation of, and adherence to, compelling values and norms."[60]

Another function of culture seems to be to transform uncontrollable "raw" fear into institutionalized "reverence", or "respectful fear". Scruton (1986, 6) sums up David Parkin's ideas in the following way:

> There are no institutional rules about how to deal with it [raw fear]—no sovereign or god to placate—so mankind must experiment, innovate, devise methods of dealing with it. In a word, create. And, by creating, transform the feral into the domesticated. In respectful fear—tamed, ordered, institutionalized—we see this emotion adapted to human purposes and interests.

As may be seen, the creative process of transforming raw fear into respectful fear (of the deity and/or social authority) is already a process of generating human attitudes, human behaviors, institutions—that is, human culture.

Culture, by virtue of the problem-solving ability outlined by so many anthropologists (see, for instance, Small, 1905), also acts as an anxiety-reducing system. It would be highly relevant to ask, however, what kind of problems culture is supposed to solve. Usually one thinks of solving the practical, physical problems of everyday life and work (with the help of the practical skills and recipes made available by culture), and the problems of behavior and interpersonal relationships (with the help of social norms and patterns of behavior). Less attention has been paid to the so-called existential problems of human life and the fact that one of the primary functions of culture has always been to offer relevant answers to the 'ultimate' questions of human life: the human condition, the fragility of the human being, the absurdity of death, the meaning and meaninglessness of human life. These questions obviously arise from existential anxiety in the world.[61]

What do we mean by "the world" here?

As already seen, anthropologists speak of the role of culture in helping people adjust to a changing environment. They usually think of the environment as the natural habitat of a group of people, or the economic, social, or political environment in which they find, and/or which they have created for, themselves. Much less attention is paid to the 'existential' environment, that is, to the world or universe as the framework of existence: an environment of anxiety and hope in which one must find freedom and peace of mind, roles and identities, faith in oneself, dignity, meaning and purpose. Comparative religion is a field of research within cultural anthropology, or related to it, in which these questions are discussed. According to an important group of scholars working in this field, the main function of myths and religions is not to further social integration or solve the practical problems of survival, as claimed by other schools of thought, but to answer the ultimate questions of the human condition.[62]

This 'existential' function of human culture and civilization, this function of helping people find answers to the ultimate questions of their lives, is at least as important, or even more important, than their role in cementing societies, supporting social integration, helping the problem-solving process, and the like. Throughout this volume I shall focus on this function and argue that existential fear and anxiety are among the major forces that generate and maintain human civilization.

PSYCHOLOGY

About Indexes Again

Sociologists and anthropologists may have some excuse for not dealing with the experience of fear and anxiety. They are more interested in institutions than in human experience, motives, and affects. Psychologists do not have this excuse. Maybe they do not need it.

In the *Psychological Abstracts* the concepts of anxiety and fear fare better than in the *Sociological Abstracts*. "Between 1967 and 1994, 46,380 articles indexed ... mentioned depression, 36,851 anxiety, and 5,099 anger" (Myers and Diener, 1996, 70). This is about 5 per cent of all the abstracts indexed. Anxiety is, undoubtedly, an important subject of research in psychology. But perhaps not in all its fields.

As a first check, let us again take a look at the indexes of a few important books, now in social psychology.[63]

In the index of David A. Goslin's *Handbook of Socialization. Theory and Research* (1969), there are 4 references to anxiety, citing 7 pages; there are no references to fear.

In the index of John Sabibi's *Social Psychology* (1992), there are 7 references to anxiety, citing 7 pages, no references to fear, and 1 reference to stress. In part three, 'The Social Motives', there are chapters on sex, altruism, justice, strategic interaction, and aggression, but none on fear or anxiety.

In the index of Karen S. Cook's *Sociological Perspectives on Social Psychology* (1995), there are no references to anxiety or fear.[64]

In the index of Lindzey and Aronson's *Handbook of Social Psychology* (1985), there is a single reference to anxiety (1 page) and 5 references to fear (8 pages).[65] As an interesting contrast, there are 49 references to 105 pages devoted to the discussion of aggression. Aggression may well be a more important social phenomenon than fear or anxiety, but the almost complete absence of the latter concepts, at least in the index of this excellent work, is hard to understand.

As a matter of fact, I did not want to believe my eyes and so I turned to a field of research where the presence of anxiety and fear can hardly be denied: the study of aging. (I could have checked other anxiety-sensitive issues as well, for instance crime, drugs, or suicide).

In the index of Ernest W. Burgess' *Aging in Western Societies* (1960) I found no references to either anxiety, fear, or stress. This may not be too surprising since this book is a strictly institutional and statistical analysis, focusing on mortality rates, care of the elderly, and so on. I therefore turned to a major book which also includes such dimensions as attitudes, motives, and affects—Matilda White Riley and Anne Foner's three-volume magnum opus *Aging and Society* (1968–72)—in which they sum up a decade of research, including survey research, on the facts and experience of aging. Curiously enough, in the indexes of the three volumes there are only 3 references (to 3 pages) to the concept of anxiety. There are no references to the concepts of fear and stress. It is a relief to find at least 14 references to

27 (out of 1,612) pages concerning death.[66] But when we turn to the text itself, we are quickly disappointed. Interpreting an enormous amount of survey research, the authors conclude that, for instance, among elderly people,

> few express ... either hope of heaven or fear of a last judgment. Indeed, few show marked fear of any sort, expressing their view rather that death is more tragic for the survivor than for the person who dies; in one United States sample of adults of all ages, scarcely 4 per cent gave evidence of fear or emotional anxiety in connection with death. (1968–1972, 332)[67]

With all due respect for survey research, this is sheer nonsense. It simply cannot be true. Maybe even 44 rather than 4 per cent would be a gross underestimate. And if 96 out of 100 respondents said that they had no fears, then they lied or deceived themselves: they did not dare say what they felt and thought, probably because they considered it to be 'bad form' (today we would say 'politically incorrect') to speak of one's fears or death, let alone a combination of the two.[68]

This is not to say that there have not been excellent studies in social psychology on anxiety, fear, and the fear of death. Let me refer only to the studies conducted among American soldiers in the Second World War (Lepley, 1947; Stouffer et al., 1949). However, I have the impression that social psychologists have not quite realized the importance of anxiety and fear in our everyday lives and in shaping human coexistence and civilization. More has been done in a number of other fields of psychological research.

Experimental Psychology

Fear is one of the most complex psychological phenomena. Scholars have serious difficulty defining what they mean by this concept, that is, what they want to study under the label 'fear'. There are scholars who consider it to be a danger signal alerting the organism to impending danger and triggering an automatic or semi-automatic response, such as escape, defense, or attack. Others think that it is an emotion, even one of the basic emotions,[69] generated by the perception of a situation, or an imminent change in one's situation that may lead to injury, frustration, failure, shame, or pain, or the impairment or destruction of one's health, social status, human environment, personality, or life. There is no consensus about fear being an innate or a learned or 'evolved' element of human behavior. Karen Horney (1939) posited the presence of an *Ur-Angst*, an "archaic anxiety" present in everybody. According to some behaviorists, on the other hand, fear is simply a learned response to particular stimuli. And so on, and so forth.

The situation is further complicated by the fact that there is a great variety of fears, ranging from St Augustine's *timor servilis* (fear of eternal damnation) and *timor filialis* (sacred fear of God) to various types of Freudian anxiety ('real' fears and neurotic anxieties, 'ego-anxiety' and inhibiting anxiety, anxiety bound to drives, feelings of guilt or the superego, to the trauma of birth and death), fear signals, panic reactions, emotional states studied by experimental psychologists, and various types of fears defined by their objects (snakes, spiders, darkness, heights, strangers, and so on—see Buss, 1997), not to mention anxiety as an ontological category as described by Kierkegaard, Heidegger, Sartre, Tillich, or Niebuhr.[70]

Despite these difficulties and complexities, there is an important body of empirical research on anxiety and fear in the various fields of psychology. In clinical and experimental psychology,[71] ethology and behavioral studies,[72] evolutionary psychology,[73] the psychology of emotions,[74] motivational research,[75] learning theory,[76] and, last but not least, Freudian and neo-Freudian research.[77]

Most of the studies in this rich fear-and-anxiety literature have focused on well-defined, concrete problems, important details of human behavior, cognitive structures, motivation, or emotional life, and have usually refrained from dealing with complex structures or from proposing more than "micro-theories" (Leary and Schreindorfer, 1997). There have been, however, important exceptions, and even a few excellent studies which have investigated the role of fear and anxiety in the generation and shaping of human civilization.

Civilization and Fear

Referring to Freud's efforts to cope with the problem of death, Otto Rank (1929, 115) remarked that it was impossible "to understand how a discussion of the death impulse could neglect the universal and fundamental death-fear to such an extent as is the case in psychoanalytic literature". In his later years, however, and especially in his late masterwork *Civilization and Its Discontents*, Freud's attention turned more and more toward the role of anxiety in the formation of human civilization (see, for example, Freud, 1961). His ideas on the role of 'Eros' and 'Thanatos' in the generation of social cooperation and of civilization in general are too well known to be repeated here.[78] His ideas were later developed in several directions—for instance, Rank's (1929, 29, 103) famous notion of the "trauma of birth" and his thesis that the main motive force and goal of culture was to establish "protective shells" which reproduced the experience of safety of the pre-birth intra-uterine state. Géza Roheim (1950) discusses in a long book the major role childhood experience, including deep frustrations and anxieties—"general anxiety", "separation anxiety", "castration anxiety", the trauma of "being left in the dark", and so on—plays in the development of the "potentially universal symbolism" of the human psyche and in defining the character of various human civilizations. Marcuse (1964) explained what he called the distortion of contemporary Western civilization in terms of a dangerously one-sided development of the human psyche since the Age of Enlightenment. Eric Fromm (1965 [1941]) interpreted the evolution of European civilization as dependent on the struggle within human beings between the striving for freedom and the anxiety-ridden escape into dependence and slavery.

After decades of disciplined and self-restricting laboratory research, recently even experimental psychologists have proposed fascinating theories, among others, theories or hypotheses on the relationship between psychological factors and the evolution of human civilization. The concepts of fear and anxiety usually do not figure among these factors, however.

In a brilliant volume edited by Barkow, Cosmides, and Tooby (1992) surveying the main results of evolutionary psychology over more than 600 pages, the concepts of fear and anxiety are practically absent. The authors convincingly argue that evolutionary psychology "constitutes the missing causal link" between biology and the social sciences. They assert that it may reveal "the psychological foundations of culture" and lay the foundations of a new, more scientific theory of culture (p. 3). They support their claim by presenting studies of a wide range of subjects. They show how perception, language, cooperation, mating and sex, parental care, conscience, learning, environmental aesthetics, intrapsychic processes, pregnancy sickness, mental imagery, face recognition, body language, deception and self-deception, play, and so on, and their role in the generation of culture, can be better understood in the light of evolutionary psychology. They also study the evolution of a few emotions—love, jealousy, and parental affection—but they practically ignore one of the fundamental emotions, fear. They do so despite the fact that an understanding of the biological and psychological evolution of this basic emotion would be extremely valuable and certainly contribute to our understanding of human culture and civilization.

In his excellent book *The Meaning of Anxiety*, after reviewing the various philosophical, biological, and psychological theories of anxiety, and before presenting his "clinical analysis of anxiety", Rollo May (1950) develops a "cultural theory" of anxiety. Starting with the Renaissance and quoting Tawney, Fromm, Kardiner, Tillich, Horney, Mannheim, Cassirer, Rizler, and others, he surveys the various "anxiety-creating cultural patterns" and states that "competitive individualism" is the fundamental value of our contemporary civilization and the primary source of anxiety.

> The weight placed upon the value of competitive success is so great in our culture and the anxiety occasioned by the possibility of failure to achieve this goal is so frequent that there is reason for assuming that individual competitive success is both the dominant goal in our culture and the most pervasive occasion for anxiety. (1950, 152–53)

Modern men's and women's anxiety is dramatically increased by the fact that their competitive failure attacks the basic value of their civilization and thereby threatens their existential security.

> We here submit that the quantity of anxiety prevalent in the present period arises from the fact that the assumptions underlying modern culture are themselves threatened ... It seems to the writer that only thus can we understand the profound anxiety which occurs in many an individual in our society at the prospect of some minor economic change, an anxiety entirely out of proportion to the actual threat. The threat is experienced not as a threat to subsistence, nor even chiefly to the prestige of the individual concerned, but is rather a threat to basic assumptions which have been identified with the existence of the culture, and which the individual, as a participant in the culture, has identified with his own existence. (1950, 188–89)

As we can see, culture and anxiety are here closely linked to one another. However, this is only a one-way relationship. Culture, or a particular cultural pattern, generates fear in people. But what about the opposite influence: Has experimental psychology not studied the role of anxiety in the generation of culture? A recent controversy has clearly shown the potential hidden in this field.

Terror Management Theory

In 1997, *Psychological Inquiry* published an important paper by Tom Pyszczynski, Jeff Greenberg, and Sheldon Solomon in which they present their recent findings supporting their "Terror Management Theory" and develop it into a comprehensive theory of human motivation. They claim that the primary drive of human beings is to cope with "an existential dilemma", that is, with the "paralyzing terror" deriving from the knowledge of "the inevitability of death". Laboratory research seems to indicate that "this terror is managed by a ... cultural anxiety buffer", that is, by boosting one's sense of personal value, by strengthening one's belief in a consistent and ordered, meaningful and just world, and by living up to the moral standards of one's society.

> Encounters with death-related stimuli lead to increased pursuit of self-esteem and faith in the cultural worldview because they signal a need for increased protection from this most basic of all fears ... (1997, 2, 4)
>
> It is our position ... that the pursuit of meaning and value is just as surely linked to self-preservation as are hunting and food gathering ... We refer to such pursuits *as symbolic means of self-preservation* because, although they do not keep the individual alive in any direct biological sense, they function to control the terror that results from knowledge of the inevitability of death ... most (but not all) of the motives studied by social psychologists are symbolic means of managing existential terror. (1997, 5)

As is usual in *Psychological Inquiry*, the article is followed by peer commentaries, giving the floor to some of the best specialists in the field: as an important attempt at theory building based on laboratory research the article is hailed by most as an important contribution to our knowledge of human motivation and behavior.[79] The critical remarks, however, are even stronger. There are three main objections. First, it is maintained that it is the reproduction of the species—and not the struggle for individual survival, with the terror of death accompanying it—that is the main, though latent, motive force of human behavior and human evolution. Second, it would be rude reductionism to consider the fear of death as the master motive of all human behaviors. Third, Pyszczynski and his co-authors work with a narrow, biological concept of death.

"Terror Management Theory is anchored in an outmoded evolutionary biology that stresses survival, but ignores reproduction", David Buss (1997, 22–23) argues. "It is now widely recognized ... that reproduction, not survival, is the engine that drives the evolutionary process ... Differential reproductive success, not differential survival success" is the main, if unconscious or semi-conscious, motivation of human behavior. In the same way, Reuben M. Baron (1997, 21) questions the validity of the authors' motivational model: "Where does prosocial behavior fit into" Terror Management Theory, he asks; and where does "preserving one's genes fit in", if it entails risking one's own life? Terror Management Theory, with its emphasis on self-preservation as the primary motive force of human beings, cannot explain the altruistic behavior of human beings, who often risk their lives for their kin or for "sacred causes" that are supposed to further the survival of the community, whereas sociobiology, focusing on the principle of reproduction, gives the right and relevant answer to this question. The existential fear of death is a secondary motive at best (pp. 21–22). Terror Management Theory is also criticized for ignoring other important motivations. Let me cite David Buss (1997, 25) once again:

> Furthermore, humans have to solve dozens of adaptive social problems, such as selecting, attracting, and retaining mates; forging coalitions; protecting families; negotiating hierarchies; forming reciprocal alliances; detecting cheaters; combating competitors; socializing children; investing in kin; and negotiating kin conflicts. Given these numerous and diverse adaptive challenges, would selection favor the evolution of so many mechanisms for the single problem of reducing anxiety?[80]

Along the same lines, Mark Muraven and Roy Baumeister (1997, 38) argue that "the view of mankind endlessly struggling in the grip of paralyzing fear of mortality is almost impossible to reconcile with the facts". If that were true, how could one explain people committing suicide, or the fact that they are often "willing to risk death" when "climbing mountains, picking fights, or marching off to war ..." (p. 37)? Besides physical death there is another, probably more important, source of anxiety: social death. "In the anxiety literature ... there appear to be two main sources of anxiety. One involves fear of injury, harm, or death, but the other (larger) one involves social abandonment and exclusion." Social belonging is "a broad and powerful motive that exists prior to and apart from self-preservation" (pp. 39–40).[81]

According to Melvin Lerner (1997, 29) it is not death that people fear, as posited by Terror Management Theory, but much more pain and suffering: "If humans have a fundamental terror, it is not of death but of Hell—of unrelieved suffering, either in this life or eternity". Many people "would or did prefer death to the misery of life". "Organized religions do not promise an escape from physical death but from eternal suffering, and they offer a reward of eternal Bliss."

The third objection concerns the way in which the authors define the concept of death. Mark Leary and Lisa Schreindorfer (1997, 28) write that the authors

> imply that existential terror emanates from a primitive fear of biological death rather than from symbolically based fears. Yet research suggests that people are often more concerned about the unknown, separation from loved ones, and eternal damnation than they are of no longer existing per se. In fact, when given a choice between living forever alone or dying prematurely surrounded by loved ones, we found that most people chose death, which suggests that fear of death often involves more than worries about no longer existing.

Mario Mikulincer and Victor Florian (1997, 34) go even further when—relying on classical existentialist writings and on the rich psychological literature on 'coping'[82]—they protest against the authors' hypothesis according to which people protect themselves against the terror of death by freezing into a rigid, conservative, conformist stance, reinforcing their adherence to an established system of beliefs, values, and norms. The experience of death may elicit just the opposite reaction. It may prompt people to positively transform and enhance their lives:

> [T]he encounter with death could lead the individual to adopt an active and constructive attitude toward life so that his or her efforts would be mainly directed toward self-expansion and the pursuit of new meanings for the self and the world ... We propose to see the encounter with death as an existential crossroads from which people can direct themselves toward inner growth and the improvement of quality of life or can adopt change-preventing attitudes and coping strategies that freeze their personal life and social milieu.[83]

What is true of individuals may also be true of human societies. Fear may be not only a paralyzing and destructive, but also a creative, force.

FEAR AND CIVILIZATION

I began my argument with what I called "the paradox of fear": the fact that, although fear seems to be a fundamental human and social experience—it is present in our everyday lives and has been dramatically present throughout the history of mankind—social scientists have paid relatively little attention to it. It has not become a major explanatory variable in mainstream sociology, social psychology, or cultural anthropology. Psychologists and psychiatrists have paid more attention to it, but few of them have realized its theoretical importance as far as human existence and the evolution of human civilization is concerned.

There have been, however, some significant exceptions. Anxiety was a major factor in Max Weber's theory of the development of capitalism and of modern bourgeois society in general. According to Borkenau (1980; 1982), every culture is determined by the answer it gives to the ultimate questions of life and death. In his later writings, Freud outlined a systematic theory of culture in which guilt-related anxiety played a major role. His colleagues and disciples Otto Rank, Géza Roheim, Herbert Marcuse, Eric Fromm, and others defined anxiety as one of the primary motive forces of human civilization. With Terror Management Theory and other hypotheses, fear and anxiety appeared as major culture-generating factors even within experimental psychology.

Let me continue the story here.

At the beginning of this chapter I proposed a hypothesis according to which fear and anxiety are the primary motive forces of human civilization. Let me now qualify this statement lest I am misunderstood. The fact that I emphasize the primary importance of fear in the genesis of culture does not mean that I want to reduce all cultural phenomena and culture as a whole to this notion: apart from anything else, I do not contest the fact that there is a wide range of other factors—social, structural, historical—which play an important role in this process. I have already discussed in this connection the Durkheimian need for social cooperation, various forms of economic and social dynamism, the necessities of social adaptation, the mechanism of challenges and responses, the dual process of differentiation and integration, the Hobbesian or Foucauldian lust for power, the autogenesis and auto-transformation of forms and structures, and I could add the natural curiosity of people, their wish to understand the world around them, to find answers to the 'ultimate concerns' of their lives, not to mention the fact that even their laziness and penchant for comfort play a non-negligible role in the generation of civilization.

On the other hand, I must also stress that I shall be working with a concept of fear, which, beyond physical annihilation, implies a wider range of human experience. The ultimate source of fear is undoubtedly the potential destruction of our lives.[84] In the social sciences, however, the concept of life cannot and should not be reduced to mean plain biological life. It is human existence taken in its broadest sense. It is human life in its wholeness and freedom, dignity and meaning. Our existence, defined in this way, is threatened even in the trivial accidents of everyday life. If one is humiliated, or if one fails to do something, one's self-esteem, that is, one's existence as a person, is impaired. If one loses one's job, it is not only one's physical existence that is threatened, but also one's social standing, one's existence as a social being. If one loses the love of somebody whose love was essential, one's deepest self is hurt, one's existence as a feeling human being is injured. If one's freedom is limited or destroyed, and one's very existence as a human person is threatened, curbed, thwarted; if the purpose and meaning of one's life becomes blurred or lost, the grounds of one's very existence are shaken and one experiences the terror of chaos and absurdity.

Whenever these threats arise, existential anxiety or fear is triggered off in us. They signal danger and mobilize our defense mechanisms. They prompt us to protect ourselves against this loss of safety, identity, self-esteem, love, freedom, meaning—not only, and perhaps not primarily, in a defensive, but also in a life-expanding and creative way.[85] They prompt us to construct and reconstruct the protective structures, physical and symbolic, of our lives. In other words, they prompt us to construct and continuously reconstruct a civilization. Our civilization.

All this sounds rather apocalyptic. Do we live in a world in which our existence is ceaselessly threatened? In a world where existential anxiety and the fear for our existence as human beings is so crucial and paramount? Do we live in such a dangerous world? Not quite. I think that the correct word is not 'dangerous', but 'alien'. We live in an 'alien world', an 'alien universe', in which it is difficult, but at the same time an exciting adventure, to live and try to survive. Culture is generated in and by this struggle for physical and spiritual survival.

In light of this hypothesis—based on the central role of fear and anxiety in generating human civilization—our civilization assumes a new character and significance. It turns out that it is not something given, it is not the sum of artifacts, beliefs, rules of conduct and coexistence. It is much more a process and action, a struggle for safety and freedom, dignity and meaning in a universe in which—outside our civilization—these values may not exist at all.

Civilization is not a luxury. It is not merely a question of civilized manners or the beauty of the Parthenon or the Duomo in Florence. It is more than kinship patterns or rites and rituals, the brilliance of Platonic and Kantian ideas, the colorful Hollywood pageantry, trains running on time, and a Mozart sonata chiming in the background. Civilization is a question of life and death. Human beings have constantly to build and rebuild their world in order to survive; in order to become, and remain, human beings. Anxiety and creative power: these may be the two poles of human existence. And they are certainly the two poles of the argument developed in this book.

Let us start with the world of symbols. Why and how have human communities of all ages surrounded themselves with symbols? And how have these symbols and symbolic systems become inalienable parts and basic structures of our civilization?

NOTES

1 Fear and anxiety are two different psychic phenomena but, in the context of the present argument, existential fear and anxiety will be used interchangeably.
2 "Animals, in order to survive, have had to be protected by fear responses, in relation not only to other animals but to nature itself. They had to see the real relationship of their limited powers to the dangerous world in which they were immersed ... early men who were most afraid were those who were most realistic about their situation in nature, and they passed on to their offspring a realism that had a high survival value. The result was the emergence of man as we know him: a hyperanxious animal ..." (Becker, 1973, 17).
3 For a good introduction to the anthropological study of fear, see Scruton (1986). For a survey of the main philosophical, biological, psychological, and cultural theories of anxiety, see May (1950).
4 In his fascinating book on the emergence of a guilt culture in Western civilization, Delumeau (1990, 1) speaks of another process of the internalization of fear. It is the emergence of "an oppressive feeling of guilt, an unprecedented movement toward introspection, and the development of a new moral conscience. The fourteenth century witnessed the birth of what might be called a 'scruple sickness', a global phenomenon that soon reached epidemic proportions ... A global anxiety ... discovered a new foe in each of the inhabitants of the besieged city, and a new fear—the fear of one's self."
5 In his *Landscapes of Fear*, Yi-fu Tuan (1979) presents a stunning picture of the ubiquitous character of anxiety and fear in human life and human history; see also Delumeau (1990).
6 For the history of the experience and concept of anxiety and fear see Haefner (1971); see also May (1950).
7 Relevant here is also the famous experiment in which classical Greek sculptures were photographed with a strong light directed from below. The beautiful and harmonious faces suddenly seemed to be convulsed in painful grimaces of anxiety and terror.

8 Quoted by Schulz (1965): "Der wahre Grundstoff allen Lebens und Daseins ist das Schreckliche."
9 This is true, of course, only if we speak of fears in the face of external dangers. As far as I know, animals, even the most developed mammals, are free from anxieties resembling those generated, in a Freudian or non-Freudian way, by the conscious and unconscious forces of the human psyche.
10 Scruton (1986, 3) explains this relative absence of fear and anxiety in the social sciences in the following way: "Since the ethnographer tends to 'see' and report the normal—the culture pattern—the absence of fear data in most reports may signal the fact that fear is not highlighted in many non-Western societies as it is in those of the Judeo–Christian tradition. Additionally, this absence may remind us of the established tradition in the social sciences of ceding the inquiry into emotions to psychology." A similar statement was made by Jeff Coulter (1979, 125): "affective states have been allowed to fall exclusively within the province of psychology". See also May (1950, 1–45, *passim*).
11 In the 'Socrates' electronic catalogue of the Green Library of Stanford University, listing about 2,500,000 titles, there are 957 citations on the subject of 'fear', and 742 citations on 'anxiety'. I shall refer to several of these works.
12 In contrast to sociology and cultural studies, fear has been an important concept and explanatory variable in political philosophy and political science as well as conflict research and political game theory.
13 After completing this article, I found an excuse for the apparent superficiality of this method in the May 1996 issue of *Scientific American*, where David. G. Myers and Ed Diener (1996; see also May, 1950, 70–72) published similar statistics on the basis of the *Psychological Abstracts*.
14 The exact figures for the last five years are as follows:

	Total number of abstracts	Number of abstracts referred to under the heading 'Fear'
1995	29,756	213
1994	29,744	196
1993	22,165	168
1992	23,667	169
1991	23,486	168

I thank Dr Dick Fritchen of the Green Library, Stanford University, for his help.
15 If we add further concepts related to anxiety and fear (for example, 'Panic': 224 citations; 'Worry': 172 citations) the outcome does not change significantly. If we extend our search to phenomena that in everyday life are likely to involve fear and anxiety—for instance, 'Death' (6,697 citations), 'Stress' (6,819), and 'Alienation' (3,020)—even if we take into account the possibility of overlap, the overall proportion of citations related to this 'negative zone' becomes larger (about 5 per cent of all citations). But the fact that the index does not refer to these articles under the heading of 'Anxiety' or 'Fear' may further justify our suspicion that there may be a lack of attention to these experiences, at least on the part of the indexers.

16 I checked the corresponding shelves in the Meyer Undergraduate Library and the Library of the Center for Advanced Study in the Behavioral Sciences at Stanford. This was an unconventional, but perhaps not altogether unjustified, way of generating a random sample of important titles in sociology. I shall return to works in social psychology later on.

17 This is a fact in spite of the anti-repressive efforts in some segments of our civilization, such as psychoanalysis, the 'sexual revolution', and so on. Think also of the educational revolution in the mid-twentieth century, which banished from families and schools threats, punishment, and fear as major tools in the disciplining and raising of children. This tolerant and 'keep-smiling' attitude has since become a must in adult life as well. Norbert Elias (1982, 326–30) would speak in this context of the civilizing process overshooting its mark: with the radical decrease in external threats, internal anxieties have dangerously increased. Consider also the fact that, for very different reasons, the concepts of fear and anxiety were practically absent in the Soviet sociological and psychological literature, even in the works of such eminent scholars as Igor Kon or L. S. Vygotsky. (Professor Csaba Pléh drew my attention to this.)

18 Since he speaks of mourning only as a social ritual he is, of course, right. The fact remains, however, that he deems the personal–emotional–existential dimension of the experience of death and its aftermath to be irrelevant.

19 "First in the world fear created the gods." Quoted from Petronius and Statius.

20 Fear and anxiety play a crucial role in the "civilizing process" described by Norbert Elias (1982, 327), but he too emphasizes the fact that fear and anxiety are "man-made" psychological states.

> The driving force underlying the change in drive economy, in the structure of fears and anxieties, is a very specific change in the social constraints acting on the individual, a specific transformation of the whole web of relationships, above all, the organization of force ... *we realize to what degree the fears and anxieties that move people are man-made* [emphasis N. E.]. To be sure, the possibility of feeling fear, just like that of feeling joy, is an unalterable part of human nature. But the strength, kind and structure of the fears and anxieties that smolder or flare in the individual never depend solely on his own 'nature' nor, at least in more complex societies, on the 'nature' in the midst of which he lives.

> The fact that the character, content, and strength of fear largely depend on the given cultural context has been discussed by several scholars. See, for instance, Douglas and Wildavsky (1982); see also Wildavsky and Dake (1990). A radically Durkheimian interpretation of fear was proposed by Scruton (1986a, 6 and 4). According to him "emotions are cultural creations, not individual ones ... they are experienced by individuals but their meaning can be found only in our collective existence ... cultures produce, communicate, and manage fear".

21 A. R. Radcliffe-Brown (1972, 81–82) went even further when he argued that rituals, myths, and religions were not instruments against, but rather the very sources of, fear and anxiety. Or both. Thus, while one anthropological theory is that magic and religion give men confidence, comfort, and a sense of security, it could equally well be argued that they give men fears and anxieties from which they would otherwise be free—the fear of black magic or of spirits, and the fear of God, the devil, and hell.

22 The fact that Durkheim studied religion only on the level of *"faits sociaux"* does not mean that he was unaware of the important role religions have played in generating human civilizations. Let me quote a relevant passage:

> They [the religious forces] animate minds and discipline them, but it is also they who make plants grow and animals reproduce. It is this double nature which has enabled religion to be like the womb from which come all the leading germs of human civilization. (1965, 255)

See also Alexander (1990, especially 156–73).

23 Originally published in 1915 as an introduction to a series of studies on the "economic ethic of the world religions" in the German *Archiv für Sozialforschung*.
24 The process, as he describes it, was much more complicated; it was not a simple, one-sided affair, but an intricate interaction between the emotional–spiritual needs of people and the economic interests of a new social system.
25 In this and the following quotations the commented passages are italicized.
26 "Since men universally seek gratification of their wishes and needs *there is the generalized problem of suffering*, of why *men must endure deprivation and pain* and so unequally and haphazardly, or, *indeed, at all*, and ... there is equally the problem of 'evil', of ... why the 'economy' of rewards and punishments fails, as it *always* does *to some extent*, to balance out ... The *sociologist is in a position to state that some significant degree of discrepancy* between expectations in both these respects and the actual state of affairs in a society is *inevitable, though it varies greatly in degree* and in incidence ... This complex of circumstances constitutes from a certain sociological point of view the primary focus of the differential significance of religion in human life ... Almost another way of putting the essential point is to say that tragedy is of the essence of the human situation" (Parsons, 1972, 93).
27 I shall treat the views expressed in this article as Parsons's own views.
28 As is well known, the belief in a just world was shown to be a dangerous illusion by Melvin J. Lerner (1980).
29 Would it be ill mannered to ask why the 72 years of average life expectancy reached by 1975 is a "full" human life? Why is it less absurd and less tragic to die at 72 than at 71?
30 In the full text there is again a cautious reservation, however: "human life is a challenging undertaking that in some respects may be treated as an adventure".
31 Neil Smelser recalls a lecture that Parsons gave at Harvard as part of his course on the sociology of religion. "He said, in a moving aside, that he could envision the possibility that a person, having lived a full life, could regard death in an aesthetic way, rather like a beautiful sunset" (letter addressed to the author, 13 February 1997). Yes, beauty has always been a powerful symbol of eternity, or at least a magic wand transforming death from a fearful and absurd experience into a melancholic, poetic, and meaningful passing away.
32 "Peter Berger ... claimed that the 'denial' of death was a basic aspect of the American outlook. We still think we were right in refusing that interpretation"; furthermore, "in our scientifically oriented civilization there is a widespread acceptance of death" (Parsons, Fox and Lidz 1978, 265 and Parsons, 1978, 349).

33 Yi-fu Tuan (1979) speaks, for instance, about various fear-situations: fear in the growing child, fear and pioneer farmers, fear and natural calamities, fear in the medieval world, fear of disease, fear of witches and ghosts, fear of violence, fear in the city, fear of public humiliation, and so forth.

34 In his book on fear and courage, Rachman (1978, 145) argues along similar lines, opposing "tangible fears" to "existentialist fears":

> In contrast to the considerable attention psychologists have devoted to the study of tangible fears, little systematic research has been applied to the nature of what are sometimes called existentialist fears. The shortage of information is illustrated by the literature on the fear of death ... our understanding of this fear has increased very little compared to the progress in other areas of psychology ...

I shall return to this issue below, when discussing psychological research.

35 See, for instance, Malinowski (1931, 1954); Van Gennep (1960); Turner (1969).

36 Which does not mean that there are no important studies of anxiety and fear on the borderline of anthropology, sociology, and social psychology. See, for instance, Spielberger and Diaz-Guerrero (1976); Rachman (1978); Tuan (1979); Scruton (1986); Marks (1987); Delumeau (1990); and Tropp (1990). See also various issues of the *Journal of Cross-Cultural Psychology*.

37 They (Kroeber and Kluckhohn, 1952, 76) remark: "Only four definitions not in the English language are included." Since the publication of Kroeber and Kluckhohn's synopsis, several surveys of recent anthropological studies have been published in various journals, but as far as our present argument is concerned they do not change the picture. See, though, among others, Clifford Geertz's severe criticism of the Kroeber–Kluckhohn classification (1973, 3–30).

38 Tylor's (1877, 1) famous definition is a characteristic example: Culture, or civilization, "is that complex whole which includes knowledge, belief, art, law, morals, custom, and any other capabilities and habits acquired by man as a member of society".

39 "[Culture] includes all standardized social procedures ... a tribal culture is ... the aggregate of standardized beliefs and procedures followed by the tribe" (Wissler, 1929, 15, 341).

40 "'Culture' ... is the total equipment of technique, mechanical, mental, and moral, by use of which the people of a given period try to attain their ends ... 'culture' consists of the means by which men promote their individual or social ends" (Small, 1905, 344–45). "The sum of men's adjustments to their life conditions is their culture, or civilization" (Sumner and Keller, 1927, 46–47). "In brief, culture consists of learned problem-solutions" (Ford, 1942, 557). "[S]hared patterns of learned behavior by means of which their fundamental biological drives are transformed into social needs and gratified through the appropriate institutions, which also define the permitted and the forbidden" (Gorer, 1949, 2). "By culture we shall understand the sum of all sublimations, all substitutes, or reaction formations, in short, everything in society that inhibits impulses or permits their distorted satisfaction" (Roheim, 1934, 216). "I now define culture with great precision as a psychic defense system" (Roheim, 1943, 81).

41 "A culture is a system of interrelated and interdependent habit patterns of response" (Willey, 1929, 207).
42 "Culture is the sum total of all that is artificial. It is the complete outfit of tools, and habits of living, which are invented by man and then passed on from one generation to another" (Folsom, 1928, 15). "[A] culture is a definite association complex of ideas" (Wissler, 1916, 197). "Culture is all behavior mediated by symbols" (Bain, 1942, 87).
43 There are, however, some important exceptions. G. P. Murdock (1940, 364–69) lists seven characteristics of culture, of which the last three refer to important functions (culture is learned, culture is inculcated, culture is social, culture is ideational, *culture is gratifying, culture is adaptive, culture is integrative* [author's emphasis]).
44 The controversy about the role of psychology has gone on ever since. See, for instance, Bock (1988).
45 Speaking of the genesis of religion, Malinowski (1931, 641; see also Malinowski, 1954, 17–92) stated that it is not born of speculation or reflection, still less of illusion or misapprehension, but rather of the real tragedies of human life. The existence of strong personal attachments and the fact of death, which of all human events is the most upsetting and disturbing to man's calculations, are perhaps the main sources of religious belief. The affirmation that death is not real, that man has a soul and that this is immortal, arises out of a deep need to deny personal destruction, a need which is not a psychological instinct, but is determined by culture, cooperation, and the growth of human sentiments.
46 See, for instance, Alexander and Seidman (1990); Smelser and Münch (1990). See also the works of Parsons, Merton, Geertz, Sahlins, Mary Douglas, E. P. Thompson, Foucault, Bourdieu, Berger, Bellah, Bell, Habermas, and others. Even Elias (1994), according to whom social changes are the main motive forces of the "civilizing process", acknowledges the importance of the "endogenous dynamic" of this process.
47 Fear and anxiety are not major variables in Simmel's model, but when he (1971, 375–93) writes about "The Conflict in Modern Culture", fear and anxiety appear as corollaries of the tensions and conflicts of this critical age.
48 See also Jaspers (1956, 213–30); Mohan (1970; especially chapter nine, 'Theology of History and the Augustinian Spirit'.)
49 See the extremely interesting article 'Kultur' in the *Theologische Realenzyklopaedie*, Bd. 20 (Berlin: de Gruyter, 1990).
50 See also Lüttge (1925); Elert (1921); Gogarten (1926).
51 See also Voltaire (1756) and Condorcet (1801). "We have become highly cultured through art and science. We are almost excessively civilized through all kinds of social manners and propriety of conduct. But we are still far from being really moralized" [Wir sind in hohem Grade durch Kunst und Wissenschaft kultiviert. Wir sind civiliziert bis zum überlästigen, zu allerlei gesellschaftlicher Artigkeit und Anständigkeit. Aber uns schon für moralisiert zu halten, daran fehlt noch sehr viel] (Kant, 1983, Bd. 9, 44).
52 This idea has been discussed by a number of philosophers, from Plato, through St Augustine, Kant, Herder, and Nietzsche, to Max Scheler and Arnold Gehlen. I shall discuss this important hypothesis in Chapter Two.

53 "There is one grand movement that encompasses not only biological and cultural evolution, but presumably the evolution of the universe itself: the course specified by the famous Second Law of Thermodynamics. But considered as closed systems, life and culture move in a different direction from that stipulated for the universe as a whole by the Second Law ... toward increase in organization, higher energy concentration ..." (Harding et al., 1960, 6). The conclusion still holds if we adopt Lotka's understanding of evolution as maximization of the energy flux. Culture, continuing the life process, appropriates free energy and builds it into an organization for survival, and like life, culture moves to maximize the amount of energy exploitation (1960, 8–9).
54 See, for instance, Wilson (1975; 1978); Barkow (1989); Boyd and Richerson (1985); Crawford et al. (1987); Dawkins (1986); Sahlins (1976).
55 The necessity of social coexistence as an important factor in generating human civilization was pointed out long ago by authors such as Vico, Hobbes, Kant, and Herder.
56 Since Montesquieu (1989 [1748]), and, later on, Taine (n. d. [1863]), many scholars have stressed the importance of the environment in shaping the culture of various societies. Arnold Toynbee (1934–61) devised a more dynamic model by arguing that human civilization is born in the interaction of challenges and human/social responses to them. The concept of human life and history as a continuous series of challenges-and-responses underlies also Popper's and Hayek's pragmatic concept of a trial-and-error process. See also Kroeber and Kluckhohn (1952, 105–111).
57 Freud, Roheim, Marcuse, and others. For a detailed analysis, see Chapter Four.
58 Durkheim and Kroeber and Kluckhohn would not contest this, though they would probably argue that these needs and emotions are not so much—or even at all—biological and psychological as social. They have been transformed— actually, most have been created—by society and its culture. They are not individual, human, but social facts. So much so that the sociologist or the anthropologist must study them as such. The *"faits sociaux"* and *"faits culturels"*, and the patterns, structures, and institutions of society are the primary factors. George C. Homans (1941, 164–72) reviews the controversy concerning the individualist versus the social interpretation of fear and anxiety. See also Hall (1994); Lessa and Vogt (1972).
59 See, for instance, Eliade (1954).
60 See also Parkin (1986), and Elias (1982 and 1994).
61 In his famous work *End and Beginning* Franz Borkenau (1980) argues that there has been a plurality of civilizations, all running their cyclical course, and each has been characterized by a specific attitude to the ultimate questions of life and death. He states also that subsequent cultures or cultural periods oscillate between a "death-accepting" and a "death-transcending" attitude ("*'todeshinnehmende'* und *'todesüberwindende' Haltung*").
62 In his brilliant book on the myth of Dionysus, McGinty (1978) puts the various interpretations into three classes: (i) the so-called genealogical interpretations (the early animistic, totemistic, magic theories) argue that myths help people answer the problems of practical–physical survival (Frazer, E. B. Tylor, Erwin

Rhode, E. R. Dodds, M. P. Nilsson, the early works of Jane Harrison); (ii) the "interpretations based on translation" translate the manifest contents of myths and religions and assert that myths and religions answer questions relating to social existence (Durkheim, Harrison in her later writings), psychological problems (Jung), or the structural patterns of life (Lévi-Strauss); and (iii) "interpretations based on rearticulation" study how myths and religions answer the ultimate questions of human existence (Frobenius, Adolf E. Jensen, Walter F. Otto, Mircea Eliade).

63 My method of selecting books was described in footnote 16.

64 In the text itself, and especially in chapter five, 'The Sociology of Affect and Emotion', there are references to 'distress', 'fear', 'embarrassment', and related concepts. There are 7 references to stress (10 pages).

65 It is interesting to note that in the second edition, published in 1968, there were many more references to these two concepts: fear (32 references to 106 pages), anxiety (51 references to 122 pages). Several factors might explain this change: (i) the second edition is almost twice as long as the third edition (3,662 pages in contrast to 1,937 pages); (ii) most of the authors are different; (iii) the indexers may have been different; (iv) defensive mechanisms may have strengthened in the two decades between the publication of the two editions; (v) something else.

66 The scarcity of these references may partly be due to terminology. There are, for example, a few references to concepts that may imply fear and anxiety, including 10 references (15 pages) to 'worry', and 6 references (12 pages) to 'isolation'.

67 Two characteristic distributions—Age 30 and under, 41–50, and 61+: "Death is not tragic for the person who dies, only for the survivors" (Agrees:) 88%, 86%, and 91% respectively; "To die is to suffer" (Agrees:) 13%, 13%, and 13%, respectively.

68 There are, of course, excellent studies on the sociology and psychology of dying in which the question of fear is thoroughly researched. See, for instance, Kearl (1989); Neimeyer (1994); Kastenbaum (1992).

69 Among others, rage, fear, happiness, love, surprise, revulsion, and grief are mentioned by experts as 'basic emotions'. See, for instance, Ekman (1994), and Watson (1925), who speaks of three basic emotions: fear, love, and hatred.

70 For an excellent survey of the history of the concepts of fear and anxiety, see Haefner (1971), already cited in footnote 6.

71 From a vast body of research see, for instance, Epstein (1967); Baumeister (1991); Vallacher and Nowak (1994).

72 See, for instance, Watson (1925); Eibl-Eibesfeldt (1975); Homans (1961); Archer (1970).

73 See, for instance, Barkow, Cosmides, and Tooby (1992); Buss (1994, 1995); Marks (1987).

74 See, for instance, Gray (1971); Solomon (1976); Izard (1977); Plutchik and Kellerman (1980); Denzin (1984); Nesse 1990); Schulman (1991); Lazarus (1991); Barkow (1989); Goleman (1995); Damasio (1994); Snyder (1994); LeDoux (1996, especially Chapters Six and Eight).

75 See, for instance, Buck (1988); Buss (1994); Peters (1958); Axelrod (1984).

76 See, for instance, Klein and Mowrer (1989, especially 158–79).

77 See, for instance, Horney (1937, 1950); Freud (1959b); Freud, Anna (1937); Fromm (1965).
78 Eros, the libido or principle of love and life, has been indispensable in creating and cementing human communities, while Thanatos, in its tamed and civilized form, has been one of the major motive forces underlying human labor and mankind's efforts to transform nature and the world (Freud, 1959a; Marcuse, 1966). I shall return to the ideas of Freud and Marcuse in Chapter Seven.
79 See, for instance, Mikulincer and Florian's (1997, 33) comment:

> This article could be viewed as the first serious attempt that social psychologists have made to incorporate the issue of death into the mainstream of the explanation of human behavior. Since the early writings of Carl Jung and some of the existential philosophers and psychologists [for example, Frankl, 1963 (1959), Heidegger, 1962 (1927), and Jung, 1959 (1934)—E. H.], social psychology usually overlooks the cognitive and emotional meaning and the motivational function of the encounter with death. One may wonder whether this attitude was the result of a cognitive–emotional barrier that social psychologists build against the threat of their own mortality, or the product of the development of mini-theories that encompass only narrow and particular social motives, neglecting the superordinate issues of life and death.

80 Buss adds: "'Avoiding death is clearly the sine qua non of survival', writes Robin Vallacher, but it is not the 'master motive' of all human behavior. There are other fundamental human concerns, including hedonism, sex, reproduction, competence, social inclusion, cognitive clarity, and personal control" (1997, 25). See also Vallacher (1997, 51).
81 See also Baumeister and Tice (1991).
82 See, for instance, Lazarus and Folkman (1984); MacCrimmon and Wehrung (1986); Mikulincer (1994); Zeidner and Endler (1995); VandenBos and Bryant (1989).
83 Let me remark that Pyszczynski and his co-authors also speak of this self-expansive motive, but it is true that they focus on the defensive, self-restricting reaction.
84 We experience the destruction of the lives of those we love, or that of life in general, as the mutilation, or destruction, of our own lives. Our existential fears may indirectly serve the survival of the species, and the mechanism of our fear responses may have been generated in the evolutionary process by the imperatives of the reproduction of the species, but this does not alter the fact that our existential fears and anxieties have played a major role in generating human civilization.
85 In his famous book on the history of sin and fear in Western civilization, Jean Delumeau (1990, 4 and 555) stresses the role of fear in enhancing people's creativity and speaks of "creative anxiety". The "intense guilt feeling" of Western man "led him to examine his own past, to know himself better, to develop his memory ... and to explore his own identity". This led to "the rise of both individualism and the sense of responsibility. A connection surely exists among guilt, anxiety, and creativity." Fear "has two sides ... it can be either salutary or destructive. As a modern philosopher wittily puts it, 'Timeo, ergo sum,' and it is true that, when viewed in clear focus, fear is a 'call to being.' It is 'creative of being'."

CHAPTER TWO

THE WORLD OF SYMBOLS

> "Society itself ... is everywhere a living myth of the significance of human life, a defiant creation of meaning."
>
> Ernest Becker, *The Denial of Death*

THIS chapter is an analysis of the ways in which human communities have surrounded themselves with spheres of symbols, under the protective shield of which they have created for themselves a world of freedom and safety, dignity and meaning—a civilization. It also discusses the social and human consequences of the impairment or collapse of these symbolic spheres during great historical transitions.

STRATEGIES

Humankind has always had to create, and continuously recreate, a micro-world for itself within a not too hospitable universe. Throughout the millennia of their history, people have developed two strategies for this purpose. Let me call the first the technical or Promethean strategy, and the second the symbolic or Apollonian.[1]

The Promethean Strategy

The technological, scientific, or Promethean strategy seeks to control the world physically and socially; to use the resources of this world to create a more or less closed human universe which protects and fosters human life and excludes everything, as far as possible, which would harm, limit, endanger, or destroy it and its comforts.

Men and women have surrounded themselves with the walls of their caves and cottages, houses and gardens, fortresses, cities, and empires. They have surrounded themselves with their tools, techniques, and institutions in order to make their own human world, lost in an austere universe, habitable, safe, and comfortable. Their achievements in this field have been important throughout their history and have become spectacular in the last two or three hundred years.

Our knowledge and skills, tools and machines, drugs and hospitals, laws and parliaments now afford us better protection against cold and heat, starvation and floods, infections and diseases, conflicts and oppression than our ancestors ever enjoyed. Our houses, with all mod cons, have become closed micro-universes, which control the elements—water and fire, heat and cold—and exclude the hostile forces of the outside world. The hyper-cities dreamt about by Le Corbusier were also meant to be self-supporting, complete, and closed worlds.[2] Modern democracies combine freedom and order better than former institutions ever did. The spaceships and space-worlds of science fiction, with which we are so fascinated nowadays, would be the consummation of this grand project of building a special world for ourselves within a universe where everything is compatible with, and created to serve, our needs and comfort.[3]

Despite all these impressive achievements, despite all the walls and dams, shelters and lightning conductors, and the protective networks of institutions, we still live in a world, which is full of factors that may hurt us, make our lives difficult or miserable, or even destroy us. Speaking metaphorically, the forces of an 'alien' world keep assailing the closed universe we have built for ourselves in the form of human suffering and misery, crime and poverty, disease and loneliness, earthquakes and epidemics, wars and civil wars, nightmares and paranoia, despair and death.

This is why we need, and have always needed, another strategy.

The Apollonian Strategy

The history of the Promethean strategy has been written in innumerable versions. We know less about the Apollonian strategy, that is, the history of how human communities have generated and continuously regenerated spheres of symbols intended to protect them in a dangerous and fearful world.

In retrospect, it is fascinating to see the diligence and obsession with which people have tried, ever since the beginning of both unrecorded and recorded history, to surround themselves not only with the walls of their caves, houses and cities, cathedrals and football domes, but also with the protective spheres of myths and religions, philosophies and sciences, knowledge and illusions, imagination and the arts. Why these efforts—why this exertion?

The most plausible answer is that the Promethean way will not suffice to fully protect us. It has more or less successfully dealt with the technical problems of our lives, but could not defeat mutability and death, our existential anxieties, the monsters in our souls, the basic uncertainties of our lives. It could not answer the ultimate questions of the human condition.

In other words, from the very beginning of human history people have had to work and fight not only for their physical but also for their 'spiritual' survival. And they have done so by surrounding themselves with spheres of symbols. Without the protection of these spheres, people could not have found peace and freedom in a world full of uncertainties, the terror of the unknown, and the anguish of a finite existence.

The importance of this protective shield cannot be overestimated. As we shall see, if this shield of symbols is impaired, if it starts to lose its relevance, if it can no longer provide meaningful answers to our questions and fears, a period of uncertainty and anxiety may follow. A cultural or spiritual crisis may develop.

In the course of our analysis, we shall see that the two strategies, the technical and the symbolic, overlap. Roman thermal baths, Gothic cathedrals, Arab mosques, and modern shopping malls are technical marvels and physically create a micro-universe for us. However, they are also full of symbolic elements generating a protective 'sphere' around us. Economic, social, and political institutions have been indispensable for our physical and social survival, but they, too, have always been densely intertwined with symbols and symbolic systems. Civilization as a whole is the interaction and sum total of these three factors: the material, the institutional, and the symbolic.

In this book, I shall focus on this symbolic strategy, on the symbolic dimension of human civilization. Even within this field, however, I shall focus on only a few cases; on some of the main confrontations between humankind and its world; on some of its most brilliant solutions and successes, but also on some of its bitter failures; on challenges and responses that have preserved their relevance even in our own day; all of which generated, and has continuously regenerated, our civilization.

Let me show first, by means of a concrete example, how these symbols and symbolic systems are created and used by human communities. The example I have chosen is a little strange, and its presentation will not be short, but it may help us understand the generation and function of an important complex of symbols.

301,665,722 Angels

In one of his treatises, Albertus Magnus, the famous thirteenth-century philosopher and theologian, estimated each choir of angels at 6,666 legions, and each legion at 6,666 angels. Other authorities before and after him came to other, no less exact conclusions. Medieval rabbinical tradition knew of 90,000 angels of destruction. In the fourteenth century, the number of angels was calculated to be exactly 301,665,722 (Davidson, 1967, xxi).

Reading these figures, I was puzzled. How did they know? How could they think that they knew? How could they compute the number of angels with such precision? Why was it so important for them to determine the number of all existing angels with such peremptory exactitude. Before I can propose a credible answer, we have to take a short lesson in 'angelology'.[4]

The adherents of the great monotheistic religions, Judaism, Christianity, and Islam, found in their God an absolute guarantee and protection for the community of the faithful against the forces of evil. He was the Creator of a universe in which people could find freedom, safety, and, ultimately, the promise of an eternal life. In principle, with such an almighty and benevolent Lord ruling over the world, all the protective creeds and practices of earlier times, totemistic, animistic, magical, and polytheistic religions and rituals, became anachronistic and superfluous. In reality, however, they survived well into the next millennia and a great number of them are still alive and active even in our hyper-enlightened contemporary societies, including the belief in angels.

In the Judeo–Christian tradition, angels are thought to be benevolent spiritual beings or entities who mediate between the realm of the sacred and transcendent, on the one hand, and the profane realm of time and space, cause and effect, on the other.[5] They are distant descendants or relatives of benevolent and sacred spirits of earlier creeds, of the lesser gods and demigods of polytheistic religions, the benevolent 'demons' of the Greeks,[6] the *amesha spentas*, holy or bounteous immortals in Zoroastrianism, and the distant relatives of the Hindu *avataras* and the Buddhist *bodhisattvas*.

In the Old Testament, due presumably to the intransigence of the new, monotheistic faith, angels did not play a major role. The emphasis was on the direct relationship between human beings and their God. Yahweh was called the 'Lord of Hosts', and these hosts of angels fought against the forces of evil and performed various missions for God, but in the canonical Old Testament only two of their leaders, two archangels, were mentioned by name: Michael and Gabriel. Two others were referred to in the apocryphal Old Testament, Raphael and Uriel, and that is it.

Later, there must have been more and more need for such mediators and messengers between mankind and God. Under the influence of Zoroastrianism, angelology—and demonology, the study of evil spirits—became more developed in Judaism during and after the Babylonian Exile (sixth–fifth centuries BCE), especially in the sects of the Pharisees and the Essenes. The real invasion—or reconquest—of the world by angels and demons came with the extracanonical writings, *pseudepigrapha*, patristic, gnostic, rabbinical–Talmudic, cabalistic, mystic, and black-magic literature and lore of late Judaism and medieval Christianity.[7] St Paul still fought against the invasion of these spirits of suspicious, pagan origin, and warned the Colossians and the Ephesians against the belief in, and cult of, angels. The Church Council in Laodicea (343–381) condemned the idolatry of angels, but St Ambrose (339–397) and St Augustine (354–430) praised them for the important role they played in the life of humankind as God's messengers. Finally, in 787, the second Council of Nicea formally approved the worship of angelic beings (Davidson, 1967, xvi, xxv). By this time, angels and demons had seized the imagination of ordinary people and theologians alike.

Why? How can we explain this angelic and demonic 'comeback'? Let me postpone the answer once more.

It is fascinating and puzzling to see the zeal and self-confidence with which church fathers and rabbis, cabalists and theologians described the realm of the angels, outlined their hierarchies, gave them names, specified the role they played in heaven and on earth (not to mention in hell). St Ambrose (1967, 336, Appendix), for instance, defined the nine orders of the celestial hierarchy as follows:

1. Seraphim
2. Cherubim
3. Dominations
4. Thrones
5. Principalities

6. Potentates (Powers)
7. Virtues
8. Archangels
9. Angels[8]

Pseudo Dionysius in *Celestial Hierarchy*, Thomas Aquinas in his *Summa Theologica*, and Dante in *La divina commedia* reproduced this list with slight variations in names and rank order. There was much less agreement, as far as the names of the seven main angels in service around God, were concerned. In Revelation (8:2) we read: "And I saw the seven angels who stand before God; And to them were given seven trumpets."

Who were they? The Old Testament, as we have seen, mentions only two of them by name. The author of the apocryphal Book of Enoch already gives the whole list: "Jophiel, Jeremiel, Pravuil, Salathiel, Sariel, Zachariel, and Zaphiel." Relying on biblical and other sources, Davidson (1967, xi, xiii) reconstructs the list in a different way: "Michael, Gabriel, Raphael, Uriel, Raguel, Saraqel, Remiel (or Camael)"; or else: "Michael, Gabriel, Raphael, Anael (Haniel), Zadkiel, Orifiel, Uzziel (or Sidriel)"; and mentions that the Koran has a different list: "Gabriel, Michael, Iblis or Eblis, chief djinn in Arabian mythology, counterpart of the Judeo–Christian Satan; Malec or Malik, principal angel of hell; the two fallen angels, Harut and Marut; and Malaku 'l-maut, angel of death, identified as Azrael."

Who was right? And how could they know so much about the names, the organization, and the ontological status of the angels, who were defined as immortal, but not eternal like God. How could they discuss their gender, their outlook, their ethereal, luminescent corporeal substance, and describe in great detail their deeds and functions?[9]

Let me stress that the question is not whether angels exist or not; their existence cannot be either proved or disproved, and so people may have good grounds for either believing or not believing in them. I ask only why people have been so much preoccupied with these spiritual beings and how they could know so much about them.

The main reason may be that people's need for protection in an empty and fearful universe has always been insatiable. Even in a monotheistic universe, living within the world of their God, they still needed further protection to quash, or at least diminish, their anxiety and increase their feeling of security. One of their means may have been to fill in the void around them with a multitude of benevolent spiritual beings, angels, who formed a luminescent, protective sphere of light and meaning, hope and freedom, love and providence. They created—or discovered—the world of angels and did everything in their power to believe in them, to convince themselves of their existence and benevolent powers. In so doing, they put into place an important piece in the puzzle, their civilization.

As already mentioned, I am also curious to know how people could know the names, the numbers, the occupation, the gender, and the secrets of the material–immaterial substance of angels. But this is the wrong question. Angels had to be given names because if they had names—if they could be given names—then they must exist. For how could they be named if they did not exist? When scholars seriously discussed whether one of the archangels, the 'regent of the sun', was called Uriel, Sariel, Nuriel, Uryan, Jehoel, Owreel, Oroiael, Phanuel, Eremiel, Ramiel, or Jacob-Isra'el (Davidson, 1967, xv), the existence of this angel came to seem more and more real. (Remember that giving names to animals and things was tantamount, in a wide range of creation myths, including Genesis, to giving life, to creation.) If 'experts' could meticulously describe the essence and character of angels, and their ranks in the celestial hierarchy; if they could tell with absolute certainty that their number was 301,665,722 and not 301,665,721 or 301,665,723; then, by this very precision, meticulousness, and almost pragmatic concreteness, their existence began to appear more and more certain.

To be sure, this is a circular argument, but circular reasoning has always been an important element of everyday civilization. Human beings are more than able to 'suspend disbelief' when they are particularly keen to do so. With this readiness to believe, they contributed to the building of a fiction, a construct, the realm of angels, which then surrounded them with its protective shield[10] and became an important part of their civilization.

SYMBOLS, MYTHS, CIVILIZATIONS

In Chapter One we saw that the protective and sheltering function of culture and civilization has not received sufficient attention on the part of social scientists; we also discovered a few brilliant exceptions. We briefly discussed the ideas of Weber, Durkheim, Parsons, Borkenau, Freud, Roheim, Fromm, Delumeau, Scruton, May, Pyszczynski, and of a few cultural anthropologists and students of comparative religion. Let me refer now to a number of other scholars who have developed important theories that may enlighten and support our working hypothesis.

'The Symbolic Animal'

According to Ernst Cassirer (1944, 222–223 and *passim*), a leading figure of twentieth-century German (and Anglo-Saxon) philosophy, the human spirit manifests itself and, at the same time, grasps the world, by means of various "symbolic forms—myth, language, art, religion, history, science". Aristotle was wrong, he argues, when he defined the human being as a "social animal". "Sociability as such is not an exclusive characteristic of man, nor is it the privilege of man alone." Ants and bees also live in societies or "animal states". Man (meaning by him human beings in general) is an *animal symbolicum*, a symbolic animal. His distinctive feature is his ability to create and use symbolic systems. "Language, myth, art, religion, science are the elements and the constitutive conditions of this higher form of society." Cassirer stresses that by their symbolic activity, human beings open a new dimension in reality; they create a cosmos of symbols, which then becomes their own world. Man

> cannot live his life without expressing his life [in symbols]. The various modes of this expression [that is, the various 'symbolic forms'] constitute a new *sphere* [emphasis mine—E. H.] ... Human culture taken as a whole may be described as the process of man's progressive self-liberation. Language, art, religion, science are various phases in this process. In all of them man discovers and proves a new power—the power to build up a world of his own, an 'ideal' world. (1944, 225)[11]

By positing not only the necessity, but also our ability, to create a world for ourselves from symbolic forms, Cassirer's work has obviously been an important source of inspiration for me, despite the fact that, instead of describing the peaceful generation of an 'ideal world', I shall try to show the almost heroic struggle of humankind to generate and maintain spheres of symbols that may protect them in an 'alien' world.

On a more empirical level, Clifford Geertz studies the role of symbols and "symbolic dimensions—art, religion, ideology, science, law, morality, common sense" in creating a human world.

> The concept of culture I espouse ... is essentially a semiotic one. Believing, with Max Weber, that man is an animal suspended in webs of significance he himself has spun, I take culture to be those webs, and the analysis of it to be therefore not an experimental science in search of law but an interpretive one in search of meaning. (1973, 30)

Eric Voegelin draws a more dramatic picture of the human condition than either Cassirer or Geertz. According to him, the human being is not an outside spectator of the universal process of being: he is "thrown into it", part of it, and desperately trying to understand it.

> But man is not a self-contained spectator. He is an actor, playing a part in the drama of being and, through the brute fact of his existence, committed to play it without knowing what it is ... There is no vantage point outside existence from which its meaning can be viewed and a course of action charted according to a plan, nor is there a blessed island to which man can withdraw in order to recapture his self. The role of existence must be played in uncertainty of its meaning, as an adventure of decision on the edge of freedom and necessity. (1956, 1)

This 'situation of ignorance' is "profoundly disturbing, for from the depth of this ultimate ignorance wells up the anxiety of existence". But the human being has a chance: he or she can grasp some aspects of being and existence with the help of symbols.

> The ultimate, essential ignorance is not complete ignorance ... The concern of man about the meaning of his existence in the field of being does not remain pent up in the tortures of anxiety, but can vent itself in the creation of symbols purporting to render intelligible the relations and tensions between the distinguishable terms of the field. (1956, 2–3)

In the course of history, various human communities have tried to understand timeless and unchangeable 'being' with the help of various sets or constellations of symbols, and these attempts have generated the rich variety of human civilizations.

> Every concrete symbol is true so far as it envisages the truth, but none is completely true in so far as the truth about being is essentially beyond human reach ... There is a magnificent freedom of variation on, and elaboration of, fundamental themes, each new growth and supergrowth adding a facet to the great work of analogy surrounding the unseen truth ... The symbols are many, while being is one. (1956, 7–8)

In the terminology of the present book we would say: Civilizations are many, while the human condition is one.

Defense Mechanisms

The fact that human beings have to protect themselves in a not too hospitable world, and the various human strategies of protecting themselves, have been studied in various disciplines. According to Nobel-prize-winning biologist S. E. Luria, humans have an innate immune system against fear. He concludes his book *Life: The Unfinished Experience* with the following statement:

> Humankind is justified, I believe, in suspecting that once again blind evolution has operated with subtle wisdom. While fashioning consciousness and exposing man to the ultimate terror [of inevitable death], it may by natural selection have also brought forth in the human mind some protective compensatory features. Human evolution may have imprinted into man's brain an intrinsic program that opens to him the innermost sources of optimism—art, and joy, and hope, confidence in the powers of the mind, concern for his fellow men, and pride in the pursuit of the unique human adventure. (1973, 150)

Psychological, social, and cultural devices may play an even greater role in this field than genetically encoded protective devices. Anxiety, and the unconscious or semi-conscious psychic mechanisms with the help of which we protect ourselves against anxiety, have been at the focus of psychiatric research since the beginning. Freud, Freudians, and other experts have discovered and defined an amazingly large number of these mechanisms.[12] They range from repression and regression to projection and introjection, identification, reaction formation, reversal, blocking and displacement, isolation, undoing, denial, depersonalization, acting out, forgetting, obsessional thinking, neurosis formation, escape into madness, paranoia, hysteria, depression, and sublimation, and even to humor and creativity, common sense and self-assuring techniques, trivialization, intoxication, and the evocation of commonly shared values.[13]

This is an impressive, even intimidating, arsenal. Only a fundamentally fearful world (and human psyche) could account for, and justify, the evolution and/or invention of so many defense mechanisms. And we may add a number of further devices and mechanisms: human beings' skills in using mimicry, masks, and camouflage, for instance; or their penchant to 'close their minds', to nurture prejudices, stigmatize, ostracize, or stereotype anything and anybody which might disturb their interests and peace of mind. Their mastery in self-deception and generating 'life lies' is no less important.[14] They profit also from the 'shortness' and selectivity of their memory, and even more from their future-blindness, their inability and unwillingness to think of the limited span and the inexorably approaching conclusion of their lives. Their reluctance to learn the truth, and their efforts to know only what confirms them in their beliefs, illusions, identity, superiority, safety, and worth, is a further important protective device.

The symbolic systems to be studied in this book have a similar function of protecting people against their existential fears and anxieties. We shall discuss in detail how they perform this function. The argument of this book would not be distorted too much if we said that civilization was the sum total, the structured whole, of these protective devices.

'The Premature Animal'

Starting from a different point, philosophical anthropologists (Scheler, 1961 [1928], Plessner, 1928, and Gehlen, 1988 [1940]) also trace the generation of culture to the precarious situation of humans in the world.

The idea that members of the human species are 'handicapped' as compared to other creatures of the animal world, and that in order to survive they have had to build up their own world, seems to be a profound, archetypal experience. It has emerged again and again, not only in the world of myths and religions—we shall discuss one such myth in the next chapter—but also in philosophy and modern scientific anthropology. According to Thomas Aquinas (1988, *I*, 76, 5), for instance, man's deficiency in innate and natural tools and weapons, such as claws, teeth, or horns, was largely compensated by his intellect and his hands, which are "the tools of tools". Kant (1991b [1784]) pointed out that nature had deprived human beings of all kinds of "animal instincts" and "innate knowledge", but had given them instead reason and free will, with the help of which they could, and had to, create themselves and their world. Two centuries later, Nietzsche (1974, vol. VII–2, fragment 25 [482], 121) spoke of the human being as an "as yet undetermined animal", which had to develop the will and the power to create itself.[15] Other examples might be mentioned.

Quoting Herder and Scheler, Arnold Gehlen (1988 [1940]), German philosopher and anthropologist, defined humans as deficient and premature beings who have to create themselves.[16] Instead of having lives, they have more and less: they have "life strategies". Human beings are the only creatures on this planet who have no "natural environment", no "niche" which would protect them. They would perish if they did not create their own world, that is, their civilization, with the help of symbols and symbolic action. They are compensated for their initial handicap and for the fearful ordeal they have to go through by freedom. While animals are enslaved by their environments and respond automatically to impulses, human beings are forced to transcend every given environment and may thereby achieve their freedom.

Scheler (1961 [1928]) went a step further when he stated that people's ability and freedom to transcend their environment, to "say no" to any given environment, also implied a serious danger.[17] Stepping out of their given world, people suddenly realized that they had fallen into a vacuum, into "absolute nothingness". Shocked by this existential experience, they had two solutions. They could try to discover the hidden structures of the "Absolute" and fit themselves into them: this is how the metaphysical theories of philosophy came about. Or, driven by their "need for shelter", they could find safety and protection by populating this empty nothingness with a wide range of imaginary beings, cults and rites, beliefs and ideas: this is how religions came about. This is also how human civilization was born.

The Angel of Death

According to Ernest Becker, an eminent follower and critic of Freud, much more was at stake in the ordeal of mankind than shelter and safety. The goal was to achieve immortality, or at least to conquer the fear of death.

In his famous book *The Denial of Death* (1973, ix) he argues that the fear of death is the main motive force in human life: "The idea of death, the fear of it, haunts the human animal like nothing else; it is a mainspring of human activity—activity designed largely to avoid the fatality of death, to overcome it by denying in some way that it is the final destiny of man."[18]

The human being is unable to accept the fatality of death and is forced by his tragic situation and the "terror of death" to assert himself, in a narcissistic way, as a unique—and as such, immortal—value in the universe. He "must desperately justify himself as an object of primary value in the universe; he must stand out, be a hero, make the biggest contribution to world life, show that he *counts* more than anything or anyone else" (1973, 7, 2, and 4). Becker (1973, 1) quotes William James (1958, 281), according to whom the world is "essentially a theater for heroism".[19] I would add that it is a theater of heroism because it is a world in which human beings can survive only if they succeed in building, with heroic efforts, their own world of safety and freedom; their protective symbolic spheres, their civilization, their society.

Becker emphasizes the primary importance of society and civilization. The main function and *raison d'être* of society is nothing else than to provide its members with meaningful roles that help them ignore the emptiness of Being and the futility of their lives.

> The fact is that this is what society is and always has been: a symbolic action system, a structure of statuses and roles, customs and rules of behavior, designed to serve as a vehicle for earthly heroism ... The hope and belief is that the things that man creates in society are of lasting worth and meaning, that they outlive and outshine death and decay, that man and his products count ... Society itself is a codified hero system, which means that society everywhere is a living myth of the significance of human life, a defiant creation of meaning. (1973, 4–5, 7)

But Becker admits that this program of heroism, though indispensable for our spiritual survival, is at the same time a fallacy. It may help us to forget, but it is unable to annihilate the fact of mutability and death. We are unable to live in a state of terror and so culture comes to our assistance; it helps us to repress our fears. It does us the favor of leading us by our noses.

> What we will see is that man ... throws himself into action uncritically, unthinkingly. He accepts the cultural programming that turns his nose where he is supposed to look ... All he has to do is to plunge ahead in a compulsive style of drivenness in the 'ways of the world' that the child learns and in which he lives later as a kind of grim equanimity—the 'strange power of living in the moment and ignoring and forgetting'—as James put it. This is the deeper reason that Montaigne's peasant isn't troubled until the very end, when the Angel of Death, who has been always sitting on his shoulder, extends his wing. (1973, 23)

Our civilization is a dazzling firework display of meaning, freedom, and the importance and immortality of humankind. It is a delusion, but it helps us survive in a universe in which there may be no meaning or freedom, and where our existence may be utterly futile.

At the end of his book, Becker (1973, 265, 269, 277 and 281) is at a loss concerning what lesson to draw from his argument. He gets entangled in a passionate debate with himself. At one moment, he is deeply pessimistic, resigned, stating that there is simply "no way to transcend the limits of the human condition" since we "are doomed to live in an overwhelmingly tragic and demonic world", we have to "accept the truly desperate situation that man is in", and that there may be no other answers than the "stoical acceptance of the limits of life". At the next moment, he rejects the "fatalistic acceptance of the present human condition" and, quoting Paul Tillich's "courage to be", he professes that humankind has the—almost cosmic or 'Teilhard de Chardinian'—vocation of transforming the "complex symbol of death" into symbols of immortality, to transform confusion into order, and nonbeing into being.

> The bold goal of this kind of courage is to absorb into one's own being the maximum amount of nonbeing ...His daily life, then, becomes truly a duty of cosmic proportions, and his courage to face the anxiety of meaninglessness becomes a true cosmic heroism. (1973, 279)

I leave it to the reader to decide which conclusion they prefer. What is important for me in the context of the present book is to show that the idea of society or civilization as the product of—and a major actor in—the heroic fight with the forces of an 'alien' world (fear, meaninglessness, the futility of human life, death) has been developed by a number of outstanding contemporary scholars.

The Social Enterprise of World Building

Peter L. Berger (1967; 1969) gives an even more dramatic account of the human condition and the human search for meaning in a universe that may in itself be meaningless. He starts from the same proposition as Scheler and Gehlen: human beings are deprived of an efficient instinctual structure. They suffer from "a built-in instability" and can "balance" themselves only by building up their own world. "Biologically deprived of a man-world, he constructs a human world. This world is, of course, culture. Its fundamental purpose is to provide the firm structures for human life that are lacking biologically ... Culture becomes for man a 'second nature'" (Berger, 1967, 5–6).

He also claims that every "human society is an enterprise of world-building" (1967, 3, 6, 19, and 27). "Every society is engaged in the never completed enterprise of building a humanly meaningful world", of imposing a "meaningful order, or nomos" upon the chaotic world of human experience. Language and religion play an outstanding role in this world-building enterprise by generating "a towering edifice of symbols".

This is, however, a fragile order and a fragile cosmos which may relapse into chaos and *anomie* at any moment. Human order, or *nomos*, is "an area of meaning carved out of a vast mass of meaninglessness, a small clearing of lucidity in a formless, dark, always ominous jungle". Human order is an "edifice erected in the face of the potent and alien forces of chaos". If this order, the social system of symbols and discourse, begins to shake, the individual is under threat of being engulfed by the surrounding chaos (Berger, 1967, 23–24).

> The socially established nomos may thus be understood, perhaps in its most important aspect, as a shield against terror ... To be separated from society exposes the individual to a multiplicity of dangers ... The ultimate danger of such separation, however, is the danger of meaninglessness. This danger is the nightmare par excellence, in which the individual is submerged in a world of disorder, senselessness, and madness. Reality and identity are malignantly transformed into meaningless figures of horror. To be in society is to be 'sane' precisely in the sense of being shielded from the ultimate 'insanity' of such anomic terror. (1967, 22)

This human world and order is also threatened by the ultimate source of chaos and meaninglessness: death. Religion is an "audacious attempt" to protect mankind also against this almost invincible anxiety by projecting human order onto "the totality of being" by "conceiving of the entire universe as humanly significant" (Berger, 1967, 28).

In order to illustrate the importance of these attempts to create a world of safety, freedom, and meaning for us, and to give an impression of the underlying human drama, let me now show the other side of the coin, and ask what happens when the protective spheres of symbols, myths, religions, philosophies, and value systems are impaired or even collapse. What happens when our safety and freedom, our human dignity and the meaning of our lives are threatened in the world we have created for ourselves?

COLLAPSE AND REGENERATION

There can be no doubt that the existence of a protective sphere of symbols is a question of life and death for human beings and human communities. If these symbolic spheres of civilization are seriously damaged, a profound spiritual and social crisis may develop. Let me give a few examples that may further illuminate this issue. I have chosen these examples at random and their discussion will be brief and almost unacceptably superficial: its only role will be to throw some light on the central thesis of this book. In subsequent chapters the reader will find a much more detailed and systematic analysis of some of these issues.

The Copernican Shock

The dramatic impact of the collapse of a major symbolic system is well illustrated by the so-called Copernican revolution, which demolished one of the basic pillars of the medieval vision of the world. In an excellent article

Karl Dienst (1976, 1094–1099) describes the shock, both positive and negative, triggered by this discovery. He shows how the baroque age interpreted the Copernican turn as the destruction of the protective "house of spheres" of antiquity and the Middle Ages, and how it experienced the new cosmic situation of mankind as the "horror of infinity".[20] He quotes Goethe, according to whom, of all scientific discoveries, none ever had a greater impact on people's thinking and their perception of the world than the ideas of Copernicus.

> Mankind had perhaps never had to cope with a greater challenge: since, due to this new knowledge, so many things vanished in vapor and smoke: a second Paradise, a world of innocence ... no wonder that ... one ... resisted such a theory, which [on the other hand] encouraged and prompted to previously unknown freedom and grandiosity of thought those who accepted it. (Goethe, 1976, 1095)

Freud was ambiguous about the role of "protective" fictions, constructs, and illusions in human life. There are contexts (1959b, 75) in which he comes to the conclusion that, since life is full of suffering, people need "palliative measures" to be able to bear these sufferings. He quotes Theodor Fontane, who said that we "cannot do without auxiliary constructions". But the main message of his lifework is that illusions are sources of suffering and have to be eliminated. He (1959b, 75, 81) described religions as "mass delusions" and asserted that the "delusional remolding of reality" by religions failed to achieve human happiness. In this same line, he praised the Copernican revolution as the destruction of a dangerous illusion and an important step towards mature, though resigned, humanity.

> The central position of Earth was [for Man] ... an instrument [by means of which he could play] a dominant role in the universe and it harmonized with his penchant for feeling himself the Lord of the World. The destruction of this narcissistic illusion attaches for us to the name of Nicolaus Copernicus ... When the Copernican revolution was generally accepted, human self-love suffered its first cosmological injury,

followed by the Darwinian and the psychoanalytical shocks, which together helped mankind to "advance towards an understanding resignation".[21]

Freedom and Anxiety

The great transitions between two civilizations—or between two major periods within one civilization—also imply the collapse of an earlier, and the generation of a new, symbolic system. The transition from the Greco-Roman to the Judeo-Christian civilization, for instance, can be well described, on the one hand, as the collapse of the myths and religions, philosophies and arts of the Greeks and the Romans, and on the other hand, as the generation of a new system of symbols constituted by a new vision of the world, a new mythology, a new religion, new moral ideals and values, and new forms of art. In between, there was a period of crisis—not only a social and economic crisis, but also a profound spiritual one in which people had already lost the protection of the old system of symbols and could not yet take refuge under the shield of a new one. They were exposed, more or less helpless, to the experience of being thrust into a dangerous and chaotic world.

The collapse of the medieval vision of the world is another enlightening example. While it remained in operation it provided people with a more or less homely universe in which they were, to a certain extent, protected against the dangers and doubts of their lives, and in which there were answers to most of their questions—from the trivial ones of individual and communal life to the ultimate questions of life and death, good and evil, and the meaning of life. The coldness and emptiness of the surrounding world was hermetically sealed off by the close-knit web of these answers, by the multiple layers of these symbolic spheres.

In the fourteenth and fifteenth centuries, the medieval vision of the world showed signs of disintegrating. The spheres of the several orders of angels, spirits, and saints, the dazzling symbols, ceremonies, and institutions of the church, the rituals and institutions of the feudal order, the sphere of myriads of everyday beliefs and superstitions, increasingly lost their protective force.

Luther, Calvin, and their followers completed the destruction, tore up the thinning veil of scholasticism and, for a moment, had the courage to look out, unprotected, into a dark, empty, and fearful universe in which there was only a single safe point of light and source of hope: God. They accepted the fact that, due to original sin, mankind lived in the Valley of Death, in an alien world. They accepted a high level of insecurity and anxiety. This was as much an act of courage as Descartes' *cogito* would be in the next century.

However, they were not—and could not have been—able to survive for long without protection. They had to generate for themselves a new protective sphere of beliefs and symbols. And they succeeded in building around themselves, both the individual and the community, the bulwarks and bastions, towers and dungeons of an austere and strict, intransigent and puritanical morality, which shielded them against the dangers and temptations of the world. They curbed human instincts with draconian rules and discipline; they developed an almost neurotic repulsion against everything which was not sterilely clean, hygienic, free of any kind of contamination by an alien and sinful world. They prompted themselves to feverish activity in order to protect themselves against their own doubts and to reduce their anxiety.[22] They cut themselves off from the world with an almost Stoic or Spinozian discipline. They thought of themselves as the soldiers of Christ marching in closed ranks through an alien country and conquering the world, the alien world, from the enemies of God, for God.[23]

If we take into account the witch-hunting rage of Protestant communities throughout the sixteenth and seventeenth centuries and the almost Manichean fury directed towards defeating the archenemy, the Catholic Leviathan, the papist Beelzebub, the ecclesiastical monster, we must assume that the success of their strategy was only partial. To give a single, trivial or tragic, example: Davidson (1967, xix, xxi) remarks that, while in post-biblical rabbinical literature, as we have already seen, the number of the "angels of destruction" was set at 90,000, "Luther's followers, in a work entitled *Theatrum Diabolorum*, not satisfied with the then current estimates of devils, raised the figure to 2.5 billion, later to 10,000 billion." In all likelihood, the forces of evil never tired of assailing the world, particularly the souls of Protestants.

The Loss of Symbols

According to many experts we find ourselves once more, at the end of the twentieth century, in an age of transition, a transition from the declining civilization of modernism and something that may, and hopefully will, emerge in the coming decades. The decomposition of the traditional European systems of thought and belief has been going on now for decades, if not for centuries; so much so that we may be arriving at the end of this long journey into night.

One of the most striking illustrations of this 'endgame'—and generally of the human condition in a world that has lost its protective spheres—is the case of Estragon and Vladimir in Beckett's *Waiting for Godot*. They are the very embodiment of the human being who has lost the protection of his world of values and symbols. They are stripped of their humanity, deprived of all the protective accessories of human life which nurture the illusion of safety and generate comfort. They are deprived of the cognitive sphere of ideas and logic since they are blockheads and have lost the ability to interpret and understand the world around them. They are deprived of the protective sphere of social norms and order: society has disappeared, the desert around them is almost completely empty. They are also deprived of the protective shell of human personality; they have lost their human identity and dignity; they are hobos. They have lost their history and their memories, which were important elements in their traditional system of defenses; they have no past and no future, only a precarious and empty present; they live after the end of human history.

They have lost their faith and their mythologies as well. The Garden of Eden has here become a wasteland, and the Tree of Life, barren. There is no spring of life bubbling at its foot. It is not Jesus Christ in his tragic glory, who is crucified; it is Estragon, the clown, who tries to hang himself on it. However, he does not even have the grace of a dignified death: the branch breaks under his weight. Is the fact that, in the second act, the tree puts out a few leaves, a sign of hope or a sardonic grimace?

Is Beckett's gloomy vision justified? Has the traditional system of symbols of Western civilization in fact collapsed? Has it really been so seriously damaged? And if it has, can it be amended, restored? Is there a chance of a new beginning? Are there new symbols and systems of symbols being generated to protect us and those who come after us?

To try to answer these questions would be the task of another book.[24] I mention Beckett's play only as an indication of what may happen to a human community if it loses its protective sphere of symbols, that is, if it loses the symbolic dimension of its civilization, which is, for the members of the community, an indispensable source of safety, freedom, and meaning.

In subsequent chapters I shall show the paramount importance of selected symbolic systems in the lives of human beings and communities. I shall also show that their importance has not diminished—in some cases it has even increased—in our enlightened, high-tech, contemporary civilization. But before doing so, I have to make a detour and devote the next chapter to the study of a concept—the 'alien world'—which

I introduced in this chapter. Beside fear and symbols, this is the third key concept in the hypothesis proposed in this book. Fear is the primary motive force in the generation of the symbolic structures of civilization since humankind lives in a world which threatens it in its well-being, even in its very existence. It is not necessarily a hostile world, only an 'alien' one, a world in which human beings and communities may have serious difficulties in feeling themselves at home.

NOTES

1. A number of authors have made a similar distinction. Let me quote only one of them. Horkheimer (1978, 47) distinguished two types of reason. His "pragmatic reason" of self-preserving efficiency might be understood in terms of the Promethean kind: through this reason "man frees himself of the fetters of nature", he writes. Man's "reflective reason", on the other hand, with its search for freedom and meaning, could be the reason that builds and maintains the symbolic spheres of the Apollonian strategy. Nietzsche's (1967) dichotomy of the Dionysian and the Apollonian refers to another duality of human civilization, although the Apollonian illusion of harmony is part of the system of symbolic protection I shall discuss in this chapter.
2. Le Corbusier planned ultra-modern building-complexes, which would contain everything that is necessary for human and communal life. The great complexes built around metro stations in great American, European, and Japanese cities, containing blocks of condominiums, hotels, banks, shopping malls, entertainment centers, and a whole range of facilities take their inspiration from Le Corbusier's ideas.
3. The, to me almost incomprehensible, success of the old and new series of *Star Trek* in America may be, at least in part, due to this search for a 'final solution' of our problems in the world. This success may also derive from a latent anxiety that we may one day lose—may already have lost—the fight on this planet, which we shall have to leave sooner or later.
4. There is a perplexingly vast literature on angels. As simple and helpful introductions to this literature see Davidson (1967); Eliade (1987, vol. 1, 282–86; vol. 4, 282–92, and other entries). Angels are 'in' nowadays. Several books are published on them each year, but few of these books give a good introduction to the history of the myths and belief systems that developed around angels.
5. See, for instance, *The New Encyclopedia Britannica*, s. v. 'Angels; Angels and Demons'. The term 'angel' derives from the Greek *angelos*, meaning 'messenger'.
6. The Greek word *daimon* had a wide range of meanings, but it mainly referred to a 'supernatural being' or 'spirit'.
7. Davidson (1967, xiii). See, for instance, the following works: The Book of Jubilees; The Book of Tobit; The Book of Adam and Eve; The Book of Enoch; Baruch III; The Martyrdom of Isaiah; The Apocalypse of Abraham; The Zohar; The Zadokite Fragments; The Sibylline Oracles; and so on.

8 Davidson (1967, xxv) remarks: "But there are other 'authoritative' lists provided by sundry Protestant writers that give seven, nine, twelve orders including such rarely encountered ones as flames, warriors, entities, seats, hosts, lordships, etc. ... Calvin summarily dismissed [all this] as 'the vain babbling of idle men'."

9 "Angels perform a multiplicity of duties and tasks. Preeminently they serve God ... But many serve man directly as guardians, counselors, guides, judges, interpreters, cooks, comforters, dragomen, matchmakers, and gravediggers ... There are instances where an angel or troop of angels turned the tide of battle, abated storms, conveyed saints to Heaven, brought down plagues, fed hermits, helped plowmen, converted heathens ... The might of angels, as made known to us in Targum and Talmud, is easily a match for the might of the pagan gods and heroes. Michael overthrew mountains. Gabriel bore Abraham on his back to Babylon ... The mighty Rabdos is able to stop the planets in their courses. The Talmudic angel Ben Nez prevents the earth being consumed by holding back the South Wind with his pinions ... As late as the 17th century, the German astronomer Kepler figured out (and somehow managed to fit into his celebrated law of celestial mechanics) that the planets are 'pushed around by angels'" (Davidson, 1967, 8). I shall return to Kepler's perplexing case in Chapter Eight.

10 This protective sphere has helped people to live with dignity and hope. According to a *Newsweek* poll taken in November 1994, as many as 33 per cent of all adult Americans "report having had a mystical or religious experience", 20 per cent "a revelation from God in the last year", and 13 per cent having "seen or sensed the presence of an angel". Kantrowity et al. (1994, 40).

11 See also Cassirer (1953, vol. 1, 11).

12 Ironically, Freud's basic theory, underlying his life work, has also been interpreted as one great defense mechanism. Relying on Otto Rank (1936, 121–22), Ernest Becker (1973, 97–100) argued that Freud was not able to face the terror of death and this is why he introduced—in his later work—the "death instinct". This was an ingenious strategy to domesticate death by transforming it from a fearful outside enemy into an integral part of a pleasure-seeking animal. Or, as Rank put it, death was thus transformed "from an unwished-for necessity to a desired instinctual goal". (Bob Scott drew my attention to this interesting Freud interpretation.)

13 Among others, see Freud (1959b); Anna Freud (1937); Horney (1937); Miller and Swanson (1960). For an excellent survey of Freudian and non-Freudian research in this field see Smelser (1987). Anxiety and panic are also important variables in Smelser's *Theory of Collective Behavior* (1962).

14 See, for instance, Lockard and Paulhus (1988), and Nesse and Lloyd (1992).

15 Quoted by Gehlen. The original German wording is: *das noch nicht festgestellte Tier*.

16 The original German term is "*ein Mängelwesen*".

17 The idea that the distinctive human characteristic is the ability to say 'no' to the given world has a long history. Let me quote here only Erich Fromm (1965 [1941], 49–53), according to whom human history began with an act of disobedience—referring to Eve and Adam—and it is not unlikely that it will be terminated by an act of obedience, meaning the penchant of contemporary mankind to "escape from freedom and look for safety in submitting itself to authority".

18 For other works based on a similar hypothesis, see Brown (1959), Lifton (1968), and Harrington (1969).
19 Becker (1973, 7) is well aware of the fact that there may also be "ignoble heroics", as in the case of "the viciously destructive heroics of Hitler's Germany".
20 Dienst cites Phillip (1963, xvi–xvii).
21 *Werke*, Vol. VI, 12ff, and Vol. XI, 294f—quoted by Dienst (1976, 1097). See also Blumenberg (1965), and Koestler (1968).
22 Fromm (1965, 111) writes about this "frantic activity and a striving to do something ... the individual has to be active in order to overcome his feelings of doubt and powerlessness ... This kind of activity is not the result of inner strength and self-confidence; it is a desperate escape from anxiety."
23 Max Weber's analysis of this struggle (1930) remains unsurpassed.
24 I deal with this issue in detail in a new book I am now working on. Its working title is *Proletarian Renaissance. A Study of Contemporary Consumer Civilization*.

CHAPTER THREE

AN ALIEN WORLD?

> "To whoever embarks on terrible seas."
> Nietzsche, *Towards a Genealogy of Morals*

THIS chapter describes the relatively low compatibility of human life with the world as it is. Humankind lives in a none too hospitable world, in an 'alien world', in which it has been rather difficult for human beings to survive, physically or spiritually. Fear and anxiety have always accompanied human existence. The struggle with external threats and internal anxieties and fears has played a leading role in the generation of human civilization.

THE WORLD

And What about Us, Sir?

Epimetheus was a benevolent god in the Greek Pantheon, but intelligence was not his strong point. He was prone to make a mess of things and, due to his foolishness, he played a woeful role in the early history of mankind. After the gods had created the animal world, Zeus, the highest of all gods, entrusted him with distributing among living creatures those tools and faculties that were necessary for their survival. Epimetheus was delighted to be given this important job and set to work immediately. He gave sharp eyes to the eagle that it may see its prey from the height of the skies. He gave the fastest legs to the deer that it may escape from its predators. He gave the ability to swim to the fish, strong claws and teeth to the panther, the ability to eat grass to the sheep, and he clothed the bear with thick fur to keep it warm; he gave every species something that enabled it to survive.

When he had finished his work, he packed his bags and was about to set off for Olympus. At that moment, he heard a low, whining voice behind his back. "And what about me, sir?" Startled, he turned around and saw a miserable, weak, naked creature, shivering in the fresh breeze as night fell. "Who the hell are you?", he asked, although perhaps, being a god, he expressed himself in a more Olympian way. "I am *Homo sapiens*, sir", the poor devil answered and looked at the departing god with panic and hope in his eyes. "Well, old boy, I am really sorry, but nothing has been left for you. You know the rules: first come, first served. Get up earlier next time. Good luck!" With that, he disappeared into the dusk.

Poor *Homo sapiens* stood there alone, shivering, unprotected, an easy prey to a thousand dangers, with no chance of survival in a cold and dark world. He looked around and asked himself, frightened: "How did I get into this world, which is not my world? What should I do to survive in this alien world?"

At this moment, a deep and majestic voice was heard, coming from behind the hills. "This is not your world, but you may build your own world within this world. I shall help you to do so because I hate injustice and hate stupidity even more. My name is Prometheus. I am the brother of Epimetheus, and so I sort of feel responsible for his mistake. Come back in a week or so and in the meantime I shall find a solution to your problem."

And so it happened. A week later, Prometheus brought with him fire and handicrafts (which he had stolen from Hephaistus and Pallas Athene) and gave them to the first man and woman and their kin. The latter did not waste any time and immediately started to carve and forge, fell trees and build houses, weave warm clothes and sharpen their weapons to protect themselves against the saber-toothed tigers, the unicorns, and—last but not least—their own belligerent neighbors. A little later on they also raised shrines in honor of Prometheus, their savior, and a number of much larger ones to Zeus (who in the meantime had cruelly punished Prometheus for having stolen the fire). Human beings began to build their own world within the alien world. A world of protecting walls, houses and cities, tools and weapons, myths, religions, and compromises.

The shock and the fear engendered by the realization that men and women are strangers in this world, that they are fragile and weak creatures, that their very existence is threatened, may always have been a deep, archetypal experience of mankind. And the same disturbing questions may have kept coming back: "How did we get into this world? Are we at home in this world? Or are we strangers here? What should we do to survive in this alien world?"[1]

Have we managed to answer any of these questions since the first men and women asked them, at the foot of Mount Olympus, or at the gates of the Garden of Eden that were closing behind them?

Spoiled by advances in technology and the comforts of modern life we tend to forget, or not to raise, these questions nowadays. We are inclined to believe, or are eager to convince ourselves, that we are at home in this universe. And we are shocked when the facts of life belie this view. We are upset, we complain, we protest, we revolt. We do not understand why there is so much pain, misery, and fear in the world.

Would it be absurd and theatrical to say that, as a matter of fact, the contrary is at least as surprising? The fact, namely, that suffering, misery, and fear are not ubiquitous; that life also provides opportunities; that there are moments of joy and comfort, and a few instances of a strange state of mind which humans call 'happiness'.

Spoiled as we are, we are inclined nowadays to forget that our start on this planet—though we know very little about how it actually happened—must have been extremely difficult. *Illo tempore*, whether we were expelled from Paradise or came out of the bush, we must have entered a rather inhospitable world. We had to get a foothold in this world, as the first bunch of grass has to strike root on an empty rocky island. Except for the few who lived in one of the scarce idyllic enclaves of the planet, where nature was more friendly and bounteous, people had to make immense efforts to adapt themselves to the adverse conditions of this world. To survive, physically and spiritually; not to starve, freeze, or die of thirst, not to be devoured by the beasts, infections and their neighbors. Or by their own fears.

Is This Our World?

It would be fine if we could answer this question with a firm and calm 'yes': 'Yes, this world is our world.' Before doing so, however, we should define what this answer would mean.

First, it could mean that the world had been created for us, the species *Homo sapiens*, and the purpose of the act of creation was our well-being and happiness. In that case, we should be in complete harmony with the world—however, that is not the case. It might be supposed that we understand something else by 'happiness' than our creator did and this is the reason we feel ourselves to be incompatible with the world. This incompatibility, this lack of harmony between the world and ourselves would then be the source of our problem and failures, fears and pains.

From the wide range of authors who have written about this incompatibility let me quote only Freud. Writing about the "pleasure principle" which, according to him, is the primary motive force of human life, he states that "its program is at loggerheads with the whole world, with the macrocosm as much as with the microcosm. There is no possibility at all of its being carried through; all the regulations of the universe run counter to it. One feels inclined to say that the intention that humankind should be 'happy' is not included in the plan of 'Creation'"(1959a, 76). Yet again, Freud may have erred when he identified the pleasure principle with human happiness.

Secondly, this universe could be our universe, and the incompatibility would be ruled out if, instead of our happiness, something else, for instance our moral perfection, was the purpose of creation. In that case this world could be our world despite the discrepancies between our wishes and our environment, and despite all the anxiety and suffering that ensue from these discrepancies.

Thirdly, perhaps we are not the main purpose of creation and this is the source of the incompatibilities we suffer from. This hypothesis would not exclude the possibility that, despite these incompatibilities, our existence has been a more or less important factor in the unfolding and consummation of a creative plan.[2]

Fourthly, we may be creatures of secondary importance in this world, dispensable toys in the hands of indifferent, mischievous, or simply irresponsible gods—as suggested, for instance, in Greek, Persian, and other mythologies. In that case, we would have good reason to feel ourselves in an alien world.

Fifthly, the world may have been created by an evil spirit, by the Devil, or by the Demiurge of Gnostic cosmology. In that case, we would experience the world not only as alien and incompatible, but also as hostile and destructive.

Sixthly, our existence in this world may have not been foreseen. We may be the products of a mistake, a coincidence, a fortuitous event or mutation—for example, the interaction of chance and necessity described by Jacques Monod (1974) and many others. In that case, we are like intruders from another world, trying to survive in, and colonize, a world which is only partly compatible. This, too, would explain the presence of pain, anxiety, and frustration in our lives.

Seventhly, the world may not have been created at all. It may have always existed, or it may have come about in the wake of a Big Bang or some other cosmological or ontological event. In that case, we may be more or less compatible with the world—compatible since we are part of this (uncreated) world. We are made of the 'star dust' whirling around in the universe and, as such, the same forces and laws operate in us as in the rest of the universe; we should have no reason not to feel at home in this world. Since life may be a qualitatively new structure, the product of a quantum jump or major mutation in the universe, however, we may have good reason not to feel quite comfortable here. Between the 'physical world' and this new form of existence there may already be major incompatibilities. And these incompatibilities may very well be the sources of existential fear and anxiety.

Finally, life feeds not only on the material world but also on itself. It is its own predator. Its various species cannibalize each other. This *bellum omnium contra omnes* is another source of fear, suffering, and death.

We need not opt for any of these answers. Since the, at least partial, lack of compatibility between the universe and ourselves seems to be an obvious fact, any of the above answers that allow for this incompatibility may be, at least in this respect, well founded. And any of them could and would explain the primary importance of fear and anxiety in our lives.

Let me stop here for a moment before we look more closely at this 'incompatibility'.

I must emphasize that this book is not intended as a panegyric on the sufferings of mankind in an alien world. On the contrary. It is the study of how people have fought, throughout their history, to survive, to respond to the threats of the world and to overcome the fears in their hearts. And how, by these efforts, they have brought about what we now call 'civilization'.

Incompatibilities

Most of us live like sleepwalkers. We hang around in a state of naiveté and nonchalance and do not realize, or do not dare to confess to ourselves, that we live in a world where the probability of hurting ourselves, and even of perishing, is rather high. We are likely to ignore the fact that we live in a world into which we do not fit too well; in a world the compatibility of which with our constitution, needs, and aspirations may be low; in a world which both supports and threatens our lives.

Let me emphasize here that the universe itself is not 'evil' in any sense of the word. It would be childish to blame the world for our ordeals. It is neither hostile nor friendly, it is simply there, existing in complete indifference to humans, their joys or pains, safety or fears, or to anything else. It is an 'alien world' which is "deaf to his [the human being's] music, just as indifferent to his hopes as it is to his suffering or his crimes", as Jacques Monod (1974, 160) remarks.[3] It is not the world itself, but our incompatibility with it that is the source of our fears and sufferings. We struggle with these incompatibilities, and when I speak in this book about our "struggle with the alien world", it will be only a form of discourse to keep the discussion as simple and transparent as possible.

As a matter of fact, the incompatibility between the world, on the one hand, and life in general—and human life in particular—on the other, is marked. The struggle for survival on this planet has been desperate, if not apocalyptic, from the very beginning. The reader should forgive me if, lest the argument become too romantic and bombastic, I briefly describe this struggle in terms of a number of wholly unromantic and matter-of-fact examples.

The major proof of our, at least relative, incompatibility with the universe is the fact that we have to die—in other words, that we have utterly failed to conquer time, one of the major dimensions of the universe. We have been slightly more successful in coping with space, though we are still able to move around only in a radius of, say, a few light seconds as compared to the billions of light years which measure the expanse of the universe.[4] With time, all our efforts have been in vain. All we can do is to measure it, but we cannot step out of it or reverse it. We are caught, inescapably, at a certain point in its flow like people clutching at a raft in the rapids of a whirling river. Only after death may we ascend into a timeless universe—or simply vanish. Inanimate objects, rocks, hills, and particles of dust are more enduring—they are eroded, destroyed, or transformed more slowly than living beings are, and so, in this respect at least, they are more compatible with the rest of the universe.[5]

When we speak of our incompatibility with the world, we also have to take into account the fact that, as far as we know, there may be relatively few planets in the universe where life may have emerged, or may emerge in the future. New discoveries may change this picture, but the chance of life emerging and surviving on a planet in this universe may be one in several million. This fact clearly bears witness to the low compatibility between the inorganic universe and organic life.

Could Planet Earth be an exception to this rule? Conditions may be exceptionally favorable for life here; there may be a high degree of compatibility between the physical environment and life. Claude Allegre (1992, 205), the famous French geophysicist, seems to confirm this hypothesis. He writes in one of his recent books:

> After all, life emerged on Earth relatively easily (one billion years were enough), while there is no trace of it on the other planets and moons of the solar system. One may conclude from this that, although we do not know how life evolved on Earth, conditions here have been specifically favorable.[6]

But if we read further in Allegre's book, we soon realize that he speaks only of *relatively* favorable conditions on Earth, meaning that even extremely low life chances are still much better than no chances at all. He shows how horrendously difficult it was for life to take root on this planet, and how desperately and stubbornly each species had to fight for survival. In the case of individual creatures, this fight inevitably and without exception ends in ultimate failure—in death. In the case of species, it ends, with few exceptions, in extinction. Life has found and conquered, even on this planet, only a tiny niche, and each living species has an even smaller niche, which may be destroyed, and in most cases has been destroyed, ruthlessly, by the indifferent forces of inanimate or animate nature.

Two hundred and seventy million years ago, at the end of the Carboniferous Age, 90 per cent of all existing species were extinguished; 65 million years ago, after having dominated the earth for almost 200 million years, practically all the dinosaurs, millions of them, starved, froze, suffocated to death within a few thousand years. In South America, almost the entire fauna was destroyed when mammals migrating from North America invaded the continent. According to Csen Jün-jüan and other experts, in the last 500 million years there have been five major cataclysms which led, on each occasion, to the global destruction of most existing species and beings.[7] The relatively favorable environment turned, time and again, into killing fields and killing waters for billions and trillions of living creatures. The world proved to be, again and again, an alien world.

Killing Fields

The destruction of life on this planet has always been almost limitless, even without cataclysms—even in so-called normal times.

Fish and birds rarely die a 'natural' death. "Their chance of surviving to an advanced age is so small that it may be statistically negligible." For instance, one estimate "places the mortality of the Atlantic mackerel during its first 90 days of life as high as 99.9996 per cent"[8]—that is, its chances of survival are only 1 in 2,500. This certainly indicates a fairly low degree of compatibility between these young fish and the world in which they are forced to live (or rather to prematurely die).

Various species of South Sea turtle have slightly better survival chances. But it may be more important to note that the cool statistics of their survival chances hide horrors of animal suffering. The turtles in question swim to their favorite beach to lay their eggs. Sharks decimate them before they reach land. When the time comes for the offspring to hatch, birds swarm over the nests and devour most of the baby turtles at the very instant they emerge from the sand. Those who manage to escape and crawl in panic towards the sea are awaited further down the beach by iguanas. Most of the few which reach the water are devoured by poisonous crabs, and in the water predator fish await the rest. If those who escape all these dangers could speak, they could repeat what one six-year-old boy once said to his mother (his words were recorded by a famous psychiatrist): "Mommy, I'd no idea when I was born that I should have such a bad time."[9]

Birds, too, have to go through an ordeal. The average annual mortality rate of songbirds is between 50 and 70 per cent (that is, 5 to 7 out of every 10 birds die within the first year of their lives). In a way they are 'martyred' since their mortality rate is highest during the period they feed their young: in these stressful weeks they are in a hurry, they cannot lose too much time being cautious, and so fall easy prey to predators.

Remember also the peaceful herbivores, the graceful antelopes or the charming and funny zebras: practically without exception they are killed by their predators. And they are happy if they are caught by lions or leopards who kill quickly; hyenas and wild dogs tear them to pieces alive. And what about the killers? Most of the beautiful big cats starve to death when they are injured or get too old to kill. Can we brush aside all the agony involved in these lives and deaths with a casual and scientific reference to the laws of the food chain?

HUMAN BEINGS

The history of the human species on this planet is as full of death and destruction as that of the other species. Its struggle with nature has not been a glorious and uninterrupted advance. And the showdown is far from being concluded. Not even the highly developed and most protected contemporary human communities are immune to the attacks of the destructive forces of nature: earthquakes, floods, tornadoes, epidemics, and the terror accompanying these ordeals. Illness and death ultimately defeat each and every individual. And the species of *Homo sapiens* itself may vanish without trace.

Dead-Ends

We know from paleontologists and anthropologists how many attempts at survival and development on the part of anthropoid, hominid, and human species have run into destructive and lethal dead-ends. The history of humankind has been fortuitous, contingent, chancy, and non-predictable, as Stephen J. Gould remarked in a recent paper, adding that extinction "is the common and eventual fate of all evolutionary lineages" of mankind (1994, 25, 27). The *Paranthropus boisei* and *robustus*, for instance, disappeared without descendants one or two million years ago. The same happened to all those species which may or may not have transmitted some of their genes to our own species, *Homo sapiens*, but became extinct: the *Australopithecus ramidus*, *afarensis*, and *africanus*, the *Homo habilis* or *Homo erectus*,[10] and even the *Homo neanderthalensis*.[11]

For two million years or more, human beings were fragile creatures, hardly surviving in this dangerous world, freezing in the winters and ice ages, starving in seasons of drought, devoured by predators much more powerful than themselves, threatened and destroyed by the unknown forces of nature. After these two million years, it was only in the last 10,000 years that the balance began to tip in their favor; by 2000 AD they have conquered—and almost destroyed—their planet. What comes next? Will these two, ten, or twenty thousand years become a frivolously, or tragically short interlude of passing glory? Will mankind be extinguished or submerge again into insignificance and anonymity? Will it be succeeded by another species?

Will Butterflies Survive Us?

Mankind may be the goal and the purpose of the created universe, but, as a matter of fact, there are species which seem to be more enduring and long-lived than we are. Let me give a frivolous, but no less shocking example.

According to biologists and entomologists, for instance, 80 per cent of all living species are insects. Some of them populated the earth as early as 350 million years ago, long before the dinosaurs; the ancestors of *Homo sapiens* appeared only 3 to 4 million years ago. They are capable of fascinating achievements. The pilgrim locust is able to fly over the Atlantic Ocean; ants carry loads twenty times their own weight; fleas jump a hundred times their own length. Insects weave the strongest silk in the world; they are masters of architecture and statics; they invented, long before humans, social organization, communication, architecture, agriculture, animal husbandry, organized wars, alcoholism, and slavery—even air-conditioning: "Myrmicine ants and certain tropical termites ... utilize the fungi to control the localized climate of the nest rather than to obtain food. In termite nests ... both the relative humidity and temperature are maintained at relatively constant, high, favorable levels as a result of the metabolic activity of the fungi."[12]

Insects are also extremely resistant and adaptable. Some of their species (cockroaches, for instance) survived the Hiroshima bomb and may survive a global nuclear catastrophe in which mankind would certainly perish. Would it be blasphemy to ask whether they are more at home on this planet than we are?

According to Claude Allegre (1992, 355, 356, 352), the relay race between consecutive dominant species has been going on ever since life appeared on Earth and it will go on indefinitely. The best-adapted species of a particular age have been replaced, again and again, by species that could adapt themselves better to the conditions of the next age. He outlines two possible, or even likely, scenarios for the future. Both may be rather shocking to members of the currently dominant species, *Homo sapiens*.

> The continents will be ruled by insects of one meter length; they will be mixtures of wasps and bees. They will be organized in societies, they will fly, swim, and walk on their hind legs, they will have four hands; having reached a certain level of thinking, and due to their high level of collective organization, they will be the absolute rulers on Earth.
>
> The Oceans [on the other hand] will be ruled by predatory dolphins [since they will be protected against ultraviolet radiation by the water and the chemical constitution of the Ocean]. Their intelligence will be more developed than that of their predecessors, they will organize themselves in societies, they will speak, think, encode their messages.

They will cultivate the sea-bed, breed algae and small fish ... they will be able to go on shore, walk on the beach, they will educate their children, they will lead a sedentary life. Will they be able to conquer the air, too?

The Earth will go on rotating. With us, or without us ...

After all, it may be not our universe.

Do We Need Space Suits in New York or Rome?

I hate to make flippant remarks, but cannot help mentioning in this context that, in a way, human beings can survive on Earth only as the astronauts survived on the Moon. We may be no more at home on this planet than they were there. Without their space suits they would have died immediately in that uninhabitable environment, just as we would quickly perish without *our* 'space suits', which protect us on this dangerous planet, that is, without our immune systems. We are disposed to forget that we are exposed to the lethal attacks of myriads of bacteria, viruses, and fungi at every moment of our lives. But the fact is that we would inevitably be destroyed by them if our immune system did not protect us: after all, they devour us as soon as we cease to live. We carry the alien world even within ourselves. It is worthwhile listening to the microbiologists. "The killers are all around", Michael D. Lemonick concludes a recent article.

> They can strike anywhere, anytime ... For wherever we go and whatever we do, we are accosted by invaders from an unseen world. Protozoans, bacteria, viruses—a whole menagerie of microscopic pests constantly assaults every part of our body, looking for a way inside. Many are harmless or easy to fight off. Others—as we are now so often reminded—are merciless killers ... The age of antibiotics is giving way to an age of anxiety about disease. (1994, 48 and 52)

Unfortunately, as Columbia University's Dr. Harold Neu observed in the journal *Science*, "bacteria are cleverer than men". Just as they have adapted to nearly every environmental niche on the planet, they have now begun adjusting to a world laced with antibiotics. It did not take long.

Pain and Suffering

If we lived in complete harmony with this world, if we did not continuously bump into its edges and corners, if we were not attacked by dangerous and destructive forces at every instant, then, in principle, this world could be a world without pain and anxiety. But even in an alien world, in a world which is not our world, we could do with less pain. We could survive with weaker fear and pain signals. Why are they so unbearably strong and so ubiquitous? Natural selection is one possible answer. Those individuals survived and propagated who had the strongest pain signals and could, therefore, avoid dangers better than others.[13]

If this is the case, we can only blame natural selection for not developing some sort of genetic gadget which would allow us to switch off pain signals once they have delivered their warning. The system keeps signaling and pains continue to torment us long after they have fulfilled their function. We are kept alive even in extreme situations in which, due to the very intensity of these pain signals, we would already prefer to die.

Is this due to a failure in the process of natural selection? The real reason may lie much more in the fact (contested by some biologists) that natural selection works according to the principle of maximizing the survival chances of the species—or of the gene—and not the well-being of individuals. This fundamental thrust of life may, and does, torture and destroy individual creatures, from amoebae to human beings, *ad libitum*. Remember Schopenhauer, according to whom the will to live—that is, the basic drive that forces us to live—is our major enemy and torturer. It compels us to live and to propagate and thereby pushes us into a hell of suffering. Its aim is not our well-being, but its own maintenance. It is a blind force. It uses us, and all living creatures, as vehicles. It lures us into cooperation. It sweetens the trap, it holds us in its power with the help of the 'pleasure principle'. And so we become the source of our own sufferings.

In all likelihood, life itself is, or has become part of, the alien world. The alien world is built into us.

THE FOUR JUNGLES

The alien world may be a more complex phenomenon than my original presentation of it assumed. We may compare it to a jungle in which it is difficult to survive. It is a tradition going back to ancient times to oppose the abode of humans, usually the city, to the surrounding wilderness; the realm of the known and the friendly to that of the unknown and dangerous. Aristotle himself opposed *nous* (reason) to *hyle*, "where *hyle* denotes the chaos antecedent to the operation of Form, but literally means 'forest'" (Piehler, 1971, 75–77; see also McClung, 1983, 16). According to commentators in late antiquity, Virgil used the word *silva* (forest) to indicate the "original chaos" and the "psychic realm of violent and primitive passions" (Piehler, 1971, 75).

Following these examples, we may say that the alien world is not only the jungle outside us, but also the psychological jungle within us. And, upon reflection, we may add a third 'jungle', the social jungle around us, and a fourth, which I propose to call the 'metaphysical jungle'. Joseph Campbell speaks in this connection of the "sickeningly broken figurations that abound before us, around us, and within us" (1968, 27). Throughout their history, people have had to struggle for freedom and peace, not only with nature, but also with the problems and conflicts of their societies and the unknown forces of their souls.

Let me emphasize the fact that, in the course of their struggle with the alien world, people themselves brought about new jungles, new realms of the alien world, some of which have become more fearful and dangerous, the sources of more human suffering, than the alien world they originally fought against. For instance, they entered into association with other people and gradually developed human society in order to be less helpless and to obtain better odds in their fight against the austerities of nature. In the course of time, society developed into a new jungle and became, according to many experts, the source of more human suffering and fear than nature or the physical world. Remember Sartre's famous phrase, "*L'Enfer, c'est les Autres*". We shall see that, similarly, the feeling of guilt came about as a protective device against 'natural evils' (disasters, diseases, death, misery, and so on), but later on it, too, became one of the main sources of human suffering and 'discontent'.[14]

The Physical Jungle

As far as the physical jungle is concerned, for hundreds of thousands of years mankind fought an almost losing battle with nature, with the physical forces of this world. In the last few centuries, though, and especially in recent decades, human beings and communities have achieved more and more brilliant victories. They have multiplied ten-, a hundred-, and in some areas a thousand-fold their power over the forces of nature. But their striving for more and more safety and comfort has become, or may become, self-destructive. They now know that they have the power, and perhaps also the propensity and irresponsibility, to annihilate themselves. And if this happens, an alien world will relapse into cosmic indifference, no longer disturbed by the foolish aspirations of this promising, or absurd, mutation of life, the human species. Remember the title of nuclear physicist Freeman Dyson's (1979) book, *Disturbing the Universe*.

The Social Jungle

Ironically, humans have been less successful in coping with the 'jungle' of the societies which they constructed for their own defense in an alien world. Their performance in this respect has been ambiguous. They have managed to solve some of the major problems of social existence and coexistence: the various forms of social organization and governance, and the recent expansion of the institutions of a democratic polity, have been important achievements. However, the social jungle has not completely receded, even in the most civilized countries. There is no human community or society in which there is no fear and brutality, oppression and misery. The sphere of inter-group relationships, relations between tribes, ethnicities, nations, and countries is even more a danger zone beleaguered by destructive conflicts. Through these rifts in the social fabric the fearful monsters of the alien world creep and burst into our universe again and again. Let me give only one example.

It might be an exaggeration to say that the history of mankind has been one of genocide, but the fact remains that the historical role of genocide is significant.[15] Tens of thousands of hordes, tribes, ethnic groups, city-states, and states have been ruthlessly destroyed by wars, invasions, and environmental disasters. Many, if not most, of them have disappeared forever without leaving the slightest trace, or leaving only some tools, broken skulls, and burial sites. Toynbee (1972, 72) mentions dozens of mighty empires which perished miserably and lists a number of great civilizations that vanished into oblivion: the Indus, the Aegean, the Hittite, the Sumero-Accadian, the Syriac, the Egyptian, the Hellenic, the Iranian, and so on.[16]

Wars have often been accompanied by genocide in modern times. The principle of *Vae victis!* has obtained in most cases. The fall of Babylon and Sumeria, Carthage and Rome, the great migrations, the Mongol and Turkish invasions, the conquest of North, Central, and South America, the colonization of Africa first by the Arabs and later by the Europeans, and so on and so forth, were all accompanied by large-scale genocides, bringing death or slavery to the defeated population. The cruel post-colonial wars in the Congo, Cambodia, Somalia, Ethiopia, Rwanda, and elsewhere have also been genocides. "There are no devils left in Hell. They are all in Rwanda", remarked one eyewitness (Gibbs, 1994, 21) of the massacres—"[f]irst it was politics ... Then it was genocide" (Gibbs, 1994, 23). In highly civilized Europe, too, possibly even worse crimes have been committed in the twentieth century: two world wars, the Russian civil war, and the concentration and labor camps were all genocidal in nature. David Walsh (1990) concludes, with reference to R. J. Rummel (1986), that twentieth-century "totalitarian governments have so far killed, apart from those who have perished in wars, more than 100 million people". Can we pretend that this universe was their universe? That it was the home and homeland of these 100 million women and children, young and old men, who fell victim to the murderous instincts of their own species?

The Jungle in Our Souls

This jungle is still running wild within us, despite all efforts since the earliest times to subdue it, tame its monsters, transform it into a well-kept garden. Even people living in the most affluent societies seem to be obsessed with the forces of chaos and evil in human beings. As somewhat frivolous, but nevertheless significant, evidence let me mention the fact that the creators of mass culture have been able to capitalize on this obsession and anxiety, offering their viewers, in dozens of television series every night, the opportunity to face and—by proxy—defeat evil. The monsters of another world, or those of the underworld, invade our world by the legion as 'aliens', 'demons', or 'Satan' himself. Instead of a single, paltry Dr Jekyll, people turn into werewolves or even more horrendous monsters by the dozen. On our television screens, crime overflows the streets, terrorists blow up cars, houses, cities, and (almost) the whole world. 'Bladerunners' chase their victims in an apocalyptic landscape, in which mankind seems to have lost its battle with the alien world.

Why this permanent witches' sabbath? Are we bored with our lives and so require excitement? Can we afford these horrendous phantasmagorias because we are already so safe and so free? Are they antidotes to our overwhelming happiness? Do we simply like to shiver at the sight of scenes of horror? Do we have to project our subconscious anxieties in order to get rid of them? Do they reduce our feelings of guilt? Do we need and enjoy these excursions into the world of the irrational and transcendental?

There may be a grain of truth in each of these hypotheses. But the almost constant emergence and re-emergence of these monsters in our world may also constitute evidence of the fact that we do not yet have full control over the jungle in our souls. It may even indicate that we are fighting a losing battle against the alien world. It may warn us that we have reached a critical stage of this confrontation; that our civilization has lost at least part of its ability to protect us against the forces of the alien world in our souls.[17]

Despite every effort, we may have less control over our minds and souls now than we have over nature and society. Some scholars contend that primeval or primitive people had a fuller mastery over their souls since they could project and elaborate their inner conflicts and anxieties with the help of rituals, myths, and archetypes. Freud (1959a) may be right when he states that in modern times human beings themselves have become the main sources of their own suffering. J. B. Russell (1981, 16) comes to a similar conclusion when he states that "we are left with the irreducible fact that the jungle remains within us. Or is it worse than a jungle? A jungle is natural. The core of evil within us may or may not be."

The Metaphysical Jungle

As to the "ultimate concerns" of our existence (Tillich, 1965), we live in a fearful jungle of ignorance and uncertainty. We do not know the answers to the most important questions of our human condition. We do not know who we are, where we come from, where we are heading. We do not know what the basic motive forces of the universe are. We do not know why we have to suffer and die, what the meaning of our lives may be, and so on. Statements about these ultimate concerns cannot be either proved or disproved. We cannot prove or disprove God's existence; we cannot prove or disprove that there is some kind of life after death; that there is some 'purpose' in the universe and our lives; that we are free to choose from real alternatives; we cannot prove or disprove that there is a moral principle working in the universe.

This being the case, it seems more than justified to consider the welter of these unanswered questions as a further dimension of the alien world; a further 'jungle', a further threat against which humankind has always had to protect itself.

THE EXPERIENCE OF THE ALIEN WORLD

It may be that the argument developed in this chapter overemphasizes the dark side of life and the alien character of the world. It seems to clash with the general feeling and atmosphere in which we have been brought up in twentieth-century Western societies, that is, the feeling that we are at home in this world, or at least that we may definitely transform this world into a pleasant, safe, and comfortable human world—a world in which there is no fear and no human suffering.

However, we should not forget that this relaxed optimism is a relatively recent experience, limited in time and space. The experience of the world not only as alien but also as hostile and dangerous has been widespread throughout the history of mankind. As we saw in the previous chapter, Jean Delumeau (1978; 1990) describes Western civilization as obsessed with fear and anxiety. Peter Berger (1967), David Scruton (1986), David Parkin (1986), and others consider fear as one of the major motive forces generating and maintaining civilizations. According to Ernest Becker (1973), the fear of death is the mainspring of all human activity. Anthropologists have found ample evidence of the importance of fear in the lives and cultures of native peoples.[18] Robert J. Lifton (1979, 136) speaks of "the extreme conflict and pain evident in the most primitive cultures", while Claude Lévi-Strauss (1961) entitled one of his books *Sad Tropics*.

The fear and anxiety that they were living in an alien world have accompanied men and women throughout the millennia and across the borders of civilizations. They have experienced their world as the Vale of Tears, the Valley of Death, the battleground of Ohrmazd and Ahriman,[19] or a world of universal suffering veiled by the cosmic and deceitful illusion of *maya*.[20]

This fearful perception of the world is present in most of the myths we know: in Greek and Renaissance tragedies, in the dramas of the absurd of modern times, in the paintings of Bosch, Goya, Toulouse-Lautrec, and Francis Bacon. It is present in the tragic visions of some of the greatest minds of humankind, in those of Socrates and St Augustine, Seneca and Sade, Pascal and Camus, Schopenhauer and Nietzsche, Freud and Kierkegaard, as well as Baudelaire, Dostoyevsky, Conrad, and many others. Samuel Johnson (who otherwise lived in the Age of Reason, the *siècle des lumières*, in the century of light and utopian hopes), illustrated the human condition with a parable describing how the gods amuse themselves by torturing human beings:

> As we drown whelps and kittens, they amuse themselves, now and then, with sinking a ship, and stand round the fields of Blenheim, or the walls of Prague, as we encircle a cock-pit. As we shoot a bird flying, they take a man in the midst of his business and pleasure, and knock him down with an apoplexy.
>
> Some of them, perhaps, are virtuosi, and delight in the operation of an asthma, as a human philosopher in the effects of the air-pump ... Many a merry bout have these frolic beings at the vicissitudes of an ague, and good sport it is to see a man tumble with an epilepsy.[21]

In a similar way, I could also quote some of the great witnesses of our own age. People who could hardly be accused of romantic *Weltschmerz* or *fin de siècle* decadence. Mircea Eliade (1954, 139–62) speaks of "the terror of history";[22] Joseph Campbell (1968, 28, 29) discusses "the terrible mutilations of ubiquitous disaster" and "the universal tragedy of man"; Albert Camus (1956) revolts against the unacceptable absurdity of a world where even innocent children have to suffer the agonies of unbearable pains and death. Jaspers (1965, 188) speaks of the "universal homelessness" of mankind in this universe. Karl Popper (1945, II, 258) concludes his discussion of the question of whether history has meaning by warning that to "maintain that God reveals Himself in what is usually called 'history', in the history of international crime and of mass murder, is indeed a blasphemy".

Let me cite one final witness. He describes our universe as "an alien and inhuman world", "a hostile universe", "a cavern of darkness"; he speaks of "the tyranny of death", and "the loneliness of humanity amid hostile forces"; he states that "the world was not made for us"; he describes human life as a "narrow raft" in a "dark ocean on whose rolling waves we toss for a brief hour", and concludes that the "life of man is a long march through the night, surrounded by invisible foes, tortured by weariness and pain, toward a goal that few can hope to reach".[23]

Whose words are these? St Augustine's? Pascal's? Kierkegaard's? In fact, these lines were written by one of the paragons of twentieth-century rationalism and—strangely enough—militant optimism, Bertrand Russell. The whole text is a beautiful *credo* concerning the power of man to live a meaningful life even in an 'alien world'.

One could, of course, discard these testimonies as examples of a moody decadence or intellectual spleen, and quietly return to one's late-twentieth-century pragmatism: we know that life is not a bed of roses, but most problems can, and should, and will, be solved. There is no reason to panic.

I, too, believe that our main task is to solve the problems which emerge in our lives and in our societies and not to brood over the tragic aspects of the human condition.[24] Nevertheless, it may be a good and pragmatic step to take these austere visions and verdicts seriously, at least for the moment. If we look at things from this angle we may learn something new about ourselves, our world, and—this is our main concern here—about our civilization. We may profit from studying human societies as communities of human beings who have constantly been engaged—in a none too hospitable world—in the everyday work of building a world of safety and freedom, dignity and meaning for themselves; of building, out of symbols, their civilization.

We shall now turn to these symbols, which are—alongside the world of material objects and institutions—the main constituents of human civilization. How are they generated? What are their functions? How do they fulfill their role of protecting people? How do they develop into essential supporting structures of human civilization?

NOTES

1 *Social Research* has devoted a whole issue to the question of 'Home: A Place in the World' (see 'Home', 1991). This is a collection of papers read at a conference in New York in October 1990.
2 Consider, for instance, the Hegelian concept of universal history according to which the Absolute Spirit could not have actualized itself without the existence, and history, of mankind. The same is true of the great "cosmic drama" of the spiritualization of the universe described by Teilhard de Chardin.

3 Bertrand Russell also speaks of "a universe that cares nothing for its [humanity's] hopes and fears" (1981, 60).

4 In coming decades, we are likely to be able to extend the radius of our maneuvers to a couple of light minutes, thanks to new generations of spaceships.

5 This incompatibility is also due to evolutionary factors: according to evolutionary psychologists, our emotional and cognitive apparatus evolved in the Pleistocene in response to the problems to be solved in that period. The process of natural selection could not adjust them to the needs of modern man, who lives in a completely different and rapidly changing natural and social environment. We live nowadays in a super-technical, post-industrial world with the emotional and behavioral responses of Pleistocene women and men.

6 An excellent introduction to the emergence and history of the various stages of life is to be found in Gould (1993).

7 The approximate dates are 455, 365, 270, 180, and 65 million years ago.

8 See *The New Encyclopaedia Britannica*, 15th ed., s. v. 'Growth and Development'.

9 Reported by Balint (1954, 118).

10 *Homo erectus* emerged 2 million years ago in Africa, spread to Europe, Asia, and Indonesia, and disappeared or developed into the archaic *Homo sapiens*.

11 *Homo neanderthalensis* may be our ancestor, but according to Stringer, Gamble, Gould, and many other experts he may be only our cousin: "[O]ne among several non-African descendants of *Homo erectus* that did not transform to modern humans, and that died essentially without issue." Coming presumably from Africa and invading Europe, *Homo sapiens* occupied the habitat of Neanderthal people who disappeared almost without trace about 30,000 ago (Gould, 1994, 25, 28); see also Stringer and Gamble (1994).

12 *The New Encyclopaedia Britannica*, 15th ed., s. v. 'Biosphere'.

13 J. B. Russell raises the same question in connection with the traditional argument of theodicy that pain is a precondition of our moral improvement: "Why are the degree and the amount of suffering so great? Would it not be sufficient to God's plan for freedom to enable us to slap or kick one another without using knife or napalm?" (Russell, 1977, 18).

14 See chapter seven on the role guilt has played in Western civilization. For a characteristic and passionate statement, see Bertrand Russell's (1946) book: *Ideas that Have Harmed Mankind*, subtitled *Man's Unfortunate Experiences with His Self-made Enemies, Including Sadistic Impulses, Religion, Superstition, Envy, Economic Materialism, Pride, Racism, Sex, Superiorities, Creeds, and Other Evil Things.*

15 Speaking of the possible extermination of Neanderthal Man by *Homo sapiens*, Jacques Monod (1974, 161–62) remarks that it "was not to be the last performance of this kind: genocides abound in recorded history".

16 See also Sorokin (1962) and Spengler (1926).

17 Kundera (1988, 11–12) believes that the monsters of history have recently become more dangerous than those of our souls.

> [After the First World War, the] time was past when man had only the monster of his own soul to grapple with, the peaceful time of Joyce and Proust. In the novels of Kafka, Hasek, Musil, Broch, the monster comes from outside and is called History; it no longer

has anything to do with the train the adventurers used to ride; it is impersonal, uncontrollable, incalculable, incomprehensible—and it is inescapable. This was the moment (just after the First World War) when the Pleiad of great Central European novelists saw, felt, grasped the terminal paradoxes of the Modern Era.

18 See our discussion of this topic in Chapter One. See also Aldrich (1931, 98) and Scruton (1986).
19 The God of Light and the God of Darkness in ancient Persian mythology.
20 In Hinduism, the illusory world of mutability and sensuality in which we live and which conceals from us the real and eternal existence in spirituality.
21 Quoted by Daiches (1960, 769). Johnson took this parable from Jenyns (1757), and interpreted it in a half-ironical way.
22 He devotes a whole chapter to the discussion of "the terror of history", adding that, since people have lost the protection of archetypes and the myth of the eternal return, and have fallen in the trap of history, "almost the whole of mankind lives prey to a continual terror (even if not always conscious of it)" (1954, p. 162).
23 Bertrand Russell (1981, 56, 57, 59, 60, 61).
24 There have been interesting attempts at pointing out the 'Gnostic' aspects of (modern) Western civilization (Voegelin, 1968; Szakolczai, 2000). My approach, however, is not a Gnostic one. When I speak of an 'alien world' I do not mean that the physical/material world is the empire of evil and death. And I do not think that the main aspiration of the human being is, or should be, to escape from the prison of the material world and of the body, and enter the sphere of pure spirituality and the divine.

According to the main hypothesis of this book, the scope of human life is both narrower and broader than this. We are unable to achieve pure spirituality in our lives (and we can only hope that we shall be able to do so after our death) but we are able to create a human world of freedom and meaning by surrounding ourselves by spheres of symbols: by a civilization. In the process of constructing our symbolic systems we may hit upon some elements of genuine, or even divine, truth. But even if everything we devise is a construct, our symbolic systems have an intrinsic value for us because they provide us with the framework of a more authentic human existence, in several ways. Let me mention here only one of them.

As we have seen, fear plays also a positive role in our lives. It challenges us and prompts us to build up, and maintain, our civilization, or to change it if necessary. It prompts us to live more intensely. It reminds us of our human situation and the precariousness of our existence. It may protect us against submerging into Heideggerian 'oblivion'. And so on. But, at the same time, fear may paralyze us, it may sap our energies, it may hinder us in developing our potentials. And, as a consequence, by protecting us against fear, our civilization, even if it is only a construct, helps us to achieve human fulfillment.

CHAPTER FOUR

THE GARDEN OF EDEN

> [The human being must] realize that, like a gipsy,
> he lives on the boundaries of an alien world.
> Jacques Monod, *Chance and Necessity*

THIS chapter describes people's attempts to control their anxiety in this world by generating the hope, the belief, the illusion that they are at the center—perhaps even that they are the very center and purpose—of the universe. These attempts have played a major role in shaping the myths, religions, belief systems, arts, and ways of thinking of all human communities we know, and they are important motive forces in forming contemporary civilization. The symbolism of the center, of paradise, and of the garden is discussed in detail.

THE MYTH OF THE CENTER

On the Periphery

Western civilization has always struggled to maintain the conviction, belief, or illusion that it is at the center of the universe, even that it is the very center, the purpose, the meaning of the universe. In all likelihood, this aspiration was present in most civilizations, but Western civilization seems to have been the most successful in developing this myth of centrality. Throughout the centuries this has been one of the most powerful shields against the terror of having to live in an alien world at the mercy of unknown and uncontrollable forces. It has also been one of the major factors in the generation of our civilization.

With all these efforts, have human beings convinced themselves that they are at the center of the universe? Or do they still fear that they are at the periphery, or at some undistinguished point of an infinitely great universe?

The facts—or at least what we imagine to be the facts—are not encouraging. Let me quote only one testimony, which is certainly worth listening to. Nobel laureate Jacques Monod concludes his book *Chance and Necessity* (1974, 160) by stating that the human being must "wake up from his millenary dream; and in doing so, wake to his total solitude, his fundamental isolation". He must "realize that, like a gipsy, he lives on the boundaries of an alien world".

Most people do not want, or are unable, to accept this gloomy prospect. Throughout their history they have made efforts to surround themselves with a complex system of symbols—their civilization—to protect themselves against the terror of a human existence at the periphery of the universe. Not an easy task, this has been a powerful motive force in putting into place the symbolic structures of our civilization.

In principle, our planet may equally be either a significant or an insignificant point in the universe. It may be—although this is unlikely—the physical or symbolic center of the universe and also an infinitesimal point somewhere on the periphery. But, living at the end of the twentieth century, we have to admit that physically it is almost nonexistent either in space or in time. So much so that we may have difficulties in conceiving its smallness in a huge universe.

The farthest points in the universe which our astronomers can see with their mega-telescopes are at a distance of about 10 billion light years from us, that is, the distance covered by a photon in 10 billion years. Since a photon travels about 10 trillion kilometers in a year (10,000,000,000,000, or 10^{13}), the farthest point we can see is about 10,000,000,000,000,000,000,000 kilometers (or 10^{22}) from us, which is already far beyond what we can understand or imagine. If we add to this that we may see, even with our largest telescopes, only a fraction of the whole universe, it is no exaggeration to say that our planet is lost in this almost boundless space. We are also lost among the myriads of stars. There are several hundred million galaxies and between one hundred million and ten billion stars and planets in each galaxy.

Fortunately, in most civilizations we know about, a wonder weapon was at hand to put this immensity in some kind of perspective: symbols and symbolic systems with which they could construct out of this fearful infinity a homely universe on a human scale.

We are also almost imperceptible in temporal terms. Our universe—and we know virtually nothing about other possible universes—was born 12 to 18 billion years ago (if the theorists are right and there was nothing before the so-called Big Bang). Our sun and planet came into being four and a half billion years ago. Life emerged three and a half billion years ago. *Homo sapiens* appeared about two hundred thousand years ago. Our recorded history goes back no more than five to six thousand years. This is a fraction of a fraction of an instant in the history of the universe.

"We are nothing in this immensity, in spite of our believing that we are all. Man is not the center of the universe, but only a tiny star dust", concludes Claude Allegre (1992, 80) in his recent book on the history of the universe. This is highly probable, but we need not accept it since it has not been proved, until which time people have the right to believe that mankind occupies a central place in the universe.

To generate and maintain this belief has always been a basic human propensity and endeavor. Not only, and probably not primarily, for the trivial purpose of feeling oneself important, but much more because humans feel lost in this vast universe and try to allay their anxiety by generating in themselves the belief that they are not insignificant and dispensable non-entities somewhere on the outskirts of the universe but, on the contrary, that the universe is revolving around them. If it does, this is indeed their universe, a human universe, and not an alien world which threatens them with destruction. They have a special place and a special role to play. In all likelihood, this longing for a central place in the universe has been a major force in generating the symbolic systems of human civilizations.

A Revolution in Reverse

At the dawn of their conscious existence, our ancestors must have felt rather helpless on the periphery of a dangerous world. It may have taken tens or hundreds of thousands of years to develop the belief or conviction that we, mankind, were at the center of the universe. Genuine human history may have begun with a Copernican revolution in reverse: if the revelations of Copernicus jettisoned us from the center of the universe, human history began with a slow and stubborn movement in the opposite direction. From their precarious situation as fragile and helpless creatures on the periphery of a dangerous world, with the help of their myths, religions, rites, ceremonies, practices, culture, and art, our ancestors forced their way to the center of the universe, at least in their imagination. It was not an exodus from, but an incursion to, the center.

In most early myths the human being appears as a newcomer, an outcast, a forlorn creature, desperately struggling with the alien forces of an unknown and dangerous world.[1] (In the 'Adamic'—or 'Garden of Eden'—type creation myths, however, the human ordeal begins only after having lost an initial, central position in the universe.) In the polytheistic cultures, human beings were in a better, though ambiguous, position. Finally, they moved to the center of the universe in the monotheistic cultures—in Judaism, Christianity, and Islam. The faith or the illusion that mankind is at the center of the universe has been one of the major constituent elements of European culture since the Middle Ages.[2] Although called into question from time to time by a few agnostics, the creed survived the collapse of Ptolemaic cosmology and the Galilean, Copernican, and Keplerian revolutions. It also survived eighteenth-century skepticism and nineteenth-century materialism, Darwinism, and Marxism.

Now, after the Copernican, Einsteinian, Darwinian, and Freudian revolutions, when we have hardly any excuse left to justify our belief that we are at the center of the universe, we still struggle for the belief, or illusion, that we are there, despite more and more evidence to the contrary. One of the basic functions of Western civilization has always been to generate and regenerate this conviction: the faith or illusion that we humans are at the center of the universe.

Where Is the Center, If There Is One?

It was not an easy task to find, or construct, the center of the universe. People living in a tribal village may have located it in the totem pole, and they continuously reinforced its sacred centrality with myths, magic, and ceremonies. Their civilization hinged on this pole and was, at least partly, generated by this mythic, magical, and ceremonial activity. For many ancient cultures, the shrine or temple at the center of the sacred capital, or a sacred tree or a sacred mountain, indicated the center of the universe. For the Greeks, it was Mount Olympus. The Hindus must have had more difficulty with answering the question since the center could not be in this world, in the world of illusion: it must have been somewhere beyond the veil of *maya*, in Nirvana. For dualistic religions such as Zoroastrianism, to locate the center of the universe may not have been simple either: was Ohrmazd (or Ahura Mazdah), the God of Light, the center of the universe, or was it Ahriman, the God of Darkness? Or was the center somewhere in between? Or was it outside their battlefield?

The Hebrews also had their difficulties. In one sense, Yahweh was the obvious center of the universe, but he was also the creator of the world, the earth, the sky, the sun, and the stars; that is, he created something outside himself, which was dependent on him but not identical with him. In this way, the universe became somewhat 'de-centered'—it lost, at least partly, its balance. The balance was symbolically restored by building the Temple of Jerusalem, the earthly abode of Yahweh, which, through the presence of the divine, could become the center of the created world as well.

God or Satan?

Christianity, with its unsolved problem of monism versus dualism—that is, the problem of whether God is the unique and almighty divine essence in the universe or battles with a powerful adversary, Satan—had an even more difficult problem to solve. This basic contradiction has played a major role in shaping Western civilization. If the earth is the center of the universe, then the central point of the earth must be the most central point of all. So far, so good; but down there, in the burning recesses deep underground, is traditionally to be found the realm of Satan: Hell. Is then Satan at the center of the universe? According to J. B. Russell (1988, 142), author of several books on the mythology of Satan, and someone who knows much more about hell and heaven than most of us:

> Like Ptolemy's, Dante's cosmos was arranged in a series of concentric spheres, the earth being the sphere at the center. Above and around the earth was the sphere of the moon and then in order those of Mercury, Venus, the sun, Mars, Jupiter, Saturn, the fixed stars, and the *primum mobile*, the sphere that moves the whole universe. Beyond and above these were heaven, the abode of God, the angels, and the blessed souls. In the center of the earth was hell, and the very center of hell, imprisoned in darkness and ice, was Satan.

Medieval theologians and cosmologists, Dante among them, solved the problem by stating that—though Satan was at the physical center of the universe—God, out there somewhere, was the real symbolic and sacred center of the universe:

> On one level this system places the Devil rather than God at the center of the universe. On a deeper level, however, Dante meant God to be placed at the real, moral center of the cosmos, though he could not represent this in spatial terms. Indeed, he took pains to insist that the moral center cannot be located in space or time ... the real center is the life and light of God, which is everywhere. (Russell, 1988, 142)

In the history of European cosmology, the alleged center of the universe was first located in the earth (geocentric universe), later it shifted to the sun (heliocentric universe), only to move even farther away to ... where? I must admit that I do not know where, according to the latest astrophysical discoveries, the 'center' of the universe is supposed to be. Is it at the point where the alleged Big Bang took place 12 to 16 billion years ago? Or, as Nicholas of Cusa asked in the fifteenth century, and mathematicians and astrophysicists have asked in the twentieth century, can infinitude have a center at all? And what if there was no Big Bang and the universe is continuously being created everywhere in a more or less homogeneous cosmic space, as hypothesized by Fred Hoyle (1950, especially Chapter 6) and others?[3] Is it not utterly absurd and unscientific to ask about the center of the world in a post-Einsteinian or Hawkingian universe?

Most of us never even give a thought to these problems. We have done our best to generate our faith in our preeminent and central position in the universe, and in various ways. In this and the following chapter I shall briefly survey some of our major strategies. First, I shall show how safe enclaves occupying a central position in the universe were isolated within the alien world by means of rites and myths of consecration. Secondly, I shall describe various types of these enclaves of human safety and freedom. I shall study, for instance, the 'paradise'-type enclaves, and then the 'garden', the 'house', the 'cathedral', and the 'shopping mall' as symbols and sites of an anthropocentric cosmos—micro-universes of safety, freedom, and human dignity within, and against, an alien world, and the essential building blocks of our civilization.

CONSECRATION

Mircea Eliade (1959) devoted a whole book to the study of the division of the world into two domains, the profane and the sacred.[4] He describes the wide range of means by which people have tried, from time immemorial, to create for themselves a micro-world of safety, freedom, and meaning within a dangerous, chaotic, and meaningless world, which—in the present book—

we call the alien world. They have used all kinds of magical, mythic, and symbolic practices to circumscribe and delineate their own world, to carve their own world out of the alien world, to isolate it from the dangers of the outside world:

> desert regions inhabited by monsters, uncultivated lands, unknown seas on which no navigator has dared to venture ... all these wild, uncultivated regions and their like are assimilated to chaos; they still participate in the undifferentiated, formless modality of pre-Creation. This is why, when possession is taken of a territory—that is, when its exploitation begins—rites are performed that symbolically repeat the act of Creation: the uncultivated zone is first 'cosmicized', then inhabited ... [It is] transformed from chaos into cosmos ... (Eliade, 1959, 9–11)

In earlier periods, these encircled human micro-universes were protected by friendly forces and spirits whose goodwill was gained by sacrifices and devotion, or who were caught and held within the confines of this world by magic. Later, with the emergence of celestial gods and more developed systems of religious ideas, these enclaves were considered to be domains of the 'sacred', and the outside world the domain of the 'profane'. The sacred domains were created by the act of 'consecration', a ceremony which opened a niche, a place, a sanctuary, a home for the divine in this world, and—by its presence—opened a realm of safety, freedom, and authenticity for people entering this place (a sanctuary, a temple, a church), or living or working in this consecrated place (a home, a city, a field, a country).[5]

People must have felt that alone they would be unable to create their own world. They needed the help and protection of a divinity. They had to implore, or constrain, the friendly spirits and forces to be with them and protect them. Later, they had to open a 'window' through which God, descending from his heavenly realm, could enter the physical world and take up his abode in the place which would be made sacred by his presence.

'Sacred' here means the presence of the divinity in an object, a place, or a human life; the presence of God in a profane world; the authentic center of an inauthentic universe. It refers to a clearing in the jungle of the alien world, the bridgehead of the divine, an enclave within the profane, an opening towards the realm of the transcendental; to a micro-world, which— due to the presence of the divine—is a blissful world of freedom and safety, meaningful and authentic human existence, surrounded by an alien world in which there is no freedom and no safety, no meaning and no authenticity for human beings.[6] It is the ordered cosmos of human civilization against the chaos of the alien world.

PARADISE

Paradise has been one of the strongest symbols of these sacred enclaves and, in general, of the human world as opposed to an alien world of fear and anxiety. It is amazing to see how mythic thinking generated a host of elements and motifs to reinforce the image of this sacred enclave at the center of the universe, and how these motives crystallized into important structures of our civilization.

First, paradise has been thought of as the sacred place par excellence (in contrast to the profane and chaotic world outside it) since God created it for Adam and Eve. "And the Lord God planted a garden eastward, in Eden; and there he put the man whom he had formed" (Genesis, 2:8). Or, in the Koranic version of the same idea: "For Him, by Him, the world was made. 'O Mohammed', God said, 'hadst thou not been, I would not have created the sky" (Campbell, 1968, 386).

People were further protected by the fact that they were believed to be the only creatures in the universe whom God had created "in his own image" (Genesis, 1:27), unlike most myths and religions, which identified their gods with non-human, semi-human, or animal beings or even monsters. God maintained a close and almost informal relationship with humankind,[7] surrounding them with his own protective aura of divinity. Furthermore, the myth transformed human beings from among the weakest and most fragile creatures into the lords of the world. "And God said: 'Let them have dominion over the fish of the sea, and over the birds of the air, and over the cattle, and over all the earth'" (1:26). The right to give names to all living beings (a motif found in many creation myths around the world), further enhanced the power of mankind over the world.[8]

Earthly paradise was opposed to the alien world also in space: various mythologies referred to different geographical locations as its site. The word 'Eden' meant 'plain' in Sumerian (Sproul, 1979, 125). In the Hebrew Genesis, the word 'Eden' may have referred to the faraway fertile plain of the Tigris and Euphrates (Genesis, 2:14). In this case, the Garden of Eden symbolized the idyllic state of the world before the Fall, before it was transformed into an alien world. In other cases, the garden of the earthly paradise had its site in the middle of an arid and deathly desert, emphasizing the contrast between this sacred and safe enclave, a world of human freedom and happiness, and the outside world, the world of danger, death, and human misery. As we shall soon see, other mythologies placed the earthly paradise on top of a sacred mountain, stressing even more its sacred and divine character with this closeness to heaven.

The Fortress of Innocence

Mythic thinking also isolated paradise from, and opposed it to, the alien world in moral terms as the realm of absolute innocence, peace, and harmony.[9] Though no immortality is promised to man and woman and to the other creatures in paradise, fear and death, illness and suffering seem completely absent from it.[10] There was no conflict, no struggle, no killing of one another in this idyllic garden. The biblical text emphasizes that all the animals were to eat only "green plants". "And to every beast of the earth, and to every fowl of the air, and to every thing that creepeth upon the earth, wherein there is life, I have given every green herb for meat" (Genesis, 1:30–31). The opposition to the real (alien) world was thus carried almost *ad absurdum*.

This protective shield of innocence was further reinforced by the fact that Adam and Eve were believed to live in the complete innocence of a world in which everything was 'good'; in which the fundamental dichotomy of good and evil—and preeminently that of moral good and evil, virtue and vice—was still absent. Their world was hermetically sealed from the outside world, as it would be after the Fall, full of suffering and conflict—kept apart from the realm of the permanent struggle of vice and virtue. In their pre-lapsarian state they were sexually innocent as well, although Genesis is contradictory on this point, quoting God as saying: "Be fruitful and multiply, and replenish the earth, and subdue it" (Genesis, 1:28), while a few verses later, in the 'J' version of the Creation myth, it is implied that Adam and Eve had been virgins before they ate of the fruit of the Tree of the Knowledge of Good and Evil (Genesis, 2:25, 3:7).

The atmosphere of timelessness, if not eternity, which filled this mythic garden to the brim further isolated it from the outside world of chaotic change and fearful mutability. The four rivers which sprang up in Eden, watered the garden and divided the world into four realms—the latter are present in many earthly-paradise myths—are symbols of life and of the ordered cosmos as opposed to the chaotic wilderness or the arid desert of death around the garden (Genesis, 2:10–14).

The threat of the alien world must have been so strong that these mythic elements and motifs did not suffice to hermetically isolate the human world and protect it against the alien world. Further motifs were needed. In several creation mythologies, for instance, a strong wall was added to enclose and protect the garden of paradise.[11] Moynihan (1979, 1) explains that the English word 'paradise' itself is a transliteration of the Old Persian 'pairidaeza', referring to a walled garden.[12] The wall separates the realm of the divine, of real life, eternal youth, happiness, order, and harmony from the outside chaos of the wilderness, the jungle, and the desert. It may also symbolize the act of separating the world of divine grace and human freedom from the enslaving chaos of the alien world.

Within the context of Christian symbolism, the wall of paradise signifies divine intervention, a redemptive interruption of the natural order (the jungle, chaos) "pointing up the power of Grace to undo the natural propensities of human will [and signifying] life-giving separation between nature and Grace" (McClung, 1983, 20).[13]

As already mentioned, in a number of mythologies the safety and the sacredness of the paradisal garden was further enhanced, and its central position reinforced, by placing it on the peak of a sacred mountain, close to heaven itself.

Sacred Mountains

Sacred mountains—such as Meru in India, Fujijama in Japan, Zinnalo in Laos, Alborj in Persia, the Qaf in Islamic tradition, the Potola in Tibet, Mount Sumeru of the Ural-Altaic people with the Pole Star fixed to it, Olympus in Greece, Mounts Sinai and Zion in the Old Testament, and Montsalvat in the Grail legends—have played an important role in the majority of civilizations,[14] and for many reasons: they were supposed to stand at the center of the world and to be the axis of the world—they connected earth and heaven.[15]

> The summit of the cosmic mountain is not only the highest point on Earth, it is also the Earth's navel, the point at which the Creation began. According to Mesopotamian tradition, man was formed at the 'navel of the earth' ... Ormazd creates the primordial ox Evagdath, and the primordial man, Gajomard, at the center of the earth ... Paradise, where Adam was created from clay, is, of course, situated at the center of the cosmos ... according to a Syrian tradition, [Paradise] was established on a mountain higher than all others ... [and] Adam was created at the center of the earth, at the same spot where the Cross of Christ was later to be set up. (Eliade, 1959, 6–17)

Sacred mountains also offered points of transcendence and ascension to heaven for saints, prophets, and—in the Christian tradition—for Jesus himself. They were also the abodes of gods and the immortal souls (Chevalier and Gheerbrant, 1969, 518–21, 582–84). Mount K'ouen-louen in China, for instance, was called by the Taoists "the Mountain of the Center of the World"—the sun and the moon were believed to orbit around it, and on its peak stood a paradisiacal garden, the Garden of the Queen of the Occident, with the Tree of Immortality growing in it. Dante placed the Earthly Paradise on the peak of an axial mountain, Mount Purgatory.[16]

The closeness of sacred mountains to heaven was an important mythic element, and the question of relative proximity puzzled many generations of priests, theologians, philosophers, and ordinary people. "Zion [was] thought to be only eighteen miles from heaven", we read in a study of ancient Jewish myths and rituals (Patai, 1947, 236–46), although later, in "more enlightened ages", the distance increased considerably. "At the beginning of the eighteenth century, Jeremias Drexel, a German Jesuit, located ... [it] 'above the whole region occupied by the stars', and computed the distance between Germany and this 'heavenly *palast*' to be exactly 10,314,085,710 miles and the depth of Paradise to be 360 million miles" (Sandmeyer, 1994).[17]

From the Garden to the City

Another question that puzzled people throughout the Middle Ages was the fate of the Garden of Eden after the Fall. Where could it be located in a fallen world? Europeans studied the maps of the Middle East and explored the Atlantic Ocean to find a trace of the garden of yore; the Chinese explored the faraway islands in the South China Sea and beyond. Discovering the Bay of Trinidad, Columbus was convinced that he had discovered the former paradise. It soon turned out that he was mistaken. But if the garden had disappeared for ever, if in a post-lapsarian world it was not to be found anywhere, there remained only one solution: to look for it, and hope for it, in the future—at the end of the history of mankind.

William A. McClung (1983) describes this shift from the past to the future paradise in his brilliant book *The Architecture of Paradise*.[18] He shows how the nostalgia for the idyllic and Arcadian Garden of Eden was gradually replaced by the vision of the celestial city, the New Jerusalem. This vision was already present in the writings of the prophets of the Old Testament, and in the Apocalypse of Saint John, but it was further developed in the Middle Ages.

> Beatrice leaves us in no doubt that Dante is going to a city: 'Vedi nostra città', she cries (*Paradiso*, XXX, 130) ... The garden is abandoned, and eventually the city is discovered, but first an intermediating vision of transfigured nature must be worked through. Dante sees a river of light, spray from which becomes rubies falling into golden flowers by the river bank (*Paradiso*, XXX, 55–69) ... The 'Rome' of heaven is then revealed as an architectural phenomenon, an amphitheater, that is simultaneously a rose; and the jeweled landscape, the *locus amoenus*, vanishes. (McClung, 1983, 38)[19]

Christian theologians realized at a very early date that in a fallen world the earthly paradise had to be protected, to be walled in, transformed into a *hortus conclusus*, or even more, into a 'fortress'. As McClung (1983, 24) puts it: "Eden survives by compromise with a fallen world, as a fortress"—or as a fortified city. This may be why most medieval illustrations of the New Jerusalem show a heavily fortified city. The sacred enclave of the divine and the human world, of real life, harmony and salvation, have to be protected with all possible means against the threats of a sinful world.

The Garden of Eden was also symbolically integrated in the strong stone structures of ecclesiastical architecture, in cathedrals, monasteries, and the *horti conclusi* of the cloisters, which, by their form, arrangement, and fountains, recalled some basic characteristics of the garden. The cloister prefigures the paradise to come, as Joachim of Fiore declared in the twelfth century (McClung, 1983, 25).

The Cross of Christ and the Skull of Adam

Let me ask two apparently simple questions. In medieval altarpieces, pictures, and frescoes the Cross was usually portrayed as standing on top of a hill and, in a considerable number of such pictures, there was a human skull at the foot of the Cross. Why does the Cross stand on top of a hill, and why did religious tradition (or mythic imagination) put the skull there? The obvious answer would be, first, that the New Testament refers to a hill near Jerusalem as the site of the crucifixion, and second, that this particular site was called "*the place of the skull*, which is called in Hebrew Gol-go-tha" (John 19:17). 'Golgotha' in Aramaic meant 'skull', and this was the name given to a hill near Jerusalem with a barren, rocky top. In Latin, it was later called '*calvaria*'.[20] The skull in the pictures may have pointed, as an emblem, to the historic site of the crucifixion.

However, there may have been much stronger forces at work. Golgotha was the site of the redeeming death of Christ, the central event in the

Christian story, and consequently it was important to emphasize and prove its central position in the universe. This may have been the reason why—using a whole range of motifs—biblical and medieval traditions over-emphasized its centrality. The hill was thought to be the peak of the sacred mountain, sunk below the surface of the earth after the Fall. And since the sacred mountain was thought to be at the center of the world, its peak was the center of the center. The cosmic mountain was also called, as were many other sites in various civilizations, the 'navel of the world' or, in Latin, the *umbilicum mundi*. It was also presumed that, *illo tempore*, it had been the site of the Garden of Eden. And since the Garden of Eden was supposed to have been located at the center of the universe, the central position of Golgotha was further reinforced. But even this was not enough: further symbols of centrality were piled one on top of the other.

According to medieval tradition, the Cross stood on the spot where, earlier, the Tree of Eternal Life had stood: at the center of the Garden of Eden, and so at the center of the universe. And here we come back to the skull at the foot of the Cross. It was not just another skull; nor was it merely the emblem of Golgotha as the 'place of the skull'. It was thought to be the skull of Adam, the first man, onto which the blood of Christ, the New Man, dropped, thereby symbolically saving Adam and Eve and humankind. In these pictures, the whole Christian drama, from the Fall to Salvation, was condensed in a single scene. The Cross stood, physically and metaphorically, at the very center of the Christian universe.

Golgotha, as part of a sacred mountain, was also the axis of the world. The Cross itself, pointing towards heaven, was an *axis mundi*. And the ascension of Jesus Christ from the summit of the hill to heaven created an even more sacred, invisible axis between earth and heaven, the temporal and the eternal, the profane and the divine. The Christian world, people's lives and hopes, Western civilization, could safely hinge on this axis which was so strong and reinforced in so many ways.

THE GARDEN

Gardens are among the most successful inventions of humankind in its endeavors to defeat fear and to feel at home in the universe. If my home is my castle, then my garden is my sanctuary. We enjoy the paradisiacal bliss of our gardens and we protect them against the outside world, the alien world, with our swords drawn, as the Archangels Michael and Gabriel protected the Garden of Eden—although we usually replace the swords with trowels.

Consider the emotional involvement, and sometimes even the fury, with which we weed our gardens, the deep pleasure we find in this activity, and the relief we feel when we have made progress. In weeding our gardens we may be doing no less than unconsciously or semiconsciously fighting against the forces of the alien world; against the chaos and disorder in the form of weeds, bugs, fungi, bacteria, and other alien beings that keep invading our world, our sanctuary, our civilization. Weeding our gardens is a relatively easy, everyday victory over the alien world.[21]

The garden is our world, a world created and controlled by us. It is an ordered and harmonious universe as opposed to the disorder and disharmony of the outside world. This is one of the few spots in our lives, and in the universe, that we really can control and keep in order. The garden is a protected enclave, enclosed by a wall, a fence, or a hedge. It is a sanctuary in which a fearful world is tamed and transformed into a friendly universe. Only those elements and beings of nature are allowed into and tolerated in it which are friendly to us—which serve our comfort. All other elements and beings are excluded, or, if they intrude, uprooted. This opposition of the inner world of the garden to the outside world was strongly emphasized in the hot climate of Persia and the Arabic lands. "High walls, trees and shrubs afforded privacy and a place for spiritual contemplation. Outside was the barren landscape, the heat and the glare; inside was shade and vegetation, symbolizing life" (Lehrman, 1980, 62).

Besides spades and sprayers, we also have other instruments with which to protect ourselves in our gardens: we have rituals, myths, and archetypes. Accordingly, gardens were considered in many civilizations as sacred places, symbols of the cosmos and divine harmony, life and eternity. This religious and mythical significance was most developed and formalized in the Persian and Islamic gardens, but it also emerged in the closed gardens of medieval monasteries, in Renaissance gardens, and in the French gardens of the seventeenth and eighteenth centuries.[22] It reemerges, in its complexity or only in some elements, in our contemporary gardens. In Italy and Spain, for instance, its presence is manifest in many places.[23]

The Enchanted Garden

Teaching at a summer school in Cortona, Tuscany, in 1994, and discussing with my students the questions we are considering here, I suddenly realized that the garden of the monastery-turned-hotel which was hosting the summer school, displayed some of the main archetypal features of traditional Persian or Islamic gardens. It was rectangular with a tiered fountain in the middle, and two paths divided it into four equal and symmetrical parts—the traditional arrangement of Persian and Islamic gardens, not to mention the mythic gardens of several other civilizations. The fountain in the middle is the sacred mountain with the spring of life bubbling at its summit. The four paths represented the four watercourses of traditional Persian and Islamic gardens, symbols of the four rivers of life which appear in the Vedas, in Genesis, and in many other sacred documents. In various cultures, the four quarters symbolized the four basic elements of the universe, and as a result, these gardens came to symbolize the cosmos.

> Long before Islam four elements were considered sacred: water, fire, air and earth. The Book of Genesis recounts that 'a river went out of Eden to water the garden; and from thence it was parted, and became four heads'. In Persian ceramics dating back approximately six thousand years, the world is depicted as divided into four sections by two axes that form a cross. At the focal point is a pool, or Spring of Life. This image may be related to the Mandala of Buddhist iconography ... The symbol of four rivers, which branch out from a common source or center in the direction of the four cardinal points, stands for fertility and timelessness ... Similarly, the flow of a river symbolizes not only fertility but the passage of time, while bathing in a sacred river was equivalent to losing the self and achieving salvation in the ocean of existence ... the four water channels not only symbolize the four rivers of life, but to a Muslim their intersection also represents the meeting of man and God. (Lehrman, 1980, 61–62)

The geometric shapes of the garden suggest that there is a strong order and harmony in this universe, and that the universe is spiritual rather than material in its essence. As we shall see in the next chapter, geometry played a particularly important role and had a deep symbolic significance in Islamic art.

The fountain is at the exact center of the garden—that is, of the universe—and so becomes the 'navel of the universe' and the sacred source of life. In Iran and Mughal India, the central cistern in the garden was also considered "part of the heavenly realms" (Schimmel, 1976, 15). Due to its height and conical shape it is also an Icarian symbol of transcendence. Pointing upwards, towards the center of the universe—the divinity—it is an *axis mundi* and a symbol of the sacred union of earth and heaven.

Being circular, the fountain symbolizes the dome of the sky, the eternal, the sacred and the spiritual as opposed to the rectangular ground plan of the garden, archetypal symbol of the secular, material, temporal world. The two together, the finite interacting with the infinite, the material with the spiritual, the temporal with the eternal, represent the universe as a whole. They form a *mandala*.[24]

The fountain of Cor stands in a circular basin and its axis holds three concentric basins or shells, each one smaller than the last as we go upwards to the fountainhead, from which the water emerges. Falling back, the water trickles and splashes down from one bowl to the next until it reaches the pool, from which it rises once again back to the top.[25] This circular motion suggests eternity, the feeling and myth of eternal return, of death and rebirth, death and resurrection.[26] It fills us with a sense of victory over fear and mortality.

This gradual descent of the water also reanimates one of the most powerful mythological motifs described by Gilbert Durand (1969) as being among the so-called chthonic myths. Free fall towards, and into, the earth is a symbol of death, he writes, and it generates fear and anxiety in humans. Myths protect them against this fear by 'slowing down' the terrible fall. In many myths this slowing down is achieved by transforming the fall into a downward spiral motion, as for instance in the first part of Dante's *La divina commedia*, in which he described his and Virgil's slow descent into Hell. Examples could be multiplied *ad infinitum*. In a great number of myths and folk tales, for instance, the hero descends into the underworld, in a spiraling motion, around the trunk of the Tree of Life.

In the case of the fountain, the slowing down is achieved by the three basins. Instead of falling down directly into the depths, the water drops and trickles down only into the next basin, by which it is softly caught and, after a while, gently given over to the next basin. The basins of the fountain are brimful. The water overflows imperceptibly and gracefully, suggesting an almost imperceptible transition between life and death. The horror of death is transformed into the poetic melancholy of transitoriness. Nothing is either final or doomed to disappear forever in this world. The lower basins and the transparent water gracefully receive the falling drops: there is salvation. Heidegger (1980, 163) was fascinated by the deep significance of this type of fountain: in his famous essay 'The Origin of the Work of Art', he quotes C. F. Meyer's beautiful poem *The Roman Fountain*:

> The jet ascends and falling fills
> The marble basin circling round;
> This, veiling itself over, spills
> Into a second basin's ground.
> The second in such plenty lives,
> Its bubbling flood a third invests,
> And each at once receives and gives
> And streams and rests.[27]

Shall I also mention that there was a pine tree in the garden? This is a late successor of the mythic Trees of Life, the cosmic trees, symbols of regeneration and immortality, Icarian symbols of transcendence and spirituality, joining earth and heaven. Add to this the beds of luscious flowers in full bloom: their beauty is a Neoplatonist transition between the sensual and the spiritual. A mystery and a mystical experience.[28]

All in all, the garden in Cortona, like the traditional, mythical garden, is a symbol of the cosmos and of the primeval earthly paradise. It has a deep emotional and archetypal significance. It is a replica of the Garden of Eden, with its trees, flowers, and fountain, and even more with its peace, innocence, and eternal harmony. In our gardens, as in the Garden of Eden, even beasts live in peace and harmony. Remember our almost celestial delight and relief when we witness the friendship of our dogs and cats: it is proof of the fact that this is our world, a good world, where the laws of the jungle, and those of the alien world, do not operate. When we are in our garden, we feel at home in this universe. At least for a few fugitive moments, a few fugitive hours. By building our garden, we build our civilization and control, curb, and defeat the monsters of a chaotic universe.

There is a single mistake in the garden of Cortona. At the top of the fountain there is a kind of *putto*, or water god, from whose jar the water spouts. This is a lapse of taste, a grave spiritual blunder, evidence of a civilization that has forgotten its sacred origins. This barbarian materialization or hominization of the spiritual and the divine would be unimaginable in the Islamic gardens of yore, where the divine hides itself behind, and radiates through, the transcendence of abstract lines and forms, or the spiritual beauty of flowers.

NOTES

1 The earliest myths were recorded no more than four to five thousand years ago, but they may reflect much earlier states of mind. The same is even truer of the myths of primitive tribes recorded in the nineteenth and twentieth centuries (see Mircea Eliade [1978–1985] or Barbara Sproul [1979]). For the difficulty or impossibility of establishing a sequence from one stage or form of mythic or religious belief to another, see the same authors and also Evans-Pritchard (1965).
2 Despite the fact that as a result of the Fall Adam and Eve forfeited their right to remain there, not to mention some hesitation now and then concerning whether Man, God, or (heaven forbid!) Satan was at the cosmological center of the universe.
3 See also Bondi (1957); Weinberg (1977); and Davies (1993).
4 See also Eliade (1954, especially the chapter entitled 'The Symbolism of the Center', 12–21), and Campbell (1968, 384–85). Yi-fu Tuan (1979, 206) writes: "Cultures differ in the ways they define space, but define it they must. The minimum requirement for security is to establish a boundary ... Closed circles are satisfyingly complete ... But the Navaho is also afraid of the closed circle. Evil may be trapped in it, and once trapped it cannot get out, nor can good enter. For this reason the Navaho favors the open circle." The Roman feast of Lupercalia and the later European tradition of 'beating the bounds' are also relevant here.
5 People consecrated their houses, fields, and churches by means of various ceremonies: sacrifices to the divinity, burning incense, sprinkling holy water (and so exorcising the place, expelling evil), praying, circumscribing or plowing around the future city (Rome), keeping magic objects, herbs, or relics in the house, having 'sacred corners' in their homes, building altars in their churches, hosting and adoring the divinity in the form of icons or statues, and so forth. All these magical rites and ceremonies served the purpose of excluding the forces of the alien world from this enclave of human safety and freedom.
6 The isolation of the sacred and safe enclave from the surrounding alien world was reinforced by the fact that the transition from the profane environment to the sacred center was imagined, and displayed, as extremely difficult. Only the most courageous heroes could attain this goal.

> The road leading to the center is a 'difficult road' (*durohana*) and this is verified at every level of reality: difficult convolutions of a temple (as at Borobudur); pilgrimage to sacred places (Mecca, Hardwar, Jerusalem); danger-ridden voyages of the heroic expeditions in search of the Golden Fleece, the Golden Apples, the Herb of Life; wandering in labyrinths; difficulties of the seeker for the road to the self, to the 'center' of his being, and so on. The road is arduous, fraught with perils, because it is, in fact, a rite of passage from the profane to the sacred, from the ephemeral and illusory to reality and eternity, from death to life, from man to the divinity. Attaining the center is equivalent to a consecration, an initiation; yesterday's profane and illusory existence gives place to a new life that is real, enduring, and effective. (Eliade, 1959, 18)

7 At least according to verses 2:4–23 of Genesis, which are attributed to the author known to scholars as the author of the 'J' (Jehovah) tradition: "[T]he other

traditions, such as the 'E' or Elohistic one, tend to depict God as remote, filling the distance between him and man with intermediaries like angels and even dreams. 'J' envisions the relationship of man and God as very close, almost informal" (Sproul, 1979, 125).

8 "[T]he Lord God formed every beast of the field and every bird of the air, and brought them to the man to see what he would call them" (Moses, 2:19–20).

9 Innocence is traditionally a strong distinguishing mark of the sphere of the divine. "In Heaven, one lives a virgin life" ["*Im Himmel lebt man keusch*"], Pope John Paul II said at a general audience in Rome in late November 1994.

10 In several other mythologies, the paradisiacal garden was the abode of the gods or of those who have achieved immortality. See, for instance, the Sumerian-Babylonian paradise or the Homeric Elysian Fields (Moynihan, 1979, 4).

11 There are mythologies in which the primeval paradisiacal garden has no walls. Genesis is not explicit on this point. As William A. McClung (1983) states, it may have been imagined as "Arcadian and open, the epitome of that nature of which it is a small part", although after the Fall—at least in medieval iconography—the archangels expelling Adam and Eve stand at the 'gate' of the garden. Solomon's garden, which was associated with the Garden of Eden, was already an enclosed garden. According to Stanley Stewart (1966), in medieval imagination and iconography the garden was usually enclosed, emphasizing the fact that after the Fall the garden became the sacred enclave of the divine in a world that, by means of the Fall, had been transformed into an alien world. In his book on the history of enclosed gardens, he (1966, 42) quotes a characteristic piece from the early seventeenth century:

> that garden far, exceeding sundry wayes,
> As perfect second woorkes, exceed things wrought before.
> All closely wall'd about, inviolately stayes,
> No serpent can get in ...
> (Rowlands, 1601)

12 'Pairi' meaning 'around', and 'daeza' meaning 'wall'. See also Lehrman (1980, 31 and *passim*). From among the countless paradise myths let me refer only to the Sumerian paradise of Dilmun; the Hindu Uttarakuta and the Island of Utnapichtim the Faraway; the Homeric Elysian Fields; and the hanging gardens surrounding the Chinese K'ouen-louen, which is the center of the universe and the gate of heaven, containing the fountain of life.

13 He quotes Stewart (1966, 59).

14 Besides the sacred mountains themselves, thousands of temples, pagodas, stupas (the sacred mound of the Buddhists), ziggurats (staged temple towers of the Babylonians), and dozens of pyramid-like structures were erected as replicas and were supposed to stand at the (symbolic–spiritual) center of the world. A great number of temples, churches, and domes were built on the tops of hills and mountains. See, for instance, the Dome of the Rock in Jerusalem, or the abbeys of the Benedictine Order throughout Europe. See Moynihan (1979, 8–9).

15 According to McClung (1983, 25) Eden was considered a heavenly space "set apart from undifferentiated nature and proximate to heaven, connected by a mountain, a tree, or a vine". See also Eliade (1959, 12).

16 Much earlier, some authorities in later Judaism had located Paradise on the summit of a sacred mountain (The Book of Jubilees 4:26; The Book of Enoch 24. See Chevalier and Gheerbrant, 1969, 519).
17 The author mentions that, according to a survey carried out in 1994, 50 per cent of Catholics, 43 per cent of Protestants, and 8 per cent of agnostics believe in the existence of Paradise (1994, 20).
18 See especially Chapter One 'Eden and Jerusalem'.
19 Or it is transformed into the "garden of love", the "*hortus deliciarum*", the "*Château d'Amour*", or the "paradise of pleasure" of medieval moral allegories, and of Renaissance and Baroque allegorical and epic poetry (*The Romance of the Rose*, Ariosto, Spenser, Tasso, and so on). See also Curtius (1953, 185ff) on 'The Ideal Landscape'.
20 In Latin, the word 'calva' means 'bald head' or 'skull'.
21 We have made the mistake of overreacting to the attacks of the alien world. First, we cut only small clearings in the jungles and woods; later, we enlarged these clearings to larger and larger fields, ending up by cutting down almost all the forests of the world, transforming the globe into a hygienic and barren laboratory, covering the last spots of nature with stone and tarmac. Then, to compensate us for the inevitable losses, we started planting small patches of green on the tops and terraces of buildings, or imitated flowery gardens with flowery carpets and meadows with artificial lawns. We have also killed almost all wild beasts, except for a few specimens which we have put behind bars and kept as thrilling reminders of the bygone and defeated alien world.
22 Renaissance and French gardens trapped nature in their mazes and embroideries of extreme artificiality. English gardens developed in the eighteenth century subdued nature in a more subtle and sophisticated way: they transformed it into an Arcadian landscape which was as artificial as the geometrical forms of the French gardens, but looked more spontaneous and natural than nature itself.
23 From the rich literature on gardens, see, for instance, Stewart (1966); Comito (1978); Thacker (1979); Moynihan (1979); Lehrman (1980); *The Islamic Gardens* (1976).
24 The *mandala* ('circle') is a complex symbol to be found in many cultures and religions. It plays a central role in the Hindu and Buddhist traditions. It is a circle, or a complex of concentric circles, enclosed in a square, or containing a pattern of squares. It symbolized the cosmos, the center of the universe, perfection, eternity, the interaction of the material and the spiritual world, the synthesis of opposite forces, space and time. It was a guide to meditation and also a tool in initiation rites. It served as a blueprint for a great number of temples and churches all around the world.
25 "This form of tiered fountain ... came late to Islamic gardens, and is more characteristic of Turkey than elsewhere" (Lehrman, 1980, 66).
26 Water was a rich and complex symbol. "It was a source of life ... [a] spiritual force ... its fluidity and purity made it an image of the soul ... the images of the passing clouds symbolize transience ..."; furthermore, "[t]he Muslims often preferred a pool to be non-transparent, since its depth was then left to the imagination and it could symbolize infinity" (Lehrman, 1980, 36–39, 89).

27 'Der römische Brunnen' (1882)

> *Aufsteigt der Strahl und fallend giesst*
> *Er voll der Marmorschale rund,*
> *Die, sich verschleiernd, überfliesst*
> *In einer zweiten Schale Grund;*
> *Die zweite gibt, sie wird zu reich,*
> *Der dritten wallend ihre Flut,*
> *Und jede nimmt und gibt zugleich*
> *Und strömt und ruht.*
>
> (Meyer, 1962, 22)

28 For Islam, the rose was the "perfect manifestation of the glory of God" (Lehrman 1980, 68). For a discussion of the symbolic role of flowers, and especially that of the rose, see Schimmel (1976).

CHAPTER FIVE

THE IMAGE OF THE WORLD

> What has the Tabernacle of Moses, the shrine of the divine, to do in our contemporary shopping malls? It is there.

THE discussion of the symbols of centrality is continued in this chapter, focusing on the mythological dimensions of architecture. How do houses and cathedrals, or contemporary buildings such as shopping centers, organize the social space around themselves? How do they assuage fears and anxieties by generating some of the basic symbolic structures of our civilization?

THE HOUSE

Besides gardens and Gardens of Eden, buildings have always played a major role in protecting us against the forces of—and our own fears in—an alien world, making us feel that we are at home in this universe and that we live in a safe, well-ordered, meaningful universe, rather than a dangerous and fearful chaos.

Promethean and Apollonian strategies overlap in the construction of buildings. Houses have had the function of protecting human beings against the forces of both the physical and the spiritual world. They have had the role of sheltering people against the cold, the rain, the heat, wild beasts, intruders, and marauders. But they have also had to protect them against evil spirits, demons, and perilous influences; against the terror of living in an unknown, mysterious, and dangerous world. It was not enough to find well-hidden caves or to build strong walls for one's hut, cottage, or house. The home had to be separated from the outside, alien world, and protected against it spiritually by various magical, mythical, and symbolic means.

In most civilizations, new houses were—and in some places still are—consecrated. These acts of consecration were important structures for all civilizations. By a magical act houses were taken out of the realm of the profane and transposed into the world of the sacred. By this means, they were isolated from the chaos of the alien world and became part of the divine order. Magical objects, icons, domestic altars and gods (the *lares* of the Romans, for instance) further reinforced this protection.

Imago mundi

Buildings were also believed to represent the center of the universe, and this central position filled the hearts of their inhabitants with the feeling of safety and significance. Norberg-Schulz (1985, 20, 22), one of the foremost experts in this field, develops this idea in his book on the "phenomenology of dwelling".

> Human life is always related to centers where actions of primary importance take place ... the settlement ... the square ... the institution ... the house ... In general, the center represents what is *known*, in contrast to the unknown and perhaps frightening world around ... As a consequence, man has always thought of the whole world as being centered. The ancient Greeks placed the 'navel' of the world (*omphalos*) in Delphi, the Romans considered their Capitol the *caput mundi*, and the *Ka'aba* in Mecca is still the center of the Islamic world. In general, the 'discovery or projection of a fixed point—the center—is equivalent to the creation of the world', Mircea Eliade says, intending that meaning and center belong together.[1]

And that is not all. Buildings also protected human communities by being symbols of an ordered cosmos as opposed to the chaos of the alien world. In public buildings this role is obvious: they are all *imagines mundi*, images of the world.

> [T]he public building is not an abstract symbol, but partakes in daily life, which it relates to what is timeless and common. In the church a general understanding of world and life is made present, in the city hall the organization of society, in the theater life as it is lived ... (Norberg-Schulz, 1985, 71)

In traditional societies—and to a certain extent in our contemporary societies as well—the ordinary house has played the same mythic and cosmic role. It has been regarded as a microcosm, the image or symbol of the macrocosm, and opposed to chaos.

> The hogan, or mud hut, of the Navahos of New Mexico and Arizona, is constructed on the plan of the Navaho image of the cosmos. The entrance faces East. The eight sides represent the four directions and the points between. Every beam and joist corresponds to an element in the great hogan of the all-embracing earth and sky. And since the soul of man itself is regarded as identical in form with the universe, the mud hut is a representation of the basic harmony of man and world, and a reminder of the hidden life-way of perfection. (Campbell, 1968, 385)[2]

The traditional Chinese house, too, was rectangular. It opened in the direction of the rising sun; there was an opening in the roof for the smoke, and a hole in the floor for the rain. The house was thus bisected by the *axis mundi*. The traditional Arab house was also rectangular (a symbol of the physical world), with a garden or a fountain within (symbols of the eternal, the celestial, the divine). The tents and yurts of nomadic people are often circular and sometimes even have a dome-like roof, symbols of the cosmos and the celestial realms. We might also mention Emperor Nero's Golden House as described by Suetonius (1967, 125): "But of all these parlors and banqueting roomes, the principall and fairest was made rounde, to turne about continually both day and night, in manner of the World", or, as his seventeenth-century English translator adds, like "heaven".[3]

According to Gaston Bachelard (1969, 6–7), the house is not only a protective, but also an integrative force. Without its shell, the human being would be dispersed and would lose himself in the contingencies of a changing world. "It is the first world of man. Before being 'cast into the world' … man is deposited in the cradle of the house."[4]

The house is a human world par excellence. It is a nucleus and generative power of civilization. It is our world, since we have built it, and—on the human scale—the building of a house may be the closest parallel to the divine creation of the world. In my home, I am the creator and the master. It is I who can say: Let there be light, and there is light the next instant. It is I who defines the days and the nights, who fixes the stars of the chandelier on the firmament of this micro-world. My house is my universe. Seeing the outside world and not being seen by it, I am in an almost divine position.

In contrast with the outside world, which is chaotic and meaningless, our world within the walls of the house is an ordered micro-universe, and—due to the presence of objects, books, photos, souvenirs—a world full of meaning. The simultaneous presence of past, present, and future allows us an intense and 'authentic' existence in the Kierkegaardian, Heideggerian, or Jaspersian senses of the word.

The interior space is further isolated from the outside world by the exterior painting of the house and the interior decoration of the walls. Outside, bright colors contrast the house with the environment. Inside, furnishings, colors, and decoration may oppose the house to an austere environment, as for instance "in the Norwegian peasant cottage where rich floral patterns remind of summer and fertility" (Norberg-Schulz, 1985, 94); or in contemporary homes, where the patterns of wallpaper are descendents or distant relatives of the wall decorations of the Roman villas, medieval and Renaissance palaces and churches, and the rich arabesque of Islamic buildings.

Nineteenth-century European middle-class homes also had a rich inner world: heavy curtains and carpets, velvet wall hangings and paneling, pictures, chandeliers, and a host of significant objects separated and sheltered it from the outside world. Modernism opened up the houses, replaced heavy walls with large windows and glass panels bringing in light and nature, proclaiming victoriously that human beings were finally at home in the universe, that they did not have to fear the forces and monsters of an atavistic and anachronistic alien world. Recently, in the emerging age of postmodernism, in the wake of the horrors of our century and the growing fear of the future, it seems that we are closing our homes, reducing the size of our windows, and locking our doors again.

It may be due to these vital functions that the loss of the home (in a war, an earthquake, a divorce) is one of the most traumatic experiences in human life. One is suddenly exposed, without protection, to the elements of an alien world. One falls out of one's civilization.

THE CITY

The City and the Wilderness

Before modern times, cities all over the world were protected by walls, fortifications, moats, and *pont-levis* against the hostile world surrounding them. Understandably, in a number of cultures and mythologies they became symbols of the world of human beings, protected by divine power against a chaotic universe outside their walls. In his fascinating study of "visionary landscapes", Paul Piehler (1971, 73, 75) speaks of "the basic psychic polarity of city and wilderness", and of "the fundamental distinction of human landscape into city and wilderness, known and unknown", rational and irrational, conscious and instinctive, order and disorder, cosmos and chaos. Epic poems in antiquity and the Middle Ages often started with "the founding of the city", that is, by fencing off an enclave to be ordered by human reason and excluding the wilderness: the forest, the ocean, the chaotic and dangerous forces of the world. It is in this way that Uruk was founded in *The Epic of Gilgamesh*, Rome in *The Aeneid*, and Heorot in *Beowulf* (Piehler, 1971, 73).

The forest or the ocean (surrounding the city, the created, ordered, rational world) were well-known symbols of chaos in early mythical and philosophical thinking. People of earlier ages were more conscious of "the fundamental conflict of man and wilderness" than we are. Creation myths often speak of the primeval waters, symbols of chaos out of which the ordered cosmos was created. And, as we saw when discussing the 'four jungles', Aristotle opposes *hyle* to *nous* (reason) "where *hyle* denotes the chaos antecedent to the operation of Form, but literally means 'forest'" (Piehler, 1971, 75).

The City and Its Archetypes

Besides the opposition of *nous* and *hyle*, ancient cities were also strengthened in their role as symbols of the cosmos as opposed to chaos *per analogiam*. They were identified, for instance, with celestial archetypes and configurations. As Eliade (1954, 7–8) points out, all "the Babylonian cities had their archetypes in the constellations: Sippara in Cancer, Nineveh in Ursa Major, Assur in Arcturus". A great number of cities were considered sacred since they were believed to stand at the center of the world and to be the gates between heaven and earth. "Babylon was literally called the gate of the gods, *Bab-ilani*", and also *Dur-an-ki*, the "Bond of Heaven and Earth" (McClung, 1983, 25; see also Eliade, 1954, 14). Babylon was also identified with paradise: the "map of Babylon shows the city at the center of a vast circular territory bordered by a river, precisely as the Sumerians envisioned Paradise" (Eliade, 1954, 10).

Jerusalem, too, had its archetype in a "Celestial Jerusalem" created by God (Baruch, II, 4:2–7).[5] "Thus, the historical Jerusalem may claim the role of 'the holy city' of the prophets (Isaiah, 48:2, 52:10)";[6] the Arabic name of Jerusalem is El Quds, 'the Holy'. Later, "Jerusalem ... yielded its historical role to Rome and to Constantinople", and finally to Charlemagne's Aachen, which was called *Nova Roma* in Carolingian documents, and ... was considered as sacred in the sense that the realm of the divine and the secular overlapped there in the person and dignity of the emperor (McClung, 1983, 71–72; see also Smith, 1956).

The faith in the sanctity of Jerusalem was so strong in the Middle Ages that in the popular imagination it was often identified with the Celestial Jerusalem of the Apocalypse. McClung (1983, 72) quotes the following anecdote. "Perhaps because they misunderstood Urban II's description of Jerusalem as 'the navel of the world', 'paradise', and 'the royal city placed in the center of the world', soldiers of the First Crusade in 1099 apparently expected to find the celestial city at the end of their road."[7] In a similar way, "during the Renaissance the *commune* of Brescia prohibited the destruction of the houses of those condemned for heinous crimes on the grounds that cities are constructed as models of Paradise" (McClung, 1983, 75).

In spite of all these physical and symbolic fortifications, all these attempts throughout human history to protect the cities as sacred enclaves in which human beings could live in safety, freedom, and dignity, the alien world has never been completely defeated. It has kept launching its attacks against the human world and, among other victories, has reoccupied parts of cities. Think of the slums of Rome or modern megalopolises, where fear and misery poison the lives of millions. People who could afford it fled back to nature, though of course only into the artificial, Arcadian nature of the Roman villas and the modern garden cities. Or they took refuge in the steel and glass office and apartment towers where they can delude themselves into believing that they hover above the smoke and stress of an alien world, in celestial heights, while the universe silently and sublimely revolves around them.

Let us not forget, however, that even in these glass and chrome sanctuaries they need myths, old and new symbols and symbolic systems, in order to feel themselves really safe and free. We shall come back to these myths, important constituents of our contemporary civilization, shortly.

THE TEMPLE AND THE CATHEDRAL

Temples and churches are the ultimate symbols of the sacred enclave, the realm of the divine on earth, the world of men and women in an alien world. And here again, we shall see the efforts, if not the obsession, of various human communities to shelter these sacred micro-universes by as many protective devices as possible; by the very site of the temple or church, by its ground plan and arrangement, the handling of its surfaces, ceremonies of consecration, the symbolic presence of divinity, and so on, and so forth. And we shall see how, by these efforts, essential elements and structures of our civilization are generated; and the fears and anxieties in people's hearts are mitigated.

The Gate of Hell

Temples or churches were often built on top of sacred mountains, thus becoming themselves part of the sacred *axis mundi*, the link between heaven and earth. We should not forget, however, that in the mythic imagination the axis of the world reached down into the underworld, into chaos, into the site of fearful dragons and monsters, and, later, into that of Satan himself.

The presence and the threat of chaos and evil were so strongly felt that people were anxious to seal it off with several protective layers and devices. In the case of the Temple of Jerusalem, for instance, the sacred mountain and its peak, the rock on which the Temple had been built, was the first protection, stopping the "mouth of chaos" or "the gate of hell".[8] As a second line of defense, there was the sacred Temple itself, with the invincible presence of God in it. Medieval cathedrals were thought to play a similar role. In India, intricate ceremonies served the same goal. Before the foundation stone of an Indian temple is laid, the

> astrologer shows what spot in the foundation is exactly above the head of the snake that supports the world [the snake is, at the same time, the symbol of chaos, of the forces threatening the created cosmos with destruction]. The mason fashions a little wooden peg from the wood of the Khadira tree, and with a coconut drives the peg into the ground at this particular spot, in such a way as to peg the head of the snake securely down ... If this snake should ever shake its head really violently, it would shake the world to pieces. (Stevenson, 1920, 354 and note)[9]

The Temple of Jerusalem—being the reproduction of the original holy Tabernacle—was also sanctified and protected by the fact that it had been built according to the instructions God had given to Moses (Exodus, 25–30).[10] It was also thought to be the symbol of the created world and to display the original divine proportions of the universe. In Judaic tradition it was described as a 'microcosm' or as the allegory of the whole cosmos; later, after its destruction, and in the Christian tradition, it became the symbol of the 'New Jerusalem', the apotheosis of the divine on earth. Given its importance, biblical and other sources were fervently searched in the hope of rediscovering its original form and proportions. As far as we know, these efforts were not crowned by success, but this failure did not prevent people from believing that their churches were essentially the reproductions of the ancient, biblical model and thus they, too, were protected by the holiness of the Temple. Helen Rosenau (1979), André Parrot (1957), and others (Gutmann, 1976; Patai, 1947) have studied these millennial efforts in the history of Christian, Jewish, and Islamic architecture.[11]

> Charlemagne's Palatine Chapel, a vaulted octagon surrounded by ambulatory and galleries ... and other medieval princely chapels were replicas of the Church of the Virgin of the Lighthouse in Constantinople, built before 768, which itself was thought to derive its form and proportions from Solomon's Temple and its model: Moses' Tabernacle. (McClung, 1983, 164, footnote 52)

Beyond being reproductions of the Temple and prototypes of the New Jerusalem, medieval basilicas and Gothic cathedrals were also believed to be images or "mirrors of the world" (Simson, 1965, 21–24). The early Christian basilica, with its "two superimposed zones: below, the colonnade or arcade accompanied by a dark aisle, and above, the high wall or clerestory pierced by large windows and covered by glittering mosaics" was an *imago mundi*, with the heavy, dark walls symbolizing the earth and the windows opening to the sky, and the golden and blue mosaics symbolizing a glorious heaven (Simson, 1965, 75).

In the early centuries Christianity was still on the defensive. Its basilicas were strong, closed buildings; they protected people against the outside, profane, alien world, and sheltered within themselves the realm of the divine and the world of humankind. The Gothic cathedral, on the other hand, with its transparent walls, magnificent gates, flamboyant towers and spires, opened up to the outside world. It trumpeted abroad the victory of the Christian God over His foes; it victoriously announced that the spirit of Christianity pervaded the world, had spiritualized matter, had defeated the alien world.

> In the early Christian basilica, the entrance was small and modest, expressing a contrast between the profane outside and the sacred inside. In the medieval cathedral it becomes grand and 'transparent', making the presence of the church in the world manifest. The Renaissance, on the contrary, does not open up, but treats the facade as a surface where the general cosmic order, which is common to the outside and the inside, is projected. (Norberg-Schulz, 1985, 78)

The Gate of Heaven

In spite of this openness, the entrance of the cathedral, the *porta coeli*, the gate of heaven, was strongly protected by a host of saints and apostles carved on the facade and sometimes on the gate itself. And within, the safety, freedom, and authenticity of human life were not only protected, but were transformed to the highest intensity by the presence of God, and by the images, statues, icons of Jesus and the choir of saints. The Devil, the evil spirit, the alien world had no chance whatever of breaking through these multiple lines of defense, of invading this sanctuary.

The entrance of the cathedral, with all the sacred symbols around it, also gave people the "sense of arrival in a place where a world is explained ... It is first of all the point where the meaning of life is revealed" (Norberg-Schulz, 1985, 79).[12] Entering the church and proceeding along the central aisle towards the altar, the site of Christ's sacrifice and the miracle of salvation, the faithful experienced and reenacted the central mystery of Christianity, which was thus also expressed in the longitudinal, Latin-cross-like ground plan of the basilicas and cathedrals. This spatial arrangement "was introduced in the first major basilica built after Constantine's decree of 313, St John in the Lateran in Rome", and remained the basic model for two millennia.

> But early Christian architecture also developed another spatial theme: the static, centralized rotunda, which does not contain any pronounced direction. The later solution was used for baptisteries and mausoleums, that is, buildings which relate to what comes before and after man's life in the world ... in the West the main emphasis was given to the longitudinal axis, whereas the East developed the Christocentric church. We may in this connection be reminded of the Latin cross of the Gothic cathedral and the Greek-cross plans of Byzantine architecture ... The Baroque aimed at full integration of path and center, and adopted the oval to solve the problem. (Norberg-Schulz, 1985, 81)

As we mentioned in the previous chapter, rectangular and circular forms have always played a major role in magical practices and the mythic imagination. In magic, the circle could encompass, invoke, and keep captive the Devil and evil spirits; or it could protect the magician—and humans in general—against the Devil and evil spirits (remember the famous scene between Faust and Mephistopheles in Marlowe's *Doctor Faustus* or Goethe's *Faust*). In mythic thinking, it symbolized the sky, the dome of heaven, the sacred, virtue, totality, perfection, eternity. The square, on the other hand, was the symbol of the earth, the material world, the created world, of stability, and also of moral fortitude, constancy, wisdom, and truth (and it, too, could be the symbol of perfection and eternity). The Temple of Jerusalem and the mythic New Jerusalem were imagined as rectangular and cubic, the Ka'aba in Mecca was cubic, and Plato's imaginary city in *The Laws* was circular. In the layout of Atlantis in the *Timaeus* and the *Critias*, square and circle were juxtaposed (McClung, 1983, 61; see also Roseanu, 1979).

As we have seen, this combination of the square and the circle, earth and sky, time and eternity in the square ground-plan and the spherical dome or cupola of Christian churches, Islamic mosques, and the sacred buildings of other cultures, was often considered to be the symbol of the cosmos in its totality and sanctity.[13]

The importance for the mythic imagination of geometrical forms and numerical proportions cannot be overemphasized. In this respect it overlaps, in a strange way, with theoretical thinking; or we may say that the philosophical and mathematical ways of thinking also have a mythic dimension. They, too, may be at least partly motivated by the hope of discovering an invisible but essential order in the universe beneath the disorder of the surface, the threatening chaos of the 'alien world'; an order that is not only understandable by the human mind, but also the essence of both the divine and the human minds. For the mythic imagination and religious faith it is the reflection of the eternal and divine order in the created universe.[14]

The millennial fascination with Pythagorean proportions, Plato's metaphor of the universe as "matter informed by geometry", the number mysticism of the Cabala and alchemy, the striving of medieval architects to recreate the divine proportions of Solomon's Temple, or St Augustine's aesthetics, which anchored "true beauty in ... the immutable numerical ratios of Pythagorean mysticism" (McClung, 1983, 69–90), the search for the 'ultimate equation' by our contemporary mathematicians and theoretical physicists: all these testify to the millennial efforts of mankind to find an inherent rational and logical order in a world which shocks us all too often with its fearful disorder and irrationality. All these things play a crucial role in building the symbolic structures of our civilization.

Arabesque

The holy site at the center of the world, the presence of God, sacred ceremonies, cosmic analogies, divine order and proportions: apparently all this was not enough to appease the fears and troubled souls of men and women of all ages. A further protective device was needed, and applied in a great number of churches, temples, mosques, and other buildings of special importance. As in the case of houses, the interior surfaces of these buildings were used to further reinforce the protection against the alien world. Icons, frescoes, stuccoes, decorations, carpets, and curtains all played an important role in this strategy. But it was in Islamic culture that this art was developed to unsurpassable perfection.[15]

As is often the case, necessity proved the mother of invention and served as source of inspiration for a great human achievement. Their faith prohibited Muslims from portraying the deity in human form, and so they were compelled to find another, impersonal way of representing the divine and the transcendental. In response, they developed the art of arabesque. They covered, or dissolved, the surface of the walls and floors of their sacred and public buildings by, or into, geometrical forms and patterns—lines and circles, checkerboards and chevrons, interlocking bands of stars, suns, and polygonal configurations, knots, medallions and rosettes, acanthus leaves and vine tendrils, or calligraphic texts from the Koran. In this way they created spaces of incomparable safety, sanctity, and transcendence. "In Islam, mathematics is the language of the intellect and its abstraction reflects the Divine Order. Man and nature are both created by God; mathematics links the structure of both and helps to explain their proportions" (Lehrman, 1980, 41).

This art of "rational abstraction" expresses in the most intense way the timelessness and presence of the divine; the "purity and perfection of symmetry" is "a contrast to man's imperfections"; geometrical forms suggest universal order and the unity of God; the intricate patterns encourage contemplation and the unending lines evoke eternity and divine infinitude. The walls, floors, and buildings lose their heavy materiality and are dissolved into the spirituality and the divine freedom of the dazzling play of lines, patterns, colors, and abstract forms. Matter is spiritualized, the world is sanctified by the presence of the transcendental and the divine (Lehrman, 1980, 21, 41, 46, 68, 74–76, 233, and *passim*). This is one of the ultimate victories of human imagination and art over the threats of an alien world. It has played an important role in assuaging people's fears and anxieties and in building their civilization.

Light

The spiritual impact of Islamic buildings was further enhanced by the sophisticated use of light and shadow. In these buildings light is usually filtered through intricate brick, stone, or wooden screens, trees and shrubbery, the falling water of fountains or cascades; and all in order to enhance their symbolic and transcendental character and the meaning of light.

> The sun, and subsequently pure light, symbolized the Absolute Being, since its illumination is the source of all existence. Pure light is indivisible, and represents the Muslim's sense of universal order ... light is metaphorically associated with life, goodness, truth and order. In sum, light leads to an understanding of the world, while it adds immeasurably to the joy of living. (Lehrman, 1980, 78)

The play and contrast of light and shadow is, of course, an indispensable element in the architecture of all ages. The reflection of light on a Greek temple, a beam of light darting into a dark basilica, the radiance and explosion of light in a Gothic cathedral or a modern glass and chrome church, may symbolize divine harmony and serenity, and they may announce the glory of God in this world, which is his world. They may also praise the courage and genius of human beings, who, by means of their brilliant lights, colors, and forms, have won a victory over the chaos of the alien world, and over the fear and despair in their hearts. They have built, out of symbols, a world for themselves. They have built their civilization.

CHAOS AND COSMOS TODAY

The World of Light and Shadow

One might easily believe that this millennial search for the center of the universe, this obsession with generating the hope, the belief, the illusion that we are at the center of the universe, has disappeared without trace in our enlightened modern age. This is not the case. The yearning for this faith has not abated, and the means of generating it may even have multiplied.

I have just mentioned the role of light in creating—the illusion of?—a sacred enclave, a human and divine cosmos within the chaos of the alien world. Let me now add that it is only contemporary humankind that has been able to build a cosmos for itself purely out of light and shadow. A world, that exists only in the eyes and minds of human beings. A world of light and shadow, which is conjured up, each night, on our television screens.

In the last few decades, television sets have become the preeminent mythic centers of our world. They may be more powerful than totem poles or holy shrines, Trees of Life, sacred cities, or cosmic mountains ever were. They have an enormous force of attraction: they pull the whole world into their gravitational center. They force everything and everybody that is important in the world onto their screens. We, the viewers, may live in the remotest part of the world, on the outskirts of the poorest suburb of the poorest megalopolis, and still we may feel that we are at the center of the universe. How could we not do so when the whole world comes into our home and pays its respects to us, day and night. Kings and admirals parade before us; prime ministers and popes personally preach to us; Hollywood stars smile and austere terrorists stare at us; wars are fought and spaceships launched in our presence; super novae and nuclear bombs explode before our very eyes (and we, god-like, remain unscathed): How could we not feel ourselves to be at the center of the world?

And television is not the only powerful means in our technological age which keeps generating in us the feeling that we are at the center of the world or living in freedom and safety within an alien world. Let me give two more examples.

The Automobile

I use the word 'automobile' instead of the more humble 'car' because its Latin origin gives it a certain solemnity and perhaps even mystery. Automobiles have this solemnity and mystery not only because they have become symbols of power and royalty, success and wealth, but also, and more importantly, because they are nothing less than mobile centers-of-the-universe.

They are not the first objects to have this capacity in human history. The portable thrones of medieval kings taken on their tribute-collecting journeys were mobile loci of sanctity. The portable Tabernacle of the Jews, before it found its permanent place in the Temple of Jerusalem, was literally a mobile center of the universe. The car is devoid of this sacred dimension—or is it?—but has developed many other features of a mythic center of the world.

It is a closed and complete universe, well protected against the hardships of the outside, alien world. A cosmos or mobile microcosm in the surrounding chaos, it cruises through the world, smooth, silent, and undisturbed, like a spaceship out in space. It protects the driver against rain, snow, and wind, and—according to a car-drivers' myth—even against the wrath of the gods, lightning. It protects him against the gaze of the multitude, the other, the crowd. He can see them, but they cannot see him: this is a position of power, earlier enjoyed only by royalty in the cushioned privacy of their équipage.[16] Cars protect us also against time, decay, and aging: if he has a better car, even the oldest driver can drive faster than the youngest. Horsepower is our power.

In a famous essay, Roland Barthes (1972) compared the latest Citroen model to a Gothic cathedral; he called it a "magic object" that "manifestly fell from Heaven" and was "a messenger from a world beyond nature". With "its completeness and unknown origin, its closed shape and radiance ... and finally its silence", it belongs "to the realm of the miraculous".

Barthes' comparison of cars and cathedrals may be sacrilegious, but it is not totally arbitrary. It is not because both cathedrals and cars are important loci, and strong symbols, of the human world of safety and freedom. Cathedrals provided safety in both the physical and the spiritual senses of the word. They were stone fortresses in times of war and siege, and were, at all times, sacred places protecting believers with the presence of God and the exclusion of Satan. Cars, on the other hand, protect people with their hermetically closed bodies against the forces of nature, and protect them also spiritually or psychologically by excluding the troubles and noises of the outside world, physical and social, and offering the driver a few moments of sacred privacy.

Both cathedrals and cars are important sources of human freedom. Cathedrals offer us freedom from everyday cares and concerns, freedom from the attacks and temptations of Satan, freedom from the burden of sins. They open up vertical transcendence for us, just as sacred mountains, Trees of Life, and other variants of the *axis mundi* do.

Cars, on the other hand, open up horizontal transcendence for us. Getting in our car, we step into a new dimension of reality. We do not walk or run, nevertheless we glide through the streets and the landscape like divine creatures. We have escaped from the realm of physical laws. The car, rolling and sweeping with us, makes us feel as if we have been freed from the force of gravitation. The more so since the springs of our car transform the rough and irresistible downward drag into a delicious rocking up and down, so defeating the forces of nature with each upward swing. Having got into our cars, we have transcended the physical world into a dimension of freedom.

Cars also free us from our social links. At work or elsewhere, we are caught in, and determined by, the network of our social relationships. Having got into our car, we step out of this network and navigate in free space, not—or at least less—determined by our social dependencies. Until, at the end of the trip, we arrive home, or elsewhere, and are caught again in the web of social relations.

Cars, as soon as they were invented, opened up a miraculous new dimension in human life. But their character as a separate, closed, human sphere within an alien world developed only step by step, over the decades. The first cars were open carriages, reveling in the experience of freedom and almost completely oblivious of safety. It was only later that they closed in upon their drivers and surrounded them with their protective shells.

The route from the first, austere black boxes to the streamlined bulbs of today's cars, with their mysteriously shining metallic paints (paints are metallic so as to be harder and better able to repel outside influences) and their silent, metaphysical elegance, has taken several decades to traverse. There has been a tendency in the history of car design from angularity to spherical, rounded, raindrop-like lines and shapes. This tendency has usually been explained as the result of technical rationality and in the terminology of 'streamlining', 'air resistance', 'fuel efficiency', and so on. But it can also be explained within the framework of our argument as a process in the course of which a more and more perfect human world has been formed within the alien world; a closed human world which has become entirely autonomous. Being perfectly streamlined, it has almost no contact with the alien world any more. It is completely independent of it (except the short stops at the gas pumps). It sails through the alien world gracefully and victoriously. It is an emblem, and a radiating center, of our contemporary civilization.

The Shopping Mall

In recent decades, a great and lucrative industry has developed with the purpose of recreating the illusion of an anthropocentric world. Think of the glossy, atrium-type shopping centers, for instance. They are small universes in themselves, closed, complete, safe, surrounding people with the metaphysical brilliance of spiraling, heavenly choirs of beauty and ecstasy: being there, it is difficult not to feel oneself at the center of a blissful universe.[17]

This may be why the mall has become—and is becoming more and more—the sacred center of contemporary life (and of the universe). As Lauren Langman (1992, 41–42) put it in an excellent article: "If the Gothic cathedral was the symbolic structure of the feudal era, and the factory [that] of the industrial, the distinct structures of today are cultural sites or theme parks like the Centre Georges Pompidou of Paris or Disneyland, and the carnivals of consumption—the shopping malls."[18]

The mall is obviously and preeminently a human world within, and opposed to, an alien world. With its open structures, beams, and girders, it emphasizes that it is a man-made world. With the lightness and courageous momentum of its lines and the breathtaking spans of its inner space, it celebrates the victory of human mind and will over enslaving physical laws. Due to the transparency of the whole building, people in the mall can virtually see how these victorious structures push the sphere of the human world outwards in order to keep the alien world at the greatest possible distance.

This is a closed and safe universe, where one can forget the threatening existence of the alien world. When inside, the only thing one can see of the outside world is the blue of the sky, filtered through, and spiritualized by, the crystal panels of the dome; this is a world of purity, transcendence, and peace. Writing about the cities of the future, the French architect Michel Ragon describes the modern structures that defeat the laws of gravity and incorporate "silence and the transparency of the sky" into the building.[19]

The shopping center is the perfect human world, a private universe, a space completely closed and protected not only by walls and a dome but also by galleries of shops running around the atrium, full of everything which is delicious, tempting, comfortable, and homely in a man-made world. They surround people with the protective sphere of an "unending stream of spectacles" (Debord, 1970).[20]

In this world, there is no snow or sleet, no thunderstorms or parching heat, there is no winter or summer, no day or night, no disturbing change or painful transitoriness. There is eternal spring here, with torrents of flowers, bubbling springs, and the refreshing breeze of Zephyrus, a benevolent and hidden deity (represented here by a lesser deity called the air-conditioning system).

Time has stopped. Mutability and death have disappeared. They have been replaced by the illusion of eternity; or even more by a combination of eternity and the Kierkegaardian or Heideggerian moment of authentic existence. People wander around the galleries, round and round, as if they were ambling along the archetypal paths of the eternal return.

The shopping center is a soft and beatific version of Utopia, "a pseudo-democratic twilight zone between reality and a commercially produced fantasy world" (Langman, 1992, 40), where everybody is anonymous and equal, where there are no feuds or conflicting interests, no social classes or inequalities, no rich or poor, no duties or responsibilities, but just the rotation of a crowd of benevolent people, who in a serene and contemplative mood roam over the galleries of the world, more as philosopher-*'flâneurs'* than consumers. The mall is a reincarnation of the *jardin des délices*, or of the island of the blessed souls of medieval and Renaissance imagination. There is no thirst or hunger, illness or destitution here; this closed world offers all the comforts and delights, goods and goodies of a world created by human beings for themselves.

It is also a world of meaning. People strolling in the galleries can revel in myriads of meanings or the simulacra of meaning since commodities are designed in such a way as to suggest purpose, meaning, and the promise of fulfillment. Posters, labels, and publicity slogans emphasize and shamelessly overemphasize this dimension of meaning; they promise more than the goods can ever deliver. But this does not prevent people from being fascinated, and deluded, by a world of meaning. It helps them forget, for a fleeting moment, their own world, outside the mall, which is chronically short of meaning.

Due to the magic of the mall and publicity, a new pullover may seem as precious as the Golden Fleece was for the Argonauts, promising fulfillment and perfection; a new lipstick may give one a new identity; a new book may hide the ultimate meaning of life; a new jewel may lend the brilliance of transcendence to one's life; a gift may be the magic wand that, back home, will fill with joy and meaning a relationship that has run out of joy and meaning.

The shopping center euphemizes and, as a result, tames and trivializes the alien world. It is full of secrets, like a jungle, but this is not a fearful but a friendly jungle full of pleasant surprises. Here the secrets are tempting and not threatening. This is the jungle of an alien world totally domesticated and transformed into a garden of joys. Here the monsters lurking behind the palm trees are huge teddy bears, toy lions, and the dinosaurs from Jurassic Park. This is a virtual world: a civilization.

Transcendental Carnival

The mall conjures up more important mysteries and mythical ceremonies as well. According to Featherstone (1991), Langman (1992), and others, consumer society—and its symbolic center, the mall—opens the gates of the archaic and anarchic forces of ancient carnivals. The mall stages "an unending series of mass-mediated fragmented 'spectacles' and carnivals that celebrate the universalization of consumption". Malls also create the myth, and generate nostalgic memories of,

> neighborhood and lost community ... of a past abundant with goods and social cohesion. The appeal to an imagined communal past is especially clear when old churches, warehouses or factories are converted to malls ... Their restaurants are often designed to replicate the cabins of wooden sailing-ships, colonial taverns ... [the] railroad dining cars of the 1930s, nineteenth-century Italian villas or ancient pagodas. (Langman, 1992, 47, 49; see also Featherstone, 1991, 75)

The mall is much more than a simple building. It is the symbol of the universe, an *imago mundi*, as medieval cathedrals were. It has a strong transcendental dimension. The golden and glass elevators ascending ceremonially into the heights of the atrium, almost up into the blue skies, suggest the glorious experience of the Ascension into the sphere of the divine. Leaving this greenhouse world of comfort and happiness for the wind and sleet of a cold winter evening is like being cast out of paradise.

Strolling in the galleries of large shopping centers, one may often see a strange construction on the ground floor, usually at the very center of the building, under the glass cupola of the atrium. It is an open structure, with four beautiful columns of imitation marble, with gilt scrolls and capitals, holding a crown-like baldachin, sheltering a fountain, or a marble table, a palm tree, or nothing at all. It is a Tabernacle, the replica of the holy tent that sheltered the Arc of the Covenant during the wanderings of the Jewish tribes in the desert.

The Tabernacle is part of the sacred heritage of both Judaism and Christianity; in Christian churches its canonical place is the altar. How and why did it get there, in the hypermodern shopping center? Is its presence at the center of our trivial and commercialized universe simply a matter of bad taste? Is it sacrilege? Not necessarily. In all likelihood it is there—even if the people strolling in the mall do not quite realize it—because the shopping mall is, or is meant to be, the holy center and shrine of our consumer civilization; and the Tabernacle is a powerful symbol of centrality and sanctity.

Tabernacles are replicas of the biblical Tabernacle ('OHEL' in Hebrew), a tent sheltering the Arc of the Covenant, and the two Tablets of the Law, which—after the settling of the Jewish tribes—was replaced by the Temple of Jerusalem, itself the symbol, and the center, of the world. They were built above the altars in medieval cathedrals and Renaissance churches (which themselves were believed to stand at the center of the world), and marked "throughout the history of ecclesiastical architecture ... the symbolic center" of the universe (Norberg-Schulz, 1985, 85).[21]

The 'transcendentalization' of malls is also served by the luxurious radiation of its inner colors and surfaces, which can be matched only by the visions of brilliant biblical and medieval mystics. McClung (1983, 15) quotes the description of the celestial city from Revelation 21:18–21: "And the building of the wall thereof was jasper: and the city was pure gold, like unto pure glass. The foundations of the wall of the city were adorned with all manner of precious stones ... And the twelve gates were twelve pearls ... and the street of the city was of pure gold, as it were transparent glass."

What was a vision in the Bible has become (virtual) reality in the opulent shopping centers with their shining golden and chrome, glass and marble surfaces. With their artificiality and geometrical forms, the brilliance of their gilt and shining surfaces, crystal panels and laser beams, marble fountains and chrome waterfalls, they are trivial replicas of the celestial city of the New Jerusalem.[22] The mall spiritualizes the world of commercial goods and commodities, just as medieval and later visionaries transformed "the stuff of commercial riches into the emblem of eternal bliss" (Langman, 1992, 46).

The Realm of the Devil

The shopping mall can also be interpreted as a negative transcendence; as the place of an ongoing black mass glorifying the basest instincts, the lascivious beast in human beings, the Evil Spirit.

If the earthly paradise is a dangerous illusion invented by Satan, then the shopping mall is his creation par excellence because it is a world in which people are lured into believing that they are innocent. And is not a world in which people live in the delusion of being innocent the world of Satan?

Theologians could certainly argue that in an innocent world there is no place for the transcendental drama described in the Old and the New Testaments or the sacred books of other civilizations; there is no place for God, Christ, or any other divinity; there is no place for remorse, feelings of guilt, a search for redemption, repentance, salvation. It is not God's world. It is a trap set by Satan to make people believe that they can enjoy paradise on earth. That they are already saved.

Without too much effort one can envision the shopping mall as a replica of the Devil's famous amusement park in which Pinocchio and his peers were changed into donkeys. Leaving the mall with our shopping booty in our hands, we should check whether we, too, have donkey's ears and tails.

No doubt, the mall is an amoral world; a world trivially beyond good and evil. In traditional and modern societies men and women were advised and disciplined by a system of moral laws. They were prompted to control and at least partly repress their instinctual drives and libidos, and to sublimate them into socially useful activities. Drives thus became major sources of social, intellectual, and artistic activity. By immediately gratifying people's appetites and wishes, Satan may shut people up in their physical and instinctual selves and obstruct their spiritual and creative development.

As we have seen, the Devil even commits the blasphemy of staging a mock-Ascension for us. And we may also be fooled into believing—what hubris!—that we are blessed souls, as we are gliding upwards into the realm of eternal bliss, on the escalators, as choirs of angels singing the glory of God. In reality, we sing the victory of the Devil over ourselves and over God.

The shopping mall, and its myth of being a human world, where people can feel themselves to be at home, at the center of the universe, may then be a dangerous illusion. People strolling in the mall may experience their own apotheosis as free and authentic personalities and the protagonists of a friendly universe, while, in reality, they may already be in the trap of Satan, *alias* the alien world. They may be losing, 'dispersing', their personalities in the Kierkegaardian sense of the word, in the whirl of shallow gratifications and trivial choices. They may be losing the Heideggerian 'centeredness' and authenticity of their being.

The Negative Myth

I do not want to take this comparison of the shopping mall and the world of evil too far. But there are scholars who literally satanize the mall and leisure society as a whole. They argue that instead of helping people create a really human universe around themselves, they are the instruments of the dehumanization of the world; they enslave people instead of liberating them. In their judgment, leisure society—and the mall within it—has become an instrument of Foucauldian domination and disempowerment. People are manipulated by political and economic power, which infantilize them into unconscious puppets caught in the vicious circle of desires generated and gratified in never-ending rotation.

> Hegemony now depends on the effective gratification provided by a mass-mediated popular culture whose themes express myriad deprivations, longings, satisfactions, aspirations and the desired experiences of particular taste cultures. There is love for the lonely, sex for the horny, excitement for the bored, identities for the empty and, typically, all are intertwined. There is a pop sociology that explains such megatrends and a pop psychology to soothe any remaining despair.
>
> This is the secret of modern hegemony: the dominant classes, via media, control norms of affective gratification and control everyday life. (Langman, 1992, 42, 54)

Due to the incessant impact of television and marketing, people are losing their social roles and identities—they are more and more becoming anonymous consumers with pseudo-identities generated by the market. They are being 'depoliticized' and 'de-socialized' and, as a consequence, more and more enslaved by the forces of power and money.

> Privatized consumption has thus become the contemporary locus of a selfhood for a hedonistic subjectivity that has withdrawn from the public realms. But this withdrawal lets the social order become more powerful with an ever more enfeebled privatized self less likely to contest major issues—as the recent Persian Gulf war showed. When the going gets tough, the tough go shopping—and at malls. It is of course no accident that after the Nintendo War, malls all over the country had celebrations of consumption for the 'heroes' of Desert Storm. (Langman, 1992, 67)

In a more morbid way, malls are also compared to modern panopticons, jails, and asylums: "Iron bars keep us from getting out of prisons, neon lights, lasers and hologram images keep us from wanting to get out of the fantastic world of malldom. Like force fields of sci-fi, the barriers are invisible and impermeable" (Langman, 1992, 48, 72). Others go as far as comparing amusement society and malls to "concentration camps" (Brittain, 1997).

If they turn out to be right, the building of mega-malls may prove an unsuccessful attempt to create a human world for late-twentieth-century customers, where they might, and should, feel free and safe at the center of the universe. On the contrary, they may realize, far too late, that they have unwittingly put themselves at the mercy of the alien world; that they are suffering "the terrors of emptiness" and "inauthenticity", from which they wanted to escape; that they are caught in a world of panic and loneliness, "delirium and anxiety" (Kroker et al., 1989, 13–17; see also Langman, 1992, 68). In an alien world. This would be a tragic failure of our efforts to build for ourselves a safe and meaningful world; a civilization.

NOTES

1 He bases his argument partly on Eliade (1954), partly on Heidegger's 'Origin of the Work of Art' (1980), in which he discusses the ability of "things" to "gather the world" into themselves thereby bestowing being upon them and so filling them with meaning.

2 We may add to Campbell's description the fact that in many cultures the octagonal represents the transition between the square, the symbol of the earth, and the circle, the symbol of the sky—that is, a transition between the earthly and the divine, the temporal and the eternal. This is why the octagonal ground plan is so important in Islamic architecture (mosques, towers), and also in Christian Gothic and Renaissance architecture (towers, spires, baptisteries).

3 Apparently, the new Shanghai stock exchange has been built in the shape of a hollowed square in order to help trap positive energies in accordance with the ancient geomantic rituals of Feng Shui.

4 "[T]he house is one of the greatest powers of integration for the thoughts, memories and dreams of mankind ... In the life of man, the house thrusts aside contingencies, its councils of continuity are unceasing. Without it, man would be a dispersed being. It maintains him through the storms of the heavens and through those of life. It is body and soul. It is the human being's first world. Before he is 'cast into the world', as claimed by certain hasty metaphysics, man is laid in the cradle of the house" (Bachelard, 1969, 6–7).

5 Quoted by McClung (1983, 25).

6 Ibid.

7 The quotation is taken from Norman Cohn (1961, 44–45).

8 "Babylon ... had been built upon *bab apsi*, the 'Gate of the Apsu'—*apsu* designating the waters of chaos before the Creation. We find the same tradition among the Hebrews. The rock of Jerusalem reached deep into the subterranean waters (*tehom*) ... And just as in Babylon there was the 'gate of *apsu*', the rock of the Temple of Jerusalem contained the 'mouth of the *tehom*'." Eliade (1954, 15–16).

9 Quoted by Eliade (1954, 19). "In fact, in certain archaic cosmogonies, the world was given existence through the sacrifice of a primordial monster, symbolizing chaos (Tiamat), or through that of a cosmic giant (Ymir, Pan-Ku, Puruse)" (Eliade, 1954, 20).

10 For the importance of the Tabernacle in the Judaic and Christian traditions, as a symbol—and the center—of the world, see note 21 below.

11 See McClung (1983, 25–30, 154–55).

12 According to Norberg-Schulz, the entrances of cities and public buildings had the same function.

13 See, for instance, Chevalier and Gheerbrant (1969), Jung (1964), and Ricoeur (1967). For a discussion of the symbolic role of the dome, the baldachin, and the tabernacle see the section 'The Shopping Mall', and especially note 21.

14 I shall return to the importance of geometry and mathematics in chapter nine, where I discuss the myth and concept of the 'rational world'.

15 Among the great number of books on the subject see, for instance, Lehrman (1980), and Moynihan (1979). In Lehrman see, among other things, illustrations 15, 18, 20, 21, 22, 23, 44, 53–56.
16 Contemporary politicians, hidden in their reinforced, steel-plated cars, are extreme cases of this safe cruising in an alien world. A caricature of this was János Kádár, First Secretary of the Hungarian Communist Party, who, after having betrayed his country in 1956, commuted between his fortified mansion and the building of the Politburo in an armored car.
17 The only predecessor of contemporary shopping centers I can think of which could match them in creating a comfortable, safe, and meaningful human world within a dreary and desolate alien world was the Roman (and also Turkish?) baths. Imagine such a bath, in a faraway border town, far to the north of Italy, on the bank of the Danube, with a fearful and unknown world over the frozen river, wrapped in darkness and mist, with the camp fires of the fierce Celtic or Teutonic tribes burning in the distance, snow and cold outside, and here we are, Roman citizens, sitting in the comfortable warm water of the circular pool, with the protective wall around and a strong dome above us, in complete safety and comfort, discussing Virgil's or Ovid's beautiful illusions of an idyllic world: this is a complete, though futile and fragile, victory over the alien world. Shopping centers did not emerge, of course, out of nothing. Nineteenth-century arcades, department stores, exhibition halls, and amusement parks were among their predecessors. See, for instance, Bailey (1978; 1986); Bennett et al. (1983); Chaney (1983); Easton, Hawkins, Laing, and Walker (1988); Gardner and Sheppard (1989); McKendrick, Brewer, and Plumb (1982); Michael B. Miller (1981); Raymond Williams (1958); and R. H. Williams (1982).
18 There is a rich and excellent literature on the symbolism of consumer culture in general, and on the shopping mall in particular. See, for instance, Kowiniski (1985); Postman (1985); Ewen (1988); Barber (1995); Gottdiener (1997); Falk and Campbell (1997); Huxtable (1997); Ritzer (1997, 1999); Baudrillard (1998).
19 "C'est la technique légère des *ossatures actuelles* qui fait virer l'expression architectonique en y incorporant *le silence et la transparence du ciel*"—quoted by McClung (1983, 46).
20 Quoted by Langman (1992, 48).
21 According to St Jerome, "the whole world is described in the sacred symbol of the Tabernacle", the four posts and four sides of which symbolize the four essential elements and the four dimensions of the universe (*Epistles to Fabiola*, 64). According to Philon of Alexandria, the tabernacle is an *imago mundi*, and also an *imago hominis* (*Life of Moses*, Book 3, 3–10). According to Origen, the tabernacle is the symbol of the whole universe as the interaction of the temporal and the eternal, the human and the divine, the visible and the invisible. Mohammed describes heaven as a cupola held by four posts. The cupola is the eternal spirit surrounding the world, the posts are the angels (Chevalier and Gheerbrant, 1969, 297; see also Lehmann, 1945). In Roman Catholic churches, the *ciborium*, sheltering the Host, often has the shape of a tabernacle even today.
22 The replicas of the Garden of Eden are to be found on tourist-catching tropical islands and in the Arcadian brochures of travel agencies.

Chapter Six

THE MORAL UNIVERSE

> "What have children to do with it, tell me, please."
> Dostoyevsky, *The Brothers Karamazov*

IN this chapter we study another important generative force of (Western) civilization: people's need to believe that they live not in a fearful and absurd, but in a 'moral', universe; that there is a kind of moral law functioning in the universe; that justice is being done in this world. We also discuss how the constant and anxious efforts of people to expel evil from the world shapes human civilization.

AMULETS AND SACRAMENTS

It is not new to state that the experience of evil—human suffering, fear, destruction, death—and the fight to control and subdue it, has been a major factor in the generation of civilizations. But it is surprising to see how little scholars have studied this factor with a view to better understanding the genesis and inner organization of human civilizations.

The experience of evil must have been overwhelming and terrifying from the very beginning. At least this is the only way to explain the diligence, or even more, the almost paranoid urge with which people all over the world have tried to expel it from their lives and world, using all possible and impossible means. It seems as if mankind has lived, throughout its history, in a permanent state of siege, assailed by innumerable foes and fiends. The number and variety of the protective devices people of all ages have invented and employed is astounding. As mentioned in Chapter Two, it would not be an exaggeration to say that, as a matter of fact, civilization is the sum total of these protective devices.

Exorcism

The belief in benevolent spirits who were thought to protect the faithful has developed in almost all cultures. On the other hand, myriads of magical practices were employed to bind, control, destroy, or scare off evil spirits and counteract their influence. Demons and devils were exorcised not only in primeval cultures, but—according to the testimony of the Old and the New Testaments—also in biblical times, and even more in the Christian Middle Ages. Exorcism is still part of Roman Catholic ritual: in the ceremony of baptism, for instance.[1] Baptism itself was one of the most powerful weapons against evil. It was thought that people who were not baptized remained the prey of demons, and that baptism resembled the miracle worked for Moses at the Red Sea. Believers pass through the dangerous waters of this world by the grace of baptism, but the Devil drowns like Pharaoh in the flood (J. B. Russell, 1981, 100–101).[2]

We have seen how houses, churches, villages, and cities were consecrated in order to protect them against the surrounding world of evil. Amulets and sacraments gave additional protection. The sign of the Cross "routed the demons" (J. B. Russell, 1981, 100). The myths and folklore about heroes going on a quest to slay evil monsters and, in a final battle, destroying them, was a further means of reassurance.[3]

Defilement and Purification

Rituals of self-purification were no less important. According to Paul Ricoeur (1967, 25), in several early cultures evil—and the impact of evil— was experienced as a 'defilement' of the human being by something coming from outside—of which one could rid oneself only by physical or symbolic ablution: "[W]e define defilement as 'an act that evolves an evil, an impurity, a fluid, a mysterious and harmful something that acts dynamically—that is to say, magically'". It is "a quasi-material something that infects as a sort of filth". Furthermore, "with defilement we enter into the reign of Terror".[4] In the terminology of the present book, we would say that we were entering into the realm of the alien world. For this impurity, this filth, this mysterious and harmful substance are, in the language of myth, symbols of the alien world which keep attacking, contaminating, defiling, and desacralizing the world of humankind.

People had to protect themselves and their communities against this threat of defilement, or had to get rid of it once the contamination had taken place. Individuals had to cleanse themselves by means of various cathartic practices, while communities cleansed themselves by excluding, expelling, or proscribing the person whose presence had defiled the community—even if he or she was not personally responsible for what had happened, as in the case of Oedipus or Orestes, for instance.

> The exile is not simply excluded from a material area of contact; he is chased out of a human environment measured off by law ... where the fatherland ends, there his defilement also ceases. To kill a murderer in the territory of the Athenian fatherland is to purify it; to kill him outside the territory is to kill an Athenian. (Ricoeur, 1967, 40)[5]

The representation of evil as defilement was later replaced by the concepts of sin and guilt, but the symbolism and discourse of defilement survived for a long time. The authors of the Old Testament, though they had developed the concept of sin, frequently expressed themselves "in the old language of defilement". In Isaiah (6:5, 7), for instance, we find "I am a man of unclean lips", and in Psalm 51 we read: "O God ... blot out my sin. Wash me thoroughly from my iniquity and cleanse me from my sin!"[6] The idea that the human being is 'defiled', 'soiled', or 'corrupted' by sin has remained with us throughout the millennia as much as the symbolism of the purifying fire of Purgatory and the myriads of superstitions and magical practices of cleansing.

Is it not grotesque—or moving, or absurd—that people have always sought to protect themselves by means of so many tactics and devices against evil, that is, the forces of the alien world? Consider, for instance, a man or a woman living in a medieval city. They were protected against the powers of evil, first, by an almighty and benevolent God; secondly, by Jesus Christ and his redeeming death; thirdly, by several angelic spheres surrounding the earth and the permanent presence of their own guardian angels; fourthly, by the choir of saints mediating between them and God, and their own patron saints whose names they were given at baptism; fifthly, by the church, with its pope, hierarchies of priests, and holy institutions; sixthly, by the walls of their city consecrated against the powers of evil, plus the patron saint of the city and that of their guild; seventhly, by their houses, which were also consecrated; and finally by the altar, crucifix, icons, and holy relics they may have kept in their houses. Beyond all this, they still had at their disposal a rich arsenal of superstitions the majority of which served to fend off the destructive influences of the forces of evil: disease, death, misfortune, accident, infertility, bad crops, natural disasters, famine, flood, infection.

Is this not too much? Is our life so miserable, so much threatened by the forces of evil that we need all these protective devices? The fact of the matter is that we seem to need yet more.

RATIONALIZATION
The Origins of Evil

How, and why, did evil come into the universe? Why do human and animal creatures have to suffer so much? Why is there so much misery and despair in the world? Why must every living creature go through the agony of death? What is the cause, or source, or meaning of all this suffering?

I do not want to say that these questions have been consciously raised since the beginning of human history, but we can safely presume that, consciously or unconsciously, they were raised as early as primeval times in all civilizations. It has always been of the utmost importance to find relevant answers since it is extremely difficult to bear pain and suffering. It is much easier to endure, and accept, them if one knows—or thinks one knows—the cause, the source, the 'meaning' of all this misery. Myths and religions came to people's succor.

One of the major functions of creation myths, for instance, has always been to explain the origin of evil in the world; to explain how and why evil invaded, or emerged in, the world. Almost without exception they have provided an explanation—and usually more than one. Explanations that must have been extremely important for people, despite the fact that in most cases these explanations were vague, blurred, self-contradictory. Let me give a few examples.

Pandora's Box

As is well known, the Greeks did not have a homogeneous mythology. Their mythology was a mixture of the myths of their various tribes and local cultures, and those of other Mediterranean, Middle Eastern, and Asian peoples. The attempts of Homer, Hesiod, and, later, Ovid to integrate these heterogeneous riches into a consistent mythology were only partly successful. The inconsistencies are manifest also in the myths about the origin of evil.

In the main, Homeric, mythology we find a great number of attempts to explain the presence of evil in the world. There are myths according to which evil came into the world by coincidence. Remember that Gaia, after having given life to a number of Titans, bore—by chance or in an inexplicable way—monsters: Cyclopes and Hecatoncheires. Uranus, her husband, was scared and shut them up in a subterranean cave called Tartaros, with disastrous consequences. In this case, the fear and weakness of a god was responsible for admitting evil into the world. Prompted by Gaia, Cronos, one of the Titans, took revenge on Uranus, and so revenge became a further link in the chain. The mutilated Uranus warned him that he, too, would meet his fate and would be thrown off his throne by his own son, Zeus. And so it happened. Thus the never-ending sequence of revenge and counter-revenge was triggered off and henceforth ran through the lives of gods and the destinies of humans.

How did mankind get involved in this fateful process? According to the best-known variant: by coincidence. We have already spoken of how Epimetheus—who was commissioned by Zeus to provide the various creatures with skills—forgot one single creature, a weak and naked being: Man. No skill was left when their turn came. Another god, Prometheus, could not tolerate this injustice, revolted against Zeus, and stole the divine fire (the symbol and instrument of craftsmanship) for them. Men and women prospered and forgot their duties towards the gods; by this impiety they, too, became responsible for the influx of evil into the world. In addition, and due to the contrivance of a wrathful Zeus and the irresponsible curiosity of Pandora, innumerable miseries and pains poured into the world. According to another variant, however, Pandora's box contained blessings, which were lost as a result of man's curiosity.

What then, finally, is the source of evil? Coincidence? Fear? The weakness, revengefulness, or irresponsibility of gods? Fate? Human impiety?[7]

Let me illustrate the confusion of Greek culture, its feverish search for answers to the question of evil, by means of Greek tragedy. The tragedies were born, at least partly, of uncertainty about the origin, and role, of evil in the world.

The heroes of Aeschylus struggled with the insoluble dilemma of fate and human freedom, divine will and human responsibility, justice (being punished for a sin) and injustice (being punished despite being innocent). In the tragedies of Sophocles, this tragic tension was further enhanced—so much so that I could irreverently say that in *Antigone*, for instance, the chorus, commenting on the events and trying to explain Antigone's tragic fate, literally talks nonsense. One moment it attributes the source of evil and of all suffering to the cold-blooded cruelty of gods; the next it cites mankind's revolt against Zeus's holy power as the cause of human suffering;[8] then it mentions fate, governed by the gods, as the cause of evil ("Pray not again. No mortal can escape the doom prepared for him"), and then blames mankind itself ("the doom he brought on himself", or "This is my guilt, all mine").[9] The chorus condemns Antigone's act as unacceptably audacious in challenging the gods, while a few moments later it praises it as an act of piety, and again, almost in the same verse, it condemns it once more as hubris:

> You showed respect for the dead.
> ....
> Your self-sufficiency has brought you down.[10]

At the end of the play, Creon struggles with his own doubts, searching for the reason for his own fall and the destruction of his family. One moment he blames himself for his "wicked heart" and "harshness", and the next he blames the gods:

> It was a god who struck,
> who has weighted my head with disaster ...[11]

Seeing these contradictions and confusion, it is understandable that, at the end of the tragedy, Creon stands broken and miserable before the incomprehensible absurdity and cruelty of human life. Two thousand years later, their counterparts were those who stood around the bodies of Hamlet or Cordelia, Othello or Desdemona, who had survived the tragic fate of their friends and adversaries. A further five centuries later, we might mention the miserable heroes of *Uncle Vanya* or *A Long Day's Journey into Night*, who gaze with empty eyes into the unfathomable misery of men and women in a dark and silent universe.

Evil in the Bible

The picture is no less blurred and contradictory in the Judeo-Christian tradition. In the interpretation of Genesis, it was the disobedience of the first man and woman that brought evil into a completely good and innocent world. Later, in the New Testament—and even more so in the medieval Judaic and Christian traditions—the serpent of the Garden of Eden came to be identified with Satan. And if the serpent was Satan, then evil had come into the world primarily and originally by means of the revolt of Satan and his fellow angels against God, after which the Fall in the Garden of Eden was a secondary event.[12]

But was it not God himself who was responsible for the invasion of evil? If somebody was able to revolt against him could he be said to have created a perfect universe? In this case, God's mistake, or his lack of power, wisdom, foresight, or omniscience was the source of evil in the world. Or was it not he who had created the angels, and Satan among them? Had they always existed, together with God? If they had, then the principle of evil, too, had always been present in a dualistic universe and mankind was an innocent victim of a *theomachia*, a war between gods, as a great number of non-Judeo-Christian myths and religions propose. Perhaps God did not even create the universe. This is the view of representatives of so-called process theology, some of whom have argued that "God's omnipotence is limited by primeval chaos, which he did not create. God is working with [an imperfect] cosmos now, prodding it along toward improvement" (J. B. Russell, 1981, 19, 80ff).

Who then is responsible for the presence of evil in this world and for all the suffering, misery, and death? Satan? God? Mankind? Or nobody, since evil belongs to the eternal essence of the world? After all, it is an alien world, and not our world.

It is not our task to answer these questions. We would not be able to do so. What is important is an understanding that, with a view to comprehending and controlling evil, human communities had to develop a rich array of beliefs and myths, theories and dogmas, ceremonies and attitudes that became important building blocks of their civilizations.

Evil Does Not Exist

The example of St Augustine is particularly enlightening. All his life he fought, stubbornly and desperately, to eliminate evil from the world; or at least for its integration into a perfectly good universe as a secondary and subordinate factor. Despite these efforts, his later writings present a gloomy and pessimistic vision of the overwhelming presence of evil in this world, a vision which would have a determining impact on Christianity—and on Western civilization in general—for more than a millennium.

In his youth, he was close to the pessimistic dualism of the Gnostics, to whom the material world was corrupt—it was the realm of evil, suffering, and death, opposed to the spirituality and freedom of the divine. Later, he adopted a more optimistic, almost evolutionist or Irenaean view of the world,[13] preaching that human history was a learning process in which evil was only a means used by God to test us and to lead us to the way of love, virtue, and wisdom. Evil would progressively be eliminated from the human world.

The fall of Rome in 410 destroyed his optimism. He lost hope in the possibility of eliminating evil step by step from the human world and of building the City of God here on earth. He did not revert to his earlier dualism. He firmly clung to the doctrine that God had created a perfect and perfectly good world and sought for new ways of explaining, and justifying, the presence of evil in the world. He developed three theories of evil. His arguments, partly taken from his predecessors and from contemporary debates, would be repeated over and over again, in many variations, by theologians and philosophers; they are found in Leibniz's *Theodicy* (Leibniz, 1966), as well as in the Sunday sermons of Catholic and non-Catholic churches today. They would be woven into the fabric of Western civilization for two millennia.

In his 'privative' theory of evil he developed the ideas of Plotinus, according to whom evil did not exist at all. It is only the lack of being—the absence of God, a lacuna, a simple negativity. It is only the perversion or corruption of goodness; it is "parasitic upon good". It is not a turning toward evil but only toward a lesser good.[14] It is a turning not toward something, but just the turning away from God.[15] "Evil has no nature; what is called evil is merely a lack of good." "Whatever is, is good; evil is not a substance, for if it were, it would be good" (St Augustine, 1966–1972, 11:9; 1960–1961, 7, 12:18).[16]

This theory was not strong enough to argue evil out of the world, and so St Augustine developed a second, 'aesthetic', theory, according to which evil is merely an illusion, a product of human beings' limited vision and ignorance.[17] The "principle of plenitude" requires that the universe contain also corruptible creatures consisting of being and nonbeing. But, seen in its totality, the universe is perfectly good and even evil contributes to this perfection. Without evil, the universe would be less perfect.

Joseph Campbell quotes Heraclitus and Blake in this connection.

> To God all things are fair and good and right; but men hold some things wrong and some right. The unlike is joined together, and from differences results the most beautiful harmony, and all things take place by strife.[18]
>
> The roaring of lions, the howling of wolves, the raging of the stormy sea, and the destructive sword, are portions of eternity too great for the eye of man.[19]

Several conclusions could be drawn from this 'aesthetic' theory of evil. The major conclusion for St Augustine was, of course, that evil did not really exist; it was only a delusion on the part of human beings, who could not see the universal purpose and harmony, which also included human suffering and death. It was also important that this argument justified God, since it proved that God had created a perfect universe.

St Augustine also formulated an early version of the 'moral' theory of evil. He stated that evil was a precondition of human freedom—there could not be real freedom and genuine choice if people could choose only between good and good.[20] He introduced two kinds of human freedom. The first, of a lower order, was *liberum arbitrium*, that is, free will and the ability to choose even the lesser good, in other words, evil. The other was real freedom, *libertas*, which was to choose God and a way of life pleasing to God. This was the freedom to believe in, and follow, God.[21]

It seems that St Augustine was unable to find a reassuring answer to the question of evil. He tried to justify even the suffering of innocent babies—they would be compensated in their afterlives; their agony may instruct and improve their parents—but finally had to acknowledge that the presence of evil in the world remained God's secret. The dark vision of his later years of a world thoroughly corrupted by original sin, his vision of the majority of people predestined to suffering in this world and to eternal damnation in the next, inspired some of the great thinkers of later ages—Pascal, Kierkegaard, Barth—but it also testifies to his final and tragic failure to solve the problem of evil.

He was, of course, not the only church father and early theologian to struggle with the problem of evil. Gregory of Nyssa, St Jerome, John Chrysostom, Ambrose, and others became involved in passionate debates on this topic, but ultimately moved around the same circle. Irenaeus developed a more optimistic approach. According to him, evil had only a temporary and instrumental existence in this world. At his creation, Adam was more like a child and he had to go through a long and painful learning process to develop his human potential and achieve mature adulthood. The Fall made his task more difficult but it was also a "fall into independence" (Hick, 1967, 138),[22] which contributed to his becoming a responsible, moral personality.

> According to the Irenaean type of Christian theodicy, the purpose of the world is 'soul-making,' an environment in which the higher potentialities of human personality may develop. To this end, it is claimed, nature is an autonomous system operating by its own laws, which men must learn to obey. If God had created a world in which natural law were continuously adjusted for the avoidance of all pain, the more heroic human virtues

[such as courage, fortitude, loyalty, honesty, caring] would never be evoked ... Indeed, it would seem that the 'rough edges' of the world—its challenges, dangers, tasks, difficulties, and possibilities of real failure and loss—constitute a necessary element in an environment which is to call forth man's final qualities. (Hick, 1967, 139)[23]

In other words, this means that the alien character of the world—the fact that we are not compatible with the world, that the world has 'rough edges' and makes us suffer—is more a blessing than a curse since it helps us actualize our human qualities.

This debate, and attempts to justify God and argue evil out of this world, went on, relentlessly and nervously, for the next millennium or more, mobilizing schoolmen and philosophers, Duns Scotus as well as Thomas Aquinas, Leibniz as well as Kant and Schleiermacher. But in spite of all the brilliant arguments in theodicy, logical fireworks, cumbersome theories, and elegant rationalization, evil, unexplained and fearful, irrational, shocking and absurd, has remained with us. Its presence, and our efforts to defeat it, have remained powerful motive forces of our civilization. In the spirit of Borkenau (1980; 1982), we could say: Each civilization is a specific response to the ultimate questions and anxieties of the human condition. The challenge is the same, only the answers are different.

SATAN

For two thousand years Satan has been a familiar figure in the landscapes of Western imagination. He—or she, or it, since angels were not believed to have a gender—has been one of the protagonists of the cosmic drama taking place in our civilization; but he has also had almost free access—through the back door of instincts and temptations—to the homes and lives of everyday people all over the world. Our civilization would be very different if human fear and hope had not created this horrendous and seductive, magnificent and villainous demon.

Why and how has he become so important in our lives and in our history? The answer is, I think, that—despite all appearances—he has been one of our major allies in our fight against evil in the world. The Lord of Darkness fights on our side against evil? Yes, we turned him around. This has been one of our most brilliant achievements in the course of our history. The 'discovery' or 'invention' of Satan was one of the most ingenious feats of humankind—or at least of those cultures which developed his myth.[24] He became one of the most powerful weapons against evil in the world. He became a powerful instrument for reducing the anxiety and suffering caused by the presence of evil in our lives.[25]

Evil Condensed

Human beings often experience the world as incomprehensible and absurd. They feel that there is too much human and animal suffering, conflict, despair, and death in this world; that there is a high degree of uncertainty and anxiety in their lives. One possible way of reducing this uncertainty and anxiety was to personify evil.

It was a clever strategy to confine the chaotic and unknown forces of evil by condensing them into virtual beings: wicked spirits, demons, devils. By identifying them and giving them names, people gained a kind of control over them. While they could not do anything with unknown, mysterious, cosmic forces, they could cope with personified evil; they could bind demons by magic, they could pray to them, exorcise them, pacify them. If demons are persons, we may believe that we understand them, that they are moved by the same motives as we are, by hatred and love, revengefulness and wickedness, vanity and appetite. Then we may hope that we can communicate with them and handle them.

As a second step, some mythologies and cultures advanced to the stage of 'mono-demonism', that is, they condensed the myriads of evil spirits and demons swarming in all corners of the world into one majestic and horrifying person, Satan. The fight against evil became thus more dramatic and apocalyptic but, at the same time, it became much more simple and promising. If all the evil of the universe was condensed in one person, then the defeat of this person would free mankind, forever, from all the evil in the world—suffering, misery, death.

In order to make it credible that Satan actually contained all evil in himself, he had to be made horrendously fearful, ugly and repellent, burdened with all possible crimes and sins in the world. This need may have been at the source of those unconscious and conscious efforts—together with other motives—that painted him in the imagination of people, and in the icons and frescoes of their churches, as the most execrable and repugnant creature in the world; comparing him to the basest animals, to serpents, toads, dragons, wolves, and monsters with tongues of fire, teeth of iron, stinking smoke, goat's hooves, and so on. The terrible suffering of sinners in Satan's power in hell reinforced this condensation of all possible evil and suffering in his person. To achieve this condensation and, in a second step, destruction of evil in one person and in one place may have been a more important motive behind the creation of the horrors of hell than our alleged sadomasochism, so often alluded to.

In a recent article, Garry Wills (1995) described nine major Italian 'Last Judgements' in mosaics and frescoes dating from the eleventh to the mid-sixteenth century. He described the morbid and desperate fascination of medieval artists and people with the torments of the damned.[26] Let me quote some passages from his article.

> In the Cathedral of Torcello, for instance, on the main mosaic (from the eleventh century), there are three compartments ... where six classes of sinners are lodged—the lustful in fire, the gluttons eating their own flesh, the angry soused in water, the envious reduced to skulls eaten by their own worms, the avaricious with their jewels, and the slothful as stray bones too lazy to recombine. These make up ... the seven deadly sins. (1995, 53)

In the Last Judgement of the Arena Chapel in Padova (1303–1306):

> Four immense rivers of fire gush out of the oval halo and race across the wall, sluicing sinners down toward a bloated Satan who eats and defecates them ... On the dragon's back other sinners are trapped by devils—the one on Satan's left is supine in agony as a devil bites into his penis ... A lustful woman is hung upside down by a hook through her genitals. A liar hangs by his tongue. A sodomite is reamed with a turning spit that enters his mouth and exits his anus ... (1995, 54)[27]

With the condensation of evil in the person of Satan, the other pole began to crystallize as well. The victorious figure of Christ the Warrior emerged.[28] The struggle between evil and good was thus transposed from the human soul to the apocalyptic level of a *theomachia*, a war of the gods, with the hope and the biblical promise that Christ would ultimately defeat Satan. This projection of evil from the human psyche onto the outside world, from our micro-world onto the cosmic battle of the gods, was an ingenious, if partly unconscious, self-defense that must have reduced the level of anxiety in people's minds. The integration of the fight against evil into the great drama of salvation reduced the power of evil even further.[29] Last but not least, Satan also played a positive role in our history because, by identifying him with the serpent of the Garden of Eden, he could be made responsible for the fall of Adam and Eve, so liberating mankind, at least partly, from the burden of sin.[30]

God's Devil

Satan was a wonder weapon but, like most weapons of this kind, a dangerous weapon as well, to be handled with the utmost care. The main problem with Satan was that he did not fit well, or at all, into the framework of a monotheistic religion. The authors of the Old Testament knew this very well and acted accordingly. Theirs being a new and fragile monotheism—the danger of relapsing into polytheism and paganism was considerable—they had to be intransigent and kept Satan out of their world, as far as possible. In the Old Testament, he is mentioned only three times,[31] and even then he is not regarded as an independent power opposing God (although the Hebrew word *ha-satan* means 'adversary', 'obstructer', 'opposer') but much more as a recalcitrant servant who runs errands on his orders, just like the other, obedient and beatific, angels (Sharma, 1987, 81).[32]

> To the Jews of Biblical times the adversary was neither evil nor fallen (the Old Testament knows nothing of fallen angels), but a servant of God in good standing, a great angel, perhaps the greatest. However, he is nowhere named. In Job he presents himself before the Lord in the company of other unnamed 'sons of God'. (Davidson, 1967, xviii)

The authors of the Talmud strongly opposed any kind of dualism (Persian and Canaanite versions of dualism were very much alive in the region). They rejected the myth of the fall of the angels and the notion of personified evil, and considered Satan more as a symbol than as a real person. They stressed the omnipotence and benevolence of God and the goodness of the world and derived the existence of evil from "the imperfect state of the created world or from human misuse of free will, not from the machinations of a cosmic enemy of the Lord" (J. B. Russell, 1981, 27). In non-canonical Hebrew literature,[33] as well as in the *Aggadah*,[34] the Cabala, and in medieval Jewish legends, Satan played a more important role, although he never developed into such a counter-power of God as in some of the medieval Christian writings, and remained throughout the Judaic tradition "'little more than an allegory' of the evil inclination among humans" (J. B. Russell, 1981, 29).[35] Despite this restraint and consistent monotheism, there was also a high level of uncertainty and many contradictions in the Jewish tradition concerning the origin of evil and the existence of Satan.

The Apocalypse

Christian thought assigned a greater role to Satan in its interpretation of, and fight against, evil. It had, from the very beginning, a strong, though latent, dualistic element, despite the fact that most of the early church fathers, Tertullian, St Augustine, and others, rejected the cosmological dualism of the Gnostics and emphasized the goodness of God and of the created world. In Christianity, Satan was

> no longer the obedient servant of God, 'the prime in splendor,' but the opponent and enemy of God, the Prince of Evil, the Devil incarnate ... This continuing conflict between God and Satan, one might add, is little more than a recrudescence, with modifications, of the dualistic system that Christianity (along with Jewish sectarians of the post-Biblical era) inherited from Zoroastrianism. (Davidson, 1967, xviii)

In the New Testament, in contrast to the Old Testament, there were many references to Satan: Satan tempted Jesus Christ; Jesus saw him "fallen as lightning from heaven"; and he and his allies played a major role in the Apocalypse (Sharma, 1987, 83).[36] The most important step was taken by St Paul, who—probably relying on the apocalyptic literature[37]—was the first Christian author to identify the serpent of the Garden of Eden with Satan (Sharma, 1987, 83). Russell remarks that there was a consensus in the early Christian tradition according to which Satan fell after Adam, and it was only in the third century, under the influence of Origen, that the idea that he had fallen before Adam's creation, and that he was identical with the serpent in the Garden of Eden, was accepted by the majority within the Catholic Church (1987, 83–84). His ontological status, character, and appearance, as well as his role in the history of the universe was precisely defined and described by the Council of Toledo in 447, but this did not end the controversies.

The myth of Satan has played a positive role in the history of Western civilization not only by contracting and destroying all the evil of the world in one person; and not only by transferring at least part of the responsibility for original sin from mankind to this mythic figure. In modern times he became a symbol of protest and revolt against orthodoxy and oppression, hypocrisy and false values. In Milton's *Paradise Lost*, he is the uncompromising spirit of freedom and revolt. In Byron's *Cain*, he questions the goodness of God, creator of a world full of suffering. In Victor Hugo's *La fin de Satan*, he is the tragic hero who suffers for the lack of real peace and harmony in the universe. Baudelaire was fascinated and deeply troubled by the tempting and intimidating beauty of Satan, by his demonic force of destruction and creation, and derided his own enlightened contemporaries who thought that Satan had never existed.[38]

THE TRANSFORMATION OF EVIL

Despite all the efforts described above to defeat or expel, rationalize or exorcise evil, it stubbornly persisted. Pain and misery, suffering and death seemed to be inalienable facts in people's lives. Further strategies were needed. One of them consisted in transforming evil from a negative into a positive factor.[39] The question was how this might be achieved. There were various solutions: the transformation of the alien world into a 'moral universe' was the most important and most successful among them,[40] and it became one of the major determinants of Western civilization.

The Moral Universe

Various civilizations created their moral universes in various ways. In general, there have been three main approaches.

First, the belief could be generated—and later the hypothesis or conviction could be developed—that the universe as a whole was governed by a universal moral law or principle, or by the (moral) providence of an almighty God. It is easy to state this but it must have taken a long time to develop and establish this belief; to convince oneself and others that, through a metaphysical, divine, or other power, justice was ultimately being done in this universe; that this was a just world, governed by an invisible moral order, which rewarded virtue and punished sin, and in which even evil had its place and ultimately played a positive role.

The Pythagoreans, Plato, the early Neoplatonists, and a major current within the Judeo–Christian tradition were the first and the most important creeds and schools of thought to develop this vision of the universe governed by an underlying, shining constellation of eternal moral laws, in light of which change and mutability, human suffering and death seemed insignificant and ephemeral. In Euripides' words:

> I am a slave, I know, and slaves are weak.
> But the gods are strong, and over them

> there stands some absolute, some moral order
> or principle of law more final still.
> Upon this final law the world depends;
> through it the gods exist; by it we live,
> defining good and evil.[41]

Secondly, one could create a moral universe within oneself, in one's soul, in one's immediate environment and actions. One could be convinced, and live accordingly, that it was only one's autonomy, the discipline of living according to the moral norms one had set for oneself, that can protect one in a world of pain, misery, and death. The Stoics were, if not the first, certainly the most consistent in building up this moral fortitude in their souls. The Protestants, too, developed this autonomy, though they anchored it strongly in an outside point, God. Nietzsche, who destroyed the faith in, or the illusion of, the existence of a moral universe, and also most of the existentialists, would argue that the individual has to create his own universe of freedom and meaning within, and despite, an enslaving, amoral, and meaningless world.

Thirdly, one could carve out and enclose a sphere of morality within an amoral world; a moral universe created by one's religion, church, or civilization, and protecting one against the attacks of the outside world of evil. This closed realm of morality was to be continuously reinforced by strengthening one's faith, exorcising evil forces, resisting temptations, praying for the help of the gods or God.

Tribal gods, or friendly gods within a polytheistic creed, could guarantee justice within these restricted spheres of morality by transubstantiating life into myth and historical events into moral parables. The Old Testament, for instance, was a brilliant instrument for raising events from the level of everyday life and history to the level of morality and transcendence. It transformed evil in the real world—disasters and defeats, suffering and death, the flight from Egypt or the Babylonian captivity—into events which were significant and positive on the level of morality. Let's take the Flood as an example.

Why Have We Forgotten the Victims?

In the last two thousand years or so, we have heard too much about Noah and his lucky family, and too little—or nothing at all—about the rest of mankind, those who miserably perished in the Flood. Why? In reality, the

Flood must have been a horrendous disaster, an orgy of the forces of evil, a terrible ordeal of human and animal suffering, despair, and death. Men and children, pets and peacefully grazing animals were drowned by the thousands or hundred-thousands in torrential waters, were crushed under collapsing buildings or choked to death by mud slides and slime, just as they are nowadays in the great floods of India and Bangladesh, or the lethal tidal waves of the Pacific Ocean. It must have been an absurd, meaningless, horrifying disaster; an intolerable experience; unacceptable evidence of the fact that mankind lived in a world in which human lives did not count, where people were dispensable entities and might be destroyed in any moment. Why have we forgotten the victims?

Probably because we, too, feel ourselves to be victims, or potential victims, and do not want to be victimized. We want to trust in the possibility of escape and victory. This may have been the main motive force that prompted mankind to develop the skill of transforming even the most negative facts and events into something positive; to transform defeat into victory.

It was in this way that decades, centuries, or millennia after the fact, the Flood was—or the Floods were—transformed by mythical imagination (on the analogy of Freud's "dream work"—it could be called "myth work") into one of the most significant, meaningful, and—in its effects—positive events in human history. It was transformed into a moral parable of sin, punishment, purification, redemption, new life. Out of terror and anxiety, it was transformed into a token of God's love; out of an experience of the destructive forces of an alien world into a proof that this is our world; that ultimately this is a good world, a moral world, a world governed by God's providential power.

The same technique was also used by Christianity—for example, in the case of martyrs. The miserable deaths of some poor fellows in faraway towns or cities, who were tortured, flogged, flayed, crucified, quartered, broken on the wheel, burnt in oil or at the stake, in dark dungeons or dirty marketplaces, were ultimately transformed into glorious reports of victory in the martyrologies and legendaries of later ages, and into the brilliance and beauty of pictures and frescoes, sparkling with gold and shining in the transcendental blue of heaven. This was a remarkable testimony to the ingenuity and stubborn will of mankind to transform the horrors of people's lives in an alien world into the victories of a human or divine universe. In other words, to transform a fearful chaos into a peaceful and meaningful cosmos; into a civilization.

And this is not the whole story. The most powerful weapon against evil was not the construction of a moral universe, or of a constellation of moral principles protecting mankind within an alien world. It was the transformation of evil into guilt.

NOTES

1 Exorcism was incorporated into the baptismal rite round 200 AD and has remained part of it ever since. See J. B. Russell (1981, 101).
2 In the third century, Tertullian "introduced the image of the Devil drowning in the water of baptism" (J. B. Russell, 1981, 101).
3 See, for instance, Campbell (1968).
4 Ricoeur (1967) quotes Pattazzoni (1931, vol. 1, 184).
5 Ricoeur (1967, 35) also stresses that "ablution is never a simple washing ... [it] is already a symbolic washing ... it is always signified in partial, substitutive, and abbreviated signs: burning, removing, chasing, throwing, spitting out, covering up, burying".
6 Quoted by Ricoeur (1967, 34).
7 People living in the Western world are inclined to forget that in pre-monotheistic civilizations a great number—if not the majority—of gods were fearsome, revengeful, destructive demons and monsters. Think of the Egyptian Seth or Sekhmet, the Mesopotamian Pazuzu, the Sumerian Lilitu, or the Persian Ahriman; not to mention the ambivalent deities, who were both destructive and life giving, such as the Indian Kali or the Greek Dionysus. Gods became purely benevolent and protective, even if sometimes wrathful, only in the great monotheistic religions, Judaism, Christianity, and Islam.
8 Sophocles (1959, lines 596–601, 604–605).
9 Ibid. (lines 1333–1334, 1260, 1316).
10 Ibid. (lines 852–855, 872, 875).
11 Ibid. (lines 1261–62, 1272–74, 1346).
12 If, and only if, Satan had fallen before Man, which was also a highly controversial issue in early Christianity. There were church fathers who argued that Satan's rebellion and fall was caused by the fact that he envied Man whom God had created in his own image, a privilege not enjoyed by the angels. In this interpretation, envy was the source of evil in the world.
13 Irenaeus (120/140–200/203) was one of the most influential church fathers.
14 Sin consists "in turning away from the higher good, namely God, to the lower good ... the will becomes evil not because that is evil to which it turns, but because the turning itself is wicked" (St Augustine, 1966–1972, 12:6).
15 See the excellent article by Hick (1967).
16 Quoted by Russell (1981, 199). Another interpretation of the nonexistence of evil comes from Hinduism, according to which the world of change, suffering, and death is an illusion, and evil is only the acceptance of this illusion as the center and goal of one's life instead of aspiring to spirituality and eternity.

17 See also Plato, *Timaeus*, 41 b–c; Plotinus: *Enneads*, III, 2, 17; as well as Leibniz and others.
18 Heraclitus, *Fragments*, 102 and 46. Quoted by Campbell (1968, 44).
19 William Blake, 'Proverbs of Hell', in *The Marriage of Heaven and Hell*.
20 It would subsequently be argued by a variety of authors that God had not, or perhaps even could not have, deprived man of this freedom. According to Schelling (1809), God cannot suspend freedom since in this way "He would suspend Himself [since freedom is His essence]; He can overcome it only by love." Quoted by Köhler (1992, 1463).
21 This dichotomy of the two freedoms would return in Isaiah Berlin's (1969) concepts of "negative freedom" (freedom to choose and to do what one wants), and "positive freedom" (freedom achieved by living according to certain principles, achieving certain goals).
22 The quotation is from Schleiermacher, who developed Irenaeus's ideas.
23 See also Hick (1966). It is important to note, however, that some scholars question the validity of Hick's interpretation.
24 According to Arvind Sharma (1987, 81–84), there is no such fixed focus of moral evil as Satan in Hinduism. In Buddhism, there is Mara, whose role can be compared to that of Satan in Judaism and Christianity. See also Boyd (1975).
25 There are too many works on Satan to be quoted here. For orientation consult Robbins (1966), and the works of Jeffrey B. Russell (1977, 1981, 1988) quoted in this and other chapters.
26 See also McGinn (1994); Delumeau (1990, especially Chapter 13 'The Tortures of the Afterlife').
27 "Caroline Walker Bynum [1995] has studied the importance of damnation as a perpetual digestion of sinners. Sinners ... are continually processed through the guts of Leviathan (whose open mouth is the gate of Hell)". Quoted by Wills (1995, 54).
28 Christ's role was sometimes, and partly, taken over by the warrior archangel, Michael, and by some warrior saints, such as St George. Beside diabology, Christology also had a rich literature in the Middle Ages.
29 This dualistic strategy against evil was well known in many mythologies and religions. It usually consisted of two steps. As a first step, one corner, one part, or even half the universe was given over to the powers of darkness and evil. At the same time, the other part of the world was made into an invincible fortress of light and goodness, which would ultimately conquer the realm of darkness and defeat the forces of evil in a cosmic *theomachia*. This was the strategy of the major dualistic creeds and religions—Zoroastrianism and Manicheism, for instance— and partly also of medieval Christianity. Consider also Freud's (1961, 85) interpretation of the God–Satan dichotomy as a mythic projection of the son's ambivalent, love–hate relationship to his father.
30 Satan became an important safety valve for guilt feelings in medieval Christianity. When, in modern times, Satan's figure began to fade and recede, the level of guilt feelings may have begun to rise in Western societies. Jung (and perhaps also Freud and Marcuse) would certainly agree with this hypothesis. Satan has played an important role in the spiritual hygiene of Western civilization.

31 In the Book of Job, where he tests Job with God's permission; in Zechariah 3:1–2, where he opposes Joshua on his own initiative; and in Chronicles 1, 21:1, where he moves David to count the people of Israel. Further, he is inferred in Psalms 109:6, and perhaps in 1 Sam. 18:10, and 1 Kings 22:21–23.
32 The Greek *diabolos* means 'adversary' and is a translation of the Hebrew word *satan*. The English 'devil' is a derivative of the Greek *diabolos*. See also Trachtenberg (1943); Ginzburg (1938).
33 The Book of Jubilees, the Testament of Reuben, the Book of the Secrets of Enoch [2 Enoch], the Testament of the Twelve Patriarchs, the Qumran documents, and so on.
34 A series of moral stories, legends, maxims, and sermons.
35 He quotes Trachtenberg (1943).
36 The original fall of Satan: Rom. 16:20, Luke 10:18. The Devil is identified with Beelzebul (Lord of the Flies), Beelzebub (Lord of Dung), and, with less critical certainty, with Lucifer: Luke 4:6. He is the prince of the world: John 14:30; the temptation of Jesus: Mark 1:13, Matthew 4:1-11, Luke 4:1-13. Several acts of exorcism: *passim*; the eschatological fall of Satan: 2 Peter 2:4, Revelation 12:7-9; he is already judged: John 16:11.
37 The genre of apocalyptic literature flourished between the second century BCE and the second century AD in Judaism and Christianity (The Book of Daniel, Revelation to John, and so on).
38 For an excellent survey of the metamorphoses of Satan throughout the centuries see J. B. Russell (1988): for references to Byron, Hugo, Baudelaire, and others see pp. 220–40.
39 St Augustine's 'moral' theory of evil, discussed above, was an attempt in this direction.
40 One of the main functions of myth has always been to transform the unconnected and meaningless events of the history of the tribe, and of everyday life, into a chain of meaningful and—in some cases—morally significant events. As we approach the great monotheistic religions, this moralization of the universe becomes more and more pronounced.
41 Euripides, *Hecuba*, lines 799–804. Quoted by Carroll (1985, 216).

CHAPTER SEVEN

THE WORLD OF GUILT

> "No civilization had ever attached as much importance to guilt and shame as did the Western World…"
>
> Jean Delumeau, *Sin and Fear*

THE great drama of guilt, repentance, and salvation has been one of the dominant factors, and a major motive force, of Western civilization for almost two thousand years. It has played a fundamental role in shaping this civilization and its history. If it loses its central place—and there are signs of such a change—this may lead to a major transformation of our civilization.

GUILT

The Great Reversal

I would like to commence this discussion of the role of guilt in the generation of our civilization with a puzzling fact, usually overlooked even by experts. Looked at in a particular way, the myth of the Fall turns out to be a reversed Christ myth: while Christ sacrificed himself for Man, in the myth of the Fall human beings sacrifice themselves for God, in the sense that they take on themselves—in the form of original sin—responsibility for the presence of evil in the world, that is, God's alleged responsibility for creating an evil world. Why did they do so? Or more precisely: Why did the myth of creation make them do so?

I have already discussed the fact that, like other creation myths, Genesis had to explain and justify the presence of evil in the world and thereby reduce fear and anxiety in the hearts of human beings. The question is, why did it lay the whole burden on the shoulders of men and women? Even more importantly, why did people accept the responsibility for evil, for all the suffering, misery, and death which afflict living creatures? There must have been extremely serious and strong motives behind the (conscious–unconscious) acceptance of this responsibility and the generation of this myth.[1] Let me suggest some of the possible reasons.

First, generalized fear and anxiety in a world permeated with the mysterious and incomprehensible forces of evil may have been worse than the burden of a well-defined, concrete guilt.

Secondly, it was conceivably in the interest of humankind to have a strong and absolutely good God, who had nothing to do with evil in the world. With the myth of the Garden of Eden and the Fall, mankind cleared God of any suspicion of having created a world of human misery and death.

Furthermore, if evil entered the world independently of, or against the will of, God, then there was the hope that God would defeat it. An innocent God would be the only real guarantor of mankind's ultimate liberation from evil.

Another argument is that, if evil was brought into the world by a human act, evil was not the primary fact—it had not existed before mankind. In this case, the original and 'normal' state of the world was innocence, harmony, and freedom—a world created by God in which human beings ought to have been completely at home. As a consequence, the alien world was accidental and the possibility of a return to original bliss existed.

More importantly, it was a stroke of genius—although, of course, not a conscious one—to transform so-called natural evil into moral evil.[2] Indeed, this may have been the crucial achievement of this myth. As a matter of fact, by the myth of the Fall, mankind transformed all evil, and natural evil par excellence—suffering, disease and death, floods and droughts, wars and epidemics—into moral evil, that is, into the result of its own acts. If a flood destroyed the crops, if the Tartars invaded and devastated a country, if people had to suffer and die, this was not inevitable, but contingent, the result of a human act that could be counteracted and remedied by another human (and/or divine) act—by faith, repentance, and expiation. By this transformation, Western civilization gained control over the main source of fear and anxiety in the world.

Paul Piehler (1971, 28, 112) gives an interesting early example of this transformation of natural evil into guilt. He shows how in the 'Psychomachia' of Prudentius, written in the fourth century, the monsters of a dangerous and fearful world were transformed into sins in the human soul.

> His [Prudentius'] explicit aim is to rationalize away the ancient fears and divert the psychic energies against those aspects of the *portenta* [monsters] that constitute sin ... His *ratio vincendi* is in fact to reduce the monsters to sins ... with the coming of the Christian era the fear of monsters becomes separated from the horror of sin, with a consequent fading of the power of the monster figure to terrify.

The power of the myth of original sin was immensely increased when the Fall of Adam was combined (as we have seen, first by St Paul) with the death of Christ and integrated into the great drama of Salvation. This cosmic vision of man relieving God of the responsibility for evil in the world at the beginning of history, and of Christ relieving man of the burden of this role and this sin at the end of history, surrounded mankind with a protective sphere of safety, freedom, and hope. This was the main reason why Leibniz (1966, 377) spoke of the Fall as a *"felix culpa"*.[3] One might be tempted to say, irreverently, that the Fall was a good deal for mankind. But has it not distorted our emerging civilization, *ab ovo*?

The Price of Guilt

On the one hand, guilt liberated man from the gnawing anxieties and uncertainties of living in an alien world. It explained the presence of evil in the world and human life. It gave people living under the wing of Western civilization a kind of control over suffering and death and offered hope to the faithful. It reduced the fearful complexity of the world to the simple and transparent drama of guilt–repentance–salvation, which could be understood even by the simplest minds. It guaranteed the help of the most powerful ally of humankind: God.

It transformed the alien world, in the most genuine sense of the word, into a universe governed by the adamant laws of morality. And it became one of the primary motive forces in Western civilization.

On the other hand, this may not have been such a good bargain after all. According to all available evidence, humankind has had to pay an exorbitant price for living in the safety of this moral universe. First and foremost, people had to accept the burden of sin and the burden of the sense of guilt, which would become extremely heavy as Judeo-Christian civilization developed.

They also had to pay a price for accepting unconditional dependence on God: this sacrifice was worth making only if in exchange one could expect safety, rewards, and ultimate redemption from God. This dependence on God later developed into the strong spiritual and social control of human lives by God's regent, the church, a situation, which continued for many centuries.

More generally, one could say that guilt has developed from a means of solving problems into a problem in its own right. It was generated as a protective device against evil and the alien world, but, ironically, it became part of that alien world. It became a new 'jungle', a new source of fear and misery—the jungle of guilt. According to Freud and others, in the course of history it has become one of the most important sources of neurosis, anxiety, and human suffering. How did it happen? How was guilt transformed from a protective device into a realm of the alien world?

On the surface, there is nothing surprising in this. As we have already seen, it is a common human experience that what we do in order to protect ourselves may turn against us and threatens us with pain and destruction. In this case, however, the underlying drama is worth our closer attention.

In what follows, I shall study this strange and unhappy mutation of the concept and role of guilt by means of a few selected examples. I shall do so in order to demonstrate that guilt has been, even in its distorted form, a major force and factor in the generation of Western civilization.[4]

In its various—positive and negative—forms, guilt has been present in every dimension of human life. It has been an everyday human experience and a key concept, not only in theology and moral philosophy, but also in jurisprudence and psychology, cultural anthropology, and even ontology. In order to give some idea of this complexity, let me quote the major types of guilt from the table of contents of an important book that deals with the role of guilt in human life (Carroll, 1985, v–vi): "Moral guilt" versus "dispositional guilt"; "persecutory guilt" versus "depressive guilt"; "superficial guilt" at an early stage of cultural evolution compared with "rampant, uncultured guilt", "parricidal guilt", and "civilized guilt" in the later stages of this evolution. And let me add, from the same table of contents, the list of "the symptoms of guilt": "remorse, reparation, purification, obsession, asceticism, psychosis, rationalization, anxiety".[5]

It must be a fearsome monster indeed to have had so many heads and to have caused so much trouble.

THE RELIGION OF GUILT
The Machinery of Guilt

As God's regent on earth, the medieval—and to a lesser extent, also the modern—church acquired almost a monopoly on running and controlling the guilt–repentance–salvation process. It played an important role in maintaining and regulating social coexistence in medieval and modern communities and also in helping people cope with a wide range of psychological problems. In this role it became one of the major institutions and constituents of Western civilization. On the other hand, it also overplayed its role somewhat, keeping people 'on the treadmill'. In various historical periods and social contexts, it could not resist the temptation of abusing its authority and exploiting the guilt machinery for its own purposes. In addition, by developing a 'guilt culture', in some cases it increased rather than decreased fear and anxiety in people's hearts.

The strange thing is that Protestantism, which revolted against the Catholic Church's domination of human souls, increased the burden of guilt even further. The founders of Calvinism and their followers stressed the eternally enslaving effect of original sin, which—according to them—had corrupted mankind *in toto* and had left open no way of improving one's chances of salvation by good deeds. The only way of escaping from sin and eternal damnation was to have absolute faith in Christ and in his redeeming power (Luther, 1525; Calvin, 1559).

Erasmus (1524), in his controversy with Luther, emphasized human freedom and stated that each individual could fall only through his or her own sin. The Catholic Church, too, left more room for the individual. According to its teaching, the impact of original sin and the power of Satan were already weakened by the sacrament of baptism; pious believers could hope for the help and mediation of the saints and the institutions of the church, and although they could not regain their innocence, by their exemplary behavior and good deeds they could improve their chances of being redeemed by Christ.

Unorthodox twentieth-century theologians have gone even further and have done a lot to divest and free the church from the onus of its powerful role as gatekeeper of heaven and hell. According to the German theologian Bonhoeffer, for instance, it is unfair to stigmatize human beings as sinful in order to be able to preach to them the grace of God (delivered by the church). Heinrich Ott (1978, 169–76), a leading personality in modern Protestant theology, follows the same line of thought. He says that "it is not the duty of Christianity to nurture a hypertrophic superego and thereby enhance in man the feeling of anxiety produced by the superego".

There are theologians who have gone so far as to reject the traditional teaching about original sin altogether. They emphasize that sin cannot be inherited, that people do not live enslaved to that ancient, mythological original sin; that Original Sin was not an historical event but an inherent characteristic of human existence.[6]

This does not mean, however, that by discarding the concept of original sin from their vocabulary contemporary theologians have also expelled guilt from our world and our civilization. If anything, they have been fighting an even more dramatic fight with guilt—and the evil lurking behind it—than their predecessors (for example, St Augustine and Pascal) did. Let me illustrate this drama with the example of Paul Tillich, one of the leading Protestant theologians of our age. I shall study his ideas in some detail in order to show how densely the various forms of guilt may be woven into the fabric of our civilization.

'A Pilgrim on Earth'

Tillich indicates two sources of human responsibility. Human beings are responsible, first, because—despite being in a situation determined by cosmic and tragic necessity—they make choices and by these choices they become responsible for whatever may result. On the other hand, they are responsible and guilty because, once in the realm of existence, they fail to do everything in their power to actualize their being, their potential essence, in the best possible way. Let us first look at the question of the initial choice.

After being created and placed in the state of "dreaming innocence" of a metaphorical Garden of Eden, men and women deliberately and freely chose human existence against this dream of "undecided potentialities". By virtue of their freedom to choose, they became responsible and guilty. This is a well-known argument in the Christian tradition.

> Man is caught between the desire to actualize his freedom and the demand to preserve his dreaming innocence. In the power of his finite freedom, he decides for actualization ... Man experiences the anxiety of losing himself by not actualizing himself and his potentialities and the anxiety of losing himself by actualizing himself and his potentialities ... The anxiety of this situation is the state of temptation. (Tillich, 1951–1963, vol. 2, pp. 34–36)

Human beings also become guilty because they fail to fully actualize these potentialities—their freedom. They are the only creatures in the world who have language with which they can liberate themselves "from the bondage of the concrete situation"; but they may fail to do so. They are free "in so far as [they are] able to ask questions about the world"; and they may ask the wrong questions. They are free "in so far as [they have] the power of deliberating and deciding"; and they may lack the courage to make real decisions. They are free "in so far as [they have] the faculty of creating worlds above the given world"; and they may lack the inspiration and the will power to do so. They are free "in so far as [they have] the power of contradicting [themselves] and [their] essential nature"; and they may succumb to their instincts and nature. "Man is free even from his freedom; that is, he can surrender his humanity", and he surrenders his freedom and humanity all too often (1959–1963, vol. 2, pp. 31–32). And there is no end to the possibilities of human freedom and failure.

Human beings may sin by "unbelief", by rejecting God as the center of their lives. They may sin by "*hubris*", by trying "to make [themselves] existentially the center of [themselves and their] world". They may sin by "concupiscence", by trying to draw "the whole of [their] world into [themselves]". Nero, Mozart's Don Juan, Faust, who wanted to know everything, and Nietzsche's *Übermensch* with his "will to power" are the classic examples of human beings in the servitude of concupiscence (1951–1963, vol. 2, pp. 47–49, 52–53).[7]

They may fail to be really alive and really present in this world. They may fail to experience time as an existential reality, as an "eternal now", and then, threatened by the demon of transitoriness, they may try "to fill the moment with as many transitory things as possible"; they may imagine "a continuation of [their lives] after the end of [their] time and an endlessness without eternity". All these are sinful, and futile, attempts to achieve eternal life, instead of bravely accepting one's finite freedom with its tragic limitations and glorious potentialities. They may also sin by losing their authentic place in the world, their "eternal here", and experience the world as "spatial contingency". They may long for a "final home", but they have no final home on earth. "He remains a 'pilgrim on earth', and finally 'his place does not know him any longer' (Job)" (1951–1963, vol. 2, p. 69).

Human beings may succumb to other "structures of despair" as well. Being tormented by anxiety, they may become a destructive force themselves by searching for absolute security and certainty in a world and in human life in which there is no absolute security and certainty. Seeing this false security and certainty threatened by "those who compete or contradict", they may panic and try to defend themselves by means "some of which are brutal, some fanatical, some dishonest, and all insufficient and destructive; for there is no security and certainty within finitude ... War and persecution are partly dependent on this dialectic" (1951–1963, vol. 2, 69, 73).

As we have seen, this is no longer the relatively simple world of traditional Christianity in which natural evil was transformed into guilt and controlled and relieved by the guilt–repentance–salvation dialectic. Here guilt, as an inherent part of the created world and a "tragic necessity", is beyond the reach of this machinery.

According to Tillich (1952), Jesus Christ is the only solution—for those who believe in him. But Tillich also has a message for all those who live in this world. We all need, he says, the "courage to be". I would add that without this courage we would not have been able to build up the protective symbolic spheres of our civilization.

THE PHILOSOPHY OF GUILT

Guilt and the Human Condition

Guilt has become a key concept in twentieth-century philosophy as well, mainly in the works of the so-called existentialist philosophers.

In the wake of Kierkegaard, Heidegger and Jaspers argued that guilt was not primarily a psychic or historical phenomenon; not the consequence of a human act or human failure; not the product of a pathological process. Rather it was an ontological category, an inalienable and essential part of human existence, fully independent of the human psyche or human history.

For them, guilt is not a "moral category"; it is not a question of good and evil, of conforming or not conforming to a system of norms; it is not the corollary of a particular act in time and space. It is a "modality of existence".[8] According to Heidegger (1962), for instance, human existence is "grounded in nothingness"; in the inevitable and tragic fact that, in each of his decisions, man has to choose just one possibility of existence and cannot help negating and annihilating all other possibilities. "The nothingness which we have in mind belongs to *Dasein*'s being-free for his existential possibilities. This freedom *is* only in the choice of one, which means not having chosen and not being able to choose the other."[9] This annihilation of potential existence is inevitable, and so people are not responsible for this "ontological" guilt. At the same time, they may become subjectively guilty if, in a state of "distraction" and "oblivion", they make the wrong choice, by which they miss the unique opportunity to discover, experience, and actualize Being as fully as possible in their own existence. Or, as Jaspers (1948, 506 and *passim*) puts it, if they do not have the courage to accept the challenge of "boundary [or 'extreme'] situations" and, as a consequence, fail to achieve an "authentic existence".

Kierkegaard spoke of this strange duality as the source of guilt long before Heidegger and Jaspers. The heroes of the Greek tragedies were sinful and innocent since guilt for them was fate and personal responsibility at the same time. For Kierkegaard—as for Niebuhr or Tillich a century later—the human being was in an intermediate situation—he was free but his freedom was limited and finite; he lived in the tension of freedom and finitude, possibility and necessity. Or as Schrag (1961, 161–66) summed up Kierkegaard's ideas about humankind's ambiguous situation: "The self *is* guilty because of its necessity or destiny (rooted primarily in its past). The self *becomes* guilty through the actualization of itself as possibility (rooted primarily in the future)."[10] This ambiguity, and the anxiety accompanying it, have been among the major motive forces of Western civilization.

Does this mean that, with guilt, evil is built into our very existence, as its fundamental modality, and so that we are inescapably caught in the world of evil, in an alien world? If our existence is limited by death, if by our very freedom and free choices we inevitably destroy part of our own potential existence, if we cannot, and will never be able to, escape our intermediate situation, a source of tension and suffering: then there may be no hope at all. Or is there any?

The answers that have been given to these questions throughout the millennia have become essential constituents of the symbolic structures of our civilization.

THE POLITICS OF GUILT

Guilt has played an important part in politics as well. It has been a fearful weapon, and a major source of human misery and suffering. Totalitarian regimes have learned a lot from two thousand years of European and non-European history. Let me give a few examples of how their guilt-generating machinery worked. I shall take my examples from a Central European country: Hungary, in the 1950s.[11]

Show Trials

The practice of show trials is too well known to require a detailed discussion here. The sense of guilt was systematically used as a tool of pressure and torture. Victims were mercilessly humiliated and accused of crimes they had never committed; or, what was even worse, vague allusions were made with no attempt to specify the crime itself. According to a wide range of witnesses, in several cases the accused, like a modern Oedipus, began to feverishly search in his or her past for something to link the accusation to, and felt almost relieved to acknowledge the 'crime' which was eventually offered. By acknowledging it, and even expressing a readiness to atone for it, he or she could hope for absolution and even to be readmitted to the community (of his on her torturers). The need to be 'forgiven' (for unspecified sins) is, of course, a common phenomenon even in our more or less 'normal', everyday lives.

Stigma

Stigmatization is an age-old method of putting people to shame and making them feel guilty. The communist regime was quick to introduce this technique. In the late 1940s and throughout the 1950s, the communists at one time or another stigmatized practically every social group in the country, on a daily basis. As a Hungarian citizen, for instance, you were branded as a member of a "fascist nation", the "last satellite of Hitler". If you belonged to the middle classes, you were called a "reactionary"; as a businessman, you were branded a "capitalist" and a "class enemy"; if you had a small business, you were a "speculator" and a "profiteer". If you happened to be a skilled worker, you were "a traitor to the working classes" and a member of the "labor aristocracy"; as an unskilled worker, you were stigmatized as a "lumpenproletarian". If you were a well-to-do farmer, you were chastised as a "kulak"; if you were happy to be only a poor farmer, you were branded nevertheless, this time as a "waverer" (if you did not enter a state cooperative quickly enough). If you tried to make a decent living and work for your family, you were stigmatized as "petty bourgeois".

To make the point even more concretely, let me list the epithets attached to so-called kulaks in a Hungarian local newspaper between 1948 and 1950:

1948 "pigheaded"; "double-chinned"; "mischievous"; "insidious"; "crafty"; "wily"; "ruthless"; "infamous"; "greedy"; "arrogant"; "braggart"; "debauchee"; "exploiter"; "parasite"; "slave-driver"; "usurer"; "reactionary"; "demagogue"; "impostor"; "swindler"; "corrupter"; "hoarder"; "black-marketeer"; "blind pig owner"; "bootlegger".

1949 "enraged"; "abominable"; "odious"; "sly"; "desperate"; "capable of anything"; "shameless"; "treacherous"; "sneaky"; "most depraved"; "stinker"; "meanest"; "aggressor"; "arsonist"; "machine breaker"; "profiteer"; "shark"; "speculator".

1950 "shameless"; "rotten"; "subversive"; "antidemocratic"; "nationalist"; "fascist"; "hoarder of bread"; "the hideous carrion-eating ravens of our working people"; "traitors born to infamy and indolence"; "vile hirelings of the child-murderers in Korea"; "these stooges of American imperialists and of the murderous gang of Tito".[12]

This practice abated in the second half of the 1950s, although some of its more moderate forms persisted for a good while. Even in the 1970s and early 1980s, broad social strata found themselves in a peculiar situation: although they were given the opportunity to pursue economic independence within the sphere of the so-called second economy, everything was done to make them feel anxious and bad about it; to make them feel that they were doing something they should be ashamed of and should hide because it did not really fit into the system of norms of a socialist society. It was usual to accuse the vendor selling hot dogs at a fast-food stand of corruption, fraud, looting, and easy and unscrupulous moneymaking.

Hidden Values

Soon after the communist takeover, another technique of guilt generation was developed (or rather, imported from the Soviet Union): the hiding of values. *Vera Angi*, a mixture of feature film and documentary made in the late 1970s, illustrates this practice very well. The action takes place at the end of the 1940s, at a party school attended by a group of enthusiastic cadres. Everything is fine until, one day, a man sent by the 'Center' appears among them. In a couple of days he shatters the self-esteem of everyone there with cool and methodical thoroughness. He pounds into them the fact that participation in the communist rebellion of 1919, membership of a past labor movement, a jail sentence, or participation in the resistance against the Germans are of no worth—on the contrary, they are the sources of individualistic pride and conceit:

> "But under the proletarian dictatorship I was commanding officer of a battalion!" one of the elder students complains, profoundly disturbed.
> "You see, comrade, you must get rid of this sectarian conceit. You must re-examine your entire past. You must learn that you're not the movement and that you still have a lot of things to learn."

Or:

> "I often talk to my colleagues about our struggles in the Resistance Movement and about our lives in prison and ..."
> "... and don't you feel, comrade, that this way you set yourself apart, place yourself above other excellent comrades? Above the leaders of our Party? You have a dangerously positive opinion of yourself."

The man from the Center keeps stressing that what is of value will be determined in every single case by the Center. After the fact. This concealment of the system of values according to which one is judged creates an atmosphere of fear and anxiety. No one knows what is good and what is evil, what is correct or incorrect behavior. "I don't know if I should say it, but I'm always and in general afraid! I never know whether what I'm saying is right or wrong", one of the students admits, in panic.

The practice of keeping people disoriented—and thereby dependent on their superiors—also had sophisticated forms before the war. According to a document I found in a county archive, for example, one of the golden rules of discipline exercised by bailiffs and overseers on the large estates was to punish peasants when they did something right and to reward them when they did something wrong; or simply to punish and reward them at random. What was important was that they, the laborers, should never know when to expect punishment and when a reward. The rationale behind this practice was that if the norms were known, then it follows that rights must also exist: a worker could say that, since he had completed a particular task according to the established norms, he was entitled to a reward. On the other hand, if there are no norms, there are no rights either: one is entirely dependent on the good (or bad) will of the supervisor and one lives in a state of subservience and uncertainty—that is, in a region of an alien world. This is a good example of how the ritual of guilt, which had been generated in order to protect people against their fears and anxieties, may become, in a distorted form, a major source of fear and anxiety.

Double Bind

In psychoanalytic praxis 'double bind' refers to the contradictory behavior of a dominant figure in one's life. The most often quoted example is that of parents who bring up their children to respect a certain norm and then punish them when they act according to this norm. The same happens in a society in which, particular norms having been laid down, it is made impossible to live according to those norms, or people are castigated for living by them. One of the major themes of the communists was that one should be a responsible, public-minded, community-oriented person. In reality, they made it impossible, if not dangerous, to be a responsible, public-minded, community-oriented person—if somebody tried to overcome the obstacles and conform to the ideal, they were quickly branded as unruly troublemakers, if not dangerous elements, leftist deviationists, counterrevolutionaries, or whatever the fashionable insult might be. Be free!—but we will punish you if you really try to be free. All men are equal!—but we will punish you if you claim anything in the name of social justice and equality.

People subjected to this double bind may become confused; they may feel guilty both when they conform and when they break the norms. Or they may become alienated from their values—they may become indifferent and cynical. This erosion of values, however, although it reduces psychic tension, may deprive people of the protection of their civilization—a civilization of which these values are indispensable components.

A Negative Social Contract

In an economy of shortage, people are constantly forced to pay tips, grafts, or bribes in order to get the goods and services they need—that is, to act illegally through no fault of their own. They are forced to break the norms and tolerate the fact that everybody else breaks them as well. This again leads to the nausea of a vague and general feeling of defilement or guilt, and, at the same time, keeps people at bay and exposed to the blackmail of those in power. In this way, instead of an open social contract (clearly specifying what is due for what in terms of social interaction) a kind of social complicity evolves, where everybody 'forgives' everybody for what they all reluctantly do. As a character in a famous Hungarian play formulated it in the mid-1970s:

> I excuse them for excusing me for excusing them ... and so on, ad infinitum. (Csurka, 1980, 483)

This passive complicity is further distorted when the system of norms not only ceases to function, but is inverted. The following anecdote is taken from a collection of jokes published in 1980.

> In a factory cafeteria it is forbidden to sell alcoholic beverages. Nevertheless, the bartender sells alcoholic drinks but reports the names of her buyers to the manager of the factory. In return, the manager closes his eyes to her selling alcoholic beverages in the cafeteria. (*Száraz*, 1980)

Here it is no longer in the individual's interest to have others conform to the norms of social coexistence. On the contrary, his or her interest lies in having others break the norms, and vice versa. The habitués of the cafeteria get their drinks; the waitress her extra profit; the management information. In the end, a social exchange of benefits develops derived from the reciprocal breaking of norms, while people maintain the appearance of the validity of the broken norms. This is the perfect inverse of a 'normal' social contract. It is the social contract of a Kafkaesque world; of an alien world; of a distorted civilization.

We may conclude that the manipulation of the feeling of guilt was a powerful instrument of political domination and a key element of state socialist culture. It transformed guilt, which had been an instrument in the fight against the evil in the world, into a part of the alien world. The fear-ridden and guilt-haunted realms of communism and fascism undoubtedly fell within the boundaries of the alien world; of the man-made 'social jungle' we mentioned in Chapter Two.

THE PSYCHOLOGY OF GUILT

According to Freud and his followers, guilt has become a central player in the human drama of anxiety and suffering, and in the gradual destruction of human happiness in Western civilization. In other words, guilt has shaped Western civilization both as a positive, protective device, and as a negative, destructive force.

Freud and Human Unhappiness

Freud belonged to a long line of thinkers—stretching from the Cynics and the Greek tragedians, through Marcus Aurelius and Seneca, St Augustine and Pascal, to Schopenhauer and Nietzsche, Heidegger and Beckett—who experienced and interpreted the world as a kind of 'alien world'.[13] He did not believe that the world of human misery could, and ultimately would, be transformed into a world of happiness. To him, the quest for the meaning and purpose of human life seemed futile and derived "from human presumptuousness". People "strive after happiness", but happiness does not have any deeper, metaphysical or ontological meaning. It is simply "an absence of pain and unpleasure", and "the experience of strong feelings of pleasure", and even in this form it is only "an episodic phenomenon". If it is prolonged, it becomes, at best, "a feeling of mild contentment" (Freud, 1959a, 75–76).

The basic motive force of human life, the pleasure principle, is at odds with reality. It is incompatible with the real world:

> [I]ts programme is at loggerheads with the whole world, with the macrocosm as much as with the microcosm. There is no possibility at all of its being carried through; all the regulations of the universe run counter to it. One feels inclined to say that the intention that man should be 'happy' is not included in the plan of 'Creation'. (1959a, 76)

In this world, we are threatened with suffering from all sides: "from our own body", "from the external world", "and finally from our relations to other men". And, last but not least, from our own psyche, in which one of the cruelest tormentors is the feeling of guilt. So much so that instead of striving for pleasure, our main goal has become to avoid suffering: "[T]he task of avoiding suffering pushes that of obtaining pleasure into the background" (1959a, 17, 77).

The question is, how can we avoid suffering? Freud enumerates a whole series of ways and means by which human beings have tried to at least palliate their suffering. He mentions the "hedonistic" attempt to satisfy all our needs; he mentions "voluntary isolation", attempts at "subjecting nature to the human will", "intoxication", the "sublimation of the instincts", religion as the "delusional remolding of reality"—but his conclusion is, in each case, that these techniques help only temporarily, or not at all. They may even deepen our suffering by generating in us excruciating feelings of guilt. Even love, which may be the source of the deepest pleasure a human being can experience, may become a source of pain and misery: "[W]e are never so defenseless against suffering as when we love, never so helplessly unhappy as when we have lost our loved object or its love" (1959a, 77).

Coming to his conclusion, Freud states with resignation that the "programme of becoming happy … cannot be fulfilled", adding "yet we must not—indeed, we cannot—give up our efforts to bring it nearer to fulfillment by some means or other" (1959a, 83). Even if we know that the fundamental antinomies of the human condition cannot be solved. Freud speaks of two of these fundamental antinomies.

Eros and Ananké

The first is that of the individual and the community. The basic motive force of human beings is "Eros", the pleasure principle, which Freud narrows down, mainly in his early writings, to sexual pleasure, also called "libido"—elsewhere he broadens it out into the much more comprehensive principle of love and life. This is his starting point. He then describes the next step in two different ways. In some contexts he argues that, forced by the necessity of survival and work (*ananké* is Greek for 'necessity') men and women have to associate with other people and live in a community. In other contexts he contends that the need to love and be loved splits the libido between the self and the other, the loving subject and the object of love; and it is this "other" that binds the individual to the community of people. "I may now add that civilization is a process in the service of Eros, whose purpose is to combine single human individuals … into one great unity, the unity of mankind … Necessity alone, the advantages of work in common, will not hold them together" (1959a, 82, 122).

However, human society has its own needs. If it wants to survive, it has to coordinate the actions of its members, and, first of all, it has to curb their libido, which would drive them to satisfy their instincts, to immediately acquire the objects of their (sexual) appetite. If these instincts and drives were not fettered and inhibited, a war of all against all would ensue and the community would be disrupted. There is no alternative solution: society has to oppress, curb, domesticate the pleasure principle in its members; and, as a consequence, it makes them more and more, and inescapably, unhappy. "On the one hand, love comes into opposition to the interests of civilization; on the other, civilization threatens love with substantial restrictions" (1959a, 103). This opposition, and the anxiety triggered by it, is a primary generative force of human civilization.

The most fearful instrument of social oppression is not the set of laws and moral norms existing in a given human community, but people's own conscience, the superego that develops in them in the process of socialization and which cruelly punishes them—by generating in them the feeling of guilt—not only for their breaches of moral norms, but also for hidden wishes that might infringe these norms. Freud speaks in this connection of the "fatal inevitability" (1959a, 122) of the sense of guilt.

Eros and Thanatos

In his later work Freud introduced a second, even more threatening antinomy: the principle of love or life as opposed to the principle of destruction or death, later called the principle of Thanatos (*thanatos* is Greek for 'death').

> I can no longer understand how we can have overlooked the ubiquity of non-erotic aggressivity and destructiveness and can have failed to give it its due place in our interpretation of life ... aggression is an original, self-subsisting instinctual disposition in man ... But ... now, I think, the meaning of evolution of civilization is no longer obscure to us. It must present the struggle between Eros and Death, between the instinct of life and the instinct of destruction ... And it is the battle of the giants that our nurse-maids try to appease with their lullaby about Heaven. (1959a, 120, 122)

Being born, the infant suffers "the trauma of birth" (Rank, 1929, 99, 103; see also Roheim, 1943, 77), and although it is propelled by Eros, the instinct of life and love, it becomes frightened and is prompted by the world to return to the safety of the maternal womb—to the Nirvana of nonbeing, a world where there is no suffering. This means that the wish to annihilate life—in other words, the instinct of destruction and death—is contemporary with the instinct of life and love. The fearful struggle of these two principles is not only the nucleus of the eternal human drama, but also the basic propelling force in the evolution of human civilization.

This evolution may be both a progress and a decline. As we have seen, the libido may be transformed into communal love, *agapé*, and as such it is an indispensable factor in integrating societies. By 'sublimation' its energies may be channeled into artistic and other forms of creation. As far as the principle of Thanatos is concerned, its destructive force has been harnessed by channeling it into socially useful work.[14]

The problem is that the instinct of destruction not only attacks the outside world, but it also—and, in fact, above all—turns inward. The human psyche, harassed by feelings of guilt, turns against itself and wants to annihilate itself. This will to self-destruction generates even more feelings of guilt, which, in turn, give new momentum to the drive of destruction. This is a vicious circle from which it is very difficult to escape. Here again we see how the feeling of guilt, which could be a protective device against human suffering, becomes a source of suffering, a part of the 'psychological jungle', a part of the alien world.

According to Freud, the sense of guilt is also increased by the fact that, as human society grows in size, its integration requires more and more norms and restrictions, which generates more and more guilt.

> Since civilization obeys an internal erotic impulse which causes human beings to unite in a closely-knit group, it can only achieve this aim through an ever-increasing reinforcement of the sense of guilt ... If civilization is a necessary course of development from the family to humanity as a whole, then—as a result of the inborn conflict arising from ambivalence, of the eternal struggle between the trends of love and death—there is inextricably bound up with it an increase of the sense of guilt, which will perhaps reach heights that the individual finds hard to tolerate. (1959a, 132–33)

Freud speaks of a strong and increasing "cultural frustration", of a cultural *"malaise"*, and states that people have to sacrifice their instincts, both Eros and Thanatos, and thus their happiness, to Ananké, to the needs of social coexistence (1959a, 97).[15] Our civilization "is largely responsible for our misery". "[U]nder the influence of cultural urges, some civilizations, or some epochs of civilization—possibly the whole of mankind—have become 'neurotic'." "It almost seems as if the creation of a great human community would be most successful if no attention had to be paid to the happiness of the individual" (1959a, 86, 144, 140).

Despite all these discouraging facts, Freud (1959a, 145) concludes his book on a positive note. He asks whether mankind will be able to master the instinct of aggression and self-destruction. It is true, he writes, that the destructive power of people has increased enormously and that

> they would have no difficulty in exterminating one another to the last man ... [But] now it is to be expected that the other of the two 'Heavenly Powers', eternal Eros, will make an effort to assert himself in the struggle with his equally immortal adversary. But who can foresee with what success and with what result?

This is the last sentence of the book, and the editor remarks: "The final sentence was added in 1931—when the menace of Hitler was already beginning to be apparent."

The 'Boiling Cauldron' of Guilt

Freud's caution was fully justified. In our century, guilt may have lost most of its positive power to protect us against the evils of nature, while developing into a fearful source of destructive forces. Pathological guilt feelings may have contributed to making the twentieth century the hell it sometimes was. Due to Stalin and the equally unhinged Adolf Hitler, for instance, the morbid potential of the human psyche may have substantially strengthened the destructive force of economic and political conflicts which ultimately ravaged the world, killed tens of millions of people, and made miserable hundreds of millions of them all around the world.

Hitler has often been cited as suffering from severe neurosis. There seems to be strong evidence supporting the hypothesis that he had depressive guilt feelings, struggled with problems of incest, felt himself impure, and was afraid that there was non-Aryan blood in him. He may have tried to defend himself against these pathological guilt feelings partly by self-punishing, masochistic rituals, partly by projecting his sense of defilement onto his enemies, primarily the Jews, in order to annihilate it, once for all, in them and with them.[16]

Henri Baruk (1954), the French psychiatrist, goes even further when he defines destructive guilt not as an individual, but as a general social phenomenon in our contemporary world. He contends that it threatens our world with an almost apocalyptic destruction. Guilt is so "unbearably painful", he says, that people want to escape from it at all costs. If they do not have a chance, or the readiness, to do penance or to make amends, then all they can do is to project their guilt and then lash out and eradicate it in someone else.

> Guilt represents a tremendous danger to society as a whole because guilt feelings lead to terrible reactions in an effort to get rid of this guilt: to accusations, against which the accused defend themselves by returning the accusations, thus creating a chain reaction of reciprocal accusations, which may in the end demoralize and destroy an entire society. (1954, 75–78)

Along the same lines, Robert Jay Lifton (1979, 35) states that the final result of this historical process is a dangerous "boiling cauldron of suppressed revolt".

'Guilt without Culture'

There are scholars who do not consider the increase in destructive guilt feelings as an historical necessity. They raise the question of responsibility, sometimes indicting Freud himself, and the cultural tradition to which he is supposed to have belonged, for having contributed to the distortion of guilt into a malignant force, which, instead of building and reinforcing human civilization, disintegrates and destroys it.

John Carroll (1985, 222), for instance, in his important book on guilt, argues that guilt has become a disruptive force and a source of purposeless human suffering as a result of the over-rationalization of Western civilization. Technical reason has gradually destroyed traditional culture; it has replaced the sacred with the secular. And a "secular culture is a contradiction in terms; it means no culture". It does not protect people against their fears and anxieties.

According to Carroll (1985, 2–3) contemporary people are lost in their world, which they do not understand and in which they are attacked by the furies of their own disrupted conscience. Dostoyevsky's Raskolnikov and Kafka's Josef K. are the symbols of this age. He contrasts this modern capitulation before guilt with the courage of the Greek tragic writers. Aeschylus, for instance, is the very opposite of Freud. "For him, knowledge, represented by the insight of Cassandra, is to live with eyes open to a fate that is 'the sheer edge of the tearing iron' ... The Aeschylean world is not subject to the logic of comfort." Its heroes do not "slide into the trough of uncultured depressive guilt" (1985, 228–29). On the other hand, the Greek tragic writers were unable and unwilling to offer a solution. They knew that truth "is brutal, it humbles, it awes". While the chorus is "pleading for mediocrity", all the heroes can do is to courageously face the mystery of guilt, evil, and human suffering.

If Carroll is right, modern men and women have lost the protection of their civilization, which traditionally controlled natural evil with the help of the concept and drama of guilt. As a consequence, they are now tormented by the furies of their own souls. They have lost an important battle with the alien world. But when Carroll and Freud conclude—for different reasons—that an increasing level of guilt feelings may irresistibly push our civilization into a profound crisis or even disruption, are they right? Do the facts support their conclusion? Not necessarily.

AN INNOCENT SOCIETY?

While Freudians and neo-Freudians have been appalled by the spread of the neurosis of guilt and have spoken of the danger of an eschatological explosion of destructive guilt feelings in our civilization, other scholars have recently outlined a different, even opposite, scenario. According to them, we may be heading towards an "innocent society", a "guiltless civilization". If this happens, it will be a major historical mutation since, for two thousand years, the concept of guilt has been one of the main organizing principles of Western, Judeo-Christian civilization.

There can be no doubt that this mutation, or at least something pointing in this direction, is already taking place. The now emerging new pattern of civilization, the present stage of which we usually label 'consumer civilization' or 'entertainment society', may also be interpreted as a response to, or a revolt against, the traditional guilt civilization. Intentionally or not, it has done everything possible to eradicate the feeling of guilt from people's minds. It has been systematically replacing the feeling of guilt with the pleasure principle, responsibility with gratification, duties with rights, self-discipline with self-actualization, the puritanical work ethic with the worship of consumption.

It is amazing to see the ingenuity and aggression with which the actors of consumer civilization have tried in recent decades to sever the two-thousand-year-old—or even much older—link between pleasure and guilt, between gratification and the fear of punishment.[17] If they succeed, this will certainly be a major landmark in the history of our civilization. It will be an important mutation. Will it also be a new start, or a sign of disintegration or decline? We still do not know. We are still seesawing between a guilt-conscious or guilt-ridden, and a guiltless or at least guilt-unconscious civilization. The twentieth century has been the century of both destructive explosions of pathological guilt neuroses, and of the emergence of the guiltless 'happyism' of the flower-power and—what a change!—shopping-mall generations.

We no longer know what to do with the feeling of guilt in our lives. Harlan J. Wechsler gives some excellent examples of how we try to hide our embarrassment in humor and self-irony. He quotes a number of jokes and punchlines, which characterize the present situation of ambiguity about guilt. Let me reproduce some of his examples.

Ziggy, the cartoon character:

> Lately I've been feeling guilty about my guilt feelings. (Wechsler, 1990, 13)

Comedian Richard Lewis:

> I wish I could feel better about feeling good. (p. 83)

An advertisement for TCBY Frozen Yogurt:

> All the pleasure. None of the guilt. (p. 20)

A book title:

> *How to Be a Guilty Parent (With Eighty-Five Guilts)* (p. 33)

Rabbi Sidney Greenberg:

> Conscience is a great servant but a terrible master. It is somewhat like an automobile horn. It is useful for warding off impending danger. But if a horn gets stuck it's a terrible nuisance. (p. 40)

Guilt has become a controversial and ambiguous concept. It may have lost its power to protect us against meaningless and absurd suffering. It may have lost its role as a major factor in generating Western civilization. People living in, and consciously or unconsciously building, our contemporary civilization may find new ways and means to protect themselves against the forces of evil in this world. They seem to be experimenting with creating (the myth of) an innocent civilization. It is both a promising and a dangerous adventure.

NOTES

1. The Greek tragic consciousness of being guilty and not guilty at the same time is an interesting—logical and not necessarily historical—transition phase in the process of transforming natural evil (which was then considered to be destiny) into moral guilt.
2. To ask whether this transformation was conscious or unconscious is to ask about one of the most complex issues in human life: How, by what kind of conscious and unconscious processes, do human communities, or mankind as a whole, solve their problems. It must usually be a long process of, first, experiencing and perceiving the problem, then of trying to understand it, followed by a mixture of instinctive and conscious attempts to solve it by trial and error.
3. I must mention that there are radically different interpretations of this 'great reversal'. Marx, for instance, described the transformation of the "concrete and non-moral fact" of the "opposition of rich and poor" into the vague moral terms of the "opposition of good and evil" as a strategy of the bourgeoisie in its class struggle with the proletariat (Marx, 1985, 220, 215).
4. In other civilizations, other factors and forces played a similar role.
5. See also the brilliant analysis by Delumeau (1983).
6. "[T]heology should reinterpret the doctrine of original sin by showing man's existential self-estrangement ... It may well be that such a task demands the definite removal from the theological vocabulary of terms like 'original sin' or 'hereditary sin'" (Tillich, 1951–1963, vol. 2, pp. 38–39). Furthermore, "theology must clearly and unambiguously represent 'the Fall' as a symbol for the human situation universally, not as the story of an event that happened 'once upon a time'" (p. 29). Finally, "the notion of a moment in time in which man and nature were changed from good to evil is absurd" (p. 41).
7. Concupiscence "refers to all aspects of man's relation to himself and to his world. It refers to physical hunger as well as to sex, to knowledge as well as to power". It "elevates him beyond his particularity and makes him universal on the basis of his particularity. The possibility of reaching unlimited abundance is the temptation of man" (Tillich, 1951–1963, vol. 2, pp. 51–52).
8. Calvin O. Schrag (1961, 154–74) gives an excellent overview of the existentialist philosophers' ideas on guilt.
9. In Heidegger's terminology, "*Dasein*" ('being-there') stands for individual human existence in contrast to "*Sein*" ('Being'), which is existence in its deepest and most general modality.
10. See Kierkegaard (1959, vol. 1, 129; 1948, 92). This inherent contradiction, this ambiguity of the human condition, has been ever present in the Judeo-Christian tradition. Man's finite freedom, his intermediate situation between the sacred and

the secular, divine perfection and animal imperfection, infinity and finitude has been described by the greatest authorities of this tradition from the prophets, through St Augustine, to Barth and Tillich.
11 In this section on the politics of guilt I rely on Chapters One and Four of my book *East European Alternatives* (1990).
12 From *Viharsarok Népe*. Quoted by Závada (1984, 157–58). It is not clear to what extent these campaigns were consciously trying to instill guilt feelings into society. They were certainly motivated by other goals: they wanted to intimidate their victims, to erode their resistance, as well as to justify the hard-line policy against them, to provoke and direct social hostility against them, to create scapegoats to relieve social tensions, and so on.
13 St Augustine hesitated, throughout his life, between a more positive and a more negative vision of the world.
14 Many psychoanalysts stress this destructive, and even violent, character of work, though they do not contest its social usefulness. Marcuse writes in this connection:

> To be sure, the diversion of destructiveness from the ego to the external world secured the growth of civilization. However, extroverted destruction remains destruction: its objects are in most cases actually and violently assailed [think of the work of the blacksmith, for instance, or that of the bulldozer], deprived of their form, and reconstructed only after partial destruction ... Nature is literally 'violated' ... Destructiveness, in extent and intent, seems to be more directly satisfied in civilization than the libido. (1966, 86)

15 The title of the German original is *Das Unbehagen der Kultur* or 'The Malaise of Culture'. The standard English title, *Civilization and its Discontents*, is a good approximation.
16 From a rich literature see, for instance, Waite (1977).
17 This process began as early as the eighteenth century—libertinism, de Sade, utilitarianism—gathered momentum in the nineteenth (Baudelaire, Nietzsche, decadence), and has become more and more dominant in the twentieth. Freud tried to eliminate the feeling of guilt with the help of reason, Fromm and Marcuse with love—consumer culture is trying to do the same thing with a new ideology, a new vision of the world and people's role in it.

CHAPTER EIGHT

THE RATIONAL WORLD

> "The only incomprehensible thing about the world is that it is comprehensible."
>
> Paul Davies, *The Mind of God*

THE present chapter deals with the fact—or fiction—of a 'rational universe', which has been particularly important for human beings in their efforts to reduce their anxiety in an unknown universe. It also discusses the contradictions and ambiguities inherent in human reason; how it is able not only to create but also to destroy 'meaning'; how it may turn against morality; how it may turn into unreason—into a force which, instead of building, destroys civilization.

TWO FACES OF RATIONALITY

Reason has always been one of our major instruments in constructing the symbolic structures of our civilization and protecting us against our existential fears and anxieties. However, despite its brilliant achievements, it has played an ambiguous role in our history.

War and Celestial Harmony

Prague, 24 May 1618. The city is in revolt. A Protestant crowd bursts into the Castle and throws the imperial regents out of the window.[1] In a couple of months, Europe will be submerged for thirty years in one of the bloodiest and most destructive wars of her history. Her cities will be sacked and destroyed, her countryside scorched, her populations decimated by starvation and epidemics.

Yet on the very same day a man called Johannes Kepler, former astronomer and astrologer of the emperor, who left Prague only a couple of years before, is sitting in his study in Linz, going through, again and again, his computations concerning the orbit of the planets. In three days, on 27 May, he will have finished his book, *The Harmony of the World*,[2] which contains his fundamental third law on the motions of the planets.

The chaos of the war and the vision of universal harmony: was this a grotesque or absurd coincidence? Not in the least. Kepler's work was meant to be a response to the miseries and horrors of his time, and of human life in general. And he was not the first, or the last, in a long series of scholars who hoped to discover the latent rationality and harmony of a universe which looked irrational and chaotic in people's everyday experience, and who tried to surround themselves and their fellow beings with the protective shield of this vision of radiant and rational harmony.

Kepler's glory and tragedy lay in this duality.[3] Throughout his life he desperately wanted to prove that, ultimately, a Pythagorean harmony governed the universe with the planets moving around the sun in circular orbits of Platonic perfection. He worked for years, making tens of thousands of computations (without a computer, of course) to prove his hypothesis. And when finally he could not help proving just the contrary, namely, the fact that the planets moved in elliptical orbits, he could not, did not want to, even could not want to, believe his own figures.[4] He spent several years trying to prove that the ellipse was in reality a circle, or in the worst case a circle slightly flattened into an oval. One of the greatest astronomers trying to turn back the wheel of time and progress: How can it be?

Towards the end of his life, almost three decades after his epoch-making discovery that the orbits of the planets were elliptical, not circular, Kepler annotated the new edition of his early *Cosmic Mysteries*. In these notes he seems to have returned to his earlier Pythagorean and Platonic conception of the world, according to which a perfectly rational and geometrical harmony underlay the universe with the celestial bodies moving in circles; they could not have moved otherwise since the circle, and only the circle, was the symbol of divine perfection. There is not a single reference to his own revolutionary first and second laws, according to which the orbits are not circular but elliptical. It was "as if Einstein, in his old age, had been discussing his work without mentioning relativity", Koestler remarks (1968, 265).

In all likelihood, Kepler needed the illusion of a universe of harmony and rationality even more than most of us—perhaps because he lived in an age of raging irrationality and disharmony. His personal life, too, was full of anxiety and suffering. Koestler (1968, 225–38) reports that he grew up in a family cursed with physical and mental illness and moral weakness. His grandmother was an "inveterate troublemaker; jealous, extreme in her hatreds, violent, a bearer of grudges". His father was a quarrelsome, vicious man, who treated his wife brutally, narrowly escaped the gallows, and finally died in exile. One of his aunts was burnt as a witch. He had six brothers and sisters—three of them died in infancy, one was epileptic. He himself was a sickly child with defective eyesight (a real handicap for somebody who was to become an astronomer), who suffered from constant stomach and gall trouble, and boils and rashes. He had a kind of paranoia, believing himself always surrounded by enemies, and he was tortured by strong feelings of guilt. He was "a neurotic child from a problem family", Koestler concludes (1968, 266). "The sufferings of a mange-eaten, chaotic childhood had left a sober thirst for universal law and harmony".

To make matters worse, he lived in one of the most troubled periods of European history. In 1595, the Turks besieged Vienna while Kepler was teaching in Graz. In 1599, he was exiled from Graz and went to Prague where he wrote his *Astronomia Nova* which he published in 1609. In 1611, he lost his position at court, was excommunicated, and moved to Linz. In 1615, his mother was accused of being a witch and, after a six-year-long ordeal, with imprisonment and threats of torture, was finally saved from the stake only by the intervention of her son.[5] In 1618, the Thirty Years' War broke out.

He died on 15 November 1630. A few years later the cemetery where he was buried was ravaged by one of the warring armies and Kepler's bones were scattered (Koestler, 1968, 422).

Kepler's life is emblematic. It represents the struggle between two rationalities in our human world: the Promethean and the Apollonian. As we have seen, the interaction of these two rationalities has played a key role in building our civilization.

Prometheus versus Apollo

The reader will remember that in Chapters Two and Three we spoke of two different—contradictory and complementary—strategies utilized by human beings in their struggle with the world. We found that with their Promethean strategy they tried to physically control the world around them, whereas with their Apollonian strategy they built spheres of symbols around themselves in order to protect themselves, emotionally and spiritually, in an alien world.

Let me state right away that both strategies are 'rational', although they work with two different sorts of rationality. In their own way, both strategies try to discover the fundamental laws of the universe, although by 'law' they understand different things. They try hard to understand the forces that move and govern the world. Both project their patterns of thoughts, hypotheses, and beliefs onto the world. And they have both been necessary for the survival of mankind in a rough and hostile world. However, they differ from one another substantially.

The Apollonian strategy builds up a world of harmony and meaning out of symbols and symbolic systems: language, myths, religions, ideas, art. With their Promethean strategy, on the other hand, people want to control the physical world and therefore they focus on facts, causal relationships, the laws of the physical universe. Ultimately they strive for safety, freedom, and harmony with this strategy as well, but their search for truth may lead them to discoveries that, at least for a while, are shocking, fearful, and may shake their belief in the harmony of the world.

The two strategies complement and obstruct each other. The technical and scientific discoveries people have made with the help of their Promethean strategy have often threatened the protective networks of symbols and beliefs people have kept weaving around themselves within their Apollonian strategy. On the other hand, the Apollonian sphere of beliefs and symbols surrounding them has often been an obstacle in the search for scientific truth. Kepler was not the first great thinker who was caught in the trap of this contradiction.

Living in an age of crisis and anxiety, Plato and his followers, for instance, dismissed the scientifically correct heliocentric conception of the universe developed by their predecessors and pushed the earth back into the center of an immobile world, surrounded by the celestial realm of planets and stars rotating around it in perfect circles, symbols of eternity and divine perfection. The belief, or the will to believe, that there was harmony and perfection beyond change and mutability became more important than the study of empirical facts. Ptolemy, the greatest astronomer of the Hellenistic age, was convinced that, as an astronomer, he had to prove that the planets moved in perfect circles and—devising complicated patterns of epicycles—he made every effort to prove that, despite all appearances and observational evidence, they did move in perfect circles.

> We believe that the object which the astronomer must strive to achieve is this: to demonstrate that all the phenomena in the sky are produced by uniform and circular motions ... because only such motions are appropriate to their divine nature ...[6]

It took a millennium and a half to break out of the iron cage of this Platonic illusion and dogma of circularity. Not only because it fitted so well into the medieval vision of a geocentric world but also because it gave people a strong sense of safety: they could feel themselves secure at the center of the universe protected by the concentric spheres of planets, angels, and the realm of the divine beyond them. The appeal of this harmonious, closed, well-protected world has remained with us.

The struggle of these two approaches, the Promethean and the Apollonian forms of rationality, has escorted mankind throughout its history. And this is not the only ambiguity characteristic of the role reason has played.

It has played a major role in creating a human world, human civilization, but at the same time, it has always had a destructive potential as well. It has been able to build up brilliant structures of facts and ideas; it has discovered some of the laws that govern our universe; it has found ways and means of mitigating human suffering and has spectacularly widened the range of human possibilities. But, in the course of its victorious expansion in the last three or four centuries, it may have destroyed some of the social and spiritual structures that may be vital for the survival of human beings and societies.

Let me give some examples of the dangerous ambiguities that are at the core of our civilization.

REASON AND MEANING

The Loss of Meaning

Instinctively, we tend to believe that reason and meaning go hand in hand; or, to put it in a different way, that if something is comprehensible, it is also meaningful. Or again, if we understand something with the help of our reason, this something must have a meaning—it must mean something. But this may not in fact be the case. Reason is certainly an instrument of comprehension, but it is not necessarily a source of meaning. Or at least we must handle the term 'meaning' with the utmost caution. If we ask, for instance, the following question: What is the meaning of life?, there is an easy answer. The word 'life' refers to a particular type of existence in this universe, the existence of animate beings. This type of existence is the 'referent', that is, the meaning of the word 'life'.

But in stating this we may disappoint some fellow creature who expects a different kind of answer from us. Imagine him or her, let it be her, having lost her spouse, or job, or hopes, and in her despair she turns to you, her only friend, and asks you: "Please tell me, what is the meaning of life?". She would certainly not be satisfied by the lexical definition of the meaning of the word 'life'. What she is interested in is whether life, not as a word, but as a human experience, has meaning. Whether it is meaningful or not. Whether there is anything in life, which makes it worth living. Whether it has a goal, a purpose.

Historically, the rational comprehension of life has also entailed that it was meaningful; that it had a meaning, a function, a purpose. Mythological and religious rationality, and most of the traditional philosophies considered and interpreted life both as comprehensible and meaningful—perhaps even more meaningful than comprehensible. The fact that it was profoundly meaningful was questioned by very few, even if its secrets might lie beyond human comprehension.

With the advent of modern scientific thought the situation has changed dramatically. The universe has become more and more understandable whereas its 'meaning' and 'purpose' have tended to recede further and further. There are people, a number of scientists among them, who bewail this loss of meaning; others hail it as progress and the defeat of anachronistic beliefs and illusions. There are also those who think—or hope—that the meaning of the universe, and that of human life, can be and should be regenerated even in the age—and the crisp light—of objective scientific knowledge. Let me give two examples.

Sometime in the late 1980s, Steven Weinberg, a nuclear physicist, who in a famous book (1977, 154) described "the first three minutes" of the universe, was flying home from San Francisco to Boston. Looking out of the window, he was fascinated by the beauty of the landscape below, with "fluffy clouds here and there, snow turning pink as the sun sets". With a certain resignation, he mused over whether our growing knowledge about the universe will destroy forever the meaningful beauty of the world as we sometimes see it from our human perspective.

> It is very hard to realize that all this is just a tiny part of an overwhelmingly hostile universe. It is even harder to realize that this present universe has evolved from an unspeakably unfamiliar early condition, and faces a future extinction of endless cold or intolerable heat. The more the universe seems comprehensible, the more it also seems pointless.[7]

The verdict of biologist and Nobel Prize winner Jacques Monod is even more austere. He discards the Apollonian illusion—and with it an essential part of our civilization—as a lie and states that we have to accept our universe, without civilizational delusions, as it is: cold, austere, meaningless.

'The Kingdom and the Darkness'

This is the title of the concluding chapter of Monod's famous book *Chance and Necessity* (1974), one of the most dramatic and shocking statements I have ever read about a universe without meaning and purpose. If I understand him well, the 'Kingdom' is the kingdom of ideas of authentic scientific knowledge, and the 'Darkness' is the darkness of a fearful universe in which we are alone, unprotected, and lost.

According to him, traditional 'animistic' knowledge, with its myths, religions, and illusions about a meaningful universe and mankind's prominent role in it, protected people against their anxieties in the universe. Science has given them authentic knowledge, and some control over nature, but destroyed this "old covenant" and forced people to face the horror of a dark and empty universe. He speaks of the "breakdown of the old covenant and the modern soul's distress" (1974, 170).

Monod is one of the few contemporary scientists who admit, with puritanical honesty and discipline, that science is not able, and in all likelihood will never be able, to alleviate people's existential fears and anxieties. It can offer them only 'objective knowledge' and not the illusion of a meaningful universe. He severely criticizes nineteenth-century scientism, which proclaimed that the course of scientific discoveries led "infallibly upward toward an empyrean noon hour for mankind, whereas what we see opening before us today is an abyss of darkness".

> Cold and austere, proposing no explanation but imposing an ascetic renunciation of all other spiritual fare, it [objective, scientific knowledge] was not of a kind to allay anxiety, but aggravated it instead ... It wrote an end to the ancient animist convention between man and nature, leaving nothing in place of that precious bond but an anxious quest in a frozen universe of solitude. With nothing to recommend it but a certain puritan arrogance, how could such an idea win acceptance? It did not; it still has not. It has, however, commanded recognition; but that is because, solely because, of its prodigious power of performance. (1974, 170)

Contemporary mankind has largely profited from the victorious expansion of modern science. Our world of comfort is built on the results of science.

But we still stick to our old illusions and do not want to, or are unable to, listen to its judgment that we are not 'at home' in this universe; that this universe was not meant for us, and that it was not 'meant' at all.

> We would like to think ourselves necessary, inevitable, ordained from all eternity. All religions, nearly all philosophies, and even a part of science testify to the unwearying, heroic effort of mankind desperately denying its own contingency. (1974, 44)

Contemporary culture is thus built on a dangerous contradiction, on a lie.[8] We still do not have the courage to face the universe as it is: indifferent, cold, alien. But sooner or later human beings must accept the message of science. They "must at last wake out of [their] millenary dream; and in doing so, wake to [their] total solitude, [their] fundamental isolation". They must realize that, "like a gipsy, [they live] on the boundary of an alien world" (1971, 171–72).

All that science can offer, beyond tremendous power over nature, is an "ethic of knowledge". But this is a great deal, since truth is a transcendental value, something beyond us, and thus the search for it may satisfy the profound human striving for something beyond what is already present and given. The ethics of defending, extending, and enriching "the transcendent kingdom of ideas, of knowledge, and of creation" may be a "utopia".

> But it is not an incoherent dream ... It is the conclusion to which the search for authenticity necessarily leads. The ancient covenant is in pieces; man knows at last that he is alone in the universe's unfeeling immensity, out of which he emerged only by chance. His destiny is nowhere spelled out, nor is his duty. The Kingdom above or the Darkness below: it is for him to choose. (1974, 180)

This is a gloomy and intimidating vision. Monod may be right. Science has made phenomenal progress in discovering some of the laws governing the universe, or at least the universe in which we live. But it seems to be still very far from answering those ultimate, or even only penultimate, questions which are really relevant from the point of view of our situation in the universe, which should be answered by our contemporary civilization if it is to keep its protective, anxiety-reducing power. How did something come out of nothing? What were the laws that governed the universe before the Big Bang? Is the universe, in time and space, finite or infinite? Where, into which dimension, will matter and energy, time and space disappear after the last moment of the Big Crunch, if any such event should occur? How did the intentionality and teleonomy of life come about in a non-intentional and non-teleonomic world? How did reflective consciousness emerge in a non-reflective universe? Or is the universe itself, in its very essence, more mental, or spiritual, than material? Did life emerge in this universe by chance, by necessity, by intention, or by any combination of these factors? Shall I continue?

Monod and his colleagues may be right, but, despite all our doubts and fears, we may still live in a meaningful universe. We may be at home in this universe.

The Meaning of Life

It is a fact, however, that—due to the weakening of our traditional belief systems, mythologies, religions, philosophies, concepts of the world—the meaning of the universe and the meaning of human life have become more and more blurred. Our civilization has lost more and more of its capacity to make us believe that there is a profound meaning and purpose underlying human life and the universe.

We may already be in a critical situation. What would we answer if we were suddenly asked: What is the meaning or purpose of life? A hundred years ago the majority of people living in Western civilization would have had an answer to this question. Today, most of us would be dumbfounded: we would not know the answer. We no longer believe in the traditional answers and have not yet found new ones.

Is this not strange or even absurd? In our everyday lives we live in a world of carefully devised meanings. We have given meaning to everything. We situate everything on a number of coordinates (animate—inanimate, physical—non-physical, artificial—natural, big—small, moving—inert, fast—slow, hard—soft, straight—curvilinear, angular—circular, regular—irregular, edible—non-edible, related—not related to a certain type of human activity, and so on), and the meaning of the given object or phenomenon is, for us, its place in this multidimensional space of coordinates. A shoe, for instance, is inanimate, physical, artificial, relatively small, curvilinear, soft and hard, visible, non-edible, related to walking, and so on.

But what about life? Is it physical or non-physical, big or small, hard or soft, fast or slow, edible or non-edible, straight or curvilinear, related to ... what activity? Our grid for situating objects and events in a space of meanings does not work in the case of life in general, or human life in particular.[9]

In our everyday lives, we have also given meaning to everything by stating its use in, and for, our lives. We have defined trees and tigers, shoes and stars, mice and mountains, space and time, earth and sky, summer and winter, angels and devils by the purpose they may serve, the function they may have, in our lives. But what is the purpose of our lives? And even before we answer this question we have to determine the wider context in which it may function. What is this wider context? Who or what is the beneficiary? Does my life have the purpose of serving me—is it 'my own' life? Would this not be a tautology? Does it serve other people, people whom I love, for instance? Many think so and define the meaning of their lives as service. My child is the meaning of my life, they would say. But then, what is the meaning of the life of your child? And that of his or her children? It would be difficult to escape from this trap.

Others think that they will find the meaning of their lives in serving a cause. The advancement of human well-being, happiness, moral perfection, freedom, democracy—these are important goals and they give us much to do; they may keep us busy for centuries. But what would be the meaning of life for a perfectly happy, free, civilized mankind, if there ever is such a human community? To enjoy its happiness, freedom, and morality? Many think so. But would this also render death meaningful? Civilization would lose its mainspring if people became resigned to the absurdity and meaninglessness of their life and death; if they gave up their search for meaning.

Let me quote a few testimonies from an interesting and puzzling book (Moorhead, 1988) which bears the proud and promising title *The Meaning of Life*, and is a collection of ideas from a selection of brilliant contemporary minds—philosophers, scientists, artists, politicians—about "the meaning and purpose of life".[10] First, here is a selection of testimonies from those who believe in the existence of a divine plan and the meaningful role we play in it.

"What is the true end of Man?", Arnold Toynbee asks, and answers with the words of the Bible: "To glorify God and enjoy Him forever." René Dubos bestows an even more important role on mankind: "I am convinced that mankind is engaged in a creative process of the kind that St Bernard had in mind for the Cistercian monks" [the monks were considered to be 'partners of God', contributing by their labors to the creative process]. Or the same idea in Christopher Fry's words: "We can only have faith that there is a purpose—that we are only part of the way in the evolutionary progression towards the fulfillment of the creative will" (Moorhead, 1988, 198, 50, 69).[11]

Others believe in a more secular, but no less cosmic, plan and in mankind's significance in the realization of this plan. Julian Huxley (Moorhead, 1988, 89, 140) assigns to mankind an eminent role in the process of evolution: "There is no purpose in living matter as such, but one of the significant facts about life is that during its Evolution it has generated purpose, and that in man, conscious purpose can become a dominant factor in further Evolution." Sigurd F. Olson writes in almost pantheistic terms about man's role in creating, and participating in, a cosmic consciousness: "I believe in the eternal quest for meaning and that the goal is the maturity of understanding, a cosmic consciousness in which one becomes a part of all life in a feeling of oneness and wholeness."

G. E. Moore gives a more precise and pragmatic definition of the role mankind may play in the cosmic history of the universe:

> A man's life is of some use, if and only if the *intrinsic* value of the Universe as a whole (including past, present, and future) is greater, owing to the existence of his actions and experiences, than it would have been if, other things being equal, those actions and experiences had never existed. (Moorhead, 1988, 128)

But do these divine or cosmic plans and frameworks exist? And if they do, do we know what they consist in? In all likelihood, we do not—though this is not a reason for not searching for them. In fact, this search may have been a major motive force of our civilization.

For some, the most sympathetic, though not necessarily convincing, answers in Moorhead's book may be those which express the belief that "the search for meaning is itself the meaning", "the meaning is in the search", or, in a more aphoristic way: "The purpose of life is to search for the purpose of life."[12]

Is this type of answer merely a play on words? Or is this search for the meaning of life the only possibility for us to become genuine human beings? Let me quote two authorities to justify this question. Steven Weinberg, whom I have already cited, speaks of the role of the scientific search for truth:

> Men and women ... build telescopes and satellites and accelerators, and sit at their desks for endless hours working out the meaning of the data they gather. The effort to understand the universe is one of the very few things that lifts human life a little above the level of farce, and gives it some of the grace of tragedy. (Moorhead, 1988, 155)

Carl G. Jung speaks more generally:

> The meaning of my existence is that life has addressed a question to me. Or, conversely, I myself am a question, which is addressed to the world, and I must communicate my answer, for otherwise I am dependent upon the world's answer. (Moorhead, 1988, 102)

Which would mean that I lose my freedom; and that the civilization in which I live has lost its power to help me find meaningful answers to the ultimate questions of my life.

Reason still has a long way to go, on both its Promethean and its Apollonian paths, to discover, or generate, the ultimate meaning of the universe. And that of human life. Or it may contribute to the construction of a civilization, which will help people live without even trying to answer their questions about the meaning of life and death.

REASON AND MORALITY

This is another relationship marked by contradiction and ambiguity. Let me discuss here only one aspect of the problem.

In *The Rebel*, Camus (1956) has painted a gloomy image of what happens to human civilization when the traditional interaction of these two principles—rationality and morality, rational interests and moral values—is disturbed; when one of them overcomes and eliminates the other.[13] According to Camus, a fundamental duality was the keystone and *sine qua non* of European civilization; the duality of soul and body, the individual versus the community, moral values versus social interests, the sacredness of human life versus *raison d'état*. Historically, the church represented the soul and the holiness of human life, while the state stood for the body and the secular interests of society.

By this duality the state was prevented from having full control over the individual, and collective interests were restrained from ignoring and freely breaking moral norms—each and every individual life was sacred. Life was an absolute value in itself, which had to be respected in all circumstances. On the other hand, the church was prevented from using its spiritual and moral power to totally subject and dominate people because they, as physical beings and members of a community, were—in principle—represented and protected by the municipality or the state. This dualism, the interaction of these two poles, was, according to Camus, the cornerstone and *primum movens* of European civilization.

Historically, this dichotomy was often contested and it became the source of serious conflicts between church and state again and again—most spectacularly in the fight about who had the right to appoint the bishops (the 'Investiture Controversy' in the eleventh and twelfth centuries), and in the fierce struggles around the separation of church and state in the eighteenth and nineteenth centuries. In other periods and contexts it was blurred, confused, hardly noticed. In any case, neither party played its role consistently and decently. The church often tried to completely dominate the individual, and states have never been entirely committed to the genuine representation and protection of social interests. However, I think that Camus was right in stating that, despite these tribulations and failures, this duality survived over the centuries and played an important role in the evolution of European civilization.

Many examples could be given of the strange working of this duality. Let me restrict myself to one or two. First, take the case of the heretics. If, in a quiz about the late Middle Ages and the Inquisition, you had to answer the question, 'Who had the right to burn a heretic?', what would you answer? 'The church' or 'the state'? The ecclesiastical or the secular power? Both answers would be false. To be precise, neither could do it on its own, because neither had full power over the human being. Ecclesiastical courts only had the right to judge the soul of the victim and they had to do their best to convince heretics to repudiate their false beliefs, to repent, and—as prodigal sons and daughters—to return to the fold of the true church. They could use the body of the heretic—to torture it, for instance—only in order to help him or her in this process and ultimately save his or her soul. They did not have the right to kill him or her. After the sentence had been passed, they handed the heretics over to the secular authorities, municipal or royal, and at the execution, at the stake, the priests of the church stood by the victims, comforting them, helping them repent and save their souls. Far from being a cynical ritual, this was the expression of the duality already mentioned, in which the church stood for the sanctity of human life, whereas the state acted in the name of (what was supposedly) 'reason of state'.

Another example, from a much later date and a different historical context, may shed light on the strength of this tradition. The scene is Hungary; the date is 6 October 1849, after the defeat of the Hungarian War of Liberation by the united armies of the Habsburg emperor and the Russian tsar. This morning an Austrian general will take his personal—and the emperor's political—revenge on the rebels. Twelve leaders of the Hungarian revolution are going to be executed; nine by hanging, three by firing squad. Now let us listen to the eyewitnesses. Béni Baló, minister of the Reformed Church, recalled:

> Colonel Tichy ordered judge advocate Zimmer to step forward and read the sentence again ... The executioner, Urticka, came forward and, in the usual manner, asked for

mercy for the condemned, repeating this procedure three times. Tichy's stereotyped response was in every instance: 'God have mercy!'

Alajos Herold, another eyewitness, recalled:

When all nine were hanged, the officer in command said to the soldiers: 'This is the reward of those ... who break their oath of allegiance to His Highness, the Emperor!' Then the command was heard: 'Kniet nieder! Zum Gebet!' That is, 'On your knees! Pray!' (*Aradi*, 1979, vol. 1, 281, 295)

Is it not amazing that the very person whose task it was to carry out the sentence, the hangman, asked the authorities for mercy for the condemned, again and again? Why did he do so? And why him? The explanation may be that he had to ritually alleviate the burden of the crime he was going to commit—that is, to take the life of human beings—even if he was authorized to do so by the legitimate authority of the state. As far as I know, this usage survived in many countries well into the twentieth century. In some places, following the execution, the executioner used to be tried for manslaughter and was acquitted in an expedited procedure. And is it not a fine example of European duality that, in the moat of a remote fortress somewhere in faraway Transylvania, it was the very representative of the state who—after having restated the rightfulness of the execution from the point of view of *raison d'état*—commanded the soldiers to pray for the souls of the executed?

Let us now return to Camus' argument. He describes the process of how the reason of the Enlightenment became both more and more philosophical and more and more murderous; how it gradually became the only principle governing societies; how people revolted against God, who had created a world of misery, injustice, and suffering, and how they replaced him with human reason, which was thought capable of creating a world of justice and well-being. He describes how *le bien commun* of Rousseau, and *le salut public* of Robespierre and company became the only objectives and the only principles governing social action. He also describes how the other pole, the sanctity of human life and the values of morality, which traditionally counterbalanced and restrained the power of social interests and reason of state, became weaker and weaker; how murder became 'logical'; how traditional European dualism was replaced with the monistic domination of efficiency, technical rationality, and genuine or bogus social interest.

He mentions the example of Russian anarchists of the end of the nineteenth century as providing one last glimpse of the traditional dualism. They sentenced to death the oppressors of the people in the name of justice and the common good and—if they had the opportunity—they 'executed' them in individual acts of terror. But they supposedly had a rule that the person who killed the selected victim had to commit suicide, or give him- or herself up, after the murder, since, however holy the cause, he or she had taken the life of a human being. And life was still thought to be sacred by these men and women: having destroyed it, they had to sacrifice themselves in exchange and expiation.

Their dualism was ruthlessly swept aside by the unscrupulous monism of Lenin and twentieth-century totalitarian regimes, for which human lives and moral values had become dispensable and only reason of state and the utopian goals of a self-elected elite counted. One human life or twenty million: both could be discounted as insignificant as compared with 'collective interest' and the totalitarian rationality of mass murder.[14] Western civilization, in this distorted form, having lost its fundamental duality, could no longer protect human life. It could not protect the victims against the terror of life and death.

Two German psychoanalysts, Alexander and Margarete Mitscherlich (1970, 33) give a stunning example of this procedure, citing one of Himmler's speeches, in which he thanked the members and leaders of the SS for shouldering the terrible but unavoidable task of exterminating millions of people.

> Most of you will know what it means to have 100 or 500 or 1000 corpses lie before you. That we have endured this has hardened us, and—with a few exceptions of human frailty—we remained decent. It is a victorious page in our history that has never been and never will be written.[15]

Mass murder is here rationalized into moral virtue, and respect for human life into moral weakness and failure. Rationality, in this context, has lost its original role and identity. Instead of protecting human life, it justified and furthered its destruction. Reason had become murderous. Instead of building, it destroyed human civilization.

REASON AND UNCERTAINTY

Discovery or Invention?

Reason, at best, may be an unreliable ally. It may deceive those who believe in it. And this is true even of the crown jewel of human reason, mathematics. It is believed to have achieved the (almost) final victory of human reason over a chaotic and alien world. From Francis Bacon to

Stephen Hawking or Edward Witten, many of the most brilliant minds of Western civilization have thought that mathematics and physics might already be on the threshold of finding the 'ultimate equation' or 'theory of everything' which would reveal, and control, the final secret of the universe.[16]

In his book *The Mind of God*, which I shall use as a guide in the next few paragraphs, Paul Davies (1992, 93–116 and *passim*) brilliantly surveys the conflicting views on the ontological status of mathematics. He speaks of the scandal, the surprise, the miracle of mathematics; of its unbelievable success in describing and interpreting the world and in predicting the outcomes of complex physical processes. How has it been able to do so?

The question to be answered is twofold. First, how is it possible that mathematics is capable of condensing and/or abstracting into a few formal equations and functions some of the basic interrelationships of an immensely complex and chaotic world? And second, how is it possible that the human mind is able to devise and understand these equations and functions? "The only incomprehensible thing about the universe is that it is comprehensible", Davies remarks (1992, 148).

But if it is, this is likely to be good news for mankind, and for at least two reasons. If the human mind is able to understand (some of) the laws of nature, there must be a certain affinity between us and the universe. And, what may be more important, if rational and logical patterns and mathematical equations are at the basis of the world (the same ones that govern the human mind), then it is probably not an alien world—it may be our world after all. We may be at home in the universe. It may have been in this sense that physicist Freeman Dyson (1979, 250) remarked: "I do not feel like an alien in this universe."

However, our situation is less good, less unambiguous, than we might imagine in our first enthusiasm. The compatibility of mathematics (and human reason behind it) with the universe is questionable. For example, are mathematical patterns, structures, and relationships inherent in the universe; are they part of the objective world; have they always been so (at least since the Big Bang)? Did we merely discover them and then crystallize them into mathematical equations (in philosophical terminology, this could be described as the 'realist' approach) or, on the contrary, are our equations fictions, constructs, which we have projected onto the world as a fisherman casts his net in the water, and (due to factors which we do not quite understand[17]), we have caught some 'fish' with this net—we have been able to control some natural processes with the help of these constructs (this would be the 'nominalist' approach). As Davies puts it, mathematics was either 'out there', and in that case we only discovered it, or it was nowhere, and we had to invent it. Did Newton "uncover something objectively real about the world, or did he merely invent a mathematical model of a part of the world that just happens to be rather useful in describing it" (Davies, 1992, 83)?

How can human beings perceive, represent, conceive, understand, 'know' the world around and within themselves: these questions have puzzled and thrilled philosophers for more than two millennia and, more recently, they have been studied by scholars working in such diverse fields as the psychology of knowledge, the theory of language, cybernetics, semiotics, the study of artificial intelligence, and cognitive science. Here, I can only briefly outline the basic problem that has been discussed with so much vehemence by the two major schools in this field, the 'realists' and the 'nominalists'.[18]

According to the 'realists'—Kurt Gödel, Roger Penrose, Alain Connes, and others—mathematics is definitely 'out there'. There exists a 'cosmic software' which is independent of us. Prime numbers, for example, "exist, abstractly, whether human beings know about them or not" (Davies, 1992, 84, 141). The same is true of the famous Mandelbrot set: it is not "an invention of the human mind: it was a discovery. Like Mount Everest, the Mandelbrot set is just there!" (Penrose, 1989, 11).[19] The number of similar examples can be multiplied.

According to the 'nominalist' approach (James Hartle and others) mathematics was invented by human beings. It is an epistemological net thrown over the universe by mankind. It is a network of Vaihingerian 'constructs', a practical 'scaffolding', an instrument not so much of discovering and understanding the world as of coping with it, handling it, controlling it in order to be able to survive in it. Mathematical laws are not absolute and eternal. Various laws may be, and have been, fitted to the same phenomena. New laws have kept replacing previous ones. Davies points out that an "alien civilization with a different evolutionary history, culture, and science might construct very different laws", and "Newton's concept of absolute universal time", for instance, "turns out to work well" only due to the special circumstance that "we move about much slower than light" (Davies, 1992, 87, 150). Quantum mechanics and quantum electrodynamics are only 'models', the products of our brains; they help us better understand the world, but they should not be mistaken for reality itself. If the realists triumphantly state that the fundamental laws of nature are mathematical, the nominalists retort that they are fundamental only because you, the realists, "define as fundamental those laws that are mathematical" (Davies, 1992, 151). Or as Bertrand Russell (1956) put it: "Physics is mathematical not because we know so much about the physical world, but because we know so little: it is only its mathematical properties that we can discover." [20]

If they are right, then even the best mathematicians are far from jotting down that 'ultimate equation'. Even if they could, we could not be sure whether it expressed the final truth about, and essence of, the universe, or whether it was only a brilliant fiction enabling us to handle those dimensions of the universe which we happen to know. The feeling of uncertainty and anxiety would remain with us. Despite the brilliance of mathematics, we would still not feel at home in the universe. And maybe we should not.

'The Wisdom of Uncertainty'

The world in which we live could well be a world of both laws and contingencies, certainties and uncertainties. One of the main functions, and abilities, of human reason—and particularly of scientific reason—is to disclose the cause–effect relationships underlying natural processes and predict their future outcomes. But the law of causality, in its traditional formulation, may not be a universal law, and predictability not a universal characteristic of the existing world. Human reason, which has always striven for certainty, and modern scientific reason, which has built its brilliant structures on the law of causality: what will they do in a world where there may be no final certainty, no general predictability, and in which causality and contingency (which may cover further, still unknown, laws, for instance of a teleological nature) interact with each other?

Human reason may, and should, master these problems; it may develop its tools to cope with this new situation. But in the meantime, its ability to protect us with the sphere of its rational structures may be seriously jeopardized.

Several outstanding scientists have expressed a growing conviction that, after the age of scientific and philosophical certainties, we may be entering an 'age of uncertainties' in which we shall have to cope with the complex and disorderly structures of the universe. The question is whether we will be able to achieve "the wisdom of uncertainty" proposed by Milan Kundera (1988);[21] whether we will be able to build up a human world of freedom, dignity, and safety in a universe of contingencies and uncertainties, a universe which is not wholly rational, or which is rational in a new way, which is built on a rationality including contingency and unpredictability. If we succeed, the outcome will be a new civilization—one built, at least partly, on uncertainty, and not on certainty.

Scholars are already working feverishly in this field. Not only mathematicians and physicists, but social scientists and philosophers as well. Let me give an example from the latter fields. There have been various attempts to develop a new way of thinking, a new practice, a new morality, a new rationality to cope with this new world—that is, with the world experienced in this new way. Some of them have been summed up under the term 'postmodern'.

Postmodernists have made a virtue of necessity. With a certain, and certainly unjust, flippancy, I could say that they have responded to the crisis of modern rationality, and to that of Western civilization in general, with a happy rage of deconstructing and destroying what was left of this rationality. They have responded to the collapse of certainty and the belief in the existence of an ultimate truth, and an ultimate goal of human evolution, by considering this new situation as an exciting challenge, a new experience, a new freedom, full of the promise of new discoveries.[22] This new experience, or experiment, is not without serious risks. It is not easy to find one's home, dignity, and freedom in a world of uncertainties. And it is not sure that a civilization may be built on uncertainty. Let me take the example of one of the outstanding thinkers of our time, Richard Rorty.

'The World Does Not Speak'

Beneath the matter-of-fact and prosaic arguments of Rorty's late-twentieth-century pragmatism and nominalism, historicism and postmodernism, there is, I think, a deep undercurrent of almost Nietzschean heroism. If Nietzsche had the courage to live in this world 'after the death of God', one hundred years later Rorty (together with a number of other contemporary thinkers and scientists) has embarked on the experiment of living in this world 'after the death of Truth'—of living in a world without the certainty that beyond mutability and contingency there is an eternal and immutable world of ideas and values. We have to resist "the temptation to look for an escape from time and chance", Rorty asserts. The fear of uncertainty has kept people captive of, and dependent on, the hope of an ultimate Truth. We should, and perhaps we shall be able to, "substitute Freedom for Truth as the goal of thinking and of social progress" (Rorty, 1989, xiii).

Rorty's basic instrument and weapon in this world of change, uncertainty, and contingency is language. His basic message is that we have to create our own truths and we may create them only by means of language, by generating new arguments, narratives, "vocabularies", in "an endless process—an endless, proliferating realization of Freedom". And to do so without hoping that we will find an ultimate argument, an all-encompassing and all-explaining narrative, "a metavocabulary which somehow takes account of *all possible* vocabularies". Truth is "made rather than found", it is a construct, yet as such it is the product of the creative power of human reason and freedom (1989, xvi, 3, 7).

We have to accept the fact that "truth is not out there" and that "where there are no sentences there is no truth". The history of our grappling with the world is the history of a series of "alternative language games", in which none of the games is more authentic than the other:

> [T]he vocabulary of Ancient Athenian politics versus Jefferson's, the moral vocabulary of Saint Paul versus Freud's, the jargon of Newton versus that of Aristotle, the idiom of Blake versus that of Dryden—it is difficult to think of the world as making one of these better than another, of the world as deciding between them ... the fact that Newton's vocabulary lets us predict the world more easily than Aristotle's does not mean that the world speaks Newtonian.
> The world does not speak. Only we do. (1989, 4–6)[23]

Language, language games, and new nets of arguments cast over an ever changing, elusive reality, are powerful means in our struggle with the forces of an alien world and with the fears of our heart. But will they be able to replace the great systems of myths, religions, morality, and universal rationality with which mankind has traditionally surrounded and protected itself in a fearful universe? Will a new civilization replace our traditional civilization? Maybe it will. The postmodern thinker and his disciples may find freedom and dignity (less safety, though) in courageously responding to all the new challenges of a world of contingencies and uncertainties.[24]

Rorty himself adds to this a great dose of self-irony and fortifies himself with the stoic attitude of facing the human condition with discipline and serenity. He finds a kind of safety in the emotional or spiritual community of benevolent people. Solidarity and human life are unquestionable values even if there is no Absolute Value in the universe. He speaks of our common hope "that suffering will be diminished, that the humiliation of human beings by other human beings may cease" (Rorty, 1989, xv).

This human togetherness and responsibility may surround us with a feeling of safety and meaning in a universe where, beyond us or without us, there may be no safety and no meaning. We need this togetherness badly in a new civilization built, not on certainty, but on uncertainty.

NOTES

1 Adumbrating the humor of Kafka, Capek, and Hrabal, the regents fell on a dunghill in the moat and so were saved.
2 *Harmonice mundi* (1618).
3 My analysis of the drama of Kepler's life is based on Arthur Koestler's fascinating study *The Sleepwalkers* (1968, part IV, 225–422).
4 I take this triple definition from the *Hamlet* analysis of Ernest Jones (1954), Freud's biographer. There are critics, he says, according to whom Hamlet *could not* act because the king was protected by his guards. According to other experts, he *did not want to* act. The real answer, Jones contends, is that he *could not want to* act because he was inhibited by an unconscious sense of identity with Claudius (suffering from an Oedipus complex, Hamlet also wanted to possess his mother and kill his father).
5 In Weil der Stadt, Kepler's idyllic birthplace, with a population of two hundred families, 38 witches were burnt between 1615 and 1629, Koestler remarks.
6 Ptolemy (1984, chapters 3 and 2)—quoted by Koestler (1968, 74).
7 More than a century earlier (Kierkegaard, [1844] 1944) had expressed a similar view: "[I]n one direction truth increases in extent, in mass, partly also in abstract clarity, whereas certitude steadily decreases."
8 "No society before ours was ever rent by contradictions so agonizing ... What ails the modern spirit is this lie gripping man's moral and social nature at the very core" (Monod, 1974, 171–72).
9 Life is, of course, not the only concept which we have difficulty situating in this multidimensional semantic universe. Some, or most, of our abstract concepts—truth, beauty, happiness, justice, and so on—need a different, and much more complex, semantic grid.
10 A few names from the roster of respondents to the question 'What is the meaning or purpose of life?': Edward Albee, Leonard Bernstein, Rudolf Carnap, T. S. Eliot, Joseph Heller, Aldous and Julian Huxley, Karl Jaspers, C. G. Jung, Bishop Hans Küng, Bernard Malamud, Margaret Mead, Henry Miller, C. Wright Mills, Karl Popper, W. V. O. Quine, Eleanor Roosevelt, Bertrand Russell, Paul Tillich, Arnold Toynbee, John Updike.
11 Needless to say, many thinkers protest against this kind of 'idealistic' vision. Let me quote only one of them, Howard Fast:

> This business of *meaning* or *purpose* is a human invention, just as the concepts of justice and fairness are human inventions, coined to make life less chaotic. Is there purpose in a rose, a cloud, a mountain? ... We are not an admirable or particularly intelligent species, and for

us to presume to enter the mind of the universe or the Almighty or God—call it what you will—is a presumption that is as arrogant as most of our fancy concepts of our importance. (Moorhead, 1988, 60)

12 See, for instance, Ira Levin, Abraham Kaplan, and James Alan McPherson (Moorhead, 1988, 121, 96, 121).
13 Have these two principles anything to do with one another? There has always been a controversy about this question. The Greek cynics and atomists, Hobbes and Nietzsche, and many modern and contemporary philosophers and scientists would argue that they do not. Socrates and Marcus Aurelius, Erasmus and Spinoza, Kant and Schiller, Jaspers and Gabriel Marcel, and a number of contemporary scientists would protest and assert that the two do go together: there is no authentic rationality without morality and there is no morality without rationality.
14 In his famous book on the spiritual crisis of our civilization, Jaspers (1965, 145) draws the same conclusion: "'There is no God', the masses shout louder and louder; and thus man becomes worthless and is murdered *ad libitum*, because he is nothing" ["Es gibt kein Gott, ist der anschwellende Ruf der Massen; damit wird auch der Mensch wertlos, in beliebiger Anzahl hingemordet, weil er nichts ist"].
15 See also Mitscherlich (1975).
16 See, for instance, Barrow (1991); Davies (1992); Torrance (1981); Weinberg (1992).
17 "'The book of nature', opined Galileo, 'is written in mathematical language.' Why this should be so is one of the great mysteries of the universe" (Davies, 1992, 140).
18 One of the latest and most exciting debates took place between two French scientists, Alain Connes, a mathematician, and Jean-Pierre Changeux, a neurobiologist (Changeux and Connes, 1989). The former represented the realist, the latter the nominalist approach. According to Connes, mathematical equations reflect the basic, abstract, and timeless structures of the universe and they are only discovered by man. Changeux, on the other hand, argues that mathematics is a product of the human brain and it might have been thoroughly different if another type of brain had invented it. Mathematics is a construct, though a useful one. See also the works and controversies of the main protagonists of various schools of thought in this field—the 'innatists', the sociobiologists, the structuralists, and so on, and the work of such, as Chomsky, Piaget, Dennett, Dawkins, Blondel, and so on.
19 Quoted by Davies (1992, 143).
20 Quoted by Koestler (1968, 534).
21 "To take, with Cervantes, the world as ambiguity, to be obliged to face not a single absolute truth but a welter of contradictory truths (truths embodied in *imaginary selves* called characters), to have as one's only certainty the *wisdom of uncertainty*, requires no less courage" (Kundera, 1988, 6–7).
22 Some of their radical critics see them in a much less favorable light. Referring to the Marxist past of some of the postmodern apostles, they argue that the logic

underlying postmodernism is the following: If Marxism is dead, then truth is dead. And then there cannot, and should not, be any other truth.

23 Or is he wrong and Lewis Carroll's Tiger-lily right?

'Oh Tiger-lily!', said Alice, addressing herself to one that was waving gracefully about in the wind, 'I wish you could talk'—'We can talk', said the Tiger-lily, 'when there's anybody worth talking to.'

24 Rorty does not question the importance of the fascinating achievements of human reason. He only questions the existence of a unique and absolute rationality, encompassing the whole universe. Or if there is one, he would probably say that we may never discover or understand it.

Chapter Nine

THE WORLD OF BEAUTY

> "Every angel is terrible."
> Rilke, *Duino Elegyies*, 1

ART plays a vital role in protecting people against their existential fears and anxieties. It surrounds them with its symbolic structures and creates for them a world of beauty and harmony (without concealing the terror underlying beauty and harmony, as Rilke reminds us). These structures mesh with other symbolic structures constituting civilization.

ART

Music

We surround ourselves not only with myths and religions, values and beliefs, ideas and visions, but also with the sounds and rhythms, melodies and harmonies of music. It fills the void around us; the void of silence; the void of nonbeing. When it stops, silence and nothingness resume their empire around us. We whistle at night in a dark forest in order to feel ourselves less alone and less unprotected in the jungle of darkness. African tribes fill the void around themselves with the rhythmic beating of drums. When we sing, the sound waves fill the space around us. With a Walkman on our belt and earphones on our head we may be walking along one of the most hectic streets of a Bladerunner's megalopolis and still feel ourselves at the center of a universe of harmony.

Various forms of music interact with silence in various ways. Gregorian chant, for instance, was the opposite of secular music. It was strictly monophonic. For those who sang it, or listened to it, its melody was a single shining track in a dark and silent universe; a lonely voice in an empty space, or a space out of which God had withdrawn after the Fall. They may have felt his presence, as if he was there, unseen, listening to the song, but keeping a terrible silence. They may have expected the light of his grace to shine at any moment and fill in the dark space of loneliness around the congregation. But plainsong resisted the temptation to try to fill this emptiness with the colorful and light harmonies of secular music and the ecstasy of dance; with the illusion of plenitude and homeliness.

Baroque music emerged at the other extreme. With their hearts full of anxiety and fear in a post-Copernican and post-Renaissance world, Baroque artists tried to fill an empty universe around them with more and more complex webs of sounds, with rich polyphony, the hysterical jubilation of their music, and the whirling and flamboyant lines and colors of their pictures, sculptures, and buildings. With the introduction of more and more brass instruments in the Romantic-period orchestras, with the appearance of the mega-orchestras of the late nineteenth and the twentieth centuries, and recently with the invasion of the mega-decibels of electronic music, this hysterical attempt to fill a deep (deepening?) vacuum around us, may have reached its apex.

Music has always flirted with disharmony, too, but only to defeat it in the final, victorious, and glorious chords. The question to be answered is whether contemporary music has gone too far in experimenting with disharmony and has inadvertently destroyed the protective sphere of harmony around us. Contemporary music may be the result, and the proof, of the coming of age of mankind, which has by now become strong enough to face the world without the illusion of an ultimately harmonious world. Its relative unpopularity, however, and the mass appeal of over-harmonious popular music (the childish revelry in disharmony of various punk, hard rock, and rap groups included)[1] seem to prove just the contrary. We may not be ready to face the terror of the world without the protection of myths and religions, beliefs and illusions, or the harmonies of music. Without the Apollonian illusion of our traditional civilization.

Horror and Beauty

If it is sacrilegious to try to say anything significant about music in a few lines, it is certainly a crime to dabble in the mysteries of beauty in the space of a few paragraphs. But it would be a serious mistake not to discuss it, even if only superficially and briefly, in a book exploring the constitution of human civilization. Art may be at the core of civilization as it is in an intense interaction with the fearful depths of human existence and nonexistence.

Let me quote a few lines from the first of Rilke's *Duino Elegyies*:

> Who, if I cried, would hear me among the angelic
> Orders? And even if one of them suddenly
> Pressed me against his heart, I should fade in the strength of his
> stronger existence. For Beauty's nothing
> but beginning of Terror we're still just able to bear,
> and why we adore it so is because it serenely
> disdains to destroy us. Every angel is terrible.[2]

These are fascinating and perplexing lines. Why are angels terrible? And why is beauty the beginning of terror?

The simplest way to answer these questions is to interpret Rilke's words within a Neoplatonist framework and state that the ultimate ideas of the universe flash up in beauty and we are shocked and terrified by their transcendental and demonic force. Another answer would be that in the beauty of angels we experience the superhuman intensity of existence, which we shall never be able to attain; we experience the nothingness of our lives in their magnificent and fearful light.[3]

There are experts—and they may be in the majority—who would question these interpretations and argue that in beauty we experience the magnificence and hope of an ultimate harmony in our universe, the celestial order of ideas, the presence of God, the infinitude of human freedom, the victory of the spirit of creation over the futilities of human life and the destructive forces of death. Beauty has nothing to do with horror and the alien world if not the fact of having the function, and the power, to protect us against them.

After admitting that psychoanalysis "has scarcely anything to say about beauty", Freud himself discussed beauty among the human tactics and devices that offer protection against suffering.

> We may ... consider the interesting case in which happiness in life is predominantly sought in the enjoyment of beauty ... This aesthetic attitude to the goal of life offers little protection against the threat of suffering, but it can compensate for a great deal. The enjoyment of beauty has a peculiar, mildly intoxicating quality of feeling. Beauty has no obvious use, nor is there any clear cultural necessity for it. Yet civilization could not do without it. (1959a, 82–83)

This apparent paradox expresses Freud's belief that beauty has no "practical" function in human life but it helps people live by hiding the dark side of existence, human suffering, and, ultimately, the terror of death. In the same passage, however, and in other contexts, he contradicts himself by referring to the practical importance of beauty in human civilization. In his earlier work he emphasized the sexual function of beauty, and later he developed his ideas on the primary importance of beauty and art as an instrument, and product, of the process of sublimation without which human societies, and human civilization in general, could not exist.

Nietzsche, before Freud, had a more complex vision of beauty. In his early masterpiece *The Birth of Tragedy* (1967) he spoke of beauty and art not only as an Apollonian veil hiding the terrible depths of existence, but also as a Dionysian force in which the demonic and tragic forces of existence well up and threaten people's everyday world of hopes and illusions at its foundations. To support this hypothesis about the fundamental duality of beauty and terror, let me recall the strange and mysterious medieval myth of Beauty and the Beast, or the discovery of beauty in evil, death, and destruction by the Romantics. I could refer also to various existentialist and structuralist theories of beauty: Roland Barthes' (1972) discussion of the unity of charm and horror in 'The Face of Greta Garbo'; or to fascinating contemporary experiments—for instance, playing tapes of classical music backwards, or pictures taken of classical Greek sculptures lit by a sharp light from below—which have brought out the demonic hidden behind, or in, the forms of beauty.

The most famous case is, perhaps, Baudelaire's *Les fleurs du mal*, a volume of poems exploring the hell and horrors of human life and transforming them into transcendental beauty. His closest relative in the visual arts is Toulouse-Lautrec, whose entire work is based on the strange and absurd antinomy of damnation and beauty, death and the transcendence of art. In his pictures, extreme human suffering and destitution parade in the forms and colors of beauty. These pictures are the real Baudelairian 'flowers of evil'. But they are also more than that. They are the products of a perverted Platonism, where the essence is perishable and the appearance radiates in light of eternity and transcendence. This is a fascinating example of the horror of the alien world—pain, mortality, the dance of death—being transubstantiated by art into beauty and harmony. Or is it the parody of the Nietzschean dichotomy of the Apollonian and Dionysian? The Dionysian energy, dynamism, and ecstasy have decayed here into the convulsive jerks and twitches of a *danse macabre*, and Apollonian harmony has degenerated into the debauchery of brilliant and irresponsible colors.

In what direction does the interaction of terror and beauty operate in these pictures? Does Lautrec overcome the terror of the alien world with the help of art and beauty? Or does he show the horrors of the alien world beneath and beyond the illusion of beauty; or express the fundamental oscillation between two basic, ontological categories of existence: life and death, hope and despair, harmony and disharmony, beauty and terror?[4]

This oscillation of terror and beauty may be there in all works of art, or in aesthetic experience in general—even if most people do not notice it— and in various artistic periods and genres it may be more or less obvious.[5] It is strong and shocking in tragedies and comedies. It is there in both the "inclusive" and the "exclusive" type of poetry as defined by I. A. Richards (1928). And it is intensely there in music: remember Schubert's famous words:

> Do you know a cheerful music? I don't know any
> [*Kennst du eine heitere Musik? Ich kenne keine*].

The dual experience of terror and beauty, harmony and disharmony, may be a powerful, archetypal motive force underlying human civilization.

TRAGEDY

Why Did Oedipus Blind Himself?

The presence of the alien world has always been felt, or at least suspected. Anxiety has always been there under the surface of our everyday lives. One way to curb this anxiety was to face the unknown and fearful world openly; to experiment with the terror of being exposed to it, unprotected. Various civilizations have had various ways and means of doing so. This was the essence, and function, of a wide range of rites and rituals. In Western civilization, a special literary genre emerged serving this purpose—tragedy.

Greek, Shakespearean, or modern tragedies may well be interpreted as showing us, in a shocking and spectacular way, what happens to human beings if the symbolic spheres surrounding and protecting them suddenly collapse. Take Oedipus or Hamlet, Electra or O'Neill's Lavinia: they are all ruthlessly jerked out of their universe, the protective shell of their everyday lives, their values and beliefs. They suddenly realize that the world, as they had perceived it, was an illusion. They are suddenly exposed to the chaos and the monsters of a world in which they are not at home; in which the laws of the jungle prevail; in which everything they had considered valuable is destroyed; in which human life has lost its meaning.

Hamlet was a happy young man, in his prime, rich and brilliant, the apple of his mother's and father's eyes, the beloved prince of the court, surrounded with loyal friends, possessing the love of the beautiful Ophelia, spoiled by his friends in Wittenberg: he was at the center of a magnificent world. And suddenly this harmonious and splendid world is ruthlessly destroyed and he finds himself in a horrendous universe of crime and betrayal, incest and murder; in a world where there is no harmony and no meaning, no love and no decency; where wives poison their husbands, friends kill and lovers betray one another. He finds himself, unprotected, in a fearful and murderous world. And finally he himself is destroyed by this world.

King Lear's world of glory and harmony collapses in the same fearful and tragic way. Wandering on the heath, stripped of his honors and losing his mind, in despair, exposed to the storm, the darkness, the cold of a hostile and chaotic world—he is the very symbol of a human being lost and unprotected in an alien world.

The shock may be so horrendous that the tragic hero is unable to face it. Oedipus' self-blinding may have expressed this unbearable confrontation with a world of terror and death.[6] None of the tragic heroes can avoid this fearful confrontation.

And what about the spectators? Why do they want to participate in these tragic ordeals? Do they seek the pleasure of a shocking experience? Do they want to gratify their sadistic or masochistic drives? Do they want to experience the intensity of human existence through the fate of these superhuman heroes? They may go to the theater for any of these reasons. But I think that the main function of tragedy is something else—something more important.

Romeo and Juliet and the Happy Ending

Human beings cannot, and should not, ignore the existence of the alien world around them. They must not be mesmerized by it, but, from time to time, they have to face it. And tragedy makes them face it.

This is not an entirely harmless experience, however. The tragic shock, with its raw force and brutality, could seriously impair people's faith in life and in the basic values of their world, their civilization. The tragic shock, unmitigated, would be too much for them. In reality, however, it does not do any real damage because tragedies belong to our civilization's arsenal of protective devices.

People are protected, first of all, by the fact that a tragedy is only a spectacle, a 'play'. They experience it only as a fiction and not as real life. Instead of actually going through the tragic emotions, they only contemplate them on the stage. They experience only the 'symbols' or forms of emotions and not the emotions themselves, as Susanne K. Langer (1953) put it.

The safety of the spectators can be further enhanced by defusing the tragedies in advance. This was common practice in the eighteenth century, when spectators were protected by prophylactic devices in vogue with the directors of the period: plays were simply adapted, rewritten, and 'improved' before being staged. The upshot invariably was that the disquieting and shocking tensions of the tragedies were resolved before they reached the stage.[7]

In a number of versions, Lear regained his throne, Cordelia was saved and married the faithful Edgar; Macbeth repented, abdicated the throne and, with moral satisfaction, watched while the real culprit, Lady Macbeth, was marched off in chains. Few tragic heroes could escape this forced 'improvement' of their fates. Romeo and Juliet were luckier: towards the end of the seventeenth century their play was performed in London with alternate tragic and happy endings. One night the friar arrived in time to save them, the next night he was tragically late.

French audiences, used to the classical decorum of Corneille, Racine, and company, were particularly sensitive to shocking spectacles. Ducis, the star translator and adaptor of the age, carefully dyed Othello almost white and made him stab Hédelmone (the French Desdemona) instead of strangling her in a brutish and utterly uncivilized manner. Despite this precaution, the first night ended in uproar: people who had never seen a murder on the stage jumped up, ladies fainted, and the actors were booed off. Ducis had to rewrite the last scenes of the play. In the new version the Doge arrived just in time to prevent the murder; he explained that Iago, who had been arrested by the state police, had confessed his conspiracy. Othello swore that he would devote his life to Hédelmone's love and to the cause of his country.[8]

In some French, German, and even English versions, Hamlet suffered the same fate of being saved. To cite Ducis again, in his adaptation Hamlet is transformed into a neo-classical French tragic hero, who, like the Cid of Corneille, has to kill the father of his lover (Ophelia being in this version the daughter of Claudius). The dilemma is solved by the discovery that it was Gertrude and not Claudius who killed his father, and so Hamlet, who would prefer to die, is forced to live happily with Ophelia and be a good king of his subjects, the Danes, who entreat him to help them. Instead of suffering a tragic shock, the spectators could go home with the politically correct and exhortatory words of Ophelia addressed to a still hesitating Hamlet:

> I do not speak to you any more about my love and myself.
> Do you dare to die? Does your life belong to you?
> Your grandeur, your duty give your life to your country.
> Don't you hear the Danes who beseech you?
> ....
> It is to you that the weak have submitted their defense.
> Punish the oppressors, support innocence,
> These are the sacred duties entrusted to you by heaven.
> Prevent and destroy the causes of their misery;
> These are your duties; die afterwards, if you dare.[9]

Desdemona's Handkerchief

People also protected themselves against tragedies by 'explaining' and pigeonholing them as problems solved or to be solved. The history of *Hamlet* criticism, for instance, with its wide range of interpretations, can be described as the history of these various ways of neutralizing the impact of the tragedy.[10]

There are critics, for instance, who try to remove Hamlet's fearful world as far from themselves as possible in time and space:[11] they say, for instance, that Hamlet was a typical man of the Renaissance and thus his fate and tragedy are not particularly relevant to us. Others neutralize the impact of the tragedy by depriving it of its universality, saying that *Hamlet* does not portray humankind's tragedy in general, but only that of a particular type of human personality.[12] It is in this way that the melancholy or the phlegmatic, the introvert or the megalomaniac, the restless or the decadent Hamlets were born. The pigeonholing of Hamlet and the defusing of the explosive power of the tragedy is even more obvious in those criticisms which treat *Hamlet* as a political pamphlet. T. S. Eliot (1927) was justified in deriding Tory or Whig, Anglo-Catholic or Protestant, conservative or revolutionary Shakespeare interpretations.

Others protect themselves against the impact of the tragedy by dehydrating it into an abstract philosophical problem.[13] It is in this way that *Hamlet* has been known as the tragedy of idealism or realism, of individualism or altruism, of abstract reflection or too much imagination. There are critics who discard him, and the forces of the alien world rampant in his fate, by seeking refuge behind their moral convictions and censuring him, now for idleness and now for rashness, for agnosticism as well as naive idealism. Indulging in their own righteousness, they state that Hamlet himself brought all the suffering upon his head; the fault lies with him and not with the world. A characteristic example of this rationalization, and arguing away, of the fact of tragedy in human life were the eighteenth-century English critics, who—supposedly after considerable racking of their brains—succeeded in solving the mystery of Othello: Desdemona's negligence was the only and ultimate cause of the tragedy; she should have taken better care of her handkerchief. There is no reason to panic. Human life is not tragic; our happiness can be protected and controlled. We may go home in peace.

Catharsis

Spectators are not left alone in their fight against the destructive forces inherent in the tragic impact. Tragedies help people escape from their encounter with the alien world. After being led through the tragic experience, the spectator is helped back to safety by what I propose to call 'catharsis machinery'. It may sound irreverent to say so, but it is nevertheless true that such 'machinery'—a pattern of signs and symbols having a cathartic effect—is built into the last scenes of practically all the tragedies we know, Greek, Elizabethan, Jacobean, Romantic, or modern.

Let me put it another way: there is a set of devices—linguistic, poetic and dramatic, formal and substantive—which have recurred regularly at the endings of tragedies since Aeschylus, through Shakespeare to Ibsen and Beckett. Elizabethan playwrights used most of them, Greek tragedians used less, and their twentieth-century colleagues have been more sparing still. Use of these devices mitigated and neutralized the impact of their tragedies.[14]

The built-in catharsis machinery has the function of transforming the destructive radiation of the tragedy into a positive human experience. In other words, the tragedians themselves help the spectators escape from the alien world in which they submerged them and retreat into their own, everyday lives, safely protected by the symbolic spheres of their civilization. They have various ways of doing this.

Justice done. As tragedies usually and necessarily have tragic endings—that is, their heroes are ultimately destroyed—the main task of the catharsis machinery is, perforce, to offset the negative impact of death and destruction. A rudimentary way of performing this task was, in some Greek, and in most Elizabethan and Jacobean, tragedies, to destroy the hero's antagonist as well, since his or her death could soothe the spectator by suggesting that there was order, justice, and harmony in the world after all.

The futility of life. Another way of transforming death into a more or less positive value consists in devaluing life. If in the last scenes of the tragedy the spectators can be convinced that life is meaningless, insupportable, not worth living, then death becomes less dreadful and more acceptable. In the last scenes of most tragedies this devaluation of life is systematically achieved. Life, after having been praised as the highest value and major goal throughout the tragedies, is suddenly called a "rack" to be tortured on in *King Lear*; "a pit of darkness" or a "dog kennel" in *The Duchess of Malfi*; "a walking shadow, a poor player" in *Macbeth*; "senseless" in *The Visit of the Old Lady*, and so on, and so forth.

Longing for death. Tragic heroes not only become weary of life in the fifth act, but in most cases they definitely yearn for death, so thoroughly transforming it from "something to be feared" into "a consummation devoutly to be wished".

A martyr's death. It is even better if the hero, instead of dying a senseless and absurd death, dies a meaningful death by sacrificing him- or herself for an ideal, a community, or for someone he or she loves (Antigone, Oedipus, Egmont, Don Carlos, Hedvig in Ibsen's *The Wild Duck*, and many others).

Poetic death. Death is, in real life, anything but poetical. But towards the end of tragedies it is, almost as a rule, euphemized into a gentle and poetic passing away. This may be achieved by using poetic symbols like withering flowers and streaming water, as is cleverly done in *Hamlet*. Or it may be done with the help of linguistic devices. The hero may "die upon a kiss" (Othello), "die in music" (Emilia), or "die smiling" (Galantha in *The Broken Heart*). Death may also alight on us as a "sweet dream", or "pure happiness" (as in Goethe's *Egmont*). It may be the hero's "native country" or the "prize of life" (as it is called in Grillparzer's *Sappho*). Or, to quote an unbeatable example from Schiller's *Cabal and Love*, it may be "a gentle Genius who lends a helping hand to the exhausted pilgrim's soul, helps him over the grave of time and opens before him the magic palace of eternal bliss ...".

Death as nuptials. Tragic authors are especially fond of the archetypal (and absurd) identification of marriage and death as a cathartic device. It is cathartic since, by this means, death, the most fearful experience, is transubstantiated into one of the most positive events of human life. In *Antigone*, this motive is repeated no less than four times. Desdemona's death-bed is made with her "wedding sheets" and she asks Emilia to "shroud" her "in one of those same sheets". In Victor Hugo's *Hernani* the "wedding bells are ringing for the burial of the hero". But Luise Miller in *Cabal and Love* is again unsurpassable when she calls the grave a "bridal bed, above which Morning spreads its golden canvas and Spring showers brilliant flowers on it". And, unbelievable as it may seem, this archetypal motive reemerges also in contemporary plays. To quote a famous example, in the last scene of O'Neill's *A Long Day's Journey into Night* Mary enters the stage with "over one arm, carried neglectfully, trailing on the floor ... an old-fashioned white satin wedding gown".[15]

Apotheosis, and even more the *self-apotheosis* of the hero at the end of the tragedy is also an effective device for the transubstantiation of death into a positive value. Tragic heroes are not only "cheering themselves up" in the last scenes, as T. S. Eliot deprecatingly remarked, but they often succeed in reinterpreting their chaotic and fragmented lives into a meaningful symbol of universal validity conveying an important message to their fellow creatures. Recall, for instance, Othello's famous "the Indian and the Pearl" monologue, Vladimir's "Astride a grave" soliloquy at the end of *Waiting for Godot*, or Jamie's quotation of Rossetti's beautiful lines in *A Long Day's Journey into Night*: "Look in my face. My name is Might-Have-Been; I am also called No More, Too Late, Farewell."

The effect of these self-apotheoses is often enhanced by the hero's rising above his or her suffering self and contemplating his or her tragic fate from a disinterested and serene distance. This *redoubling of the self* becomes quite explicit in some tragedies where, in the final scenes, the heroes begin to speak of themselves in the third person. Antigone: "Luckless Antigone"; Creon: "Creon has ceased to exist"; Hamlet: "His madness is poor Hamlet's enemy"; Othello: "That's he who was Othello"; and so on.

The cathartic effect is also boosted by the *transformation-of-the-hero* device. As a matter of fact, a more or less sudden, and usually unmotivated, change takes place in the hero's character towards the end of the tragedy. In *Antigone*, an arrogant and self-righteous Creon becomes a repentant and humble Creon between lines 1063 and 1095. The bloodthirsty Hamlet of act four comes back from England, in the first scene of act five, as a gentle and melancholy prince. A cowardly Macbeth changes into a fearless hero during the intermission between acts four and five. A vengeful Lady Milford in *Cabal and Love* is metamorphosed into a noble and self-sacrificing martyr in scene eight of act four. And so on, and so forth.

How can we explain the recurrence—over more than two thousand years—of these more or less 'cheap' cathartic devices in the most moving and authentic masterpieces of world literature?[16] How can we explain this historical conspiracy on the part of tragic playwrights? How do they help their spectators to get over the fear and shock they experience while in the claws of tragedy so easily? How do they cheat their spectators into believing that the tragic contradictions of human existence may be, and are being, solved?

They do so because the tragic vision of human existence, in its raw and brutal force, would be unbearable. People living in Western civilization are unable to look death in the face; they are unable to face a world of destruction, absurdity, and meaninglessness. They are attracted by this vision, but they also protect themselves against it. Tragedies invade the realm of death and despair, but they also help us find our way back to our everyday world of meaning, hope, and life-sustaining illusions—to our civilization.

NOTES

1 In this type of music, an overemphasized and obsessive rhythm usually offsets the absence of harmony and provides the illusion of order and certainty in a chaotic world.

2 Rainer Maria Rilke, *Duineser Elegien* 1 (English translation by J. B. Leishman and Stephen Spender, *Duino Elegies*, London: Chatto and Windus, 1975):

> *Wer, wenn ich schriee, hörte mich denn aus der Engel*
> *Ordnungen? und gesetzt selbst, es nähme*
> *einer mich plötzlich ans Herz: ich verginge von seinem*
> *stärkeren Dasein. Denn das Schöne ist nichts*
> *als des Schrecklichen Anfang, den wir noch grade ertragen,*
> *und wir bewundern es so, weil es gelassen verschmäht,*
> *uns zu zerstören. Ein jeder Engel ist schrecklich.*

3 There are experts who think that only beauty in art has this profound duality and that natural beauty (a landscape, a flower, a face) is purely positive. Others include natural beauty in the duality hypothesis.

4 In postmodern art this dichotomy has become shamelessly obvious in the mixture of ecstasy and panic. See, for instance, Kroker et al. (1989).

5 In medieval religious art the duality of terror and beauty is obvious. Think of the gloomy visions of Christ's agony, the torture of martyrs, or the horrendous scenes in hell. But in pictures with biblical or hagiographic subjects the real counterpoint of the horrors depicted is divine grace and not beauty, which plays only a secondary role.

6 Or am I mistaken? Was it a moral duty for him to punish himself? Perhaps, but mythic thinking is not ethical and moral. Was it a social convention and duty that forced the sinner to give up his autonomy and his citizenship by blinding himself and thus making himself dependent on other people like a slave? However, mythic thinking is not sociological. Did he blind himself because he did not have the strength to look at his own defiled face and person any longer? Perhaps, but mythic thinking is not psychological; it is ontological; it raises the ultimate, existential questions of human existence.

7 For eighteenth-century Shakespeare adaptations, see Branam (1956). See also Lirondelle (1912); Widmann (1931); Conklin (1947); Benchetritt (1952); Mander and Mitchenson (1953).

8 "Let us go, I am being reborn, I live again to love Hédelmone and serve my country" [Allons, je crois renaître, et je reprends la vie/Pour aimer Hédelmone, et servir la patrie]. From the text of the 1792 Paris performance of *Othello*.

9 From Ducis' adaptation performed first in Paris in 1769. See Paul Benchettrit (1956).

> *Je ne parle plus de mes feux ni de moi.*
> *Mais pour oser mourir, ta vie est-elle à toi?*
> *Ta grandeur, ton devoir la livre à ta patrie,*
> *Entends à tes côtés le Danois qui te crie.*
> ....
> *C'est à toi que le faible a commis sa défense.*
> *Punir les oppresseurs, soutenir l'innocence,*
> *Protéger les sujets contre leurs ennemis,*
> *Voilà les droits sacrés que le ciel t'a remis.*
> *De leurs malheurs cachés préviens, détruis les causes,*
> *Ce sont là tes devoirs, meurs après, si tu l'oses.*

10 See, for instance, Malone (1923); Ralli (1932); Conklin (1947); Halliday (1950); Mander and Mitchenson (1953).
11 See, for instance, the studies of L. L. Schücking, F. P. Wilson, W. Stroedel, L. B. Campbell, and others.
12 See, for instance, the psychological *Hamlet* interpretations of Otto Ludwig, F. T. Vischer, F. Paulsen, F. Gundolf, and others.
13 See, for instance, the *Hamlet* theories of Hegel, Schopenhauer, H. Ulrici, G. G. Gervinus, and others.
14 A much more detailed analysis of tragic catharsis is to be found in Hankiss (1977a). Novels have similar 'catharsis devices' built into their last chapters—see Hankiss (1977b).
15 'Lovers-dying-together' scenes, 'mad' scenes, or 'music intoned' in the last scene have the same strong cathartic effect.
16 Most of these devices are widely used also by contemporary film directors, even in TV dramas and thrillers.

CHAPTER TEN

THE WORLD OF PLAY

> "To put it simply, the birds sing
> much more than Darwin permits."
> Friderich Buytendijk, *The Meaning of Play*

IN this chapter we discuss the role of play in Western civilization, and the ways in which plays and games create their own symbolic space, an enclave within civilization, which offers especially strong protection against fear and anxiety and is brimful with freedom and meaning.

HOMO LUDENS

In a Strange Land

Jürgen Moltmann (1972, 2), who wrote an important book on play, starts his argument by quoting an old spiritual from slave days:

"How can I play, when I'm in a strange land?"[1]

This is a beautiful and moving line, but I think that, at the same time, it asks the wrong question. To be in a strange land is no reason not to play. On the contrary, it may be our main reason to play. We play, and may have to play, precisely because we live in a strange land. Play creates for us a virtual world of safety and freedom within a strange land where safety and freedom are hard to find.

Do not try to look up this definition in the *Encyclopaedia Britannica*. Most experts would not agree with it; they would consider it to be too broad and too romantic. They can provide us with dozens of stricter and more scholarly definitions. The phenomenon of play has always puzzled philosophers—and even some great theologians—and has perplexed psychologists, sociologists, and anthropologists since they entered the intellectual scene in the nineteenth century. They have described and analyzed play in many different ways (readers interested in these attempts to define the content, and the social role, of play will find a survey of the major theories in the Appendix at the end of this chapter), but in my view most of them miss their mark and ignore the main function of play; the main motive force behind it. There is, however, a major exception.

'Under the Sign of Play'

Jan Huizinga (1950), the Dutch historian, wrote a brilliant book on the role of play in human civilization. The book has a Latin title, *Homo Ludens*, which is meant to emphasize the fact that the human being is at least as much a 'playing being' as a 'knowing being' (*Homo sapiens*).[2] It was first published in 1938 and has been translated into many languages. Huizinga's work is much more important than the (lack of) attention given to it by most contemporary psychologists and physiologists of play would indicate.[3]

He well knew, but did not spend much time discussing, the various biological, physiological, and social theories of play current in his time.

> By some, the origin and fundamentals of play have been described as a discharge of superabundant vital energy, by others as the satisfaction of some 'imitative instinct', or again as simply a 'need for relaxation'. According to one theory, play constitutes "a training of young creatures for the serious work that life will demand later on ... Some find the principle of play in an innate urge to exercise a certain faculty, or in the desire to dominate and compete. Yet others regard it as an 'abreaction'—an outlet of harmful impulses, as the necessary restorer of energy wasted by one-sided activity, as 'wish-fulfillment', as a fiction designed to keep up the feeling of personal value, and so on. (Huizinga, 1950, 2)

He was not convinced by these theories. Or, at least, he thought that the important questions lay elsewhere. He was much more interested, first, in the formal characteristics that could be found in all kinds of playful activities, and, second, in the role that play had 'played', as a result of these characteristics, in the history of human civilization. He was convinced that human activities, and human civilization as a whole, had been permeated and propelled by the spirit of play from the very beginning.

Myth and ritual, for instance, "are rooted in the primeval soil of play" and so are all those institutions and activities that historically derive from them, such as "law and order, commerce and profit, craft and art, poetry, wisdom, and science". Culture can be studied adequately only "*sub specie ludi*", "under the sign of play" (Huizinga, 1950, 5).

> Ritual grew up in sacred play; poetry was born in play and nourished on play; music and dancing were pure play. Wisdom and philosophy found expression in words and forms derived from religious contests. The rules of warfare, the conventions of noble living were built on play-patterns. We have to conclude, therefore, that civilization is, in its earliest phases, played. It does not come from play like a babe detaching itself from the womb: it arises in and as play, and never leaves it ... Genuine, pure play is one of the main bases of civilization. (Huizinga, 1950, 173, 5)

How can play have such an important role in our lives? Huizinga asks. Because play is, or opens, an essential—we could even say ontological—dimension of genuine human existence and human civilization. It allows people to "step out" of ordinary life, transcend "the immediate needs of life", break down "the absolute determinism" of the material world, and enter the "sacred sphere" of spirituality and freedom, self-mastery, fairness, and dignity (Huizinga, 1950, 3, 9, 14, 211).

He goes even further (Huizinga, 1950, 212) when he identifies play and rite and states that, in this "sacred space", the human play somehow represents and re-enacts the cosmic "play", the play of God. And then he concludes that: "Instead of the old saw 'All is vanity', the more positive conclusion forces itself upon us that 'all is play'."

Not All Is Play

Under the spell of this brilliant analysis it is difficult to reject its author's conclusion. Nevertheless, we cannot accept it in its entirety. I think Huizinga is right when he states that play is an essential dimension of human life; that it "sparkles" between matter and mind, frivolity and ecstasy; that it creates a sacred space and has something metaphysical and divine in it. At the same time, he may be mistaken when he concludes from all this that "play is older than culture"; that the "great archetypal activities of human society are all permeated with play from the start"; and that "all is play" (Huizinga, 1950, 1, 4, 212).

Play is one of the major generating forces of human civilization; but it does not antedate civilization. Play and the other "archetypal activities" of mankind do have something in common. But—as we shall see in a moment—this common element resides in a structural and functional similarity and not in the alleged fact of play "permeating" all other activities. Finally, it is a beautiful and elevating aphorism to say that "all is play" instead of repeating, with bitterness or melancholy, that "all is vanity". But unfortunately—or fortunately—it is not true. Not all is play.

Play is not omnipresent in our world. It is not dissolved in the material of the world. Quite the contrary: it contrasts sharply with the rest of the world. It is its counterpole. It opens, in a flash, with fascinating ease and brilliance, the gate of a human world of freedom and safety, meaning and dignity.

Huizinga tantalizes us. In his introductory chapter, where he develops his thesis, he stresses the major importance of this contrast between the "ordinary world" and the "sacred space" of play. His insights are invaluable for the understanding of the phenomenon of play; I shall largely draw upon them in my analysis. But in the main body of the book he seems to have forgotten this contrast, this tension between the two worlds, and is more interested in showing the role of play in generating, and intertwining with, various activities and institutions of our civilization.

In reality, play has contributed to the generation of our civilization in a different and much more dramatic way. It has done so by opposing its own world of freedom, peace, and meaning to a world short of freedom, peace, and meaning. Like other symbolic systems—myths, religions, philosophies, arts—it has surrounded us with its protective sphere.

'Don't Kiss the Engine, Daddy ...'

To be opposed to the ordinary world, and the alien world behind it, as water is opposed to fire, or the sacred to the secular, belongs to the very essence of play. All kinds of play start with 'marking off' a space for play, with drawing a magic circle, square, rectangle, or other shape around the field of play. Huizinga makes this point quite clearly.

> All play moves and has its being within a playground marked off beforehand ... The arena, the card-table, the magic circle, the temple, the stage, the screen, the tennis court,

the court of justice, and so on, are all in form and function play-grounds, that is, forbidden spots, isolated, hedged round, hollowed, within which special rules obtain. All are temporary worlds within the ordinary world, dedicated to the performance of an act apart. Inside the playground an absolute and peculiar order reigns. (Huizinga, 1950, 10)

This act of marking off is obvious in the case of competitive and rule-based games, which are the main objects of Huizinga's attention. But what about games of imitation and identification? As far as theater plays and movies are concerned—and Huizinga includes them in this category—their space is clearly and sharply delineated. In the case of children playing soldiers, doctors, or daddy, the demarcation is more flexible but no less real: under the spell of identification children move around within the transparent bubble of their imagined identities, as sleepwalkers; the 'real world' does not exist for them any more. The world of play lies beyond the confines of the alien world.

Stepping over into the realm of play, people escape from the servitude of the material world and enter the realm of freedom. They leave behind their everyday concerns and needs, the constraints of their own interests, the necessities of physical survival. They escape from the Schopenhauerian life flux into the cool and serene world of symbols. They leave behind the burdensome, oppressive fears and hopes of their own lives.[4]

They also escape from the "absolute determinism" of the real world since the realm of play has its own laws and is not subject to the physical causality dominating the outside world. There is a gap, a discontinuity, between the two worlds. The realm of play is not 'caused' by the outside world. It is superfluous and autonomous, disinterested and free (Huizinga, 1950, 3, 7, 8, 9).[5]

It is free and escapes from the iron law of causality also by oscillating between reality and semblance; by being a world of "as if". This "sparkling" or oscillating between two worlds is brilliantly illustrated by an anecdote Huizinga tells us of a father "who found his four-year-old son sitting at the front of a row of chairs, playing 'trains'. As he hugged him the boy said to him: 'Don't kiss the engine, Daddy, or the carriages won't think it's real'" (Huizinga, 1950, 8).

Stepping over into the world of play, we also escape from the 'social jungle'. The world of play is a world of joyful irresponsibility. There are no fathers and children here, no poor relatives, no duties and public responsibilities. This is a purely individualistic world, where we cooperate only with those with whom we have voluntarily made a contract. In this world, there is only me, my interests, my goals, my joys, my success, my happiness. This is the world of pure and undisturbed individualism and selfishness. In the words of Eugen Fink (1980, 227): "Play is moved and motivated by an almost 'pagan' lack of concern, by a pleasure of the senses, a mysterious delight in semblance, in the glitter of colors, in the peach skin of things."

But, curiously enough, it is at the same time the only world of perfect justice. In the world of play everybody, each participant, has exactly the same rights and opportunities. A complete and ideal equality of opportunities is achieved here. This is the only existing, and perhaps the only possible, Rawlsian world.[6] Here the 'initial choice' has taken place. The future actors have chosen and accepted the rules of the game before they know which part they will play. Whether they will be lucky and privileged or unlucky and underprivileged participants in the game. Within this equality of opportunity, the play allows people to maximize their chances. They may freely choose the world in which they can excel. If they happen to limp, they will not choose football as their favorite game, but chess or Monopoly, at which they can be the best. Life is much more unjust and cruel.

A World of Innocence

The 'psychological jungle', too, is excluded from the world of play. This is a world free from sin and guilt, inhibitions, neuroses, pathologies. There are no tall and small, beautiful and ugly, neglected and beloved women and men here. There is no depression; there is no paranoia, Oedipus complex, or painful repression. There is no torturing superego, and no subconscious either, with its painful turbulences, since there is nothing to be repressed here. There is nothing that the ego could not tolerate or support.

This is a world of amoral or pre-moral innocence; a Garden of Eden before the Fall.[7] This is a world where a pure and unlimited childish selfishness is not a sin, but is the rule; it is not scorned, but encouraged. Here one can be selfish without sinning and feeling guilty. Here one has escaped from the world of original sin. In this world, one is not only allowed, but prompted, to cheerfully defeat or ruin one's partners. One can gratify one's aggressiveness, cruelty, thirst for success, power and domination, and do all this without sinning, without being caught in the net of guilt and humiliation. The Erinyes are not allowed into the sanctuary of play.

With the help of play we also escape from the 'metaphysical jungle' of our ultimate concerns, the harassing questions of life and death. In the world of play the fearsome tyrants of our real lives—time, transitoriness, death—do not exist. Or, due to the magic of play, they become harmless and reversible. Time and life can be started and restarted here again and again. Death loses its sting when we pass over from our ordinary world into the realm of play.

And play can do even more than that. It is, in itself, an act of creation. It creates a new world, a world of symbols, having its own autonomous laws. And it may even create new lives for the player. It offers him or her 'roles', that is, alternative forms of human identity and existence.[8] In this way it helps him or her escape from the trap of Heideggerian or Sartrian "negativity"; from the need to choose a single existence and thereby annihilate all other potential existences.[9] If Heidegger and other existentialists were right in asserting that this annihilation of potential forms of being is the 'ontological sin' of mankind, then play may even possess a redemptive power. And even if it does not redeem us, it may increase the intensity of our lives. We have just referred to identification-based play in which people assume new identities. We may now add that they usually identify themselves with intense, strong, fascinating roles; roles that give them the feeling of power, authenticity, fulfillment. Think of our children, who most often identify themselves with their fathers or mothers, an almighty family doctor, or with other powerful symbols of energy, life, freedom: the fireman, the soldier, or the pilot, the horse, the locomotive, or the airplane.

Chance and Cherries

We do strange things when playing. The strangest of all is that we voluntarily introduce uncertainty, contingency, chance into our lives.[10] In our 'ordinary' lives we usually do just the opposite: we fear, and try to avoid, uncertainty. It threatens our safety, it fills us with anxiety, it reminds us that we live in a world beyond our control. This is why human communities have always tried to reduce the presence and power of uncertainty in their lives. One of the main functions of myths and religions, science and technology, art and literature has been to reduce human anxiety by reducing uncertainty. Why then do we do the opposite when we play?

On the one hand, we do not do the opposite since one of the main functions of play is to reduce uncertainty and anxiety. Passing from the real world to the world of play means to pass from a world of confusion and chaos to a transparent world of order governed by clear and safe rules; from a world of uncertainty and dissonance to a world of safety, "rhythm and harmony" (Huizinga, 1950, 10).

Yet, paradoxically, we also introduce uncertainty and chance into our lives when we enter the realm of play. Why do we do so? First, particular forms of uncertainty have their own appeal. Chance, for instance, is 'ticklish', fascinating, exciting. In real life, to take a chance may be too risky; we, or our plans, may be ruined by it. In the world of play (with the exception of hard gambling[11]) its scope is limited; it can be switched off at any moment; it is defused, neutralized; the loss one may incur is reasonably limited. And, as we shall see, the joy we may derive from playing with chance is maximized in many ways.

Another reason put forward by many experts on play is the fact that our everyday lives tend to be 'boring'; they have a low intensity and human beings suffer from the lack of sufficient arousal and stimulation.[12] In the world of play, the excitement of chance increases the intensity of our lives. And intensity of life is something which we enjoy.

We are sometimes prompted to take a chance even in our real lives. We courageously, or foolishly, jump out of the safety of our lives, because we are fed up with routine. These jumps, though hailed by existentialist philosophers, are too dangerous and relatively rare. Play offers a realm within which taking a leap into the unknown is much less risky. We can enjoy the thrill of leaping into the precipice of chance and freedom without risking our careers, fortunes, or lives.

The thrill and joy are further increased if chance and human will interact with one another. I remember that when I was a naughty boy of about ten, instead of decently eating cherries, I used to throw them up in the air, one after the other, and try to catch them with my open mouth. I enjoyed the exercise tremendously, both when I succeeded and when I failed. In other words, I willfully created uncertainty. I introduced contingency and chance into an action which would otherwise have been entirely controlled, determined by myself (taking the cherry and putting it in my mouth). Why did I do so? Perhaps because human beings may unconsciously or semi-consciously experience the burden and the pain of being bound by, and imprisoned in, a rigid system of causes and effects. They may sometimes be prompted to try to escape, at least for a fleeting moment, into freedom, that is, into a sphere where the causal system in which they and their acts are embedded, does not work.

I may be reading too much into a young boy's juggling with some red cherries on a beautiful summer afternoon, decades ago, somewhere in Europe, but I think that on that afternoon, without knowing it, I experimented with two mysterious metaphysical categories—chance and freedom. I threw the cherry out of a causally determined world into a world of contingency and chance. Or, more precisely, I threw the cherry over into another system of causality in which I could no longer control its trajectory. And I felt a thrill in watching its dangerous and beautiful free flight. But the real thrill was still to come.

It came when I succeeded in catching the cherry with my mouth. There was something more to it than merely the joy of a successful performance. In this happy coincidence, in this happy crossing of two trajectories—that of the cherry and my own movement—the hidden harmony of the universe may have flashed up for a fleeting moment. I may also have enjoyed the shiver of hazarding the destruction of something valuable and perfect, of a beautiful red cherry, a symbol of life; not to mention the shiver of narrowly escaping this danger, this destruction, the irruption of chaos and nonexistence into my world.

From time to time we need to jump out of the causal networks which tightly control our real lives. Play helps us jump out into uncertainty, chance, and 'freedom', without hazarding too much.[13] It is a world of 'as if', and so the losses one may suffer therein will have no lasting effects. Yet even in the world of play, we are cautious enough to reduce the risks further. We usually do not risk our good or bad luck by throwing a gold Cartier watch in the air and trying to catch it. Too high a risk would destroy the joy of play. Cherries have just the right market value for this kind of sport.

The Paradox of Freedom

It may sound paradoxical, but it is a fact that we may generate freedom for ourselves by limiting our initial freedom. This self-limitation is an important factor in the world of play.[14]

As a matter of fact, when we enter the realm of play we voluntarily limit our freedom in order to generate, in the end, more freedom for ourselves. This is particularly true of rule-based play. When we create, or accept, the rules of a game, we narrow our sphere of random action. At the same time, we thereby widen the range of possible combinations and generate freedom for ourselves.

The rules of chess, for instance, limit the players' movements on the board to a few legitimate moves. At the same time, they also multiply the possible variations and combinations of their movements by a billion times. If there were no rules, the pieces would just stand there, or they could be moved in a random order or disorder. Think of how quickly a young child, who does not yet know the rules, gets bored by shoving the pieces around and how quickly he abreacts his frustration by overturning the board. Initiates, on the other hand, can enjoy, for a lifetime, the fascinating freedom of exploring the unlimited possibilities within a space of eight times eight small squares. It is almost like experimenting with infinity.

Or think of playing pool. To keep shooting the ball directly into one of the pockets would soon become tedious. This is why the rules of play limit the player's original freedom by forcing him or her to strike the cue ball against a second ball with the aim of getting the second into the pocket. This limitation creates a wide range of possible variations: it creates freedom. And this is not all. A further source of joy in this game is that it offers players the possibility of putting the 'forces of nature' into motion. With one simple push, they can trigger off a rich interplay of kinetic forces. The balls, bouncing back from one another, rebounding from the cushion, criss-crossing the table in interesting geometric patterns, make the action of the forces of nature almost visible. They show us nature as transparent, ordered, harmonious. They help us cope with the chaos of an alien world. At play, civilization is at its best.

SOCCER

Sacred Rules

The game begins by marking off a field in the world; a microcosm of human freedom, order, and spirituality from the chaos of a world of confusion and materiality. The instant the game begins, this field becomes sacred, separated from the rest of the world by a magic spell, an impenetrable symbolic wall. And the sacred rules of the game begin to obtain and operate within the field, which the profane are forbidden to enter. Remember the shock and the uproar, if not the terror, when a non-initiated, a profane, person all of a sudden crosses the boundaries of the field. Or remember the complicated rituals by which the referee may allow a physician or a coach to enter the field in case of injury. The border between the realm of the profane and that of the sacred should not be transgressed.[15]

This is a world of freedom generated by restrictions. The basic rule is very simple. It specifies that the ball has to be moved, from the center spot, into one of the goals at the two ends of the field. That's all. But if the ball could roll from the center point straight into one of the goals, its track would be, or would seem to be, strictly determined. To generate freedom, rules are established which put obstacles in the way of the ball and complicate its movement.

The first set of obstacles is introduced by putting two teams of eleven players on the field with the task of getting the ball into the goal. So far so good. But they have the task of getting the ball into opposite goals: team A has to kick the ball into the goal of team B and vice versa. To further complicate the game, the two teams have the right to try to hinder the other team, within certain limits and observing a few further rules, in achieving their goal.

Add to this the fact that the 22 players are not automatons; they are independent beings, with their own will and skills. These 22 autonomous players, making countless decisions at every moment, increase the number of possible combinations almost without limit. After this, only one further factor is needed to multiply the number of possible combinations practically to infinity. And this factor is in play from the very beginning: the ball.

The Ball

Balls are among the most important 'freedom generators' in our everyday lives. The ball is freedom, or chance, embodied. It is a demon; not Maxwell's boring and industrious demon, but a jolly goblin. When fans say to each other 'the ball is round', they mean that anything may happen on the football field. Even the favorite may lose. Yes, the ball may bounce in any direction. It seems to have its 'own will'. It seems to be autonomous. One cannot predict or control its movements entirely. It is an object and, nevertheless, it seems to be free. Free of determinism. Objects are subject to the force of gravitation. The ball is among those few objects which look as if they could challenge the forces of nature. By bouncing off the ground again and again, and by bouncing, insolently, in the most unexpected directions, it seems to be freeing itself, again and again, from the iron law of gravitation. It moves as if it were weightless; it can choose the most beautiful and glorious trajectories, it may fly at unlikely distances; it has the Platonic perfection of spheres.

It also has an almost metaphysical function. It spiritualizes the fight between human beings. It plays the role of a catalyst between two or several players. In a real fight, the adversaries try to physically defeat, subdue, if not destroy, one another. In football (or basketball, tennis, and so on) the fight is no less fierce, but it is not destructive. Thanks to the ball, it is defused and spiritualized. According to the rules, players, who otherwise are robust and aggressive athletes, have to behave as impeccable gentlemen and gentlewomen. They must not hinder one another in their free movement and even in the heat of the fight they have to avoid, as far as possible, physical contact. If they do not, they are penalized and can even be excluded from play. There is a kind of vacuum between them, a spiritual sphere, the sphere of the ball and its movements, which keeps them apart and mediates between them. The player can touch only the ball, not his or her adversary, and the ball and its movements express, in a symbolic and indirect way, the interaction of human intentions and forces deployed in the struggle.

By introducing the factor of chance and unpredictability into the struggle, the ball transforms a bitter and down-to-earth human fight into an epiphany of spirituality and freedom. In the brisk movements of the ball, chance and human will interact, dance, somersault with each other. The ball integrates in itself human will and chance, human freedom and limitation, success and failure, hope and the loss of hope for a brief moment to be regained in the next.[16]

Dionysus versus Apollo

The sacred does not exist without the profane. The football field has to be marked off and opposed to the surrounding world. The football match fails to achieve its goal if it is not watched by spectators; if there are no fans to yell or boo, jubilate or despair. The experience and the sacred ceremony remain incomplete if the tension between the field and the grandstand is missing. If the clean emerald field, sparkling in a crystal light, and the transparent rationality and freedom of the game is not opposed, in sharp and shocking contrast, by the howling and raving mob in the darkness of the stands, burning red torches and being pulled, from one minute to the next, between ecstatic joy and hellish misery.

In our everyday lives, reason and passion are mixed. Soccer (like some other games) separates and opposes these two realms. All the passions, emotions, and instincts are pushed over to the side of the spectators. They are supposed to be excited, passionate and raging, desperate, miserable and happy, enraged, hating and furious, loving, admiring and adoring: they may, and have to, let off steam, they may attain Dionysian raptures, they may rage and love, cavort and explode, and finally achieve catharsis (if their team wins) or descend into hell (if their team loses).

At the same time, they must experience the freedom of the Apollonian or Platonic spirituality of the game going on down on the pitch.

The players move around in a world of spirituality; in a transparent world of clear and perfect rules, rules freely accepted by them and by everybody present. They live and act in a freedom born of the fascinating interaction of human will and chance; in the freedom of a world of infinite combinations. They act according to clear and sacred rules. While they are playing, they are supposed to act as pure rational beings who have left behind, off the field, their everyday passions and emotions, personal wishes or fears. They perform the roles that have been allotted to them and are supposed to be moved only by the sublime goal of winning the match. To this end, they have to subordinate everything; they serve only the cause, as angels serve God.

They move in a world of pure morality and justice. A world of justice and total impartiality, of perfect equality of opportunity which is never achieved in our everyday lives. Even the advantage deriving from the direction of the wind is balanced in a just way: the two teams change ends after the first half. When and where do we, privileged and underprivileged, change sides in the real world? And there is a referee, with divine powers, who sees that justice is done, who is unbiased and incorruptible. The whole ritual, the sacred ceremony of the game, is threatened if the suspicion arises that he may be biased. The players are supposed to obey the rules. If they break the rules, they are immediately punished and, if they do it again, they are excluded from play. They are expelled from the sphere of spirituality and we see them disappearing into the chilly Hades of the locker room.

The real expulsion from paradise comes, however, only if the sanctity of the play is profaned; if the spell is broken; if the illusion of play is destroyed—by the players falling out of their angelic roles and starting a fist fight on the field; by a cheating referee; by people realizing that the match is rigged; by spectators invading the field. Such events may do lasting damage to people and to the human community. Huizinga writes in this connection:

> It is curious to note how much more lenient society is to the cheat than to the spoil-sport. This is because the spoil-sport shatters the play-world itself. By withdrawing from the game he reveals the relativity and fragility of the play-world in which he had temporarily shut himself with others. He robs play of its *illusion* ... The play-mood is *labile* in its very nature. At any moment, 'ordinary life' may reassert its rights. (Huizinga, 1950, 11, 21)[17]

I think there is much more at stake in this case. Not simply the play-world, but the human world we have built for ourselves collapses if somebody cheats or steps out of the game. It is a bitter shock to suddenly realize the fragility of our world of freedom, spirituality, and dignity; the fragility of our civilization. And to awake again in an alien world.

American Football

American football works with sharper contrasts. At first sight, it is not a world of freedom. It is a world of butting and struggling, a world of chase, an ecstasy of aggression and destruction. But, on closer inspection, it transcends into a glorious epiphany of freedom, and in several ways.

The iron wall of the defense negates all freedom; it tries to obliterate even the slightest possibility of motion; to completely immobilize its adversary; to freeze it in its mortal embrace. But in spite of the efforts of this Leviathan, the alacrity of the human mind, and the nimbleness of human limbs, find the propitious moment to break out of this embrace and zigzag their way to liberty.

Here again the ball has a central role to play. Most of the time, the demons in the service of the evil power attack and hound the knights of King Arthur, who protect the ball, their Holy Grail. They force the ball to the ground again and again; they want to subdue, captivate, conquer it. Once in a while, however, the ball escapes from this earthly turmoil: it flies up in the sky, free, glorious, spiritual and divine, drawing a perfect and beautiful arc in the air: this is the ecstasy of Ascension, the epiphany of freedom, the experience of the divine.

And that is not the end. While it is flying high, one of the knights is sprinting along the ground and the real ecstasy comes when the divine trajectory of the ball and the zigzagging human course of the knight meet in the holy moment of a successful reception. This is a real consummation, the sudden and momentary union of the divine and the human. This is the apotheosis of the human being, who had the will, the skill, the courage, to cross the trajectory of the divine. Who 'went and caught a falling star' ...[18]

PLAY AS WORLD SYMBOL
The Cosmic Ball Game

Some of my readers may think that I am exaggerating or even joking. I am not. I am only drawing upon the rich treasures of mankind's mythological imagination. Hugo Rahner mentions, for instance, the ball game of Eros and Aphrodite, described by Apollonius Rhodius in the third book of his *Argonautica*. Jakob Bachofen (1926), a leading expert on religious symbolism, interpreted this scene in the following way:

> In Apollonius' account the ball thrown by Urania describes a line of fire through the air like a star. In a fragment of Sappho it is described as having a color like that of purple fire. These are flights of fancy, but they still convey clearly their primitive cosmic significance.[19]

He and various other scholars gave further examples of the cosmic and mystic symbolism of the ball. Robert Stumpfl (1936, 136ff) described, for instance, how in the Middle Ages the bishops and their priests led a sacred ball game in the choirs of their cathedrals on Easter Day, in reminiscence of early ceremonial dances, the dance of the angels around the throne of God, and unconsciously re-enacting also the old Germanic rite of the Easter ball game, where the ball symbolized the glorious sun being resurrected after the dark winter months.[20]

We might also recall all those scenes and pictures in which an infant god holds in his hands the globe as a ball, or plays with the planets as if they were balls.

> Here is the significance of those pictures of the infant Jesus in medieval art that show him carrying the sphere of the world in his hands—the 'apple' in this divinely light-hearted game with the cosmos. Similarly, the putti of baroque art, playing like tiny giants with the ball of the Earth, are symbols in human form of the nature of that original thought in the mind of God that hurled forth the tremendous pyrotechnics of creation; they are the last residual vestiges of the attempt to clothe in visible form God's mighty playing with the world. (Rahner, 1965, 18)[21]

God at Play

God playing with the world? Why would he do so? Or let me ask rather: Why does the image of the playing god occur so often and so forcefully in the myths of various civilizations? If I add that in a great number of myths gods not only play with the world, but create the world through playing and dancing, then the question becomes even more puzzling. Why has play acquired such an important role in mankind's mythic imagination? How could playing and dancing be identified with the holy act of creation?

The hidden and unconscious motive behind this identification may have been to further enhance the protective force inherent in play. I have argued in this chapter that the easiest way of escaping the alien world and stepping over into the safe enclave of a human world of freedom was to start to play. The possibility of associating the world of play with the realm of the divine, and not only with the realm of the human, opposed it even more to the real world and reinforced its power to protect mankind against the forces of that world.

Even if we accept this hypothesis, we have to ask the further question of how play, and dance as a form of play, could have been associated with the sacred and the divine.[22] The answer proposed by scholars is that playing and dancing have some characteristics that are absent, or extremely rare, in the real, physical and secular world, and thus they suggest something that seems to be different, 'metaphysical', divine; something that opposes them to the real, the alien world. Joy and serenity, elegance and grace, freedom, disinterestedness and creativity are among these features.

Interpreting Plato's ideas on human play, Rahner writes that Plato referred to the human being as a "plaything of God", and saw in this the highest perfection a creature could attain.

> There is a real perception in this, for if the highest attainable form of human development consists in the possession of those qualities which we especially associate with the idea of play, a lightness and freedom of the spirit, an instinctively unerring command of the body, a certain neatness and graceful nimbleness of mind and movement, then—platonically speaking—it is precisely through such things as these that man participates in the divine, or it is precisely in such things as these that he achieves the intuitive imitation and the still earth-bound recovery of an original unity he once had with the One and the Good. (Rahner, 1965, 11)

If we may participate in the divine, if there was an original unity between the secular and the sacred, the human and the divine, then people may feel fundamentally at home in this universe—the presence of the alien world is contingent and ephemeral. And if Eugen Fink (1980) is right, and play is a "world symbol", then joy and freedom reign and not the destructive and chaotic forces of an alien world.

Play and dance could help people identify themselves with the cosmos in various ways. By playing the role of spirits, demons, and gods, by re-enacting cosmic events—the rotation of the Sun, the Moon, the stars, the rhythm of the seasons, the decay and resurrection of life—they may have felt that they were being reintegrated in the harmony of the great cosmic order and would thereby be protected against the forces of an alien world. The cosmic dance of the stars and planets was re-enacted in the dancing choirs of the Greek mysteries; the ceremonial dances of a variety of civilizations expressed the movements and gestures of gods and cosmic powers. The belief in the magic force of ritual plays and dances—that were supposed to reinforce the cosmic order as opposed to the chaos of an alien world—was almost universal in early civilizations. Huizinga, for instance, refers to the Chinese belief that "the purpose of music and the dance is to keep the world in its right course and force Nature into benevolence towards man" (Huizinga, 1950, 14).

In the Judeo–Christian tradition the ceremonial dance has had a much lesser role—it was banished for almost two millennia—though the dance of David before the Ark of the Covenant, and the dancing choir of angels around the throne of God, were remembered throughout the Middle Ages.[23] Recently, ceremonial dancing has re-emerged and become a dominant feature in some of the evangelical churches of America. Harmony and rhythm, music and dance, the words of love and the hope of salvation fill these crystal cathedrals to the brim and leave no space free for the forces of the alien world.

But all this may not have been enough. People in several civilizations seem to have needed even more security; they needed an even stronger guarantee that they lived in a safe and ordered cosmos; that they lived in their own world. This may explain the fact that the mythic imagination has enhanced the transcendental power of play and dance even further, not only envisioning them as re-enacting, and controlling, cosmic events, but also presenting a magnificent vision of them as participating in the very act of creation.

Creation through Play

The vision of a god creating the world through playing and dancing appears in a wide variety of myths.[24] The role of infant gods in these myths is especially important—they emphasize the play character of creation.

One of the most puzzling texts is to be found in Proverbs, in the Old Testament. The text has several translations and a wide range of interpretations. Most interpreters agree, however, that the text refers to Divine Wisdom (*Hochmah* in Hebrew), who was the child of God, or God's creative spirit—later also called the infant Logos—who participated in the creation of the world by playing and/or dancing, or only rejoicing before

God while he was creating the universe. The standard English translation of the text is the following:

> When he established the heavens, I was there ...
> when he marked out the foundations of the earth,
> then I was beside him, like a little child;
> and I was daily his delight,
> rejoicing before him always,
> rejoicing in his inhabited world
> and delighting in the sons of man.[25]

Rahner (1965, 20) also quotes the Douay Version of the Vulgate, which uses the word "playing" instead of rejoicing, and—referring to other *loci* in the Bible—he proposes that the word could also be translated as "dancing".

> I was with him forming all things:
> and was delighted every day,
> playing before him at all times,
> playing in the world ...
> I was daily his delight;
> I danced before him always;
> I danced upon his round earth.

How could play and the playing child become symbols of creation? A wide range of answers has been proposed.

The deep and undisturbed absorption of the playing child, for instance, may have suggested the solemnity of the holy act of creation. More importantly, it may have suggested the freedom of the creative act. In his *Theology of Play*, Jürgen Moltmann (1972) argues that 'God is not a *"Deus faber"*, who must always be doing something in order to exist. He was as free as a playing child to create something or not to create anything at all. "He did not have to create something to realize himself."

The question of the freedom of God has been discussed since the early centuries of Judaism and Christianity. Was he absolutely free? So free that he could have created another world or not have created any world at all? Most eminent scholars are inclined to believe that there could have been no previous cause that made God create the world, since God was the ultimate cause. Neither could he have had a definite goal or purpose with the creation of the world since such a purpose would have determined his action and limited his freedom. The act of creation was as free and absorbed, as serious and serene, as meaningful and meaningless as the play of the child or the joyous ecstasy of dance.[26]

This vision works in two ways. If the world was created with the ease and joy, freedom and harmony of play and dance, then it may not be an alien world. On the other hand, if play and dance have—in their ease and joy, freedom and harmony—something essentially divine in them, then women and men can escape from the alien world at any time by entering the sacred realm of play and dance.

This may, of course, be an illusion, part and parcel of the spheres of symbols that have protected us against the terror we feel in a world that may be not our world. But even in this case it may have been a life-preserving illusion. It may have helped us live our lives with less fear and anxiety—and with more dignity.

The Loss of Play

The image of a god creating the world playing and dancing is the product of the mythic imagination. It may, however, express something important about the universe. It may express its eternal and calm indifference; it may also express a divine freedom and serenity of which we are hardly capable in our everyday lives. It may have the message for us that we could achieve the bliss of real freedom and of genuine, though mortal, existence if only we could escape from the servitude of our needs and interests, which harass and chase us to death. Play may help us 'switch off' from this murderous struggle for survival and domination; it may help us relax and achieve the divine serenity and seriousness that is the essence of play.

If God created the world playing, or if it emerged as the playful and free interaction of cosmic forces, then we should not be too concerned about our lives either. It may be dangerous hubris to take ourselves too seriously. Socrates and Plato, and a long line of Judeo–Christian, Buddhist, Taoist, and other thinkers have warned us that nothing human is really serious.[27] Modern men and women may have forgotten this warning.

We have seen that, according to Huizinga (1950, 173), Western civilization was born, and survived for two millennia, "*sub specie ludi*".[28] Triumphal processions and '*circenses*', sumptuous banquets and splendid theaters in Rome and the hippodrome in Byzantium; church ceremonies and courtly love, chivalry and marketplace farces in the Middle Ages; pageants and pastoral theaters, *commedia dell'arte* shows, Senecan tragedies and public festivities, Boccaccio, Aretino, and Erasmus, Cervantes and the comedies of Shakespeare in the Renaissance; allegorical plays and operas, masquerades and the parade of periwigs in the Baroque age: all these centuries were "brimful of play", they "radiated the play-spirit" (Huizinga, 1950, 173–94). Since the eighteenth century, however, the play spirit has been increasingly eroded. Utilitarianism, the "prosaic efficiency and the bourgeois ideal of social welfare", the Industrial Revolution and Marxism, this "grotesque overestimation of the economic factor", increasingly diminished the spirit of playfulness. Liberalism and socialism, church and state, analytical science and philosophy "were all pursued in deadly earnest in the nineteenth century".

> Realism, Naturalism, Impressionism and the rest of that dull catalogue of literary and pictorial coteries were all emptier of the play-spirit than any of the earlier styles had ever been. Never had an age taken itself with more portentous seriousness. Culture ceased to be 'played'. (Huizinga, 1950, 191–92)

Huizinga judged the situation in his own age—he published his book in 1938—to be even more critical. He complained that "the play-element" had been lost. Instead of a genuine spirit of playfulness, Western civilization was hallmarked by "Puerilism ... that blend of adolescence and barbarity", and by "the insatiable thirst for trivial recreation and crude sensationalism, the delight of mass meetings, mass-demonstrations, parades"; as well as by "gregariousness ... yells, or other signs of greeting, the wearing of badges and sundry items of political haberdashery, walking in marching order or at a special pace and the whole rigmarole of collective voodoo and mumbo-jumbo" (1950, 205).

Communists were no less bad-tempered, remarked Jürgen Moltmann (1972, 11). The socialist revolution fostered "a spirit of joyless *tristesse* in the various paradises of the working class. In Prague the 1948 revolution closed down 2,000 coffeehouses, restaurants, and beer gardens."

Developing the ideas of Huizinga, David L. Miller (1969) devoted a whole book to the analysis of this decadence of the play spirit. Although we live in a consumer society, saturated with 'entertainment', we have lost our genuine ability to play; we have lost "the divine gracefulness of a child" at play (1969, 103). We should relax. We should let things happen. We should admit chance and freedom into our lives and let the world create itself. Instead of feverishly and perpetually doing something, we should learn simply to be. We should learn from the profound absorption and tranquility of the playing child. The goal of life is "not to win the game (we are all going to lose the game of life anyway), but simply to play and to play simply" (1969, 130).

> Life is a kind of hit and run game—according to those who cannot see that life is the game of life. For them it is the end, the purpose, that has value ... Why not hit and run just to hit and run ... ? What did you do today? I played. What did you play? I just played. Why did you do that? Just for fun. (Miller, 1969, 127–28)[29]

To achieve this freedom, this serene lightheartedness, may be a fascinating strategy against our own fears in this world. But is it not an illusion? A self-deception? Can we cross the street, in happy blindness, not caring about the cars rushing by? Can we pass through the traps and minefields of our lives with a happy nonchalance? Certainly not. But anxiety and panic, and the convulsive urge to succeed, to become and achieve something, may reduce our chances of survival in a difficult world.

Frivolity and Ecstasy

The message of play, and its role in our civilization, may be more complex than that. Huizinga, Fink, Rahner, Miller, and other experts on play emphasize its essential duality. Huizinga (1950, 21) speaks of "frivolity and ecstasy" as "the twin poles between which play moves". Miller (1969, 119) writes of play's "original unity of seriousness and non-seriousness". According to Eugen Fink (1980, 62 and *passim*) the basic, Heraclitean dualities of life and death, creation and destruction, semblance and reality, time and eternity flash up and the profound structures of the universe and being emerge in play as a "world symbol".

Hugo Rahner, too, regards play as the ultimate symbol of human existence; of an existence that is glorious and tragic at the same time. Man (and Rahner means here, of course, both men and women) at play is a "grave-merry" man; he is "two men in one".

> [H]e is a man with easy gaiety of spirit, one might almost say a man of spiritual elegance, a man who feels himself to be living in invincible security; but he is also a man of tragedy, a man of laughter and tears, a man, indeed, of gentle irony, for he sees through the tragically ridiculous masks of the game of life and has taken the measure of the cramping boundaries of our earthly existence. (Rahner, 1965, 27)

He concludes his argument in a tone of stoic resignation, Christian hope, and existentialist courage. Referring to two main aspects of life that are revealed, and experienced, in play, he writes:

> The first is that existence is a joyful thing because it is secure in God; the second, that it is also a tragic thing, because freedom must always involve peril ... and ... the game may be lost. (1965, 26–27)

Yes, the game may be lost. But play, as a realm of freedom and disinterested joy, may remain one of the safest refuges of human beings in this world. It is a sanctuary, a virtual civilization of safety and freedom in an age in which our 'real' civilization has partly lost its ability to help us answer the ultimate question of human existence.

APPENDIX

As I promised at the beginning of this chapter, the reader will find here a brief survey of some of the major theories of play.

Karl Groos (1898, 1901) author of one of the earliest systematic studies of animal and human play, classified human play as the "playful exercise" of the following: *sensory organs* (sensations of contact, temperature, taste, smell, hearing, or sight); *motor apparatus* (playful movement of the bodily organs, playful movement of foreign bodies, such as hustling things about, rolling, spinning, shoving, and skipping foreign bodies, throwing at a mark, destructive movement-play, playful endurance, and so on); *higher mental powers* (memory, imagination, attention, reason); *feelings* (physical pain, mental suffering, surprise, fear); *will*; *socioeconomic impulses* (fighting play [physical fighting, mental rivalry, teasing, hunting, witnessing fights, the tragic], love play [courtship, love play in art, sex in comedies], imitative play [playful imitation of simple movements, dramatic imitation in play, plastic or constructive imitative play, inner imitation], social play).

Half a century later, Roger Caillois (1961) divided plays into four categories, "depending upon whether, in the games under consideration, the role of competition, chance, simulation, or vertigo is dominant. I call these *agon*, *alea*, *mimicry*, and *ilinx*, respectively. All four indeed belong to play. One plays football, billiards, chess (*agon*); roulette or a lottery (*alea*); a pirate, Nero, or Hamlet (*mimicry*); or one produces in oneself, by a rapid whirling or falling movement, a state of dizziness and disorder (*ilinx*)."

Both Groos and Caillois go far beyond simple classification; they try to distinguish play from other human activities and look for the main factors that are at work in the generation of playful activities. In doing so they continue the work of many of their predecessors. Recently, M. J. Ellis (1973) has given an excellent historical survey of the most important approaches and hypotheses in this field.

Among the "Classical Theories of Play" he mentions the following five:

(i) According to the *surplus energy theory of play*, animal and human organizations need a safety valve, a way to reduce their energy surplus which accumulates in those parts and functions of their bodies which are not used for a certain period of time.

(ii) The *instinct theory of play* maintains that play is simply an instinct, an inherited capacity and drive to "emit playful acts".

(iii) According to the *play as preparation theory*, the main drive and purpose of play is to prepare the young animal, or the young human being, to cope with the tasks of adult life.

(iv) The *theory of play as recapitulation* contends that the player unconsciously recapitulates situations, actions, events that were important in the development of the species. What was originally ritual, myth, or serious work has become play.

(v) Proponents of the *theory of play as relaxation* argue that, after a certain period of activity, "the organism needs to emit other responses that allow the fatigued elements to regenerate".

Ellis discusses the next group of theories under the heading of "Recent Theories of Play".

According to the *theory of task generalization*, "players transfer to play or leisure behaviors that are rewarded in another setting": in work, in private or public life.

The *theory of compensation* maintains that people play in order to "satisfy psychic needs not satisfied in, or generated by, working behaviors".

According to the *catharsis theory of play*, play is generated by "the need to express disorganizing emotions in a harmless way by transferring them to socially sanctioned activity". Groos speaks of the need to safeguard the integrity of the individual; Menninger argues that "competitive games provide an unusually satisfactory social outlet for the instinctive aggressive drive", and so on.

Various *psychoanalytic theories of play* agree in stressing the importance of play in processing and assimilating difficult experiences, strengthening the ego and helping it to master the environment.

The *theory of the cognitive dynamics of play* is based on Jean Piaget's theory of the development of the child's relationship to reality. According to him, in his early years the child is overwhelmed by outside reality; he is forced to 'accommodate' himself to the world. Later, he becomes more and more able to apply his mental structures to reality, that is, to 'assimilate' and master reality. In ordinary life, accommodation and assimilation are more or less balanced. "Play occurs when the child can impose on reality his own conceptions and constraints."

The *theory of play as learning* asserts that play is the product of a learning process and its function is to reduce tensions between the child and his environment. These learning processes may vary strongly according to the tensions to be solved. In cultures which inculcate in children a strong sense of duty—and, as a result, leave "little scope for individuality or creative problem solving"—games of chance will prevail. In cultures emphasizing the value of performance, the stress deriving from the pressure for achievement will be resolved by games of skill. Finally, in cultures built on obedience, the aggressive tendencies generated by this constraint will develop games that "provide opportunities to force obedience on others".

Among the "Modern Theories of Play" Ellis discusses first the *theory of play as arousal*. According to this theory human beings need an optimal level of stimulation, and play is one of the means of generating the missing amount of stimulation. Play, ranging from the "rough-and-tumble play of young animals" to the "epistemic" games of puzzles, problem solving, day-dreaming or acting, generate "novelty, complexity, and/or dissonance, i.e. information"; and information is stimulation.

The last theory Ellis mentions relates to the *competence/effectance motive* of play. He quotes White, who claims that play belongs to those activities which are "motivated by a need to demonstrate a capacity to control or produce effects in the environment". "Play is caused by a need to produce effects in the environment. Such effects demonstrate competence and result in feelings of effectance." And "effectance is pleasant". Groos spoke in the same connection of the "joy in being the cause".

NOTES

1 He also quotes Psalm 137: "How shall we sing the Lord's song in a foreign land?"
2 See also Buytendijk (1933).
3 See, for instance, Caillois (1961); Ellis (1973).
4 As Eugen Fink (1980, 80) remarks: "Play ... raises life, full of obligations, into the light and floating ether of the 'non-obligatory'."
5 Quoting a wide range of experts, Ellis (1973, 9–17) speaks in this connection about play as "voluntary", "trivial", "fruitless", "not under the control of known contingencies", "nonproductive", "aimless", "self-sufficient", and so on.
6 See Rawls (1971).
7 According to Huizinga (1950, 6) play "lies outside the antithesis of wisdom and folly, and equally outside those of truth and falsehood, good and evil. Although it is a non-material activity it has no moral function. The valuations of vice and virtue do not apply here."

8 "When we play, we experience a strange act, and the happiness, of creation: we may become everything, an infinite range of possibilities is open before us, we have the illusion of a free and unlimited beginning" (Fink, 1980, 78).

9 To quote Eugen Fink once more (1980, 79): "The child is the undetermined all, the old man the determined few—one is born as many and one dies as one."

10 There are many ways of introducing chance into the world of play. Dice have been used for this purpose since time immemorial. Dealing and drawing cards will do as well as turning the 'Wheel of Fortune' or playing football with an egg-shaped ball instead of a decent round one (which also has a close relationship with chance). I shall return to these balls in a moment.

11 In gambling, the powers of chance may break through the walls of play and destroy (or, in a few cases, save) the real life of the gambler.

12 See the discussion of the "modern theories of play" by Ellis in the appendix. See also Ellis (1973, 80–100).

13 As Tuan (1979, 202) remarks, "surprise and anxiety can be pleasant as long as we have ultimate control".

14 This is also true in the social sphere. When people enter a human community, they have to accept the rules of the community, which limit their individual freedom. On the other hand, these rules, and the survival of the community, may create for them a wide range of new possibilities from which they can freely choose.

15 There are many extremely interesting interpretations of soccer. Here I refer the reader only to Buytendijk (1952) and Denny and Riesman (1955).

16 The ball used in rugby or American football increases the role of chance at the expense of human intentions. In an article entitled 'The Lure of Pinball', Julius Siegal (1957) describes the player at the pinball machine as Everyman, pitting himself against the oppressively omnipotent American Industry and trying to defeat the monster-machine.

17. Huizinga remarks that "illusion" is "a pregnant word" since it derives from the Latin "inlusio", "illudere", "inludere", and "means literally 'in-play'".

18 In the presence of a wonderful touchdown perhaps even John Donne would excuse me for citing his beautiful poem 'Go, and Catch a Falling Star', in this context.

19 Quoted by Rahner (1965, 17–18).

20 Quoted by Rahner (1965, 84).

21 He also gives examples of Greek and Hellenistic mythology and literature.

22 "All play has somewhere deep within it an element of the dance" (Rahner, 1965, 66). In the German original this is expressed even more strongly: "Alles Spiel ist irgendwo am Grunde seines Wesens ein Tanz"—literally, 'all play is, in its essential being, a dance', *Eranos-Jahrbuch* (1949), p. 59.

23 Rahner (1965, Chapter IV, *passim*). He mentions a few examples of ceremonial dancing in the Christian liturgy even in the nineteenth and twentieth centuries.

24 Rahner (1965, 99) and others quote Vedantic, Sanskrit, and other examples. See Miller, David (1969, 106).

25 Proverbs 8, 27–31.

26 In his book *The Mind of God*, physicist Paul Davies (1992, 191–93, 194–222) surveys various views about God's possible role—and freedom—in creating the universe. Contradicting Einstein, and siding with the adherents of quantum mechanics, he

argues that, yes, "God plays dice with the universe". He also discusses the question of God's freedom to create various kinds of universe or not to create a universe at all. See also Torrance (1981); Dyson (1979).

27 Let me quote only a passage from Plato's *Laws*: "To be sure, man's life is a business which does not deserve to be taken too seriously; yet we cannot help being in earnest with it, and there's the pity. Still, as we are here in this world, no doubt, for us the becoming thing is to show this earnestness in a suitable way" (1961 VII, 803).

28 Without refuting Huizinga's argument, Rahner (1965, 91–105), Miller (1969, 108–117), and others show that the spell of play has not been equally strong throughout European history. The "serious serenity" of Greek civilization, for instance, was followed by the austerity and seriousness of early and medieval Christianity, which loathed and condemned frivolous gaiety ("Woe upon you who laugh now; you shall mourn and weep", Luke 6:25). The ribaldry of jokes and theaters was considered the realm of the devil.

29 To illustrate his point, Miller quotes some lines from a book about a cat written in the style of a nursery rhyme:

This was no time for play.
This was no time for fun.
This was no time for games.
There was work to be done.
....
Do you know where I found him?
You know where he was?
He was eating a cake in the tub!
Yes he was!

The hot water was on
And the cold water, too.
And I said to the cat,
'What a bad thing to do!'
'But I like to eat cake
In a tub,' laughed the cat.
'You should try it some time.'
Laughed the cat as he sat.
....

And then I got mad.
This was no time for fun.
I said, 'Cat! You get out!
There is work to be done.
I have no time for tricks.
I must go back and dig.
I can't have you in here.
Eating cake like a pig!
You get out of this house!
We don't want you about!'
Then I shut off the water
And let it run out.

CHAPTER ELEVEN

THE WORLD OF JOKES

> "Never to be born would be best for mortal man. But hardly one man in a hundred thousand has this luck."
>
> Quoted by Freud

EVEN such seemingly trivial things as jokes are indispensable factors in a civilization. They flirt with people's existential anxieties and with the 'alien world': they break through the protective shields of civilization but, after a moment of hilarity–terror–freedom, they let people escape back into the safety of their everyday lives. By this exercise they renew and reinforce the normative and symbolic structures of civilization.

JOKES AND LAUGHTER

Jokes belong to the *ephemerida* of our lives. They seem to provide us with brief moments of hilarity, flashing up for an instant and then fading away without leaving a trace. I shall argue, however, that they are powerful allies in our efforts to curb and control our fears and anxieties in a world where we do not quite feel at home. And they are indispensable constituents of our civilization.

Did Moses or Christ Ever Laugh?

They may have, but it is not at all likely.[1] Moses is portrayed in the Old Testament as an austere and forbidding man, majestic and morose, visionary, care-ridden, suffering from the enormous weight of responsibility. He was too busy disciplining his people and bringing them out of the desert to have much time for fun. And he may have not been the type of man to enjoy life. Did he at least smile when, after forty years of wandering in the desert, and a few minutes before his death, he was allowed to look down onto the Promised Land from Mount Nebo? It is almost impossible to imagine it. According to the testimony of Deuteronomy, in his last days and hours he was tossed between fears and hopes, visions of victory and destruction, God punishing or saving his sinful but chosen people.

Jesus Christ has usually been portrayed as a serious and grave young man, looking at us with sad and pensive eyes. On the other hand, he brought to his followers the Gospel, and he may, or should, have smiled as the messenger of the 'Good News'. If he did, this smile was not recorded by his biographers, the four evangelists, and was forgotten, or even ignored, by those who laid down the foundations of the institutions of his church. Most of the early church fathers were convinced that human beings had no reason to laugh and had no excuse for joking. Living in the vale of tears and in the shadow of original sin, weeping and mourning became men and women much better than laughing and joking.

If we assume that we live in a world with which we are not entirely compatible—and this assumption is part of the working hypothesis of this book—should we not agree with those holy authorities? Not necessarily. There may be niches and moments of pleasure and joy even in a universe that is far from ideal. And, if we succeed in building up our own human world of safety, freedom, and meaning within this 'alien universe', we may have good reason to laugh, joke, and rejoice.

At the same time, we had better watch our step when we enter the world of jocularity. The church fathers may have been right to declare that jokes have something to do with the Devil—or at least with the unknown depths of our existence. They may send us off on strange adventures. They may be dangerous.

Are Jokes Trivial?

Let me start with a silly, trivial joke.

> Cannibal boy to his Mom: "But Mommy, I don't like my little brother."
> Cannibal mother to her son: "Shut up and carry on eating."

Listening to this joke, when we reach the last phrase, we burst out laughing. But after a few seconds, the impact of the joke fades away and we resume our everyday business. In most cases, we forget the joke forever as something ephemeral, negligible, trivial. We are not aware of the fact that something important has happened to us in the moment we experienced the joke. We do not realize that even the simplest joke is a complex and, at the same time, dangerous set of machinery.

There are no innocent jokes, although there is innocent laughter. We may laugh when we are suddenly relieved of anxiety, a tension, a burden; we may laugh when we meet with friends we have not met for a long time; when we get the job of our lives; when our children do something funny; when our beloved smiles at us; when we just feel happy.

But there are also other sorts of laughter. Our laughter may be wicked, as well as innocent. It may be sarcastic or sardonic, as well as angelic. We may laugh from bitterness as well as from joy. We laugh when we are happy and also when we should rather weep. We may laugh at people whom we love and at those whom we scorn. We laugh the laugh of love and the laugh of malice. We may laugh when relaxed as well as when we are embarrassed. We laugh when we hit the jackpot and when somebody else misses the jackpot. We laugh when we are experiencing the profoundest love of our lives and we also laugh when we are merely tickled.

We laugh when we feel free, happy, masters of the world, lords of life; when life is beautiful; when we feel at home in this universe. But, as we shall see, we may also laugh, strangely enough, when we fall out of our lives and our universe; when we are pushed, even if only for a fraction of a second, off the precipice into an unknown and alien universe. And jokes do push us over the edge. They are not mere 'kidding'. They are not trivial. There is a destructive and liberating demon in them. They are dangerous.

How could a joke as simple and silly as the cannibal joke I just quoted be 'dangerous'? Where could a 'demon' hide itself in such an insignificant and transparent triviality? Let us take a closer look at it.

Why do we laugh, if at all, when we listen to this joke and arrive at the final instruction: "Carry on eating"? Metaphorically, I could say that it is at this point that we light the punch line and detonate the joke, which in turn blows up something important in our world or in our psyches. Strangely enough, we react to this explosion by laughing. The explosion is brought about by a simple trick. The joke starts a train of thought and then, suddenly and unexpectedly, it derails this train and jerks it over to another track. This is the basic machinery of the majority of jokes.[2]

In this particular joke, the explosion takes place within the word 'like'. At the beginning of the joke, we think that we are listening to an everyday conversation between a mother and her son about the latter's emotional relationship to his younger brother—that is, our train of thought is proceeding on the level of social relationships. And then, the mother's closing remark derails us and—after a brief and frontal clash with absurdity—makes us jump over to another level of meaning. Instead of referring to the lack of brotherly love, the statement "I don't like my brother" suddenly turns out to express culinary displeasure: "I don't want to eat more of the chop or rib or leg of my stewed, fried, or roasted little brother ..."

So far so good, but why do we respond to this sudden change of meaning by bursting into laughter—into joyful and, almost at the same instant, embarrassed laughter?

When I told this joke to a group of students (most of them Americans), all of them laughed; but one, a woman from Kazakhstan, although laughing, buried her face in her hands. Why did she do so? Was she embarrassed, or ashamed, by the fact that she could laugh at such a scene? Or was she more sensitive than the others and could not face the horror of the scene? Was she scared by the sudden emergence of another world, the monsters of an alien world?

Dozens of books and hundreds, if not thousands, of studies have tried to solve the enigma of jokes. Let me discuss here only the ideas of Freud (1938), who wrote one of the best studies in this field.[3]

Freud and Jokes

At the beginning of his study Freud (1938, 661–63) argues that the "deviation of the trend of thought", or the "displacement of the stream of thought" is pleasant because to be consistent or logical requires a large amount of psychic energy.[4] By breaking the logic of the argument, jokes help us economize on psychic energy and we feel pleased if we succeed in doing so.

> It is quite obvious that it is easier and more convenient to turn away from a definite trend of thought than to stick to it; it is easier to mix up different things than to distinguish them; and it is particularly easier to travel over modes of reasoning unsanctioned by logic. (1938, 717)

This is a characteristic late-nineteenth-century idea. Freud himself will, at least partly, dismiss it at the end of his study. But we should not rule it out completely as a possible source of pleasure and laughter.

Later in his study, and relying on earlier theories of wit developed by Herbert Spencer and others, Freud distinguishes a large category of jokes as "tendency jokes", in which the switch between two levels takes place between a "higher" and a "lower" level. At the punch line, the train of thought suddenly and unexpectedly drops from a level of reality that stands higher in the social hierarchy of values to a lower one.[5] In our joke, it is a switch from the level of social relationships and feelings of love and loyalty to the level of material needs and their satisfaction.

In the second part of his study Freud develops his own, psychoanalytic theory of wit. If in the first part of the study he indicated the saving of psychic energy as the main source of pleasure and laughter, here he focuses much more on the liberating impact of jokes. He argues that jokes set a trap for us. They hide the illogical in the logical and thereby elude the control of reason, outwit the superego, and release, even if only for an instant, the repressed emotional and instinctual contents of the subconscious.[6] This brief release of control and the welling up of libidinal and aggressive energies is a delightful experience of liberation, and therefore we laugh.

In the concluding part of his study, Freud (1938, 719, 738) goes further and points out important parallels between jokes and childhood experience. He contends that the main function of wit and jokes may be to help people return to the world of childhood, a world of irrationality and incongruity, free of the control of logic and morality. Under the spell of a joke, "the adult again becomes a child who derives pleasure from the free disposal of his mental stream without being restricted by the pressure of logic". He relishes "the pleasure in 'freed nonsense'", which in adult life "rarely dares manifest itself". This relapse into the freedom of yore is pleasant and laughter is the physiological expression of this pleasure.

In the same way, Freud (1938, 761) points out similarities between jokes and dreams. They 'work' with the same, or similar, tools—displacement, condensation, brevity, indirect expression, and the like—and they both play a role in the psychological household of human beings. There are also important dissimilarities between them, however.

Despite its apparent unreality, the dream retains its relation to the great interests of life; it seeks to supply what is lacking through a regressive tour of hallucinations; and it owes its existence solely to the strong need for sleep during the night. Wit, on the other hand, seeks to draw a small amount of pleasure from the free and unencumbered activities of our psychic apparatus, and later to seize this pleasure as an incidental gain. It thus *secondarily* reaches important functions relative to the outer world. The dream serves preponderantly to guard against pain, while wit serves to acquire pleasure; in these two aims all our psychic activities meet.

With all my admiration for Freud's brilliant analysis of wit, I have to say that I disagree with his final conclusion. The formulation of its first half is dangerously misleading. Its second half misses its point or is simply mistaken.

THE COMIC DESTRUCTION OF REALITY

As far as dreams are concerned, in a trivial sense they do help us sleep and stay asleep. But their essential function is something else. It is to help us stay, not asleep, but alive. It is to help us resume our lives next morning.

Freud has shown better than anybody else the apocalyptic struggle we wage in our dreams with the monsters of the night, the monsters of our souls and the world. He has shown how dreams transform, curb, neutralize these destructive forces that keep invading our world. He has shown how dreams process those conflicts, tensions, frustrations that we experienced during the day and that threatened the peace of our souls.

In the terminology of the present book, he has shown how dreams reduce the stress of living in a dangerous world. He has shown how dreams fight the monsters of our subconscious—we have seen in Chapter Three that even our own psyche may become part of the 'alien world'—and how they regenerate in us the feeling that we are at home in this universe—that this is our world. What is really difficult in this world is not to sleep, but to live.

As far as jokes are concerned, Freud (1938, 761) concludes a long and brilliant analysis by stating—as we have seen—that jokes generate "a small amount of pleasure" and trigger off laughter by liberating the psychic apparatus from various repressive mechanisms, controls, and social routines. While dreams protect us against pain, "wit serves to acquire pleasure".

I think that in this conclusion Freud underestimates the role jokes (and the whole comic arsenal) play in our lives. Jokes do generate pleasure, but they also have another, latent, function which may be far more important. They do the same thing as dreams: they, too, are instruments or weapons in the fight against the threatening forces of the world; the 'alien world' outside, and within, us.

If mythologies, religions, and philosophies are the heavy weaponry, jokes are the light cavalry in this fight. They only touch upon, or flirt with, the alien world. They do not engage in frontal attacks against it. They break into it only for a fraction of a second and, the next moment, they escape back into the safety of our everyday world of time-tested routines.

This is an adventure, not without serious risks. Jokes experiment with the destruction of the basic structures of our human world. They blow up, just for a fleeting instant, the rational and causal structures of our universe; the system of social conventions and values; the moral codes and political hierarchies of our societies.

Logical jokes push us, for a brief moment, into the realm of the irrational and the absurd. Political jokes foray into the free and dangerous world of anarchy. Sexual jokes open up in us the delightful but dangerous world of instincts. Cynical, skeptical, and blasphemous jokes experiment with the destruction of decorum and truth, social values and institutions.[7]

If this is really the case we have to explain why we enjoy these risky excursions into the alien world; why we respond to them by laughing.

I shall come back to this problem later and shall argue that laughter is not always a sign of pleasure and happiness; that it is a much more complex and ambiguous phenomenon. But before doing so I shall attempt to show how the "comic destruction of the world" is brought about by jokes. First, I shall discuss the destruction of logic, and second, that of the causal structures of the world.

The Destruction of Logic

The first joke I quoted at the beginning of this chapter was a clear and simple example of how jokes lead us to a logical collision, an instantaneous embarrassment about whether we understand what we have heard or not, into nonsense which we cannot simply ignore since it seems to have some sense nevertheless. Let me give three examples, from the simple to the more complex; with the third joke we will literally crash into the realm of the irrational and absurd. The first comes from a play by Oscar Wilde, the two others from Freud's collection of jokes.

The first is a very simple witticism:

Charity, dear Miss Prism, charity! None of us are perfect. I myself am peculiarly susceptible to draughts. (Oscar Wilde, *The Importance of Being Earnest*)

Here, our train of thought is thrown off track at the last moment, by the last word, 'draughts'. Listening to what is being said, we think that the character is speaking of a moral flaw. But suddenly and unexpectedly we crash into something illogical, nonsensical, absurd: into the word 'draughts', which—according to the rules of our everyday logic—does not have anything to do with morality. For a brief instant we are perplexed and our perplexity is expressed by an embarrassed laughter.[8]

The second:

> A gentleman entered a shop and ordered a fancy cake, which, however, he soon returned, asking for some liqueur in its stead. He drank the liqueur, and was about to leave without paying for it. The shopkeeper held him back. 'What do you want of me?' he asked. 'Please, pay for the liqueur,' said the shopkeeper. 'But I have given you the fancy cake for it.' 'Yes, but you have not paid for that either.' 'Well, neither have I eaten it.' (Freud, 1938, 666)

This joke also leads us by the nose into the world of nonsense; into a conflict with our rational, logical, and moral universe. For a moment, we enjoy the freedom of anarchy, irrationality, and amorality, but in the next instant we are in haste to get back to our world of no nonsense and of morality.

The third:

> Two Jews met on a train at a Galician railway station. 'Where are you traveling?' asked one. 'To Cracow,' was the reply. 'Now see here, what a liar you are!' said the first one, bristling. 'When you say that you are traveling to Cracow, you really wish me to believe that you are traveling to Lemberg. Well, but I am sure that you are really traveling to Cracow, so why lie about it?' (Freud, 1938, 707)

Here again we run into a maze of absurdities; into a world of contradictions and paradoxes; into a world where people lie when they tell the truth, while they should lie to tell the truth; a world where to be honest (not to lie) is to be dishonest; a world where breaking the rule is the rule. And so on. The logical course of the argument is broken again and again until we lose the thread and start laughing, both pleased and embarrassed:[9] pleased because, for a moment, we enjoy the collapse of the logical structures of our universe, and embarrassed because, the next instant, we become scared by the collapse of the logical structures of our universe.

The Destruction of Causality

We need, and at the same time suffer from, the causal order of our world. We could not live without it and we are imprisoned by it. It is an indispensable constituent of the human world; it is the supporter and structure of order in the cosmos. It makes planning, decision making, conscious and goal-oriented action possible. But it is also a cage, a jail; it limits our freedom. It enslaves us in a world of determinism. To disrupt it, to blow it up, is a delightful, liberating experience. At least for a fleeting moment. But again: its lack is terrifying. If it ceased to work, the chaos of the alien world would engulf us. Our problem is that we have to build a human world where there is predictable, causal order and, at the same time, we wish to escape, again and again, from the iron grip of this causal order.

Jokes and other genres of comedy thrive on this ambiguity of causality in our world and lives. They help us jump out of this order for a brief instant and then they help us return to the safety of our world of order. Let me illustrate this with the example of animated cartoon punch lines.[10]

There can be no doubt whatsoever that cartoon punch lines attack the causal structure of our world with great vehemence and reckless ingenuity. They go out of their way to disturb, derail, or upset the automatic cause-and-effect linkages of our thinking. Let me give some characteristic examples.

CAUSE → unexpected EFFECT

In a famous cartoon series Gus, the clown-hero, is much too lazy to get up and uses a boomerang to angle for his newspaper lying in the hall: he throws the boomerang (CAUSE), which flies toward the newspaper, circles over it, seems to be about to pick it up (intended EFFECT), but only continues to circle over it and in the end sweeps the jars off the shelf (unexpected EFFECT 1) and then, breaking through the window, leaves the apartment (unexpected EFFECT 2).[11]

CAUSE → the opposite of the EFFECT expected

Hardluck Harry, another cartoon hero, tries to pick up a horseshoe he has caught sight of in a bush, because a horseshoe (CAUSE) brings luck (+ EFFECT). However, in this case the horseshoe happens to be still attached to the hoof of a horse grazing in the bush, and the horse kicks poor Harry up into the air—that is, finding the horseshoe brings not good luck but hard luck (– EFFECT).

Interchange of CAUSE and EFFECT

This occurs, for example, in a Walt Disney cartoon in which Donald Duck, as captain of a ship, tries to raise the anchor lodged in the seabed with the help of a winch and in his earnest efforts does not notice that, instead of hauling up the anchor, he is pulling down, and so sinking, the ship, together with the winch and himself (from being the subject who CAUSES the action Donald Duck becomes the object who suffers the EFFECT of the action).

The CAUSE changes yet the EFFECT remains the same

A lion tamer performs the usual stunt:
    First: He opens the mouth of the lion and puts his head into it; after the show he bows (CAUSE) → the audience applauds (EFFECT).
    Second: Again, head in, head out, bow (CAUSE) → applause (EFFECT).
    Third: Head in, the lion bites off the lion tamer's head, the lion gracefully bows to the audience (a new CAUSE) → the audience applauds (the same EFFECT).

CAUSE → exaggerated EFFECT

The absurd exaggeration of the effect may also break up the automatic relationship between cause and effect. A medieval knight wants to save the kidnapped princess (CAUSE), but when he has slain the dragon, hundreds of kidnapped princesses rush out of the dragon's cave and run after him, and he flees in panic, shouting "Help, I have won!" (multiple EFFECT).
    The world of motion pictures offers a classic example of this type of gag. Laurel and Hardy are building a house. When the house is finished the two builders look on, satisfied, and are waiting to be paid for their work. Meanwhile a small bird alights on the chimney (CAUSE), which trembles under its weight and begins to sway; finally the whole house collapses (a ludicrous disproportion between CAUSE and EFFECT).[12]

CAUSE and EFFECT reversed

One of the greatest burdens of life is that one cannot undo what has already occurred. Cartoons, however, consistently make a mockery of this iron law of reality. They triumph over causality and determinism by reversing the relationship, and direction, of cause and effect. They defeat the final irreversibility: death.

In cartoons everything is reversible and hence time, death, and causality lose their very essence, their 'sting'. The hero is struck down and he gets up; a brick falls on his head and he walks on; he is run over by a truck and flattened like a pancake but the next moment he resumes his original shape. Tom, chasing Jerry, runs into a huge pot which explodes into a thousand tiny pieces, but the next instant all the pieces graciously fall back in place and the pot resumes its original shape as if nothing had happened. And we, looking on, laugh happily. We are thrilled by, and enjoy, both the momentary dissolution, and the rebirth, of causal order.

And the thrill can be still further enhanced.

A Clown's Leap into Freedom

It may have been unintentional, yet it certainly was no coincidence that one of the most famous European cartoon heroes was named Gus, Gustave, or Auguste, which is the French name for the naive and hapless circus clown (as opposed to the Mephistophelean 'white clown').[13]

Clowns always try to be crafty, to trick others, but on the brink of success they tend to find themselves cast into the pit of failure. They think, with enormous self-confidence, that they know the laws governing the world and believe that they control the course of events. But, at the last moment, the strategies they have carefully built up collapse, they fall out of their logic into another logic in which they are not the victorious actors but the suffering objects of the action: they are the ones who land on their face, who get a kick in the behind; the water intended for others is poured over their heads, the fire-cracker they maliciously light burns their own pants. And we laugh at them, but this is not the laughter of superiority and condescension but that of sympathy.

We love them because they are free; they are free from the 'original sin' of selfishness that would injure others. They can harm only themselves. In their simplemindedness they are the only members of the human race who can never assert their own selfish will. They are the only adult persons who are comically or tragically unable to handle the cause–effect relationships that would give them control over other people and the world. They are the very symbols of the tragic and/or comic incompatibility between the human being and the world.

In their clumsiness they keep stumbling out of the logic of rational action, they move back and forth between the rational and the irrational, the possible and the impossible, the predetermined and the accidental.

Jokes, cartoons, and clowns play, experiment, or frolic with the accidental, the fortuitous—with chance. They jump, or fall, out of our safe world of rationality and causality: they jump, or fall, over into the unknown, the free; into a no-man's-land.

They are like trapeze artists, who start the show by swinging to and fro, emphasizing the interaction of human efforts and the laws of physics. And then, suddenly, they let the bar (and the causal order) go and begin to fly and spin in a space 'free of causality' (we have always considered flying as the symbol of freedom from the laws of the physical world). Seeing this flight, people experience the ecstasy, and also the thrill and danger, of breaking away from this world, into the realm of the fortuitous, the dangerous, the alien. And then, the next instant, they sigh with relief seeing that the acrobat catches hold of the other trapeze and re-enters the safety of our everyday world with its familiar system of calculable causes and effects.

The show is still more effective if it is performed by a clown acrobat who is hair-raisingly clumsy on the first trapeze, then, as if by accident, he lets go of it and wriggles in the air with comic desperation, until finally, again as if by accident, he catches hold of the other trapeze. Frightened by the flight into another world, through a dangerous alien world, and happy with his lucky escape, he mops his brow—and we laugh. Why?

Flirting with the Alien World

Something similar happens in a famous scene from Chaplin's *Modern Times*, in which he, blindfolded, roller-skates on a platform on the top floor of a department store, unprotected by rails, making beautiful curves, with complete nonchalance, carried away by the experience, in beatific innocence and irresponsibility, totally unaware of the danger that with each curve he gets nearer the edge of the platform and risks falling down into its abyss.

This is one of the most effective scenes ever filmed, provoking laughter and thrills at the same time. It has been interpreted and reinterpreted in several different ways. Within the present argument it could be discussed as another way of challenging the causal order of our world. A beautiful and seemingly innocent but slightly wider curve would trigger off a terrible chain reaction: an inch more and he would fall over the edge of the platform down into the precipice and destroy himself: a trivial CAUSE leading to an apocalyptic EFFECT. The scene could also be interpreted as teasing the powerful cause–effect mechanism: with each widening curve the causal mechanism is ready to snap and destroy its victim, who escapes the trap, again and again, by the skin of his teeth. We flirt here with nonexistence, with being annihilated, with something beyond our world, with an 'alien world'.[14]

Do we enjoy the thrill of it? Why do we laugh when we see the comic hero drop out of his everyday world? And why do we laugh when he finally notices the pit and, panic-stricken, tries to get away from the edge of the precipice and crawl back to the safety of our everyday world?[15]

In his famous book on laughter, Henri Bergson (1911) discusses the phenomenon with a simple example. An elegant man is walking in the street. He suddenly slips on the skin of a banana and falls. We, who have witnessed the scene, burst out laughing. Why? Do we gloat over him? Do we take delight in his shame? Do we take an aggressive pleasure in his defeat? According to Bergson we enjoy and, at the same time, abhor the sight of his falling. In the first fraction of a moment we enjoy it and laugh since it is ludicrous to see somebody fall from his dignified role as an honorable citizen (both Spencer and Freud would agree). But the next instant, we take fright at the sight of somebody being suddenly transformed from an autonomous and free human being into a puppet or object at the mercy of blind physical forces.

Let us go through the experience once more. A man is walking in the street as an autonomous human being, free to decide where he goes, what he does; he is master of himself. In the instant he slips, he loses not only his equilibrium but also his autonomy, his freedom, his dignity as a person. The forces of the physical world burst through the surface of human civilization and pull him down into their own realm, where there is no human freedom, no autonomy, no dignity. This is like a horror film in which the aliens suddenly break into our world and pull us down into the abyss of the unknown, the non-human, the horrific. And our laughter turns into a shriek of terror.[16]

We could even say that in this simple, everyday scene we experience the collapse of the human world, of human civilization, with its protective spheres of human dignity and freedom, decorum and autonomy, which has been laboriously built up throughout history and which we painstakingly reinforce and maintain throughout our lives.

Laughter and Terror

Laughter is a complex phenomenon. When we laugh at a joke, a cartoon gag, or the stunt of a clown–acrobat hurling himself about in the air and all but missing the trapeze, we go through a wide variety of experiences.

Under the impact of the joke, for a fraction of an instant, when the punch line hits us, we are confused by the absurdity of the situation and laugh embarrassedly. At the same time, we enjoy the experience of being liberated from the oppressive rules and norms of reason and logic, the physical universe and society, and we laugh the laughter of liberation. The next moment, we luxuriate in the lush jungle of the instinctual, the irrational, or the anarchic, and we laugh for pleasure. However, after a brief moment, we take fright at the chaotic and unknown forces of the jungle and are in haste to return to our everyday world of rules and order, routines and discipline. Being back in the safe grounds of our everyday lives and civilization, we look back at, and dismiss, what we have experienced as something absurd, nonsensical, irrelevant. And we laugh from a sense of relief.

"No nonsense with nonsense, please! ... humor is a serious business!", a famous Hungarian humorist once remarked, and he was right.[17] Jokes, gags, and clowns play with fire; they flirt with the alien world. They catapult us, for a fraction of an instant, outside our world, but let us escape back to safety the next instant. To listen to a joke or a gag, or to watch a clown–acrobat's stunt, is like riding a roller coaster. First, when we begin to roll downhill, we start laughing, as if we were tickled, and we experience the ecstasy of freedom. As we accelerate and more and more get the feeling that we are falling out of our world, our laughter goes over into a hysterical shriek. Then, the next instant, our free fall is slowed down by a graceful curve in our trajectory; we triumphantly return to our everyday world and laugh, relieved. What would happen in case of an accident? If the rush of the coaster were not stopped? If we were running to our destruction? If it were not merely a joke that boys eat their younger brothers for lunch? If the comic impact—the essence of which is to be ephemeral—were to prolong itself and stay with us? It would be horrendous.

Jokes, gags, and clowns, however, are merciful. After the surprise trip through a strange and alien world, they let us return to our own world. They remind us of the fragility of our civilization, which we have constructed and maintain with so much care and zeal. They remind us of the unknown and fearful depths of our existence and our universe, but just for a moment, and then let us go. They only flirt with the alien world, and so strengthen our civilization.

NOTES

1 Medieval theologians raised the question "whether Christ ever laughed", as Hugo Rahner (1965, 37) reminds us in his book on play. He refers to Theodor Haecker, according to whom humor "constitutes the real human background of the civilization of European Christendom" (Rahner, 1965, 35).
2 Lukes and Galnoor (1985, x) describe the same process in the following way: "Their effects, when successful, always seem to include some flash of recognition and illumination ... caused by an abrupt switch of a train of thought to a different track."
3 Among the innumerable studies on jokes and laughter, let me mention only two fascinating essays: one is in German, Plessner (1950), the other in English, Koestler (1964, 25–97).
4 In a long chapter entitled 'The Technique of Wit', Freud (1938, 639–87) examines a whole arsenal of deviating instruments: mixed words, condensation of two words in one, double meanings, plays on words, puns, nonsense, sophistic and faulty thinking, automatic errors of thought, representation through the opposite, indirect expression by allusion, omission, and so on.

Schopenhauer interpreted the role of incongruity in a radically different way. According to him we laugh at the incongruity of jokes because we find it amusing that speculative rationality acts confusedly, makes blunders, and proves incapable of grasping concrete, lifelike reality (of which only sensory learning and, ultimately, "contemplation" is capable).
5 According to Herbert Spencer (1946, *passim*) "descending incongruity" is always and necessarily present in jokes; it is an incongruity which transports the human psyche from a level of reverence, greatness, solemnity, or generality to a level demanding less spiritual energy (such as the level of triviality, smallness, ordinariness, or uniqueness), and the surplus spiritual energy thus freed finds an outlet in laughter and in the intense movements accompanying it.
6 In political jokes, for instance, oppressive social discipline, censorship, self-censorship, and fear are outwitted by the joke machinery.
7 "In the first case [obscene wit] it overcomes the inhibitions of shame and decorum ... In the second case [aggressive wit] it overthrows the critical judgment ... In the third and fourth cases [cynical and skeptical wit] ... it shatters the respect for institutions and truths in which the hearer had believed" (Freud, 1938, 723).

8 Several other wheels of the joke-machinery already mentioned are also turning in this joke. Running parallel with our embarrassment, we also enjoy our sudden escape from the cage of our everyday logic and routines, and laugh for joy. Furthermore, the sudden switch-over from the level of moral decorum to that of everyday trivialities (like catching cold) liberates us, for an instant, from the oppressive control of our moral inhibitions and we laugh from relief.

9 'You know that I know that you will want to cheat me and therefore you lie to me by telling me the truth. You say that you are going to Cracow to make me believe that you are going to Lemberg, while in fact you plan to go to Cracow.'

10 I shall take my examples mainly from European animated cartoons.

11 The humorous impact is increased by delaying the climax. The moment we see the jars, we know what will happen, but the boomerang continues to circle slowly and majestically before, at long last, it shatters the jars. This delayed effect is a favorite trick of animated cartoonists.

12 This is a favorite motive in American cartoons as well. Remember all those cartoons in which some trivial thing causes enormous destruction reaching almost apocalyptic dimensions. The final big chase scenes in Walt Disney's or Hanna and Barbera's burlesques teem with such chain reactions of destruction, in the course of which the order of causal relations is crushed.

13 See Fellini's charming film, *The Clowns*.

14 Lukes and Galnoor (1985, xii), too, stress the underlying presence of anxiety in jokes, though they discover a 'boundary situation' only in black humor: "Black or 'gallows' jokes come close to the boundary on the other side of which one finds alienation, total despair and self-hate."

15 In contrast to the tragic borderline situation frequently referred to by the existentialists, here we are dealing with a 'comic borderline situation'. The clown does not jump, but falls, into the precipice of freedom (or destruction).

16 Let me remind the reader of the dual mask of dramatic art, which looks in two opposite directions: one of the faces laughs, the other is distorted in a tragic grimace. What do they have in common? Are they not two extremes, each excluding the other? They are and, at the same time, they are not. We have all experienced how easily laughter turns into crying, and how often tears brighten up into a happy smile. Despite a basic contradiction, comedy and tragedy, laughter and tears have somewhere, deep in the human soul, a common source. In the terminology of this book I would say that jokes flirt with an alien world, while tragedies experiment with a complete and open confrontation with it.

17 Frigyes Karinthy, Hungarian humorist (1887–1938). Lukes and Galnoor (1985, x) quote Mark Twain in this context: "'A German joke', Mark Twain once said, 'is no laughing matter'. Not only is this in itself a good political joke, it also captures one central theme of this collection: that joking about politics is a serious, often deadly serious business."

Chapter Twelve

THE WORLD OF TRIVIALITIES

> Trivialities are sometimes not trivial at all.

In this chapter we discuss a contemporary mythology, the mythology of perfumes, a system of feelings and beliefs, ideas and symbols created by the advertising industry. In the course of this analysis it turns out that even trivialities may be indispensable building blocks of civilization.

Vanity fair is not a fair of vanities. It is not a fair of frivolous and unimportant things. Vanities may be a deadly serious matter. So much so that instead of *vanitatum vanitas* we should rather talk of *vanitatum gravitas*—the importance and seriousness of vanities. They, too, play a crucial role in building around us protective spheres which help us survive in an alien world.

In the course of history, people have surrounded themselves not only with idyllic gardens and city walls, cathedrals and football domes, myths and religions, but also with a shining cloud of vanities.

In order to show that vanities are not trivialities, I have chosen as an example something which was born in the very heart of our vanities. I shall argue that even perfumes, and the mythology created by and around perfumes, have played an important role in our age-long, and contemporary, struggle for meaning, safety, and freedom. They have helped us build our civilization.

PERFUMES AND THE HOLY GRAIL

Scents may be pleasant, even delightful. The world would certainly be a much less agreeable place to live in without them. But in themselves, in their natural state, they would play only a modest role in our lives. However, if and when they are transformed into 'fragrances', they may gather an almost transcendental power. How does this strange transubstantiation take place?

There is a simple answer. The magic may simply be due to chemistry. Recent experiments have shown that various scents may exert a strong and direct impact on our psyche. They play with our emotions and subconscious practically uncontrolled. They may accelerate and slow down our heartbeat. They may make us feel happy or unhappy. Menthol, eucalyptus, and cypress are stimulants; lavender, chamomile, cinnamon, rosemary, and lemon have, on the contrary, a soothing, tension-releasing effect. Orange reduces anxiety; musk-nut oil and musk rose reduce stress. Peppermint helps concentration; and a wide range of scents have a strong 'sex-appeal' or even aphrodisiac effect. Scientists at Duke University are reported to be experimenting with scents that may reduce aggression, while Estée Lauder and Shiseido are allegedly working on the development of a scent that would boost optimism. A whole aroma-industry has grown up called 'aromochology'. Laboratories and aroma firms are making huge profits by pumping and spraying various scents in department stores, boutiques, offices, hospital wards, or casinos to trigger off the right response in shoppers (to buy more), employees (to work more), patients (to relax), and gamblers (to risk more).[1]

However, this is only part of the answer. Beyond a chemical procedure, scents also have to go through a mythological transformation. They must be transubstantiated into a magic liquid which has the power of creating a new and shining micro-universe for human beings. This is a sophisticated, archetypal process. Gilbert Durand (1969), the famous French anthropologist, describes myths in which a stormy sea that is on the point of engulfing the hero and his ship is suddenly and miraculously transformed into crystalline, holy water in a chalice—or even into the blood of Christ in the Holy Grail—which the hero holds in his hands. In other words, a hostile and external world, surrounding human beings and threatening them with destruction, is transformed into something which they control and which even has redemptive power.

Perfumes, too, work according to this mythological principle. They are catalysts. They transform the world that surrounds us into the elixir of life. First, everything that is precious and friendly in our world—sunshine, flowers, the summer sky, beauty, youth, energy, innocence and sensuality, purity and maturity—are distilled into a fragrance. Then, as a second step, when the bottle is opened, the fragrance surrounds us with a protective sphere and creates around us a microcosm of safety and bliss, beauty and plenitude.

It must be as highly condensed, strong, and pure as a noble and old liquor. In most cases its color is golden yellow, radiant as an elixir of life, as the sunshine, as the precious essence of mature grapes. The bottle should be, and in most cases is, transparent, crystalline, shining with the brilliance of beauty, purity, and spirituality. The form of the bottle is also an important factor in the mythological transubstantiation. We shall look at a great number of examples.

When the bottle is opened, the fragrance may emerge, spread, and begin the enchantment. It must create a protective sphere, a micro-universe around us. How can it work this magic?

It could not do it by itself. Even the best perfumes would remain only a few fluid ounces of fragrant liquid in more or less well-shaped bottles. They would remain pleasant but not particularly significant substances, providing some brief moments of comfort but not doing much more than that. In order to be able to exert a magic power, first they have to be transformed by the spell of imagination, and by the mythology provided, consciously and unconsciously, by the creative artists of the advertising industry.

CREATION AND PLENITUDE

It has always been so important for human beings to believe that they are at home in this world that in a great number of creation myths they made themselves co-creators of the world. This wish has been so strong that it has led to a couple of powerful visions of creation, even in the world of perfumes. In one of the posters of Yves Saint Laurent's 'Y', for instance, a woman in black almost literally repeats one of the most majestic acts of creation, that of separating the darkness and the light. She is standing in the middle of the picture, raising her arms and pushing apart the black walls of darkness, while an exuberant light pours gloriously into our world.[2]

A great many posters and commercials also suggest that the world of perfumes which surrounds and protects us is a complete and harmonious universe in itself. This may be the reason for the frequency of sun and sky motifs. Dozens of golden perfumes are contained in sun-shaped bottles with transparent blue covers or stoppers symbolizing the sky or the spheres. Paloma Picasso's 'Mon Parfum' is a golden sun in the embrace of a dark and shining universe. The bottle of 'Vanderbilt' is a glorious sun and on its opaque and bluish stopper there is a swan radiating plenitude, harmony, and freedom. Van Cleef and Arpels' 'First' has a sun-like bottle, with a ring-shaped blue, transparent stopper, which may symbolize the infinity of the universe. Perry Ellis' '360', a perfume of golden color, fills a transparent spherical bottle, with a transparent round cover. Within this cover, there is a light blue, round stopper, a micro-universe within the greater universe, redoubling the feeling of safety and harmony.[3]

ICARIAN SYMBOLISM

Decay and death are major sources of our anxieties and sufferings. To liberate oneself from the bondage of earthly life, to defeat the laws of the physical world, to break away from the earth, has always been one of the most profound aspirations of humankind. Consequently, the symbols of flying, of soaring into the skies, of the sun, of arrows, spears, and rockets shooting up into the blue sky, of spires and skyscrapers pointing towards heaven, of shamans climbing up the Tree of Life and courageous men hiking snowy peaks of almost transcendental purity have always played an important role in our mythologies.[4] They have also found their way into the world of perfumes. The classic example is a poster for Giorgio's 'Wings', on which a young woman is jumping or flying up into the sky, while the text runs: 'Set your spirit free.'[5]

A 'JOOP' poster shows a young woman climbing up a ladder (remember the ladders of the shamans!), but, in order to enhance the Icarian effect, the ladder itself is flying; it is attached to a balloon which is soaring up into the sky. On other posters, the bottles themselves fly up as golden suns in a blue sky, evoking the bliss of escaping into transcendence and eternity.[6]

TRANSCENDENCE

The breaking away from the earth and material life has been developed almost into a cult of transcendence and celestial perfection. The names and slogans of a wide range of perfumes flash the concepts of infinity, perfection, or the sublime. Think, for instance, of Caron's 'Infini' and 'Parfum Sacré', Jean Patou's 'Sublime', Guy Laroche's 'Horizon', Dijon's 'Perfection', or L'Oréal's 'Plenitude'.

Other perfumes offer even more: the promise of a spiritual experience. They suggest that in the universe created by the fragrance one can get rid of the burdens of the material universe and discover one's spirituality. Nino

Cerruti offers 'a perfume for the soul', and Vanderbilt prompts his customer to 'Let it [the perfume] release your splendor'. Under the obvious impact of Nina Ricci's 'L'Air du Temps' a young woman is etherialized into an angelic being who, in her robe of tulle, fades away into the white and blue universe; the same transubstantiation is repeated visually by the perfume bottle itself. Another young woman on a poster for Nina Ricci's 'Nina', in a white lace robe, with long white handkerchiefs and a faraway look, is on the point of entering, like a modern Eurydice, the world of spirituality through a transparent white veil. The young woman of Estée Lauder's 'White Linen', clad in blissfully white linen, is absorbed in deep meditation in a white and blue Olympic setting.[7]

Spirituality is also suggested by the gleaming transparency of the bottles and by the deep, golden radiation of the perfume within them. In European civilization gold has always been the color and symbol of the sacred, the divine, the spiritual, and so its lavish use as the color of perfumes, stoppers, boxes, and posters, which are flooded with gold, adds to the spiritualization of the world of fragrances.

SPIRITUALITY AND SENSUALITY

In the world of perfumes, however, spiritual ecstasy comes close to the ecstasy of earthly love. Spirituality and sensuality transcend each other. As in Renaissance Neoplatonism, here too the spiritual is sensual and the sensual spiritual. This combination of spirituality and sensuality is an important element of the universe created by fragrances. It enhances the contrast between this universe and the real world, which lacks both spirituality and sensuality, and lacks even more the bliss of their combination. A poster for Lagerfeld's 'Chloé' is a classic example of this sophisticated, perverse, or Botticellian and innocent, combination of sensuality and spirituality. A beautiful woman is immersed in a state of dreamy contemplation, while her floating hair and sensuous limbs are dissolved in the soft white light of spirituality. This duality is enhanced by the fragrance bottle itself, which is sensuously round and full of rich, golden perfume, but through its opaquely white stopper, in the shape of wings, it transcends itself to attain spirituality.[8] If I add that there is a second layer of meaning, an opposite movement, from spirituality to deep, erotic, and narcissistic sensuality—with a woman of angelic beauty leaning over a phallic symbol (the stopper), which is reaching down into a symbol of femininity (the round bottle)—then it turns out that we have here a picture of almost artistic complexity and of a powerful and disturbing emotional attractiveness.[9]

SENSUALITY AND LOVE

There is also much sensuality in the world of perfumes. Many perfumes and posters suggest that this world is a luscious jungle of the senses and encourage initiates to surrender themselves to the pleasures of its voluptuousness. Elizabeth Arden's 'Sunflowers' "recharges the senses" and promises "a deep flowering of pleasure"; 'Venezia' would "seduce the senses"; Etienne Aigner's "Private Number" prompts us to "surrender to the senses"; while 'Asja' is an "Oriental empress of sensuality" and 'Opium' promises "sensuality to the extreme".

The world of perfume promises, instead of the rude and boring chores and routines of everyday love, the genuine love of tenderness or passion, or both. Cacharel's 'Anaïs, Anaïs' promises "all the tenderness of a perfume" (*toute la tendresse d'un parfum*), and 'Loulou' is a perfume which is a 'caress' (*quand le parfum se fait caresse*). Hermès' perfume is "a tender and stormy" 'Amazone' (*tendre et fougueuse amazone*), and the young woman on the poster of Guy Laroche's 'J'ai Osé' ("I dared"), standing, with large blue eyes, beside a panther with large blue eyes, is "as tender and savage as her perfume" (*tendre et sauvage comme son parfum*).

In other cases strong passions prevail. The world of perfume is, or may be, also the world of irresistible, blazing passions. This is suggested by Valentino's 'Vendetta', Dior's 'Poison', Calvin Klein's 'Obsession', Etienne Aigner's 'Explosive', Cacharel's 'Panthère', Dior's 'Eau Sauvage', or Elizabeth Taylor's 'Passion'. Oscar de la Renta's 'Volupte' encourages women to "Trust [their] senses", while 'Caliente' prompts them "to discover the rich, sexy, feel-good fragrance that sets your soul afire".

In a few cases, direct sexual symbols appear as well. Montana's perfume for women is contained in a bottle suggesting the curved shape of a woman, while the bottle of his perfume for men, with its pyramidal shape, is a stylized phallic symbol. The majority of bottles of perfumes for women suggest femininity with their rounded, curving lines, and in some cases become obvious, but artistic, symbols of female sexuality, as in the case of Margaretha Ley's 'Escada'.[10] There are a couple of perfumes which develop an almost perverse, but refined and highly artistic, sexual symbolism.[11]

Compare Chloé's 'Narcisse', for instance, which is a masterpiece of its genre. The transparent bottle shines and glitters with innocence and virginity. Yet the bottle also has the shape of an egg, which is a symbol of fertility. This symbolism is enhanced by the golden plenitude of the perfume within it. This opposition would be appealing in itself. But it is only part of the story. The stopper of the bottle is a beautiful flower, opening its white, opaque calyx, another symbol of female sexuality. And even this is not enough. There is a green stamen in the calyx, the filament of which reaches deep down into the liquid within the egg, linking, in this way, the two symbols of sexuality and fertility, the egg and the flower. If we add that, from a particular perspective, caught in several posters for this perfume, a meandering line on the bottle seems to spiral up around the green filament of the stamen, like the snake around the Tree of Knowledge in the Garden of Eden in medieval iconography, then we have to acknowledge that here we encounter a masterly combination of the motifs of innocence and loss of innocence, and several symbols of sexuality and fertility. Those posters for the same perfume which portray young men and women in passionate intimacy do not add much to, and may even reduce, the impact of this rich symbolism.

Bad taste is a rare exception in the world of spiritual sensuality, elegance, and beauty. Usually the allusions are refined and discreet. One of the advertisements for Elizabeth Arden's 'Red Door'—on which the red cover of the bottle opens and the perfume spurts out of it—is close to becoming one of these exceptions.[12] In the world of perfumes for men, sexual symbolism is more direct and sometimes shockingly explicit. Take, for instance, Pierre Cardin's 'Pour Monsieur', which is a rude phallic symbol. One of its posters goes even farther, showing a young man standing, with elegant nonchalance, within this phallic symbol.

ESCAPE FROM TIME AND MORTALITY

Decay, death, and the agonizing evanescence of time constitute one of the major sources of our anxieties in this world. As we have seen in previous chapters, one of the main functions of human civilization is to protect people against these anxieties. Perfumes, too, play a role. They offer an escape and create a new universe around us, in which there is no decay and no death; in which time is meaningful and life is eternal. The world of perfumes is full of life symbolism, including sun-shaped bottles and golden fragrances. Other kinds of life symbol abound. Elizabeth Arden's

'Sunflowers' is a "celebration of life"; Givenchy's 'Amarige' is a "celebration of laughter, love and happiness"; and Estée Lauder's perfume is called 'Youth Dew'. Others offer the delight of life, like 'C'est la Vie', or Jean Patou's 'Joy'; and the happy and beautiful young women and men in the posters have the same message for us.

Perfumes offer rebirth to a new life. Perry Ellis' '360' prompts and helps you to change your life: "Life is how you change it." Lanvin's 'Clair de Jour' not only announces "The Eau de Toilette of New Mornings" (*L'Eau de Toilette des Nouveaux Matins*), but also creates a fascinating vision of rebirth, showing a blue and infinite ocean, with the bottle of fragrance rising in the morning haze like a glorious sun, and a young woman, in a trance, ready to give herself to the Sun God or to the new light (or simply doing her morning exercises).

Mortality is also defeated by the power of perfume to transform the empty and evanescent time of the real world simultaneously into magnificent eternity and meaningful and intense moments. Calvin Klein's perfume is 'Eternity' itself, while Chopard's 'Casmir' is "the magic of the moment".[13] Finally, Scherrer's 'Perfume' wins the prize by synthesizing the meaningful moment and eternity. It promises both "the passion of the moment" and the Faustian "eternal feminine" (*La passion du moment. L'éternel féminin*).

ESCAPE FROM EVERYDAY LIFE

Perfumes may also offer women an escape from the boredom, vulgarity, and emptiness of their everyday world. They suggest, with a wealth of allusions, that the world of perfumes is a world of exotic mysteries and pleasures. Mystery is offered by 'Mystère' and 'black magic' by 'Magie Noire'.[14] Under the spell of the fragrance, a woman suddenly finds herself in the twilight world of the most exotic Oriental queens, goddesses, and mysteries; in the world of 'Anaïs Anaïs', 'Samsara', 'Shalimar', 'Yatis', or 'Amarige'. She finds herself in the 'Byzance' of Rochas, the 'Indian Nights' of Scherrer, or in the court of 'Asja' (Fendi), "the Oriental empress of sensuality", who gives her a guidebook introduction to this exotic world: "The Orient is fascination, mystery, magic and ancient traditions. An enchanted world, rich in colorful suggestions and intense sensations."[15]

The same wish to escape from a world of harsh realities is served by suggesting that fragrances create an enchanted world of dreams and fantasies. Elizabeth Taylor's 'White Diamonds' is the "fragrance dreams are made of", and Ted Lapidus' 'Fantasme' opens the mysterious world of the unconscious: "The unconscious has its perfume" (*L'inconscient a son parfum*).[16]

THE EPIPHANY OF PERSONALITY

In her everyday life, a woman (the same is true, of course, of men) often struggles with uncertainties and doubts about herself. Her identity may be blurred, her self-esteem undermined. She may not find her genuine role and identity, her true personality. The world of perfumes promises an easy and quick recovery from this state of anxiety and malaise. Under the spell of the perfume, within the shining, protective sphere it creates, she undergoes a profound metamorphosis. She all of a sudden becomes beautiful and elegant, pure and fresh, innocent and voluptuous, divine and immortal, free and happy, the object of glowing passions and tenderness.

Molineux's 'Quartz', for example, liberates her from her complexes—after all, it is an "*Eau de parfum* without complexes" (*L'eau de parfum sans complexe*). Daniel Hechter offers her 'Caractère' and Jil Sander's 'Background' exhorts her to "discover your background". Slava Zaitsev's 'Maroussia' prompts her to become a "new woman" and to discover her "new self" (*Eine Frau entdeckt ihr neues Ich!*). Jil Sander's 'Parfum No. 4' helps her to be "the spirit of her time". Montana's perfume prepares her for 'Success'. Hermès' fragrance makes her feel like an 'Amazone'. Ungaro's 'Diva' lends her the glamour of a star or a goddess, while Thierry Mugler's perfume transforms her into an 'Angel', or a 'femme fatale'. It warns us: "Beware of angels ..." (*Méfiez-vous des anges ...*). Finally, Gres' 'Cabotine' encourages her to be herself in almost Nietzschean terms: "I am as I am" (*Je suis comme je suis*).[17]

In the world of perfumes she may feel herself as elegant as the jet set in 'Roma' and 'Paris' (Fendi, Biagiotti), or the sophisticated crowd on the 'Rive Gauche' (Yves Saint Laurent).[18] She may feel relaxed as Giulio's 'Nonchalance' and as beautiful as the legion of dazzling young women in the advertisements, or like Estée Lauder's 'Beautiful'. She may feel herself to be wise, like Estée Lauder's 'Knowing', and as fresh as 'White Linen', or the "fresh" 'JOOP', and the "clean and classic" 'NAVY'.

Above all, she may feel herself to be a real woman. She is prompted to be as capricious and tempting as Chanel's 'Coco' or Cacharel's 'Loulou'; to be suavely and "overwhelmingly feminine" like Fendi's 'Asja'; voluptuous and crazy like Krizia's 'Krazy' (playing chess with a panther); "tender and savage" like Guy Laroche's 'J'ai Osé'; full of dreams and fantasies like the young woman of Azzaro's '9'; or irresistibly elegant, unapproachably seductive, and eternally feminine like Jean-Louis Scherrer's model. Challenging the real world, in which life is often neurotic, loveless, and unfeeling, perfumes create a micro-universe around her, where she is encouraged to love not only her partner, but also herself. The world of fragrances is a feminine world where she may feel herself at home. She may almost identify with these beautiful and sparkling bottles, the round and curving forms of which suggest femininity.[19] By portraying women caressing themselves, as on the poster of Ted Lapidus' 'Fantasme' and many others,[20] the narcissistic character of this world is enhanced even further. The frequent appearance in perfume ads of twins, or women looking at their reflection in a mirror, has the same effect.[21] The act of spraying, with which she wraps herself in a cloud of perfume and encloses herself in the enchanted sphere of the fragrance, has a narcissistic side. The bottles with glass stoppers are less sophisticated technically but perhaps more sophisticated psychologically. With the stopper she has only to touch herself and the magic is done: she is transformed into a goddess who is protected by her own radiant divinity.

DELUSION OR CREATION?

Is this creation of the mythological world of perfumes nothing other than the calculated and cynical strategy of the creative artists and publicity managers of the perfume laboratories who want to dupe women (and men) into buying their brands?

There can be no doubt that they eagerly and systematically search for visual and verbal motif which may have a strong emotional appeal for potential buyers. It may be enlightening, however, to refer in this context to Carl Jung, who once noticed that it was not Goethe who wrote Faust, but Faust who 'wrote Goethe'—meaning that, due to the poet's extraordinary sensitivity, the Faustian archetype (the eternal, and eternally failing, human aspiration to perfection and perfect happiness) could emerge from the collective consciousness and guide Goethe's hand in recreating Faust's legend. It would be too flattering to say that designers and publicity managers have the same sensitivity and are able to tap the rich resources of archetypes. But they do search for motifs that may mobilize powerful emotions in people, and such motifs will often have their roots in the hidden sphere of archetypes. If they drew more on this submerged world of powerful emotions and common human experience, they might considerably strengthen the impact of their publicity campaigns.

May we say, after all, that women (and men in another way) are deluded by this mythology of fragrances? Are they duped by the creators of perfumes? Yes and no. They are, because this is an artificial world, a world of illusions and fantasy, dreams and nostalgia. And they are not if this world of illusions and fantasy helps them feel happy, free, strong, and at home in this universe. If it fills their lives with meaning and harmony. If it helps them discover their true selves and explore new possibilities.

Trivialities are sometimes not trivial at all. They are indispensable constituents of our civilization; of a civilization that surrounds us with its symbolic spheres and protects us against our fears and anxieties in an alien world.

NOTES

1 International Flavors and Fragrances in New York; Test and Smell Treatment and Research Foundation (Chicago); Takasago (Tokyo); Haarmann and Reimer (Germany); and so on.
2 Torrente's 'Perfume' repeats, in a more static way, the same separation of light and darkness, while Ted Lapidus is more direct and matter-of-fact when he names his perfume simply 'Creation'.
3 See also Lanvin's 'Clair de Jour', Giorgio's 'Wings', Montana's 'Perfume', Guerlin's 'Shalimar', or Priscilla Presley's 'Experiences'. There are also more complex solutions. Boucheron's 'Women's Line', has a ring-shaped bottle, filled with golden perfume surrounding a dark universe, and has a transparent violet stopper.
4 Jung, Bachelard, Ricoeur, Eliade, Durand, and others discuss these symbols in detail.
5 The TV ad redoubles the Icarian symbolism: the woman first runs up a spiraling staircase (first Icarian motif) and then jumps from the top of the staircase (second Icarian motif).
6 'Wings', 'JOOP', and so on. The wing-shaped stoppers evoke the flight into freedom and eternity (Lagerfeld's 'Chloé', Nina Ricci's 'L'Air du Temps', Vanderbilt's 'Vanderbilt'). The monogram of Yves Saint Laurent's 'Y' perfume is in itself an Icarian symbol. Similarly, the conic bottles of Fendi's 'Eau d'Issey', Hayman's '273', or the Eiffel Tower on the poster of Yves Saint Laurent's 'Paris', where flying doves enhance the same Icarian symbolism even further.
7 The woman of Fendi's 'La Passione di Roma' gives, in a platonic rapture, a kiss to a Greek or Roman god in white marble. And many other perfumes feature women who, under the spell of a perfume, are in a serene trance of spirituality ('Amarige', 'Eternity', 'Fragrant Jewels', 'Chloé', 'Azzaro 9', 'Lalique', 'L'Air du Temps', 'Trésor', and so on).

8 Nina Ricci's 'L'Air du Temps' uses almost the same symbolism.
9 'Iceberg Femme' combines the principles of spirituality and sensuality in a different way. The name evokes the mysterious silence and purity of icebergs, and the sharp, clear edges and facets of the bottle suggest purity, discipline, and spirituality, while the round, purple stopper suggests sensuality and passion. Aramis' 'Tuscany' refers to the same duality when it quotes Dante: "It draws the fire to the Moon".

Elizabeth Taylor's 'White Diamonds' combines the two principles by identifying the perfume with jewels. "Brilliance, splendor, a rich sensual fragrance. Endless brilliance of a rare jewel." Jewels, and especially diamonds, have this duality in themselves. They have the pureness and brilliance of spirituality, but, at the same time, a deep fire burns within them. This is a "cold fire", however, combining the serene coolness of spirituality with the fire of human passions. See also Revlon's new 'Fire and Ice' ("Play with fire, skate on thin ice").

The perfume in the bottle has this same duality. The transparent bottle glistens like a jewel—it is frequently cut like a diamond or a crystal (Azzaro's 'Oh Lala', Yves Saint Laurent's 'Paris', or Van Cleef and Arpels' 'Van Cleef')—while the golden perfume within it has a deep, sensuous radiation. Designers fully exploit this affinity between perfumes and jewels. Tiffany's 'Tiffany' is a "jewel for the senses", Boucheron's 'Women's Line' is "more than a perfume, a jewel", Van Cleef and Arpels' perfume is a 'Gem', and Lancôme's perfume a 'Trésor'. (This identification has, of course, a more prosaic, and less mythological, reason as well. By associating the perfumes in the minds of their clients with precious and costly jewels, producers can charge several times more than the production costs of their fragrances.)
10 The bottle of Ted Lapidus' 'Fantasme', with its soft concentric lines and longish, pointed stopper, is a combination of female and male symbolism.
11 Dijan's perfume for women, for instance, in its ring-shaped bottle with a ring-shaped stopper, is a dual symbol of femininity. His perfume for men, on the other hand, contained in a ring-shaped bottle, but with a full, round stopper has a discreet bisexual symbolism. The clear and highly stylized lines of the bottles save them from any trace of vulgarity.
12 Another advertisement for the same perfume—which portrays the bottle with the key and a young woman in a seductive position, with the invitation: "Open it"—is only slightly more discreet.
13 Laura Biagiotti's 'Roma' is a "breath of eternity", while Elizabeth Taylor's 'White Diamonds' promises "endless brilliance". On the other hand, Lancôme's 'Trésor' is "the perfume of precious instants"; Dior's 'Dune' is "a moment of dream"; and Yves Saint Laurent's 'Y' is "a fragrance for moments of intense emotion".
14 Remember also "the magic of the scent" of 'Noa Noa' (Otto Kern); the "pure charisma" of 'Parfum No. 4' (Jil Sander); or "the secret scents of the forests of Mysore" of the perfume of Roger and Gallet. 'JOOP' goes even further by promising a whole drama of initiation into the world of mystery: "Fresh at first, the fragrance deepens into an expression of mystery, sensuality and allure."

15 *L'Oriente è fascino, mistero, magia e antiche tradizioni. Un mondo incantato, ricco di suggestioni colorate e di sensazioni intense ...*
16 Perfumes also offer an escape into the past, into the world of romantic secrets of 'Incognito' (Cover Girl), where "intrigue never ends"; where 'L'Effleur' helps us "discover romance in all its fragrant forms"; and 'Petit Point' (Wiener Bouquet) brings us back to the Rococo or Biedermeier world of lace and bouquets. Music and dance, 'Jazz' (Yves Saint Laurent), 'Samba Nova' (Mambo), and 'Rumba' (Babor) complete the magic of this world. Even more poetically, a fragrance may be music and dream at once, like Muelhen's 'My Melody Dreams', or it may become, in a mystical and divine way, the "melody of time" itself, like Nina Ricci's 'L'Air du Temps'.
17 'Cabotine' in French is a woman full of life, caprice, and exuberance.
18 The Left Bank, traditionally the seat of Paris intellectual life.
19 Like, for example, Estée Lauder's 'Beautiful' or Ungaro's 'Diva', which are shaped like busts; Ungaro's 'Senso', which is like a woman's body in a pleated dress; or the bottle of 'Escada', already mentioned, which strongly suggests the sensuous lines of female hips.
20 'Eau de Rochas', Ungaro's Eau de Toilette, Givenchy's 'Amarige', Carolina Herrera's 'Flore', and so on.
21 Max Factor's 'Geminesse', which invites you to "reflect the other you"; Cacharel's 'Anaïs Anaïs'; Lillie Rubins' 'Perfume'; Alberta Ferretti's 'Femina'; and so on.

CHAPTER THIRTEEN

SYMBOLS AND CIVILIZATION

> "True, we need hope ... But we do not need more, and we must not be given more. We do not need certainty."
>
> Karl Popper, *The Open Society and Its Enemies*

I HAVE argued that existential fear is one of the main generative forces of human civilization. It seems to play a much more important role in this process than is usually assumed by social scientists. To protect themselves against the threats of an 'alien world', and against their own fears and anxieties, human beings and communities surround themselves with systems of symbols. The constellation of these symbolic systems is one of the main components of human civilization.[1]

I hope that I have shown convincingly that studying human civilizations from the angle of this hypothesis sheds new light on its various aspects. The hypothesis explains the importance and the amazing survival of myths even in high-tech contemporary societies. It puts the major myths of various civilizations—the myth of centrality, the myth of the morality and rationality of the universe, and so on—in a new light. It reinterprets the cosmic drama of guilt and redemption; the role of the arts, play, and jokes; and even the paraphernalia of our contemporary consumer civilization. It helps us better understand how civilizations come about and how they function.

Before concluding this book, however, let me check our hypothesis once more. Can we prove that symbols and symbolic systems do 'protect' people against the dangers of the world and against their own anxieties and fears; and that this protection is the primary function of the symbolic structures of civilizations? The answer depends on how we define the concepts of 'symbol' and 'protection'.

CAN SYMBOLS PROTECT US?

In everyday language—but also in the social sciences—there is a certain confusion about the use of the term 'symbol'. There are disciplines which use the terms 'sign' and 'symbol' interchangeably. Others make a clear distinction between the two, using 'sign' for something which stands for or denotes something else, and 'symbol' when a primary sign is used to refer to, or suggest, a further, secondary meaning. The word 'rose', for instance, is a sign that refers to a concrete flower or species of flower (to the flower as an object or concept); however, when we employ the word, or the concept, or the flower itself, to indicate or suggest, for instance, love, or beauty, or the mystery of existence, we are using it as a symbol. In this book, the term 'symbol' is used in the latter sense.

In a way, both signs and symbols can 'protect' people. Traffic signs, for instance, can protect us from accidents, injuries, and even death. Signs or symbols on medicine bottles may save us from poisoning ourselves. Symbols or signs used in science and technological blueprints can protect us against the dangers of ignorance or from walking over bridges that might easily collapse. In a much more general way, the symbols or signs of our language can protect us from an infinite number of dangers by transmitting to us the experience of our fellow beings and predecessors; they can save us from the ordeal of solitude by helping us communicate with others; they can also save us from the prison of the *hic et nunc*, the present situation, by allowing us to conceive of other possible situations and worlds; and so on.

In this book, symbols—mainly complex configurations of symbols—have been studied as performing less a practical, more an 'existential' function. Myths and religions, visions of the world and works of art, moral norms and the rituals of guilt, plays and the folklore of jokes have been described as systems of symbols that have helped us to survive spiritually in this universe. They have alleviated our anxiety, reduced our fears, fostered hope, and generated meaning and purpose in our lives. They may have done even more. They have built a human world of relative safety and freedom, dignity and meaning in a universe in which there may be no freedom, no dignity, and no meaning outside this human microcosm.

The trouble is that all this may be an illusion. We may be deluding ourselves. Symbols and systems of symbols may form a radiant haze, a world of fantasy around us, a virtual world we call civilization, which hides the threatening darkness and emptiness beyond it. They may lull us into the illusion that there is freedom, meaning, and human dignity in this world.

Mythic heroes, religious beliefs, moral values, visions of the world, works of art, the miracle of play, and the impertinence of jokes may help us, for brief moments, to suffer and fear less and to feel at home in this universe, but the forces of the alien world, pain and mortality, will ultimately and inevitably defeat us. Even the most brilliant symbols and symbolic systems, the richest and strongest civilizations are unable to stop time and defeat death; they are not able to generate meaning and purpose which do not perish together with our lives in an empty and meaningless universe. Or are they? Before I even try to answer this question, let me introduce an important concept.

CONSTRUCTS

Hans Vaihinger, the German philosopher, published an extremely interesting book in 1911 (Vaihinger, 1924), in which he argued that mankind would not be able to survive in this world without generating and using 'fictions'.

According to Vaihinger, fictions are constructs of the human mind and imagination: concepts, classifications, relationships, logical devices, and 'laws'. They are ideas which have no counterpart in reality, but which enable us to deal with it better than we otherwise could (Ansbacher and Ansbacher, 1956, 77). They are tools, catalysts, guideposts, which help us orient ourselves and survive in this world. They constitute a scaffolding around an unknown reality. They must be discarded "if no longer needed", that is, after they have helped us to handle—and not necessarily understand—the piece of reality in question. They are not 'true' in the sense of 'adequately representing reality'. They misrepresent reality, they are 'errors', but "expedient errors ... of great practical value", without which we could not control reality (Ansbacher and Ansbacher, 1956, 83; Vaihinger, 1924, 108, 145).

From among the many examples analyzed by Vaihinger, let me mention the lines of longitude and latitude: they do not exist in reality but are indispensable instruments for navigation. The parts of the day, 'morning' and 'evening', or the very concept of time as we use it, not to mention our everyday concept of space, are constructs without which we could barely have survived. Zero-degree centigrade is also a useful but artificial construct, just as the rules of logic, the juristic fiction of laws, utopias, or works of art are fictions, but useful fictions. Myths and religions, the concept of the 'soul' in psychology, and the concept of human freedom in philosophy are, according to Vaihinger, fictions, but also indispensable preconditions of moral responsibility and social coexistence (Vaihinger, 1924, xiii, 28, 147).

Vaihinger states that fictions appeared relatively late in the history of European thought because their existence implied "an emancipation from immediate perceptions and from the belief that thought is identical with reality". Plato recognized the fictional character of myths, and Aristotle that of some mathematical abstractions. In scholastic philosophy, the nominalist school emphasized the fictional character of ideas. But "fictions were first extensively employed from the seventeenth to the nineteenth century, particularly in the fields of mathematics, physics, sociology and philosophy" (1924, xvi, 135–42, 145, 153).

After the initiatives of Leibniz, Hobbes, Locke, Hume, and others,[2] Kant was already working extensively with fictions, although he was still reluctant to acknowledge the major role fictions played in the world and in his thinking. Nietzsche was the first to proclaim the omnipresence and importance of fictions, emphasizing the overwhelming significance of fictions or constructs in human life in his early work, when he spoke of the role of "Apollonian illusion" and stated that "he who destroys illusions within himself and in others is punished by the most severe of tyrants, nature". He deplored "the mythless existence" of the contemporary world. Throughout his later work, he would state again and again that the freedom of the will was "a necessary delusional concept" and "moral freedom is a necessary illusion". Life in general, and the life of the *Übermensch* in particular, is impossible without "the belief in illusion", "the joy in illusion", and last but not least, "the will to illusion" (quoted in Vaihinger, 1924, 343, 344, 356).

Is it not strange that Nietzsche, the great destroyer of lies and illusions, at the same time sang the praise of illusions? As a matter of fact, he attacked the lies and illusions that may harm and destroy life, but protected the illusions which help life prevail. He put existence before essence, life before truth. In Vaihinger's interpretation, he "place[d] himself not only 'beyond good and evil' but also beyond 'truth and falsehood'" (1924, 352). Vaihinger goes even further and states that to bring about life-generating and life-protecting illusions is an act of creation. We have created, and have to create, our world out of ideas, illusions, fictions.

> Catastrophe: what if falsehood is something divine? Whether the value of all things may not consist in the fact that they are false? Whether we should not believe in God not because he is true, but because he is false? ... What if it be not just the lying and falsifying, the reading in of meanings, which constitutes a value, a sense, a purpose? (Vaihinger, 1924, 362)[3]

This is almost a prelude to Sartre's theory of negativity. It claims that the source of freedom is in nonbeing—in something that does not exist, that is not 'given'. The only and ultimate freedom for a human being is to have the courage to create his or her own world and existence out of his or her own ideas, goals, and authentic choices. He who fails to do so will be overpowered and enslaved by the routines of the everyday world, where there is no freedom, no meaning, and no human dignity.

In recent decades, with the development of postmodern thinking—with its penchant for relativism, pluralism, and nominalism—'fictions' and 'constructs' have made a spectacular comeback. In Chapter Eight I discussed Richard Rorty's ideas about the "death of Truth", and the revolution in modern thinking which replaced truth with freedom, risk, and the adventure of searching for better and better 'vocabularies', 'language games', or 'arguments'. It is these vocabularies, games, and arguments that create, if not the world, at least the interaction between the world and us. This interaction may be the only real and authentic existence for human beings.

Here we return to the question of how, if at all, symbols can protect us.

CIVILIZATION: A BRILLIANT CONSTRUCT?

The symbolic systems of our civilization may be mere constructs of the human mind. There may be, but there is no necessary correspondence between our ideas, concepts, symbols, hypotheses, and theories, on the one hand, and so-called reality, or the laws of nature, on the other. The issue is highly controversial. No one has yet convincingly proved that there is an essential correspondence between the constructs of our minds and the fundamental laws and ultimate secrets of the universe, although no one has conclusively proved the contrary, either.[4]

However, the argument developed in this book hopefully supports the hypothesis that, even if our symbolic systems are mere fictions, the essential importance of the role they have played in our history, and in our lives, cannot be questioned. In all likelihood, without them there would have been more human suffering and agony in this world—even if they have sometimes turned into fearful jungles and have become sources of human suffering and anxiety.[5] The final balance has still to be drawn, however.

Symbols, as a matter of fact, can change the world. They can change it indirectly through the activity of human beings. People, when they are prompted by symbols, when they communicate through symbols, when they try to understand the world through symbols, when they set goals for themselves with the help of symbols, do change the world. They could not change the world if they did not possess an arsenal of symbols. On the other hand, symbols can have a direct influence, not on the world, but on human beings, and thereby change people's relationship with the world. It is this relationship that counts, that is essential for humans. It is this relationship that they experience as their lives in the world.

Myths and religions, scientific theories and works of art have changed people's vision of the world and, as a consequence, their relationship to the world. They have thereby reduced people's anxiety in an unknown and dangerous universe which may be devoid of meaning and purpose. People's belief in a moral universe has introduced the principle of justice in a universe in which there may be no justice and injustice, but only the blind rattling of physical forces and laws. With the help of the rituals of guilt, human beings have transformed natural evil into moral evil and have thereby acquired some control over human suffering and mortality. They have achieved an almost divine serenity and seriousness in their brief moments of play, sanctuaries in a world full of trouble and discord. Jokes and tragedies have helped them to explore the universe beyond the boundaries of our everyday world: jokes, by taking them on a brief roller coaster trip into the alien world; tragedies, by prompting and helping them face its fearful depths with courage, resignation, and hope.

All in all, they have changed the balance—or let us say imbalance—between the world and humankind. The systems of symbols with which they have surrounded themselves have transformed them from helpless, weak, fragile creatures, living in a fearful and powerful world, into conscious human beings who have the strength and courage to control the forces of the world. At least to a certain extent.

Symbols and symbolic systems may be fictions or constructs, but this does not obliterate the fact that, to a considerable degree, it has been through them that human beings have become what they are. It is by assiduously working on the construction of a world consisting of, and protected by, symbols that men and women have become *Homo sapiens* in the sense that they are creatures who know—or at least are supposed to know—who they are and what their business might be in this universe. It is through this process that they have become *Homo culpabilis*, a being able to take responsibility for what is happening in the world; or *Homo ludens*, who can create freedom and harmony for him- or herself in a universe of disharmony and bondage; or *Homo tragicus* or *comicus*, able to look into the absurd and tragic depths of fate with resignation and serenity. Human beings would not recognize themselves if the shining constellations of symbols they have built suddenly disappeared from around them and from within their minds.

It may turn out that castles built in the air, or built of symbols, are 'real' castles after all. Sometimes they may be stronger than castles built of stone. A civilization may survive in its symbols even when its stone buildings have already fallen into dust. Forms and structures created by the human spirit, though fragile and perishable, may have a reality and an importance that we still do not know and cannot fully understand. This reminds me of a story I heard a few years ago. Let me conclude these pages by recounting it here.

> One evening, a lady entered the Dior shop on Fifth Avenue in New York and asked for a hat that would match her elegant, *haute couture* evening dress. She was obviously late for a party or the theater and went nervously through the whole collection without finding something to her taste.
>
> Christian Dior, who happened to be in the shop, watched her ordeal and after a while—retaining his incognito—offered her his help. He took a piece of tulle and pressing it here, patting it there, conjured up a fascinating hat in a trice. She was stunned and delighted.
>
> "How much is it?", she asked the unknown master. "Five thousand dollars, Madam", he replied. "Oh, no, this is ridiculous!", she cried. "So much for this ... this ... nothing? For this ... triviality?" "Very well, Madam," said Dior, who then took the 'hat', smoothed it out again, folded it into a neat kerchief, said: "Please, accept this as a gift of the house," and took his leave.[6]

To create something brilliant out of nothing; to build up galaxies of symbols, perhaps out of nothing; to build up a world of freedom, meaning, and human dignity in a universe where there may be no freedom, no dignity, and no meaning outside our microcosm: this has been a task worth doing. Our civilization is the outcome—a brilliant construct?—of this fascinating human adventure.

NOTES

1 Other basic needs, such as the need for comfort or social cooperation, also generate symbols and symbolic systems but—as we have seen in chapter two, and without falling into the trap of a primitive reductionism—most of these needs can be traced back to an underlying existential fear.
2 In his criticism of Newton, for instance, one of Berkeley's main points of attack was that Newton's basic concepts were only fictions. "He maintained that Newton's 'true

mathematical space' was in fact no more than an imaginary space, a fiction of the human mind" (Cassirer, 1944, 44).

3 I give here the German original of this difficult text: *Katastrophe: ob nicht die Lüge etwas Göttliches ist: ob nicht der Welt aller Dinge darin beruht, dass sie falsch sind? ob man nicht an Gott glauben sollte, nicht weil er wahr, sondern weil er falsch [ist]? ... ob nicht gerade das Lügen und Falschmachen (Umfälschen), das Sinn-Einlegen ein Wert, ein Sinn, ein Zweck ist?* (Vaihinger, 1913, 789).

4 Think, for instance, of the views and disagreements of mathematicians, physicists, biologists, philosophers, and theologians, such as Barrow and Penrose, Einstein and Heisenberg, Gödel and Russell, Heidegger and Tillich, Weinberg and Dyson, Changeux and Connes, and Dennett and Gould, or of the unending controversy about the truth-content and hidden message of mythologies as seen by Frazer and Eliade, Lévi-Strauss and Jung, and Dumézil and Ricoeur.

5 Myths, religions, and ideologies are among the most powerful symbolic systems, and we know that their role in human history has not always been positive, to say the least.

6 I heard this story from the well-known Hungarian fashion designer, Kati Zoob.

BIBLIOGRAPHY

Aldrich, Charles Robert. 1931. *The Primitive Mind and Civilization*. New York: Harcourt, Brace and Co.
Alexander, Jeffrey C. 1990. *Structure and Meaning. Rethinking Classical Sociology*. New York: Columbia University Press.
Alexander, Jeffrey C., Bernhard Giesen, Richard Münch, and Neil J. Smelser, eds. 1987. *The Micro-Macro Link*. Berkeley: University of California Press.
Alexander, Jeffrey C. and Steven Seidman, eds. 1990. *Culture and Society. Contemporary Debates*. Cambridge: Cambridge University Press.
Allegre, Claude. 1992. *Introduction à une histoire naturelle. Du big Bang à la disparition de l'Homme*. Paris: Fayard.
Ansbacher, Heinz L., and Rowena R. Ansbacher, eds. 1956. *The Individual Psychology of Alfred Adler*. New York: Basic Books.
Aradi vértanúk [The martyrs of Arad]. 1979. Budapest.
Arato, Andrew, and Eike Gebhardt, eds. 1978. *The Essential Frankfurt School Reader*. New York: Urizen Books.
Archer, J. 1970. 'The Organization of Aggression and Fear in Vertebrates', in *Perspectives in Ethology*, ed. Bateson and Klopfer, pp. 231–99.
Augustine, Saint. 1966–72. *The City of God against the Pagans*, vols. 1–7, trans. G. E. McCracken and W. M. Green. Cambridge, Mass.: Harvard University Press.
——. 1960–61. *Confessions*, vols. 1–2, trans. William Watts. Cambridge, Mass.: Harvard University Press.
Axelrod, R. 1984. *The Evolution of Cooperation*. New York: Basic Books.
Bachelard, Gaston. 1969. *The Poetics of Space*. Boston: Beacon Press.
Bachofen, Johann Jakob. 1926. *Urreligion und Symbole*. Leipzig. Quoted by Rahner (1965, 17–18).
Bailey, P. 1978. *Leisure and Class in Victorian England*. London: Routledge and Kegan Paul.

———. 1986. *Music Hall: The Business of Pleasure*. Milton Keynes: Open University Press.
Bain, R. 1942. 'A Definition of Culture'. *Sociology and Social Research* 27.
Balint, Alice. 1954. *The Early Years of Life. A Psychoanalytic Study*. New York: Basic Books.
Barber, Benjamin R. 1995. *Jihad vs. McWorld*. New York: Times Books.
Barkow, Jerome H. 1989. *Darwin, Sex, and Status: Biological Approaches to Mind and Culture*. Toronto: University of Toronto Press.
Barkow, Jerome H., Leda Cosmides, and John Tooby, eds. 1992. *The Adapted Mind. Evolutionary Psychology and the Generation of Culture*. New York: Oxford University Press.
Barnard, Frederick M. 1968. 'Culture and Civilization in Modern Times', in *Dictionary of the History of Ideas*, ed. Wiener, vol. 1, pp. 613–21.
Baron, Reuben M. 1997. 'On Making Terror Management Theory Less Motivational and More Social'. *Psychological Inquiry* 8 (1): pp. 21–22.
Barrow, John D. 1991. *Theories of Everything. The Quest for Ultimate Explanation*. Oxford: Clarendon Press.
Barth, Karl. 1926. 'Die Kirche und die Kultur. Vortrag am Kongress des kontinentalen Verbandes für innere Mission zu Amsterdam, 1. Juni 1926'. *ZZ* 4: pp. 365–84.
Barthes, Roland. 1972. *Mythologies*. New York: Hill and Wang.
Baruk, Henri. 1954. *Psychoses et névroses*. Paris: Presses Universitaires de France.
Bateson, P. P. G., and P. H. Klopfer, eds. 1970. *Perspectives in Ethology*. New York: Plenum Press.
Baudrillard, Jean. 1998 [1970]. *The Consumer Society. Myths and Structures*. London: Sage.
Baumeister, Roy F. 1991. *Escaping the Self: Alcoholism, Spirituality, Masochism, and Other Flights from the Burden of Selfhood*. New York: Basic Books.
Baumeister, Roy F., and D. M. Tice. 1991. 'Anxiety and Social Exclusion'. *Journal of Social and Clinical Psychology* 9: pp. 165–95.
Becker, Ernest. 1973. *The Denial of Death*. New York: The Free Press.
Benchetritt, Paul. 1952. *A History of Hamlet in France*. Dissertation, University of Birmingham.
———. 1956. 'Hamlet at the Comédie Française, 1769–1896'. *Shakespeare Survey* 9.
Bennett, T. et al., eds. 1983. *Formations of Pleasure*. London: Routledge and Kegan Paul.
Berger, Peter, L. 1967. *The Sacred Canopy. Elements of a Sociological Theory of Religion*. New York: Doubleday. (Reprinted in 1990 as an Anchor Book.)
———. 1969. *The Rumor of Angels*. New York: Doubleday. (Reprinted in 1990 as an Anchor Book.)
Bergson, Henri. 1911. *Creative Evolution*, trans. Henri Louis. New York: Holt.
Berlin, Isaiah. 1969. *Four Essays on Liberty*. New York: Oxford University Press.
Blumberg, Hans. 1965. *Die Kopernikansche Wende*. Frankfurt am Main: Suhrkamp. Quoted by Dienst (1976, p. 1097).
Bock, P. K. 1988. *Rethinking Psychological Anthropology: Continuity and Change in Human Action*. New York: Freeman.

Bondi, Hermann. 1957. 'Theories of Cosmology'. In Munitz (1957, 405–412).
Borkenau, Franz. 1980. *End and Beginning: On the Generation of Cultures and the Origins of the West*. New York: Columbia University Press.
——. 1982. *Formation and Civilization*. Oxford: Blackwell.
Boyd, James W. 1975. *Satan and Mara: Christian and Buddhist Symbols of Evil*. Leiden: Brill.
Boyd, R., and P. J. Richerson. 1985. *Culture and the Evolutionary Process*. Chicago: Chicago University Press.
Branam, George C. 1956. *Eighteenth-Century Adaptations of Shakespearean Tragedy*. Berkeley: The University of California Press.
Brittain, A. 1997. *The Privatized World*. London: Routledge and Kegan Paul.
Brown, Norman O. 1959. *Life Against Death. The Psychoanalytical Meaning of History*. New York: Viking Books.
Buck, R. 1988. *Human Motivation and Emotion*. 2nd ed. New York: Wiley.
Bultmann, Rudolf Karl. 1962. *History and Eschatology*. New York: Harper and Row.
Burgess, Ernest W. 1960. *Aging in Western Societies*. Chicago: Chicago University Press.
Burke, P., ed. 1973. *A New Kind of History*. London: Routledge and Kegan Paul.
Buss, David M. 1994. *The Evolution of Desire*. New York: Basic Books.
——. 1995. 'Evolutionary Psychology: A New Paradigm for Psychological Science'. *Psychological Inquiry* 6: pp. 1–30.
——. 1997. 'Human Social Motivation in Evolutionary Perspective: Grounding Terror Management Theory'. *Psychological Inquiry* 8 (1): pp. 22–26.
Buytendijk, Friedrich J. 1933. *Wesen und Sinn des Spieles*. Berlin: Kurt Wolff.
——. 1952. *Le Football*. Paris.
Bynum, C. W. 1995. *The Resurrection of the Body in Western Christianity, 200–1336*. New York: Columbia University Press.
Caillois, Roger. 1950. *L'homme et le sacré*. Paris: Gallimard.
——. 1961. *Man, Play, and Games*. Glencoe: The Free Press.
Calvin, Jean. 1559. *Institutio religionis christianae*, 11, 1, 7.
Campbell, Joseph. 1968. *The Hero with a Thousand Faces*. Princeton: Princeton University Press. Bollingen Series XVII.
Camus, Albert. 1956. *The Rebel*. New York: Knopf.
Carroll, John. 1985. *Guilt. The Grey Eminence Behind Character, History and Culture*. London: Routledge and Kegan Paul.
Cassirer, Ernst. 1944. *An Essay on Man. An Introduction to a Philosophy of Human Culture*. New Haven: Yale University Press.
——. 1953 [1923–25]. *Die Philosophie der symbolischen Formen*. 2nd ed. Vols. 1–3. Darmstadt: Wissenschaftliche Buchgemeinschaft.
Chaney, D. 1983. 'The Department Store as a Cultural Form'. *Theory, Culture and Society*, 1/3.
Changeux, J.-P., and Alain Connes. 1989. *Matière et pensée*. Paris: Jacob.
Chevalier, Jean, and Alain Gheerbrant, eds. 1969. *Dictionnaire des symboles*. Paris: Laffont. (English translation: *Dictionary of Symbols*. Oxford: Blackwell.)
Cohn, Norman. 1961. *The Pursuit of the Millennium*. 2nd ed. New York: Harper and Row.

Comito, Terry. 1978. *The Idea of the Garden in the Renaissance*. New Brunswick, N. J.: Rutgers University Press.
Comte, Auguste. 1830–42. *Cours de philosophie positive*. Paris.
Condorcet, Antoine Nicolas de. 1801. *Esquisse d'un tableau historique des progrès de l'esprit humain*. Paris.
Conklin, P. S. 1947. *A History of Hamlet Criticism*. London: Cass.
Cook, Karen S. 1995. *Sociological Perspectives on Social Psychology*. Boston: Allyn and Bacon.
Coulter, Jeff. 1979. *The Social Construction of Mind*. New Jersey: Rowman and Littlefield.
Crawford, C. B., M. F. Smith, and D. L. Krebs, eds. 1987. *Sociobiology and Psychology*. Hillsdale, N. J.: Erlbau.
Csurka, István. 1980. *Házmestersirató* [Lament for the janitor]. Budapest: Szépirodalmi.
Curtius, E. R. 1953. *European Literature and the Latin Middle Ages*. New York: Pantheon.
Cusanus, Nicolaus. 1440. *Learned Ignorance*.
Daiches, David. 1960. *A Critical History of English Literature*. Vols. 1–2. New York: Ronald Press.
Damasio, Antonio. 1994. *Descartes' Error. Emotion, Reason, and the Human Brain*. New York: Putnam.
Davidson, Gustav. 1967. *A Dictionary of Angels. Including the Fallen Angels*. New York: The Free Press.
Davies, Paul. 1993. *The Mind of God. The Scientific Basis of a Rational World*. New York: Simon and Schuster.
Dawkins, Richard. 1982. *The Blind Watchmaker*. New York: Norton.
Debord, G. 1970. *The Society of the Spectacle*. Detroit: Black and Red.
Delumeau, Jean. 1978. *La peur en Occident: Une citée assiégée*. Paris: Fayard.
———. 1990. *Sin and Fear. The Emergence of a Western Guilt Culture, 13th–18th Centuries*. New York: St. Martin's Press, 1990.
Denny, Reuel, and David Riesman. 1955. Autumn. Football in America'. *Perspectives USA* 13: pp. 108–129.
Denzin, Norman K. 1984. *On Understanding Emotion*. San Francisco: Jossey-Bass.
Devereux, Georges. 1966. *De l'angoisse à la méthode dans les sciences du comportement*. Paris: Aubier.
Dienst, Karl. 1976. 'Kopernikanische Wende', in *Historisches Wörterbuch der Philosophie*, ed. Ritter and Gründer, vol. 4, pp. 1094–1099.
Dirks, Nicholas B., Geoff Eley, and Sherry B. Ortner, eds. 1994. *Culture/Power/History. A Reader in Contemporary Theory*. Princeton: Princeton University Press.
Ditfurth, Hoimar von, ed. 1965. *Starnberger Gespräche*. Stuttgart: Georg Thieme.
Douglas, Mary, and Aaron Wildavsky. 1982. *Risk and Culture: An Essay on the Selection of Technological and Environmental Dangers*. Berkeley: University of California Press.
Durand, Gilbert. 1969. *Les structures anthropologiques de l'imaginaire*. Grenoble: Dunod.

Durham, W. 1991. *Coevolution: Genes, Culture, and Human Diversity*. Stanford, Cal.: Stanford University Press.
Durkheim, Emile. 1951. *Suicide*. Glencoe, Ill.: The Free Press.
———. 1965. *Elementary Forms of Religious Life*. New York: The Free Press.
Dyson, Freeman. 1979. *Disturbing the Universe*. New York: Harper.
Easton, Susan, A. Hawkins, S. Laing, and H. Walker. n. d. *Disorder and Discipline. Popular Culture from 1955 to the Present*. London: Temple Smith.
Edwards, Paul, ed. 1967. *The Encyclopedia of Philosophy*. Vols. 1–8. New York: Macmillan.
Eibl-Eibesfeldt, I. 1975. *Ethology: The Biology of Behavior*. 2nd ed. New York: Holt, Rinehart and Winston.
Ekman, Paul, and Richard Davidson, eds. 1994. *Questions About Emotions*. New York: Oxford University Press.
Elert, Werner. 1921. *Der Kampf um das Christentum: Geschichte der Beziehungen zwischen dem evangelischen Christentum in Deutschland und dem allgemeinen Denken seit Schleiermacher und Hegel*. München: C. H. Beck.
Eliade, Mircea. 1954. *The Myth of the Eternal Return*, trans. W. R. Trask. Bollingen Series XLVI. New York: Pantheon Books.
———. 1959. *The Sacred and the Profane*, trans. W. R. Trask. New York: Harper.
———. 1978–85. *A History of Religious Ideas*. Vols. 1–3. Chicago: Chicago University Press.
———, ed. 1987. *The Encyclopedia of Religion*. Vols. 1–16. New York: Macmillan.
Elias, Norbert. 1982 and 1994. *The Civilizing Process. The History of Manners, and State Formation and Civilization*, trans. Edmund Jephcott. Oxford: Blackwell (German original: 1939.)
Eliot, T. S. 1927. *Shakespeare and the Stoicism of Seneca*. Shakespeare Association Lectures. London: Oxford.
Ellis, M. J. 1973. *Why People Play*. Englewood Cliffs, N.J.: Prentice-Hall.
Epstein, S. 1967. 'Towards a Unified Theory of Anxiety', in Mahrer (1967).
Erasmus. 1524. *De libero arbitrio*, in *Opera omnia*. Leiden (1703–1706), vol. 9. (Reprinted: 1961–62.)
Evans-Pritchard, E. 1965. *Theories of Primitive Religions*. Oxford: Clarendon Press.
Ewen, Stuart. 1988. *All Consuming Images. The Politics of Style in Contemporary Culture*. New York: Basic Books.
Falk, Pasi, and Colin Campbell, eds. 1997. *The Shopping Experience*. London: Sage.
Featherstone, M. 1991. *Consumer Culture and Post Modernism*. London: Sage.
Febvre, Lucien. 1973. '"Civilization": Evolution of a Word and a Group of Ideas', in ed. Burke, pp. 219–57.
Feifel, H., ed. 1959. *The Meaning of Death*. New York: McGraw-Hill.
Fichte, Johann Gottlieb. 1964. 'Theorie der Subjektivität', in *Gesamtausgabe der Bayerischen Academie der Wissenschaften*, ed. Reinhard Lauth and Hans Jacob. Stuttgart: Frommann.
Fink, Eugen. 1980. *Spiel als Weltsymbol*. Stuttgart: Kohlhammer.
Fletcher, Jonathan. 1997. *Violence and Civilization. An Introduction to the Work of Norbert Elias*. Cambridge: Polity Press.

Folsom, Joseph K. 1928. *Culture and Social Progress*. New York: Longmans, Green and Co.
Ford, C. S. 1942. 'Culture and Human Behavior'. *Scientific Monthly* 55.
Frankl, V. E. 1963. *Man's Search for Meaning*. Boston: Beacon Press.
Freud, Anna. 1937. *The Ego and the Mechanisms of Defense*. London: Hogarth Press.
Freud, Sigmund. 1938. 'Wit and Its Relation to the Unconscious', in *The Basic Writings of Sigmund Freud*, ed. A. A. Brill, pp. 631–761. New York: Modern Library.
——. 1959a. 'Civilization and Its Discontents', in *The Standard Edition of the Complete Psychological Works of Sigmund Freud*, ed. James Strachey, vol. 21, pp. 59–148. London: Hogarth Press.
——. 1959b. 'Inhibitions, Symptoms and Anxiety', in *The Standard Edition of the Complete Psychological Works of Sigmund Freud*, ed. James Strachey, vol. 20, pp. 73–174. London: Hogarth Press.
——. 1961. 'A Seventeenth-Century Demonological Neurosis', in *The Standard Edition of the Complete Psychological Works of Sigmund Freud*, ed. James Strachey, vol. 19, pp. 275–300. London: Hogarth Press.
Fridja, N. H. 1986. *The Emotions*. Cambridge: Cambridge University Press.
Fromm, Erich. 1965 [1941]. *Escape From Freedom*. New York: Avon Books.
Gardner, C., and J. Sheppard. 1989. *Consuming Passion: The Rise of Retail Culture*. London: Unwin Hyman.
Geertz, Clifford. 1973. *The Interpretation of Cultures. Selected Essays*. New York: Basic Books.
Gehlen, Arnold. 1988. *Man: His Nature and Place in the Universe*. New York: Columbia University Press.
Gerth, H. H., and Wright C. Mills, eds. 1958. *From Weber: Essays in Sociology*. New York: Galaxy Book.
Gibbs, Nancy. 1994. 'Why? The Killing Fields of Rwanda'. *Time Magazine*, International Edition (16 May): pp. 21–27.
Ginzburg, Louis. 1938 [1913]. *The Legends of the Jews*. Philadelphia: The Jewish Publication Society of America.
Goethe, Johann Wolfgang. 1976. *Materialen zur Geschichte der Farbenlehre, I, 4. Zwischenbemerkung*. In Dienst (1976, p. 1095).
Gogarten, Friedrich, 1926. *Illusionen. Eine Auseneinnandersetzung mit dem Kulturidealismus*. Jena.
Goleman, Daniel. 1995. *Emotional Intelligence*. New York: Bantam Books.
Gorer, Geoffrey. 1949. *The People of Great Russia; A Psychological Study*. London: Cresset Press.
Goslin, David A. 1969. *Handbook of Socialization. Theory and Research*. Chicago: Rand, McNaily and Co.
Gottdiener, Mark. 1997. *The Theming of America. Dreams, Visions, and Commercial Spaces*. Boulder, Col.: Westview Press.
Gould, Stephen Jay. 1994. 'So Near and Yet So Far', *The New York Review of Books*, 41, No. 17 (20 October): pp. 25–27.
——. ed. 1993. *The Book of Life*. New York: Norton.

Gray, Jeffrey. A. 1971. *The Psychology of Fear and Stress*. London: Weidenfeld and Nicholson.
Groos, Karl. 1989. *The Play of Animals*. New York: Appleton.
——. 1901. The Play of Men. New York: Appleton.
Gutmann, Joseph, ed. 1976. *The Temple of Solomon: Archaeological Fact and Medieval Tradition in Christian, Jewish and Islamic Art*. American Academy of Religion: Society of Biblical Literature. Religion and the Arts, 3. Missoula: Scholars Press.
Haefner, H. 1971. 'Angst, Furcht', in Ritter and Gründer, vol. 1, pp. 310–14.
Hall, Stuart. 1994. 'Cultural Studies: Two Paradigms', in ed. Dirks et al., pp. 520–38.
Halliday, F. E. 1950. *Shakespeare and his Critics*. London: Duckworth.
Hankiss, Elemér. 1977a. 'Túl vagy Innen Jón és Rosszon? A tragikus katarzis társadalmi funkciójáról' [This side of or beyond good and evil? The social functions of tragic catharsis], in Hankiss, *Érték és társadalom*, pp. 167–202.
——. 1977b. 'A halál és a happy ending. A regénybefejezések értékszerkezetéről' [Death and the happy ending. The value structure of novel endings], in Hankiss, *Érték és társadalom*, pp. 203–30.
——. 1977c. *Érték és társadalom. Értékszociológiai tanulmányok* [Values and societies. Essays in the sociology of values]. Budapest: Megvető.
——. 1990. *East European Alternatives*. Oxford: Clarendon Press.
Harding, Thomas G., David Kaplan, Marshall D. Sahlins, and Elman R. Service, eds. 1960. *Evolution and Culture*. Ann Arbor, Mich.: University of Michigan Press.
Harrington, Allan. 1969. *The Immortalist*. New York: Random House.
Hegel, Georg Wilhelm Friderich. 1975. *Lectures on the Philosophy of History. Introduction, Reason in History*, trans. H. B. Nisbet. New York: Cambridge University Press.
Heidegger, Martin. 1962. *Being and Time*. London: SCM.
——. 1980. 'The Origin of the Work of Art', in Heidegger, *Basic Writings*, ed. D. F. Krell, pp. 139–212. London: Routledge and Kegan Paul.
Herder, Johann Gottfried. 1784–91. *Ideen zur Philosophie der Geschichte des Menschen*. In *Sämtliche Werke*, vol. 13.
Hick, John. 1966. *Evil and the God of Love*. London: Macmillan.
——. 1967. 'The Problem of Evil', in Edwards, vol. 3, pp. 136–41.
Homans, George C. 1941. 'Anxiety and Ritual: The Theories of Malinowski and Radcliffe-Brown'. *American Anthropologist* 43: pp. 164–72.
——. 1961. *Social Behavior: Its Elementary Forms*. New York: Harcourt, Brace and Co.
'Home: A Place in the World.' 1991. *Social Research* 58.
Horkheimer, Max. 1978. 'The End of Reason', in Arato and Gebhardt, pp. 26–48.
Horney, Karen. 1937. *The Neurotic Personality of Our Time*. New York: Norton.
——. 1939. *New Ways in Psychoanalysis*. New York: Norton.
——. 1950. *Neurosis and Human Growth: The Struggle Toward Self-realization*. New York: Norton.
Hoyle, Fred. 1950. *The Nature of the Universe*. New York: Harper.
Huizinga, Jan. 1950. *Homo Ludens. A Study of the Play Element in Culture*. New York: Roy Publishers.

Huxtable, Ada Louise. 1997. *The Unreal America. Architecture and Illusion*. New York: New Press.
Islamic Garden, The. 1976. Dumbarton Oaks: Trustees for Harvard University.
Izard, Caroll E. 1977. *Human Emotions*. New York: Plenum Press.
James, William. 1958. *Varieties of Religious Experience: A Study of Human Nature*. New York: Mentor.
Jaspers, Karl. 1948. *Philosophie*. Heidelberg: Springer.
——. 1956. *The Origin and Goal of History*. New Haven: Yale University Press.
Jaspers, Carl. 1965. *Die geistige Situation der Zeit*. Berlin: Walter de Gruyter.
Jenyns, Soame. 1757. *Free Enquiry into the Origin and Nature of Evil*. London.
Jones, Ernest. 1954 [1949]. *Hamlet and Oedipus*. Garden City, N.Y.: Doubleday.
Jung, Carl G. 1959. 'The Soul and Death', in Feifel, pp. 3–15.
——. 1964. *Man and His Symbols*. New York: Dell.
Jusserand, J. J. 1898. *Shakespeare en France sous l'ancien régime*. Paris: Colin.
Kant, Immanuel. 1983. *Werke* in 6 Bänden, ed. Wilhelm Weischedel (Ed.). 5. Aufl. in 10 Bänden. Darmstadt.
——. 1991a. 'Conjectures on the Beginnings of Human History', in *Political Writings*, ed. Hans Reiss. Cambridge: Cambridge University Press.
——. 1991b. 'Idea for a Universal History with a Cosmopolitan Purpose', in *Political Writings*, ed. Hans Reiss. Cambridge: Cambridge University Press.
Kantrowity, Barbara et al. 1994. 'In Search of the Sacred'. *Newsweek* (24 November): pp. 38–45, 40.
Kastenbaum, R. 1922. *The Psychology of Death*. New York: Springer.
Kearl, M. 1989. *Endings: A Sociology of Death and Dying*. New York: Oxford University Press.
Kierkegaard, Søren. 1944. *The Concept of Dread*. Princeton, N. J.: Princeton University Press.
——. 1948. *The Gospel of Suffering*. Minneapolis: Augsburg Publishing House.
——. 1959. *Either/Or*. New York: Anchor Books.
Klein, Stephen B., and Robert R. Mowrer, eds. 1989. *Contemporary Learning Theories*. Hillsdale, N. J.: Lawrence Erlbaum.
Klemke, E. D., ed. 1981. *The Meaning of Life*. New York: Oxford University Press.
Kluckhohn, Clyde. 1962. 'Conceptions of Death Among Indians', in Richard Kluckhohn, pp. 134–49.
Koestler, Arthur. 1964. *The Act of Creation*. London: Hutchinson.
——. 1968 [1959]. *The Sleepwalkers*. New York: Macmillan.
Köhler, Joachim. 1992. 'Schuld; Neuzeit', in Ritter and Gründer, pp. 1456–1466.
Kowiniski, William S. 1985. *The Malling of America: An Inside Look at the Great Consumer Paradise*. New York: W. Morrow.
Koyré, Alexander. 1957. *From the Closed World to the Infinite Universe*. Baltimore: Johns Hopkins Press.
Kristeva, Julia. 1980. *Pouvoirs de l'horreur. Essai sur l'abjection*. Paris: Seuil.
Kroker, Arthur, Marilouise Kroker, and David Cook. 1989. *The Panic Encyclopedia. The Definitive Guide to the Postmodern Scene*. London: Macmillan.
Kroeber, A. L., and Clyde Kluckhohn. 1952. *Culture: A Critical Review of Concepts and Definitions*. New York: Vintage.

Kundera, Milan. 1988. *The Art of the Novel*. New York: Grove Press.
Langer, Susanne K. 1953. *Feeling and Form*. New York: Scribner.
Langman, Lauren. 1992. 'Neon Cages. Shopping for Subjectivity', in Shields, pp. 40–82.
Lazarus, R. S. 1991. *Emotion and Adaptation*. New York: Oxford University Press.
Lazarus, R. S., and S. Folkman. 1984. *Stress, Appraisal, and Coping*. New York: Springer.
Leary, Mark R., and Lisa S. Schreindorfer. 1997. 'Unresolved Issues with Terror Management Theory'. *Psychological Inquiry* 8, No. 1: pp. 26–29.
LeDoux, Joseph. 1996. *The Emotional Brain. The Mysterious Underpinnings of Emotional Life*. New York: Simon and Schuster.
Lehmann, Karl. 1945. 'The Dome of Heaven'. *Art Bulletin* 27: pp. 1–27.
Lehrman, Jonas. 1980. *Earthly Paradise. Garden and Courtyard in Islam*. Berkeley: University of California Press.
Leibniz, Gottfried Wilhelm. 1966. *Theodicy, Abridged*. Indianapolis: Bobbs-Merill.
Lemonick, Michael D. 1994. 'The Killers All Around'. *Time International* 37 (12 September): pp. 48–55.
Lepley, William M., ed. 1947. *Psychological Research in the Theaters of War*. 17 volumes. USAAF Aviation Psychology Research Report, No. 17. Washington D.C.: US Government Printing Office.
Lerner, M. J. 1980. *The Belief in a Just World: A Fundamental Delusion*. New York: Plenum.
——. 1997. 'What Does the Belief in a Just World Protect Us From: The Dread of Death or the Fear of Undeserved Suffering?' *Psychological Inquiry* 8, No. 1: pp. 29–32.
Lessa, William A., and Evon Z. Vogt, eds. 1972. *Reader in Comparative Religion. An Anthropological Approach*. 3rd ed. New York: Harper.
Lévi-Strauss, Claude. 1961. *Sad Tropics*. New York: Criterion.
Lifton, Robert Jay. 1968. *Revolutionary Immortality. Mao Tse-Tung and the Chinese Cultural Revolution*. New York: Vintage.
——. 1979. *The Broken Connection. On Death and the Continuity of Life*. New York, Simon and Schuster.
Lindzey, Gardner, and Elliott Aronson. 1985. *Handbook of Social Psychology*. 3rd ed. New York: Random House.
Lirondelle, André. 1912. *Shakespeare en Russie*.
Lockard J. S., and D. L. Paulhus, eds. 1988. *Self-Deception. An Adaptive Mechanism?* Engelwood Cliffs, N.J.: Prentice Hall.
Lukes, Steven, and Itzhak Galnoor. 1985. *No Laughing Matter. A Collection of Political Jokes*. London: Routledge and Kegan Paul.
Lumsden, Charles J., and Edward O. Wilson. 1981. *Gene, Mind, and Culture. The Coevolutionary Process*. Cambridge, Mass.: Harvard University Press.
Luria, S. E. 1973. *Life: The Unfinished Experience*. New York: Scribner.
Luther, Martin. 1525. *De servo arbitrio [The Bondage of the Will]*. (English edition 1931, London: Sovereign Grace Union.)
Lüttge, Willy. 1925. *Das Christentum in unserer Kultur*. Leipzig.
MacCrimmon, K. R., and D. A. Wehrung. 1986. *Taking Risks: The Management of Uncertainty*. New York: Free Press.

Mahrer, B., ed. 1967. *Progress in Experimental Personality Research*. New York: Academic Press.
Malinowski, Bronislaw. 1931. 'Culture', in Seligman and Johnson, pp. 634–42.
——. 1954. *Magic, Science and Religion and Other Essays*. New York: Anchor Books.
Malone, Kemp. 1923. *The Literary History of Hamlet*. Heidelberg: Winter.
Mander, Raymond, and Joe Mitchenson. 1953. *Hamlet Through the Ages. A Pictorial Record from 1709*. London: Rockliff.
Marcuse, Herbert. 1964. *One-Dimensional Man. Studies in the Ideology of Advanced Industrial Society*. Boston: Beacon Press.
——. 1966. *Eros and Civilization. A Philosophical Inquiry Into Freud*. Boston: Beacon Press.
Maritain, Jacques. 1957. *On the Philosophy of History*. New York: Scribner.
Marks, Isaac. M. 1987. *Fears, Phobias, and Rituals*. New York: Oxford University Press.
Marx, Karl. 1985 [1844]. *Ökonomisch-philosophische Manuskripte*, in *Marx-Engels-Werke*, Bd. 40, Berlin.
May, Rollo. 1950. *The Meaning of Anxiety*. New York: Ronald Press.
McClung, William A. 1983. *The Architecture of Paradise. Survivals of Eden and Jerusalem*. Berkeley: University of California Press.
McGinn, Bernard. 1994. *Antichrist: Two Thousand Years of Human Fascination with Evil*. San Francisco: Harper.
McGinty, Park. 1978. *Interpretation and Dionysos. Method in the Study of a God*. The Hague: Mouton.
McKendrick, N., J. Brewer, and J. H. Plumb. 1982. *The Birth of a Consumer Society: The Commercialization of Eighteenth-Century England*. London: Europa.
Mennell, Stephen. 1992. *Norbert Elias. An Introduction*. Oxford: Blackwell.
Meyer, Conrad Ferdinand. 1962. *Gedichte*. Tübingen: Niemeyer.
Mikulincer, Mario. 1994. *Human Learned Helplessness: A Coping Perspective*. New York: Plenum.
Mikulincer, Mario, and Victor Florian. 1997. 'Do We Really Know What We Need? A Commentary on Pyszczynski, Greenberg, and Solomon'. *Psychological Inquiry* 8, No. 1: pp. 33–36.
Miller, Daniel R., and Guy E. Swanson. 1960. *Inner Conflict and Defense*. New York: Holt.
Miller, David L. 1969. *Gods and Games. Toward a Theology of Play*. New York: The World Publishing Company.
Miller, Michael B. 1981. *The Bon Marché. Bourgeois Culture and the Department Store*. Princeton: Princeton University Press.
Mitscherlich, Alexander. 1975. *The Inability to Mourn*. New York: Grove Press.
Mitscherlich, Alexander, and Margarete Mitscherlich. 1970. *Eine deutsche Art zu lieben*. Munich.
Mohan, Robert Paul. 1970. *Philosophy of History. An Introduction*. New York: The Bruce Publishing Co.
Moltmann, Jürgen. 1974. *Theology of Play*. New York: Harper.
Monod, Jacques. 1971. *Chance and Necessity. An Essay on the Natural Philosophy of Modern Biology*. Glasgow: Collius–Fontana.

Montesquieu. 1989. *The Spirit of the Laws*, trans. Anne M. Cohler, Basia C. Miller, Harold S. Stone. Cambridge: Cambridge University Press.

Moore, Barrington, Jr. 1973. *Reflections on the Causes of Human Misery and upon Certain Proposals to Eliminate Them*. Boston: Beacon Press.

Moorhead, Hugh S., ed. 1988. *The Meaning of Life*. Chicago: The Chicago Review Press.

Moynihan, Elizabeth B. 1979. *Paradise as a Garden in Persia and Mughal India*. New York: Braziller.

Mumford, Lewis. 1963. *Technics and Civilization*. 2nd ed. New York: Harcourt and Brace.

Munitz, Milton K., ed. 1957. *Theories of the Universe*. Glencoe. Ill.: The Free Press.

Muraven, Mark, and Roy F. Baumeister. 1997. 'Sex, Terror, Paralysis, and Other Pitfalls of Reductionist Self-Preservation Theory'. *Psychological Inquiry* 8, No. 1: pp. 36–40.

Murdock, J. P. 1940. 'The Cross-Cultural Survey'. *American Sociological Review* 5: pp. 364–69.

Myers, David G., and Ed. Diener. 1996. 'The Pursuit of Happiness'. *Scientific American* (May): pp. 70–72.

Neimeyer, Robert A., ed. 1994. *Death Anxiety Handbook: Research, Instrumentation, and Application*. Washington, D.C.: Taylor and Francis.

Nesse, Randolph. M. 1990. 'Evolutionary Explanations of Emotions'. *Human Nature*, No. 1: pp. 200–215.

Nesse, Randolph M., and Alan T. Lloyd. 1992. 'Evolution of Psychodynamic Mechanisms', in Barkow et al., pp. 601–624.

Niebuhr, Reinhold. 1941. *The Nature and Destiny of Man*. New York: Scribner.

——. 1951. *Faith and History*. New York: Scribner.

Nietzsche, Friedrich. 1967. *The Birth of Tragedy: and The Case of Wagner*. New York: Vintage.

——. 1968. *The Will to Power*, ed. Walter Kaufmann. New York: Random House.

——. 1969. *On the Genealogy of Morals*. New York: Vintage.

——. 1974 [1967–]: *Werke. Kritische Gesamtausgabe*, Bd. VII-2. Berlin–New York: De Gruyter.

Norberg-Schulz, Christian. 1985. *The Concept of Dwelling. On the Way to Figurative Architecture*. New York: Electa/Rizzoli.

Ott, Heinrich. 1978. *Das Reden vom Unsagbaren: Die Frage nach Gott in unserer Zeit*. Stuttgart: Krenz.

Parkin, David. 1986. 'Toward an Apprehension of Fear', in Scruton, pp. 158–72.

Parrot, André 1957. *The Temple of Jerusalem*. London: SCM Press.

Parsons, Talcott. 1972. 'Religious Perspectives in Sociology and Social Psychology', in Lessa and Vogt, pp. 88–93. (First published in 1994.)

——. 1978. 'Death in the Western World', in Parsons, *Action Theory and the Human Condition*, pp. 331–351. New York: The Free Press.

Parsons, Talcott, Renee C. Fox, and Victor M. Lidz. 1978. 'The "Gift of Life" and Its Reciprocation', in Parsons, *Action Theory and the Human Condition*, pp. 264–99.

Patai, Raphael. 1947. *Man and Temple in Ancient Jewish Myth and Ritual*. London: Thomas Nelson.

Penrose, Roger. 1989. *The Emperor's New Mind*. Oxford: Oxford University Press.
Peters, R. 1958. *The Concept of Motivation*. London: Routledge and Kegan Paul.
Petazzoni, Raffaele. 1931. *La confession des péchés*. Paris.
Phillip, E. 1963. *Das Zeitalter der Aufklärung*. 1963, Quoted by Dienst (1976, p. 1098).
Piehler, Paul. 1971. *The Visionary Landscape. A Study of Medieval Allegory*. London: Edward Arnold.
Plato. 1961. *Laws*, trans, A. E. Taylor. Princeton: Princeton University Press.
Plessner, Helmuth. 1928. *Die Stufen des Organischen und der Mensch. Einleitung in die philosophische Anthropologie*. Berlin: De Gruyter.
———. 1950. *Lachen und Weinen*. Bern: Francke.
Plutchik, R., and H. Kellerman, eds. 1980. *Emotion: Theory, Research, and Experience*. New York: Academic Press.
Popper, Karl. 1945. *The Open Society and its Enemies*. 2 volumes. London: Routledge and Kegan Paul.
Postman, N. 1985. *Amusing Ourselves to Death*. New York: Viking.
Ptolemy. 1984. *Almagest*, trans. G. J. Toomer. New York: Springer.
Pyszczynski, Tom, Jeff Greenberg, and Sheldon Solomon. 1997. 'Why Do We Need What We Need? A Terror Management Perspective on the Roots of Human Social Motivation'. *Psychological Inquiry*, 8, No. 1: pp. 1–20.
Rachman, S. J. 1978. *Fear and Courage*. San Francisco: Freeman.
Radcliffe-Brown, A. R. 1972. 'Taboo' [The Frazer Lecture, 1939], in Lessa and Vogt, pp. 72–83.
Rahner, Hugo. 1965. *Man At Play*. New York: Herder.
Ralli, Augustus. 1932. *A History of Shakespearean Criticism*. London: Oxford University Press.
Rank, Otto, 1929. *The Trauma of Birth*. New York: Harcourt, Brace and Co.
———. 1936. *Will Therapy and Truth and Reality*. New York: Knopf.
Rawls, John. 1971. *A Theory of Justice*. Cambridge, Mass.: Harvard University Press.
Richards, I. A. 1928. *Principles of Literary Criticism*. New York: Harcourt, Brace and Co.
Ricoeur, Paul. 1967. *The Symbolism of Evil*. Boston: Beacon Press.
Riley, Mathilda White, and Anne Foner. 1968–72. *Aging and Society*. New York: Russel Sage Foundation.
Ritter, Joachim, and Karlfried Gründer, eds. 1971–95. *Historisches Wörterbuch der Philosophie*. 9 volumes. Basel: Schwabe.
Ritzer, George. 1997. *The McDonaldization Thesis. Explorations and Extensions*. London: Sage.
———. 1999. *Enchanting a Disenchanted World. Revolutionizing the Means of Communication*. London: Sage.
Robbins, Rossel Hope. 1966. *The Encyclopedia of Witchcraft and Demonology*. New York.
Roheim, Géza. 1934. *The Riddle of the Sphinx. Our Human Origins*. New York: Harper and Row.
———. 1943. *The Origin and Function of Culture*. New York: Nervous and Mental Disease Monographs 69.

——. 1950. *Psychoanalysis and Anthropology*. New York: International University Press.
Rorty, Richard. 1989. *Contingency, Irony, and Solidarity*. Cambridge, Cambridge University Press.
Rosenau, Helen. 1979. *Vision of the Temple: The Image of the Temple of Jerusalem in Judaism and Christianity*. London: Oresko.
Rummel, R. J. 1986. 'War Isn't This Century's Biggest Killer'. *Wall Street Journal* (7 July): p. 11.
Russell, Bertrand. 1946. *Ideas that Have Harmed Mankind, Man's Unfortunate Experiences with His Self-Made Enemies, Including Sadistic Impulses, Religion, Superstition, Envy, Economic Materialism, Pride, Racism, Sex, Superiorities, Creeds, and Other Evil Things*. Girard, Kan.: Haldeman.
——. 1956. *An Outline of Philosophy*. New York: Vintage.
——. 1957. *Why I Am Not a Christian*. New York: Simon and Schuster.
——. 1981. 'A Free Man's Worship', in Klemke, pp. 55–62.
Russell, Jeffrey Burton. 1977. *The Devil. Perceptions of Evil from Antiquity to Primitive Christianity*. Ithaca: Cornell University Press.
——. 1981. *Satan. The Early Christian Tradition*. Ithaca: Cornell University Press.
——. 1988. *The Prince of Darkness. Radical Evil and the Power of Good in History*. Ithaca: Cornell University Press.
Sabibi, John. 1992. *Social Psychology*. New York: Norton.
Sahlins, Marshall D. 1976. *The Use and Abuse of Biology: An Anthropological Critique of Sociobiology*. Ann Arbor: The University of Michigan Press.
Sandmeyer, Peter. 1994. 'Der lange Marsch ins Paradies'. *Stern*, No. 52 (December): pp. 16–28.
Scheler, Max. 1961. *Man's Place in Nature*. Boston: Beacon Press.
Schelling, Friedrich Wilhelm Joseph. 1809. *Philosophische Untersuchungen des Wesen der menschlichen Freiheit*.
Schimmel, Annemarie. 1976. 'The Celestial Garden in Islam', in *The Islamic Garden*, pp. 11–40.
Schrag, Calvin O. 1961. *Existence and Freedom. Towards an Ontology of Human Finitude*. Chicago: Northwestern University Press.
Schulman, M. 1991. *The Passionate Mind*. New York: Free Press.
Schulz, W. 1965. 'Das Problem der Angst in der neueren Philosophie', in Ditfurth, pp. 1–23.
Scruton, David L., ed. 1986. *Sociophobics. The Anthropology of Fear*. Boulder: Westview Press.
Seligman, and Johnson, eds. 1931. *Encyclopedia of the Social Sciences*.
Sharma, Arvind. 1987. 'Satan', in Eliade, vol. 13, pp. 81–84.
Shields, Rob., ed. 1992. *Lifestyle Shopping. The Subject of Consumption*. London: Routledge and Kegan Paul.
Siegal, Julius. 1957, October. The Lure of Pinball. *Harper's 215*, 1289, 44–47. Quoted by Caillois (1961, 183).
Simmel, Georg. 1971. *On Individuality and Social Norms. Selected Writings*, ed. Donald N. Levine. Chicago: University of Chicago Press.
——. 1978. *The Philosophy of Money*. London: Routledge and Kegan Paul.

———. 1980. *Essays on Interpretation in Social Science*, trans. Guy Oakes. Manchester: Manchester University Press.

Simson, Otto von. 1965. *The Gothic Cathedral: Origins of Gothic Architecture and the Medieval Concept of Order*. 2nd ed. Bollingen Series 48.

Small, A. W. 1905. *General Sociology*. Chicago: University of Chicago Press.

Smelser, Neil J. 1962. *Theory of Collective Behavior*. London: Routledge and Kegan Paul.

———. 1987. 'Depth Psychology and the Social Order', in Alexander et al.

Smelser, Neil J., and Richard Münch, eds. 1990. *Theory of Culture*. Berkeley: University of California Press.

Smith, E. Baldwin. 1956. *Architectural Symbolism of Imperial Rome and the Middle Ages*. Princeton: Princeton University Press.

Snyder, C. R. 1994. *The Psychology of Hope. You Can Get There From Here*. New York: Free Press.

Solomon, Robert C. 1976. *The Passions*. Garden City, N.Y.: Doubleday.

Sophocles. 1959. *The Complete Greek Tragedies*. Volume 2. Chicago: University of Chicago Press.

Sorokin, Pitrim A. 1962 [1937–1941]. *Social and Cultural Dynamics*. 4 volumes. New York: Bedminster.

Spencer, Herbert. 1946. 'The Physiology of Laughter', in Spencer, *Essays in Education and Kindred Subjects*. London: J. M. Dent.

Spengler, Oswald. 1926. *The Decline of the West. Perspectives of World History*. 2 volumes. New York: Knopf.

Spielberger, Charles D., and Robelio Diaz-Guerrero, eds. 1976. *Cross-Cultural Anxiety*. Washington, D.C.: Hemisphere.

Sproul, Barbara. 1979. *Primal Myths*. New York: Harper.

Stevenson, Margaret Sinclair. 1920. *The Rites of the Twice-Born*. London: Oxford University Press.

Stewart, Stanley. 1966. *The Enclosed Garden*. Madison: University of Madison Press.

Stouffer, S., et al. 1949. *The American Soldier: Combat and Its Aftermath*. Princeton: Princeton University Press.

Stringer, Christopher, and Clive Gamble. 1994. *In Search of the Neanderthals: Solving the Puzzle of Human Origins*. London: Thames and Hudson.

Stumpfl, Robert. 1936. *Kultspiele der Germanen als Ursprung des mittelalterlichen Dramas*. Berlin: Junker und Dunnhaupt. Quoted by Rahner (1965, 84).

Suetonius. 1967. *History of Twelve Caesars, Translated into English by Philemon Holland, Anno 1606*. Charles Whibley, ed. New York: AMS Press. Quoted by McClung (1983, 76–77).

Sumner, W. G., and A. G. Keller, eds. 1927. *The Science of Society*. 4 volumes. New Haven: Yale University Press.

Szakolczai, Árpád. 2000. *Reflexive Historical Sociology*. London: Routledge.

Száraz, György. 1980. 'Jokes'. *Élet és Irodalom* (5 April). [In Hungarian.]

Taine, Hippolyte. n. d. *History of English Literature*, trans. Henri Van Laun. New York: A. L. Burt.

Teilhard de Chardin, Pierre. 1959. *The Phenomenon of Man*. New York: Harper and Row.

———. 1964. *The Future of Man*. New York: Harper and Row.
Thacker, Christopher. 1979. *The History of Gardens*. Berkeley: University of California Press.
Thomas Aquinas, Saint. 1988. *Summa theologiae, I.* 76, 5. (original work written 1265–1273). Quoted by Gehlen (1988).
Tillich, Paul. 1936. *The Interpretation of History*. New York: Scribner.
———. 1951–63. *Systematic Theology*. 3 volumes. Chicago: University of Chicago Press.
———. 1952. *The Courage to Be*. New Haven: Yale University Press.
———. 1965. *Ultimate Concern. Tillich in Dialogue*, ed. T. M. Brown. New York: Harper and Row.
Torrance, Thomas. 1981. *Divine and Contingent Order*. Oxford: Oxford University Press.
Toynbee, Arnold. 1934–61. *A Study of History*. 12 volumes. New York: Oxford University Press.
———. 1972. *A Study of History*. New ed., revised and abridged by the author and Jane Caplan. Illustrated. London: Thames and Hudson.
Trachtenberg, J. 1943. *The Devil and the Jews*. New Haven: Yale University Press.
Tropp, Martin. 1990. *Images of Fear: How Horror Stories Helped Shape Modern Culture (1818–1918)*. Jeffers, North Carolina: McFarlan.
Tuan, Yi-fu. 1979. *Landscapes of Fear*. New York: Pantheon Books.
Turner, Victor. 1969. *The Ritual Process*. Chicago: Aldine.
Tylor, E. Burnett. 1877. *Primitive Culture; Researches Into the Development of Mythology, Philosophy, Religion, Language, Art, and Custom*. New York: Henri Holt.
Vaihinger, Hans. 1913 [1911]. *Die Philosophie des Als-Ob. System der theoretischen, praktischen und religiösen Fiktionen der Menschheit auf Grund eines idealistischen Positivismus*. 2. Aufl. Berlin: Reuther und Reichard.
———. 1924. *The Philosophy of 'As If', a System of the Theoretical, Practical and Religious Fictions of Mankind*. London: Routledge and Kegan Paul.
Vallacher, Robin R. 1997. 'Grave Matters'. *Psychological Inquiry* 8, No. 1: pp. 50–54.
Vallacher, Robin R., and A. Nowak, eds. 1994. *Dynamical Systems in Social Psychology*. San Diego: Academic Press.
Van Gennep, Arnold. 1960. *The Rites of Passage*. Chicago: University of Chicago Press.
VandenBos, G. R., and B. K. Bryant, eds. 1989. *Cataclysms, Crises, and Catastrophes: Psychology in Action*. Washington, D.C.: American Psychological Association.
Voegelin, Eric. 1956. *Order and History*. Volume 1, *Israel and Revelation*. Baton Rouge: Louisiana State University Press.
———. 1968, [1959]. *Science, Politics and Gnosticism*. Chicago: Henry Regnery.
Voltaire. 1756. *Essai sur les moeurs et l'esprit des Nations*. n. p.
Waite, R. G. L. 1977. *The Psychopathic God: Adolf Hitler*. New York: Basic Books.
Walsh, David. 1990. *After Ideology. Recovering the Spiritual Foundations of Freedom*. San Francisco: Harper.
Watson, J. B. 1925. *Behaviorism*. New York: Norton.
Weber, Max. 1930. *The Protestant Ethic and the Spirit of Capitalism*. London: Allen and Unwin.

———. 1958. 'The Social Psychology of the World Religions', in Gerth and Mills, pp. 267–301.
Wechsler, Harlan J. 1990. *What's So Bad About Guilt? Learning to Live with It since We Can't Live without It*. New York: Simon and Schuster.
Weinberg, Steven. 1977. *The First Three Minutes. A Modern View of the Origin of the Universe*. New York: Basic Books.
———. 1992. *Dreams of a Final Theory*. New York: Pantheon.
White, Leslie A. 1949. *The Science of Culture. A Study of Man and Civilization*. New York: Grove Press.
Widmann, Wilhelm. 1931. *Hamlets Bühnenlaufbahn. 1601–1877*. Leipzig: Tauchnitz.
Wiener, Philip P., ed. 1968–1974. *Dictionary of the History of Ideas*. 5 volumes. New York: Scribner.
Wildavsky, Aaron, and Karl Dake. 1990. 'Theories of Risk Perception: Who Fears What and Why?'. *Daedalus* (Fall): pp. 41–60.
Willey, M. 1929. 'The Validity of the Culture Concept'. *American Journal of Sociology* 35.
Williams, Raymond. 1958. *Culture and Society 1780–1950*. Harmondsworth: Penguin.
———. 1976. *A Vocabulary of Culture and Society*. London: Fontana.
———. 1981. *Culture*. London: Fontana.
Williams, Rosalind H. 1982. *Dream Worlds: Mass Consumption in Late Nineteenth-Century France*. Berkeley: University of California Press.
Wills, Garry. 1995. 'Hunt For the Last Judgment'. *New York Review of Books* (20 April): pp. 53–58.
Wilson, Edward O. 1975. *Sociobiology: The New Synthesis*. Cambridge, Mass.: Harvard University Press.
———. 1978. *On Human Nature*. Cambridge, Mass.: Harvard University Press.
Wissler, Clark. 1916. 'Psychological and Historical Interpretations of Culture'. *Science* 43.
———. 1929. *An Introduction To Social Anthropology*. New York: Holt and Co.
Závada, Pál. 1984. *Kulákprés. Dokumentumok és kommentárok a parasztgazdaság történetéhez* [Squeezing the Kulaks. Documents and commentaries on the history of peasant farms]. Budapest: Művelődéskutató Intézet.
Zeidner, Moshe, and Norman S. Endler, eds. 1995. *Handbook of Coping*. New York: Wiley.

INDEX

advertising industry, 263, 270–271
Aeneid, 117
Aeschylus, 141, 176–177, 214
agapé, 174
age of uncertainties, 198, 200
Albee, Edward, 201
Albertus Magnus, 50
Aldrich, Charles Robert, 6, 89
Alexander, Jeffrey, C., 40, 42
alien world, 36, 48, 54, 60, 64–66, 69–92, 110, 122, 132–133, 171, 187–188, 196, 219, 235, 244, 246, 256–259, 275–277,
    and cataclysms 75
    experience of, 85–87
    and extinction of animal species 78, 82–83
    and extinction of civilizations, 82–83
    and genocide, 82–83
    a "hostile universe", 86
    a hypothesis, 1–3
    and killing fields, 56
    and mortality, 74–79
    and space, 74
    and "Terror of History", 89
    and time, 74
    transformed into a Moral Universe, 151–154
alienation, 38
Allegre, Claude, 75, 88, 93
Ambrose, St., 50
American football, 232
    aggression and the sublime, 232
amesha spentas, 50
Ananké, 172–173
angels, 50–53, 66–67, 217
    belief in, 67
    in Talmudic literature, 67
    "they are terrible", 207
Angel of Death (Becker, Ernest), 58–59
animal symbolicum (Ernst Cassirer), 54–55
animated cartoons,
    comic destruction of the world, 250–255
    triumph over causality, 255–256
anomie, 10, 60
Ansbacher, Heinz L., 277
Ansbacher, Rowena R., 277
anthropology, philosophical, 57
Antigone, 141–142, 214–216
anxiety, 83, 123, 133, 147, 162, 165, 187, 219, 237, 245, 275, 279

anxiety *(cont.)*
  age of, 184
  creating cultural patterns (May, Rollo), 31
  creative, 45
  existence, 55
  and freedom, 63–64
  Freudian, 29
  ontological, 29
  reduction, 50–53
  and social death, 33
  theories of, 31
anxiety, *see also* fear
Apocalypse, The, 150–151
Apocrypha, 50–53, 156
Apollo, 230–231
Apollonian illusion, 206–208
  music, 206
Apollonius Rhodius, 233
Arabesque, 122
Arató, Andrew, 283
Archer, J. 44
archetypes of the city, 117
architecture
  "mirror of the world", 120
  symbolic, 113–136
Aretino, 238
Ariosto, 110
Aristotle, 81, 200, 278
Aronson, Elliott, 27
"as if", the world of, 227, 277–281
Athenian politics, 200
Atlantis, 122
Augustine, St., 21, 29, 42, 50, 86–87, 122, 143–145, 150, 154, 156, 162, 171, 180
authentic existence, 165
authenticity, loss of, 133
automobile
  and cathedrals, 126
  center of the world, 125–127
  "horizontal transcendence", 126
  and "human world", 125–127
  symbol of the cosmos, 125–127
  symbolism, 125–127
avataras, 50

Axelrod, R., 44
axis mundi, 105, 119, 126

Bachelard, Gaston, 115, 134, 271
Bachofen, Johann Jakob, 233
Bacon, Francis (the painter) 86
Bacon, Francis (the philosopher), 195
Bailey, P., 135
Bain, R., 42
Balint, Alice, 88
ball, 243
Baló, Béni, 193
baptism, 154, 161
Barber, Benjamin, 135
Barnard, Frederick M., 284
Barkow, Jerome, H., 30, 43–44
Baron, Reuben, M., 33
Barrow, John D., 202, 281
Barth, Karl, 21, 145, 180
Barthes, Roland, 125, 208
Baruk, Henri, 175–176
basilica, 120–121
Bateson, P.P.G., 284
Baudelaire, Charles, 86, 150–151, 156, 180, 208
Baudrillard, Jean, 135
Baumeister, Roy F., 33, 44–45
beauty
  in art, 217
  and divine grace, 217
  and horror, 207–209, 217
  intoxicating, 208
  natural, 217
  sexual function, 208
  and sublimation, 208
  world of, 205–218
Becker, Ernest, 2, 37, 47, 58–60, 67–68, 85
Beckett, Samuel, 65–66, 171, 214
Bellah, Robert, 42
Benchetritt, Paul, 217
Bennett, T., 135
Beowulf, 117
Berger, Peter L., 2, 14, 40, 42, 60–61, 85
Bergson, Henri, 20, 257
Berkeley, George, 281

Berlin, Isaiah, 155
Bernard, St., 190
Bernstein, Leonard, 201
Bible, *see also* Old and New Testaments
Big Bang, 73, 93, 96, 188, 196
Big Crunch, 188
Birth of Tragedy, The, 208
Bladerunners, 84
Blake, William, 144, 155, 200
Blumberg, Hans, 68
Boccaccio, Giovanni. 238
Bock, P.K., 42
bodhisattvas, 50
Bondi, Hermann, 108
Borkenau, Franz, 2, 35, 43, 53, 146
Bosch, Hieronymus, 7, 86
Bossuet, Jacques-Bénigne, 21
Botticelli, Sandro, 265
Bourdieu, Pierre, 42
Boyd, James W. 43, 155
Branam, George C., 217
Brewer, N.J., 135
Brittain, A., 133
Broch, Hermann, 88
Brown, Norman O., 68
Bryant, B.K., 45
Buck, R., 44
Buddhism, 155, 237
Bultmann, Rudolf Karl, 21, 24–25
Burgess, Ernest W., 27
Buss, David M., 29, 32–33, 44–45
Buytendijk, Friedrich J., 219, 242–243
Bynum, Caroline Walker, 150, 155
Byron, George Gordon Noel, 156

Cabal and Love (Schiller), 215–216
Caillois, Roger, 240, 242
Cain (Byron), 150
Calvin, Jean, 63, 67, 161
Campbell, Colin, 135
Campbell, Joseph, 81, 86, 108, 115, 134, 144–145, 154–155
Campbell, L.B., 218
Camus, Albert, 7, 86, 192–193
Capek, Karel, 201
car, *see also* automobile

Carnap, Rudolf, 201
carnivals of consumption, 128
Carroll, John, 156, 160, 176–177
Carroll, Lewis, 203
Cassirer, Ernst, 2, 31, 54–55, 67, 281
cataclysms, 75
catharsis, 213
cathartic devices, 213–216
cathartic "machinery", 213–216
cathedral, 120–121, 126
    imago mundi, 119–122
    symbol of the sacred, 119–122
center of the world, *see also* myths of centrality
    moral, 95–96
    physical, 95–96
    where is it?, 94–96
certainty and uncertainty, 198–201
    see also uncertainty
Cervantes, Saavedra, Miguel de, 202, 238
chance
    and freedom, 227
    and play, 225–227, 229, 243
    of survival, 78
Chance and Necessity (Jacques Monod), 187–188
Changeux, Jean-Pierre, 135, 202, 281
chaos
    and cosmos, 60, 97, 115, 117, 119–121, 124–133, 227, 232, 253
    hyle, 81
    silva, 81
Chaplin, Charlie, 256–257
Charlemagne, 120
Chevalier, Jean, 101, 110, 134–135
Chomsky, Avram Noam, 202,
Christianity, 59, 94, 154–156
    see also Judeo–Christian tradition
Church and State, 192
church, *see also* cathedral
civilizing process (Norbert Elias) 42
Cid, le, 212
city
    archetypes of, 117
    imago mundi, 116–118

city *(cont.)*
    symbol of the cosmos, 116–118
        the sacred, 117–118
Civilization, *see also* "culture"
    and "alien world", 69–90
    as a construct, 275–282
    and fear, 34–37
    generation of, 36–37
    Greco–Roman, 63
    Judeo–Christian, 63
    and meaningful roles 186,189
    modern and Gnostic, 89
    and "Moral Universe", 137–156
    and myths of centrality, 91–136
    and play, 219–244
    and "Rational World", 181–204
    and religion, 40
    as sum total of protective devices, 57
    and "world of guilt", 37, 157–180
        beauty, 205–218
        jokes, 245–260
        symbols, 47–68, 275–282
        trivialities, 261–274
Civilization and Its Discontents (Sigmund Freud), 180
civilizations, their collapse, 61–66
civilizing process (Norbert Elias), 6, 24
clowns, 255
Cohn, Norman, 285
comic destruction of the world, 250–255
Comito, Terry, 110
competitive individualism, 31
Comte, Auguste, 22
Condorcet, Antoine-Nicolas de, 42
Conklin, P.S., 217–218
Connes, Alain, 197, 202, 281
Conrad, Joseph, 7, 86
consecration, 96, 108
constructs, 4, 197, 277–281
    culture as a ..., 17, 275–282
consumer civilization, 238, 261–275
contingency, 200
    see also chance
Cook, K.S., 27
Copernican revolution, 61–62, 93–94
Copernicus, 61–62, 93–94

Cordelia (King Lear), 211
cosmic ball game, 233–237
cosmic drama (Teilhard de Chardin), 87
Cosmic Tree, 107
Cosmides, Leda, 30, 44
cosmolgy, 94–96
cosmos
    and chaos, 60, 97, 115, 117, 119–121, 124–133, 227–232, 253
Coulter, Jeff, 38
Courage to Be (Paul Tillich), 164
Crawford, C.B., 43
Creation myths, 235–237, 263–264
Creon (Sophocles), 216
crime in the cities, 84
crisis,
    age of, 184
    cultural, 63–66
    spiritual, 63–66
cultural anxiety buffer, 32–34
cultural patterns, 23
culture, *see also* civilization
    as adjustment, 41
    as artifact, construct, 17, 275–282
    autogenesis, 19
    a "codified hero system", 59
    a constellation of symbols, 47–68
    contradictions of, 42
    definitions of, 17–19, 41–45
    as domination, 23
    as a "dynamic system", 22
    as "enterprise of world building", 60–61
    and entropy, 22–23, 43
    and environment, 43
    existential dimension of, 11–16, 24–26
    functionalist approach, 23
    functions of, 42
    genesis of, 19–26
    and genetics, 23
    Islamic, 123–124
    and meaning, 54
    motive forces of, 35
    as problem solving system, 41
    psychological definitions, 17

culture *(cont.)*
    as second nature, 22, 60
    social genesis of, 23–24
    as social heritage, 17
    and social integration, 10–11, 23
    and sociobiology, 23
    structures, 23
    as sum of acts of sublimation, 41
        patterns of learned behavior, 41
    as sum total of artifacts, 42
    a "symbolic action system", 59
    as a system of adjustment, 17, 23
        habit patterns, 42
        rules, 17
    theories of, 35
    and thermodynamics, 22–23, 43
    tragic contradictions, 20
culturgens, 23
culturology, 22
Curtius, E.R., 110
Cusanus, Nicolaus, 96
Cynics, 171, 202
Csurka, István, 170

Daiches, David, 89
Dake, Karl, 39
Damasio, Antonio, 44
dance, 234–237
    in the Judeo–Christian tradition, 235
danse macabre, 7, 209
Dante, Alighieri, 51, 95, 106, 191, 272
Darwin, Charles, 5. 62,
Darwinian revolution, 94
Darwinism, Neo-, 14, 23
Dasein, 164, 179
Davidson, Gustav, 50, 64, 66–67
Davies, Paul, 108, 181, 196–198, 202, 243
Dawkins, Richard, 5, 43
death
    acceptance of, 40, 43
    denial of, 40, 45
    of God, 199
    ignoring it, 45
    mourning, 10, 13

"premature", 12–14
    and religion, 42
    and social psychology, 45
    terror of, 58–60, 67
    of Truth, 199, 279
Debord, G., 128
decadence, 86
deconstruction, 199
defense mechanisms, 36, 41, 55–57, 67
    see also protective devices
defilement, 138–140
Delumeau, Jean, 37, 41, 45, 53, 85, 155, 157, 179
delusion, mass, 62
delusional remolding of reality, 62
Demiurge, 72
demons, 64, 50, 66–67, 84, 147
Denial of Death, The (Ernest Becker), 58
Dennett, Daniel C., 202, 281
Denzin, Norman K., 44
Denny, Reuel, 243
Descartes, René, 63
Desdemona, 212, 215
Devereux, Georges, 286
Devil, 121–122, 131–132
    God's, 149–150
    see also Satan
Diaz-Guerrero, Robelio, 41
Diener, Ed, 38
Dienst, Karl, 62, 68
Dionysus, 43, 154, 230–231
Dior, Christian, 281
Dirks, Nicholas B., 286
Disneyland, 128
Ditfurth, Hoimar von, 286
Divine Wisdom, 235
Dodds, E.R., 44
Don Carlos, 214
Don Juan, 163
Dostoyevsky, F.M., 7, 86,137, 176
Douglas, Mary, 39, 42
Dr. Jekyll, 84
drama of the absurd, 86
Drexel, Jeremias, 101
Dryden, 200

duality
    of Church and State, 193
    European, 192–195
    of human person and the raison
        d'état, 192–195
    of individual and society, 192–195
    of sacred and profane, 192–195
Dubos, René, 190
Ducis, Jean-Francois, 211–212, 217
Duino Elegies, (Rainer Maria Rilke), 207, 217
Dumézil, Georges, 281
Duns Scotus, 146
Durand, Gilbert, 196, 262, 271
Durham, W., 23
Durkheim, Émile, 1, 5, 10–11, 23, 25, 35, 39, 40, 43
Dürrenmatt, Friedrich, 214
dying, sociology of, 44
Dyson, Freeman, 82, 196, 244, 281

Easton, Susan, 135
Egmont (Goethe), 214–215
Eibl-Eibesfeldt, I., 44
Einstein, Albert, 282
Eisteinian revolution, 94
Einsteinian universe, 96
Ekman, Paul, 44
élan vital, 20
Electra, 210
Elementary Forms of Religious Life, The, (Émile Durkheim), 10
Elert, Werner, 42
Eley, Geoff, 286
Eliade, Mircea, 2, 43–44, 86, 96–97, 108–109, 117, 134, 271, 281
Elias, Norbert, 4, 6, 24, 39, 42–43
Eliot, T.S., 291, 213
Ellis, M.J., 240–243
Elysian Fields, 109
emotions, "basic", 44
energy and form, 20
enterprise of world building, 60–61
Epimetheus, 69–70
Epstein, S., 44
Erasmus, 202, 238

Eros and *Thanatos*, 30, 45, 173–175
eternal return, 106, 128
Euripides, 151–152, 155–156
European "duality", 192–195
Evans-Pritchard, E., 108
evil 3, 11, 83, 137–156,
    in the Bible, 142–143
    condensation of, 148
    it does not exist, 143
    it is not a substance, 144
    origins of, 149–146
    role in generating civilization of, 137, 138
    sources of, 140–146
    rationalization of, 140–146
    transformation of natural evil into sin, 157–159
    transformed into positive human experience, 151–154
    theories of (St. Augustine), 144
évolution créatrice, L', 20
Ewen, Stuart, 135
existential problems, 24–26
exorcism, 154
extracanonical writings, 50–53

faits sociaux, 11, 16, 40, 43
Falk, Pasi, 135
Fall, *see* original sin
Faust, 122, 163, 270
fear, *see also* anxiety
    and aging, 27–28
    and altruistic behavior, 33
    and anthropology, 16–26, 37
    and civilization, 1–4, 5–37, 29–32
    and coping, 34
    and death, 27–28
    of dying 34
    in ethology, 29
    and evolutionary biology, 32–34
    in evolutionary psychology, 29–34
    existential, 15–16, 34–37, 41, 45
        and civilization, 24–26
    and existential terror, 32
    and experimental psychology, 28–29, 32–34

fear *(cont.)*
   and Freudianism, 29
   history of the concept, 44
   in learning theory, 29
   man-made, 39
   in motivational research, 29
   paradox of, 6–7, 34
   in political science
   as produced by culture, 39
   and psychology, 26–34
   in psychology of emotions, 29
   "situational", 15–26
   and social adaptation, 33
   and social psychology, 26–28
   and sociology, 8–16
   of suffering, 33
   and survival, 32–34
   types of, 25, 29–30, 41
Featherstone, Michael, 29–130
Febvre, Lucien, 4
felix culpa, 159
Fellini, 260
Fichte, 22
fictions, *see* constructs
Fink, Eugene, 239, 234, 242–243
Fleurs du Mal, Les (Charles Baudelaire), 208
Flood, the, 152–153
Florian, Victor, 34, 45
Folkman, S., 45
Folsom, Jospeh K., 42
Foner, Anne, 27
Fontane, Theodor, 62
football, 228–232
Ford, C.S., 41
Foucault, Michel, 1, 5, 23, 41–42, 132
Foucauldian domination, 132–133
Frazer, James George, 43, 281
freedom, 1–5, 49, 55, 62–64, 97, 125–127, 145, 152, 155, 163–5, 184, 199, 200, 207, 219–244, 261, 276
   and anxiety, 63–64
   and the ball, 229–230, 232
   and chance, 227
   of clown, 255–256

   escape from, 67
   of God, 235–237
   loss of, 160
   and necessity, 55
   negative, 155
   paradox of, 227–228
   positive, 155
Freud, Anna, 45, 67
Freud and human unhappiness, 171–172
Freud, Sigmund, 1, 5, 9, 18, 29–33, 39, 43, 45, 53, 56, 62, 67, 72, 84, 86, 153, 168, 171–177, 200, 207–208, 245, 257, 259
Freudian revolution, 64
Frobenius, Leo, 44
Fromm, Erich, 30–31, 35, 45, 53, 67–68, 180
Fry, Christopher, 190

Galilean revolution, 94
Galileo, Galilei, 202
Galnoor, Itzhak 259–260
Gamble, Clive, 88
Garden of Eden, 71, 91–113, 135, 148, 150, 158
   after the Fall, 101
garden
   cosmic symbol, 105–107
   enchanted, 105–107
   enclosed, 109
   French, 104, 110
   as human universe, 103–107
   iconography of, 109
   of love, 110
   Persian and Islamic 104–107
   Renaissance, 104, 110
Garden, Solomon's, 109
Gardner, C., 135
Geertz, Clifford, 2, 4, 41–42, 54
Gehlen, Arnold, 25, 42, 57, 60, 67,
gene-culture coevolution, 23
Gervinus, G.G., 218
Gheerbrant, Alain, 101, 110, 134–135
Gibbs, Nancy, 83
Gilgamesh, 117
Gnostic cosmology, 72

Gnosticism, 89, 150
God, 108, 111, 120–124, 131, 143, 152–153, 233–237
  as center of the world, 95–96
  dancing, 235–237
  freedom of, 235–237
  at play, 233–237
  responsibility of, 143
God and play, 233–237
Gödel, Kurt, 197, 281
gods, 154
Goethe, Johann, Wolfgang, 62, 122, 215, 270,
Gogarten, Friedrich, 42
Golden Apple, 108
Golden Fleece, 108, 129
Goleman, Daniel, 44
Golgotha, as the center of the world, 102–103
Gorer, Geoffrey, 41
Goslin, David A., 27
Gottdiener, Mark, 135
Gould, Stephen Jay, 88, 281
Gray, Jeffrey, 44
Greek mysteries, 235
Greenberg, Jeff, 32–34
Gregorian chant, 206
Gregory of Nyssa, 145
Greta Garbo, 208
Grillparzer, Franz, 215
Groos, Karl, 240–242
Grünewald, Mathias, 7
guilt, 3, 5, 157–181, 224–225, *see also* sin
  "boiling cauldron" of, 175–176
  in Christian tradition, 161–164
  and consumer society, 177–179
  and crisis of western civilization, 176–177
  and culture, 37
  and destruction, 180
  depressive, 176
  and double bind, 169
  feeling, 45
  and generation of western civilization, 157–180
  and hiding of values, 167–168
  and human responsibility, 162–164
  and innocent society, 177–178
  and libido, 172–173
  as "modality of existence", 164
  as moral category, 164
  and negative Social Contract, 169–170
  and neurosis, 160, 171–177
  pathological, 173–177
  philosophy of, 164–165
  politics of, 165–170, 180
  price of, 159–161
  psychology of, 171–177
  religion of, 161–164
  —repentance–salvation, the drama of, 159–160
  and show trials, 166
  socially disruptive, 173–177
  source of suffering, 174–177
  and stigma, 166–167
  and suffering, 171–172
  and unhappiness, 171
  types of, 160
guiltless civilization, 177–179
Gundolf, F., 218
Gutmann, Joseph, 120

Habermas, Jürgen, 42
habitus (Norbert Elias), 24
Haecker, Theodor, 259
Haefner, H., 37, 44
Halliday, F.E., 218
Hamlet, 201, 210, 212, 214, 218
  adaptations, 211–213
Hankiss, Elemér, 180, 218
Hanna and Barbara, 260
happiness and unhappiness, 71–72, 208
happy ending, 211
Harding, Thomas G., 23
harmony
  and disharmony, 181–185
  in music, 205–206
  and neurosis, 181–185
  Pythagorean, 182
  in universe, 182, 227

Harmony of the World, The, 182
Harrington, Allan, 68
Harrison, Jane, 44
Hartle, James, 197
Hasek, Jaroslav, 88
Hawking, Stephen, 196
Hawkingian universe, 96
Hawkins, A. 135
Hayek, Friedrich August von, 43
Heaven, 95, 100
    Gate of, 121–122
Hedvig (Ibsen: *Wild Duck*), 214
Hegel, Georg Wilhelm Friedrich, 14, 21, 87, 218,
Heidegger, Martin, 7, 9, 13, 29, 45, 89, 106, 116, 132, 134, 64, 171, 179, 225–281
Heisenberg, Werber Karl, 281
Hell, 95, 148
    Gate of, 119–121, 155
Heller, Jospeh, 201
Heraclitean dualities, 239
Heraclitus, 144, 155
Herder, Johann Gottfried, 1, 5, 22, 42–43, 57
Herold, Alajos, 194
Hesiod, 141
Hick, John, 145, 154–155
Himmler, 195
Hinduism, 89, 94–95, 154, 155
Hitler, 68, 175
Hobbes, Thomas, 35, 43, 202, 278
Hochmah, 235
Homans, George C., 43–44
Homer, 141
hominid species, 88
Homo ludens, 219–221, 280–281
Homo sapiens, culpabilis, tragicus, comicus, 280–281
Horkheimer, Max, 66
Horney, Karen, 29, 45, 67
horror, *see also* fear
    and beauty, 207–209, 217
    of dark and empty universe, 187
    of infinity, 62
hortus deliciarum, 110

house
    as *imago mundi*, 113–116
    as symbol of the human world, 134
Hrabal, Bohumil, 201
hubris, 142, 163
Hugo, Victor, 150, 156, 215
Huizinga, Jan, 220–223, 226, 231–232, 235, 237–239, 242–244
human adventure, 56
human condition, 13, 59, 87
humankind
    a handicapped species, 57, 60
    an "as yet undetermined animal", 57
Hume, David, 278
humor, *see* jokes
Hungarian War of Liberation, 193–194
Hungary, politics of guilt, 165–170
Huxley, Aldous, 201
Huxley, Julian, 191, 201
Huxtable, Ada Louise, 135
Hoyle, Fred, 96
hyle, chaos, 81
hyperanxious animal, 7

Ibsen, Henrik, 214
Ideal Landscape (Curtius), 110
Illusion
    joy of, 278
    will to, 278
image of the world, 113–137
imago mundi, 113–137
immortality, 128, 267–268
impressionism, 238
incompatibility of life and the physical world, 72–80
Industrial Revolution, 238
innocent society, 177–178
Inquisition, 193
instinct
    of death, 173–175
    of destruction, 173–175
    of life, 173–175
intensity of existence, 207, 210
Investiture Controversy, 182
Irenaeus, 144, 154–155
Islam, 94, 154

Islamic culture, 123–124
Islamic Gardens, The, 110
Izard, Caroll E., 44

James, William, 58–59
jardin des délices, 129
Jaspers, Karl, 42, 86, 116, 164–165, 201–202
Jefferson, Thomas, 200
Jensen, Adolf E., 44
Jenyns, Soame, 89
Jerome, St., 135, 145
Jerusalem, 118
    Celestial, 117
    Temple of, 95
Joyce, 88
John Chrysostom, St. 145
John Paul II, 109
Johnson, Samuel, 86, 89
jokes
    and childhood experience, 249
    and clowns, 255–256
    as "comic borderline situations", 260
    comic destruction of the world, 250–255
    cynical, 251
    derailing the train of thought, 246–255
    destruction of causality, 253–256
    and "descending incongruity", 259
    and dreams, 249–250
    flirting with the alien world, 251, 256–259
        with terror, 256–259
    and freedom, 248–255
    and Freud, 248–252
    and human autonomy, 257
    and laughter, 245–245
    logical, 251
    machinery of, 246–248, 257–259
    obscene, 259
    political, 251, 259
    and psychic energy, 248–249
    a "serious business", 258
    sexual, 251
    switching between levels, 249
    techniques of wit, 259
    tendency jokes, 249
    and terror, 257–259
    theories of, 259
    they are dangerous, 246–248
    triumph over causality, 253–256
    types of, 251
    world of, 245–260
Jones, Ernest, 201
Judaism, 50, 94, 110, 154–156
Judeo–Christian tradition, 237
Jung, Carl G., 44–45, 134, 155, 201, 270–271, 281
jungle,
    as chaos, 81
    metaphysical, 84–85
    physical, 82
    psychological, 83–84
    social, 82–83
Jurassic Park, 129
justice, 11

Kádár, János, 135
Kafka, Franz, 7, 88, 176, 201
Kant, Immanuel, 1, 5, 15, 21–22, 42–43, 57, 146, 287, 292
Kantrowity, Barbara, 67
Kaplan, Abraham, 202
Kardiner, Abram, 18, 31
Karinthy, Ferenc, 258
Kastenbaum, R., 44
Kearl, M., 44
Keller, A.G. 41
Kellerman, H., 44
Kepler, Johannes, 67, 94, 181–185, 201
Keplerian revolution, 94
Kierekegaard, Sören, Aabye, 7, 13, 29, 86–87, 116, 132, 145, 164–165, 179, 201
killing fields, 76, 79
King Lear, 210, 214
Klein, Stephen B., 44
Klemke, E.D., 290
Kluckhohn, Clyde, 4, 17–19, 41, 43
knowledge,
    Kingdom of, 188

Koestler, Arthur, 68, 182–185, 201–202, 259
Köhler, Joachim, 155
Kon, Igor, 29
Kowinski, William, 135
Koyré, Alexander, 290
Kristeva, Julia, 1980
Kroeber, A.L., 4, 17–19, 41, 43
Kroker, Marilouise, 133, 217
Kulturreligion, 21
Kundera, Milan, 88–89, 198, 202
Küng, Hans, 201

La divina commedia, 51
La fin de Satan (Victor Hugo), 150
Laing, S., 135
Langer, Suzanne K., 211
Langman, Lauren, 128–133, 135
language, 200
language games, 200
laughter
    and terror, 257–259
    and Judeo–Christian tradition, 245–246
    laughter, a dynamic process, 257–2560
    types of, 247
Lavinia (Eugene O'Neill), 210
Lazarus, R.S., 44–45
Le Corbusier, Charles-Edouard Jeanneret, 48, 66
Leary, Mark, 33
LeDoux, Joseph, 44
Lehrman, Karl, 104–105, 109–111, 123–124, 135
Leibniz, Gottfried Wilhelm, Freiherr von, 144, 146, 159, 278
Lemonick, Michael D., 291
Lepley, William M., 28
Lerner, Melvin J., 33, 40
Lessa, William A. 43
Leviathan, 155
Levin, Ira, 202
Lévi-Strauss, Claude, 85, 281
Lewis, Richard, 178
liberalism, 238

liberum arbitrium, 145
libertinism, 180
life
    as an adventure, 40
    expectancy, 40
    emergence of, 88
    enhancement of, 14
    holiness of human, 192
    lies, 56
    meaning of, 181, 189–192
    purpose of, 181, 189–192
    tragic, 40
    unfinished experience, 56
Lifton, Robert Jay, 68, 85, 176
light, as symbol, 124
Lindzey, Gardner, 27
Lirondelle, André, 217
Lloyd, Alan T., 67
Lockard, J.S., 67
Locke, John, 278
Logos, 235
Long Days Journey Into Night, A (Eugene O'Neill), 142, 215
love, 171–174, 180
    and perfumes, 266–267
    source of suffering, 172
Ludwig, Otto, 218
Lukes, Steven, 259–260
Lumsden, Charles J., 23
Luria, S.E., 56
Luther, Martin, 63, 161
Lüttge, Willy, 42

Macbeth, 214, 216
Macbeth, Lady, 211
MacCrimmon, K.R., 45
Malamud, Bernard, 201
Malinowski, Bronislaw, 19, 41–42
Malone, Kemp, 218
mandala, 110, 105–106
Mandelbrot set, 197
Mander, Raymond, 217–218
Manicheanism, 64, 155
manipulation of the consumer, 131–133
Mannheim, Karl, 31
Marcel, Gabriel, 202

Marcus Aurelius, 171, 202
Marcuse, Herbert, 30, 35, 43, 45, 180
Maritain, Jacques, 21
Mark Twain, 260
Marks, Isaac M., 41, 44
Marlowe, Christopher, 122
martyrs, 153–154
Marx, Karl, 5, 15, 22, 179, 202–203, 238
mathematics and the universe, 196–198
Mauss, Marcel, 14
Maxwell's demon, 229
May, Rollo, 7, 31, 37–38, 53.
maya, 86, 94–95
McClung, William A., 81, 100–102, 109, 118, 122, 131, 134, 135,
McGinn, Bernard, 155
McGinty, Park, 43
McKendrick, N. 135
McPherson, James Alan, 202
Mead, Margaret, 201
meaning , 3, 47, 54–55, 59–61, 181, 271, 276, 276, 282,
   creation of, 59–61
   of life, 186–192
   loss of, 63–66, 185–187
   and meaninglessness, 26
   and reason, 185–192
   "webs of significance" (Clifford Geertz), 54
   search for, 54–55
meaningful order, 60
meaningful roles, 190
meaningful universe, an illusion, 187
meaninglessness, 60, 186
Mecca, 122
Merton, Robert, 42
Meyer, Conrad Ferdinand, 111, 106–107
Michelangelo, 7
Mikulincer, Mario, 34, 45
Miller, Daniel R., 67
Miller, Davis L., 238–239, 243–244
Miller, Henry, 201
Miller, Michael B., 135
Mills, C. Wright, 201
Milton, John, 150

Mind of God, The (Paul Davies), 196–198, 243
Mitchenson, Joe, 217–218
Mitscherlich, Alexander, 195, 202
Mitscherlich, Margaret, 195
Modern Times (Chaplin), 256–257
Mohan, Robert Paul, 42,
Moltmann, Jürgen, 219, 236, 238
Monod, Jacques, 74, 88, 91–92, 147, 201, 187–189
mono-demonism, 147
Montesquieu, Charles-Louis de Secondat, 43
Moore, Barrington, Jr., 292
Moore, G.E., 191
Moorhead, Hugh S., 190–192, 201
Moral Universe, 3, 137–156
morality and reason, 192
Moses, 245–246
mosques, 122–124
mourning, 39
Mowrer, Robert R., 44
Moynihan, Elizabeth B., 109–100, 135
Mozart, Wolfgang Amadeus, 163
Munitz, Milton K., 293,
Muraven, Mark, 33
Murdock, J.P., 42
music, 205–207
   baroque, 206
   contemporary, 206
   Gregorian, 206
   as a symbolic sphere, 205–206
Musil, Robert, 88
Myers, David G., 38
mystery and perfumes, 268–269
myth, 49, 108, 275, 280
   of Beauty and the Beast, 208
   of center of the world, 3, 91–137
   and civilization, 53
   Christian, 157
   of Creation, 117, 263–264
   of the Fall, 157
   functions of, 156
   of "Moral Universe", 137–156
   Pandora's Box, 140
   of "Rational World", 181–203

myth *(cont.)*
  of world of perfumes, 261–276
  theories of, 43–33
  work, 153

naturalism, 238
naval of the world, 100, 103, 114, 118
Neimeyer, Robert A., 44
Neo-Platonism, 151, 207, 265
Nero, 183
Nesse, Randolph M., 44, 67
New Jerusalem, 101–102, 120, 122, 125, 131
Newton, Isaac, 197, 200, 281,
Nicholas de Cusa, 96
Niebuhr, Reinhold, 21, 24, 29, 165
Nietzsche, Friedrich Wilhelm, 15, 42, 57, 66, 69, 86, 152, 171, 180, 199, 202, 208, 278
Nilsson, M.P., 44
nomos, a meaningful order, 60–61
Norberg-Schulz, Christian, 114, 116, 120–121, 131, 134
Nowak, A., 44

Oedipus, 139, 166. 210, 214, 217
Oedipus complex, 201, 224
Old Testament, "J" and "E" versions, 99–100, 108–109
Olson, Sigurd F., 191
Olympus, Mount, 94
Ophelia, 212
Orestes, 139
Origen, 150
original sin, 145, 157–159, 161–162, reinterpreted, 161–164, 179
Ortner, Sherry B., 286
Othello, 214–217
Ott, Heinrich, 161–162
Otto, Walter F., 44
Ovid, 135, 141

pain, 80
palliative measures, 62
  see also protective devices
Pandora's Box, 140

panic, 38
Paradise Lost, (John Milton), 150
Paradise, 71, 96, 98–102, 107, 109, 118, 130–131
  as Fortress of Innocence, 99–100
  myths, 109
Paradisiacal garden, 109
Parkin, David, 25, 43, 85
Parrott, André, 120
Parsons Talcott, 10, 12–15, 40–41, 53,
Pascal, Blaise, 13, 86–87, 145, 162, 171
Patai, Raphael, 101, 120
Pattazzoni, 154
Paul, St., 150, 159, 200
Paulhus, D.L., 67
Paulsen, F., 218
Penrose, Roger, 197, 281
perfume, 261–276
  chemistry, 262–263
  and Creation myths, 263–264
  epiphany of personality, 269–270
  and escape from time and mortality, 267–268
  and eternity, 268
  experience of plenitude, 263–264
  and femininity, 269–270
  and harmony, 271
  and the Holy Grail, 261–263
  Icarian symbols, 264
  and illusion, 270–271
  and immortality, 267–268
  and the magic, 268–269
  and mystery, 268–269
  and mythology, 4, 261–276
  and passions, 266
  posters, 261–276
  research, 271
  and romantic love, 266–267
  and sensuality, 265–266
  and sex, 266–267
  and spirituality, 265
  sun symbols, 263
  symbols of life, 263, 267–268
  symbols of transcendence, 263–265
peripheral position of humankind, 92–93
personality, the epiphany of, 269–270

Peters, R., 44
Petronius, 39
Philon of Alexandria, 135
philosophical anthropology, 57
Piaget, Jean, 202, 241
Piehler, Paul, 81, 117. 158
pinball, 243
Pinocchio, 131–132
Plato, 122, 151, 155, 184–185, 234, 237, 244, 278
Platonic perfection, 182
Platonic spirituality, 231
play, 3, 219–244
    in the 20th century, 238–239
    American football, 232
    as basis of civilization, 220–221
    and chance, 225–227
    chess, 228
    in consumer society, 238–239
    cosmic ball game, 233–237
    Creation through..., 235–237
    dance, 234–237
    definitions, theories, 220, 240–242
    and Dionysian raptures, 231
    Easter ball game, 233
    for its own sake, 238–239
    and freedom, 219–244
    frivolity and ecstasy, 239–240
    and God, 233–237
    Homo ludens, 219–221
    as a human world, 219–244
    in history, 237–238
    as illusion, 222–224, 237, 243
    and immortality, 225
    interaction of chance and the human will, 225–227
    loss of, 237–239
    not all is play, 221–222
    pinball, 243
    pool, 228
    as a protective device, 219–244
    role of the ball, 229–237
    and rules of the game, 227–229, 231
    sacred and profane, 228–237
    a sacred ceremony, 231–232
    as a sacred place, 221, 228–237
    and self-limitation, 227
    soccer, 228–232
    and spirituality, 231–232
    spiritualization of conflict, 229–230
    symbol of human existence, 239
    tension between Apollo and Dionysus, 230–232
    and tragic experience, 239
    and uncertainty, 225–227
    versus reality, 221–224
    a victory over the laws of nature, 229–230
    a virtual world, 219–220
    a world of justice, 223–224, 231
    a world of innocence, 224–225
    as world symbol, 233–237, 239–240
pleasure principle, 72, 89
Plessner, Helmuth, 57, 259
Plumb, J.H., 135
plurality, devices 199
Plutchik, R. 44
poetry
    "exclusive", 209
    "inclusive, 209
polytheism, 149, 152
Pompidou, Centre Georges, 128
Popper, Karl, 43, 86, 201, 275
porta coeli, 121–122
Postman, N., 135
postmodernism, 199, 279
Prague
    "defenestration", 181–182
    the revolution of 1968, 238
premature animal, 57
process theology, 143
profane and the sacred, 96–97, 108, 134, 192–195, 228–229, 230–237
Prometheus, 70
protective devices, 62, 66, 198, 118–121, 137–140, 172, 205–206, 275–282
    arabesques, 123
    baptism, 138
    beauty, 207–208
    Bowdlerization of tragedies, 211–213
    "cathartic machinery", 213–216
    exorcism, 138

protective devices *(cont.)*
　jokes, 245–260
　in the Middle Ages, 139–140
　perfumes, 261–276
　physical 47–48
　play, 219–244
　purification, 138–140
　rationalization of evil, 140–146
　Satan, 146–151
　Shakespeare adaptations, 211–213
　Shakespeare criticism, 212–213
　symbolical, 47–53
Protestant discipline, 64
Protestant Ethic and the Spirit of Capitalism, The (Max Weber), 12
Proust, Marcel, 88
Prudentius, 159
pseudepigrapha, 50–53
Pseudo Dionysus, 51
Psychological Abstracts, 27
Ptolemy, 94–95, 184–185, 201
purification, 154
Pyszczynski, Tom, 32–34, 45, 53
Pythagorean mysticism, 122
Pythagoreans, 151

Quine, W.V.O., 201

rabbinical literature, 50–53
Radcliffe-Brown, A.R., 39
Ragon, Michel, 128
Rahner, Hugo, 233–236, 239–240, 243–244, 259
raison d'état, 192
Ralli, Augustus, 218
Rank, Otto, 29–30, 35, 67, 173–174
Rational World, The, 3, 181–293
rationality
　Apollonian, 183–184
　of evil, 140–146
　and mass murder, 195
　murderous, 195
　Promethean, 183–184
　two faces of, 181–185
rationality, *see also* reason
Rawls, John, 224, 242

realism, 238
realists versus formalists, 202
reason
　formalist approach, 196–198
　and harmony of the universe, 181–185
　and meaning, 185–192
　and morality, 192
　pragmatic and reflective, 66
　realist approach, 196–198
　and uncertainty, 195–201
　and unreason, 192–195
Rebel, The, (Albert Camus), 192
religion
　genesis of, 42
　as mass delusion (Freud), 62
　origin of, 10–11
　sociology of, 11–12
resignation, 62
Revelation, 51
Rhode, Erwin, 44
Richards, I.A., 209
Richerson, P.J., 43
Ricoeur, Paul, 134, 138–139, 154, 271, 281
Riesman, David, 243
Riley, M.W., 27
Rilke, Rainer Maria, 3, 205, 207, 217
rites of passage, 108
rituals, protective, 108
Ritzer, George, 135
Robbins, 155
Robespierre, Maximilien, 194
Roheim, Géza, 35, 2, 18, 20, 30, 41, 43, 53
Roman bath, as *imago mundi*, 135
Romance of the Rose, The, 110
Rome, 118
Romeo and Juliet, 211–212
Roosevelt, Eleanor, 201
Rorty, Richard, 199–201, 203, 279
Rosenau, Helen, 120, 122
Rossetti, Dante Gabriel Charles, 215
Rousseau, Jean-Jacques, 194
Rowlands, Samuel, 109
rules of the game, 227–229, 243

Rummel, R. J., 83
Russel, Bertrand, 86–89, 198, 201, 281
Russel, Jeffrey Burton, 84, 88, 95–96, 138, 143, 149, 154–156
Russian anarchists, 194–195

Sabibi, John, 27
sacred, and the profane, 96–97, 108, 134, 192–195, 228–229, 230–237
Sacred Mountains, 100–101, 110
Sade, Marquis de, 86, 180
Sahlins, Marshall, D., 23
salvation history, 24–25, 86
Salvation, the great drama of, 159
Sandmeyer, Peter, 101
Sappho (Franz Grillparzer), 215, 233
Sartre, Jean-Paul, 7, 29, 81, 225, 279
Satan, 84, 108, 121, 125, 131–132, 154–155
   as center of the world, 95–96
   in Christian thought, 150–151
   a human invention, 146–151
   in Judaic tradition, 149
   in literature, 150–151
   in the Kabala, 149
   a protective device, 146–151, 155
   in the Talmud, 149
   in The New Testament, 156
   in The Old Testament, 156
Scheler, Max, 2, 25, 42, 57–5860
Schelling, Friedrich, Wilhelm Joseph von, 7, 155
Schiller, Johann Christoph Friedrich, 202, 214–216
Schimmel, Annemarie, 105, 111
Schleiermacher, Friedrich, 6
Schopenhauer, Arthur, 80, 86, 171, 218
   on laughter, 259
Schrag, Calvin O., 165, 179
Schreindorfer, Lisa, 34
Schubert, Franz, 209
Schücking, L.L., 218
Schulman, M., 44
Schulz, W. 38
Scruton, David L, 25, 37–39, 41, 53, 85, 89

Seidman, Steven, 42
Sein, 179
Seneca, 7, 86, 171, 179, 237
Service, Elman R., 23
sex and perfumes, 266–267
Shakespeare, 214, 238
   adaptations, 211–213, 217
   criticism, 212–213
Shanghai stock exchange, an *imago mundi*, 134
Sharma, Arvind, 149, 150, 155
Sheppard, J., 135
shopping center
   as center of the world, 127–133
   as cosmic symbol, 127–133
   and eternity, 128
   as "human world", 127–133
   as *imago mundi*, 127–133
   as *jardin des délice*, 129
   as jungle, 129
   manipulation of the consumer, 131–133
   myths, 130
   negative myth, 132–133
   as Realm of the Devil, 131–132
   as a sacred place, 127–133
   as transcendental carnival, 129–131
   a Utopia, 129
shopping mall, *see* shopping center
Sidney Greenberg, 178
Siegal, Julius, 243
significance, 61, *see also* meaning
silva, chaos, 81
Simmel, Georg, 20, 42,
Simson, Otto von, 120
sin, 11, 148
   original 3
   reversal of, 157–159
   and stigmatization, 161
sin, *see also* guilt
Sleepwalkers, The (Arthur Koestler), 201
Small, A.W., 25, 41
Smelser, Neil J., 40, 67
Snyder, C.R., 44
soccer, 228–232
sociobiology, 23

Sociological Abstracts, 8–9, 27
Socrates, 86, 202, 237
solidarity, 200
solitude of humankind, 92, 188
Solomon, Sheldon, 32–34, 44
Solomon's Temple, 120, 122
Sophocles, 141–142, 154, 214–216
Sorokin, Pitrim A., 88
Spencer, Herbert, 249, 257, 259
Spengler, Oswald, 22, 88
Spenser, Edmund, 110
Spielberger, Charles D., 41
Spinoza, Baruch, 7, 64, 202
Sproul, Barbara, 98, 108–109
Stalin, 175
Star Trek, 66
Statius, 39
Stevenson, Margaret Sinclair, 19, 119, 134
Stewart, Stanley, 109–110
stigmatizing, 166–167
stoicism, 10, 14, 64, 152, 239
Stouffer, S., 28
strategies
    Apollonian, 47–50, 66, 113, 192
    Dionysian, 66
    Promethean, 47–48, 66, 113, 192
stress, 38
Stringer, Christopher, 88
Stroedel, W., 218
Stumpfl, Robert, 233
Suetonius, 115
suffering, 40, 80, 88
Sumner, W.G., 41
survival
    of individual, 80
    of species, 80
Swanson, Guy E., 67
symbolic action system, 59
symbolic animal, 54–55
symbolic forms, 54
symbolic means of self-preservation, 32
symbolic spheres, 47–68, 271, 279
    the collapse of, 61–66, 210
symbolic strategies, 47–50
symbolic structures of culture, 47–68

symbolic systems, their collapse, 61–66, 210
symbolic voyages, 108
symbols, 2, 47–68
    architectural, 113–137
    and automobile, 125–127
    of center of the world, 91–137
    Chinese houses, 115
    of chaos, 134
    and city, 116–118
    and civilization, 53–66, 275–282
    of cosmos, 110
    definition, 276–277
    of eternity, 110
    functions of, 276–281
    and garden, 103–107
    and house, 113–116
    Icarian, 107, 264, 271
        perfumes, 264, 271
    of immortality, 59
    as protective devices, 47–53
    of life, 227
        perfumes, 263
    and light, 124
    loss of, 63–66
    and music, 205–206
    Navaho houses, 115
    Nero's Golden House, 115
    networks of, 184
    play as world symbol, 233–237, 239–240
        symbol of human existence, 239
    perfumes, 261–276
    and shopping mall, 127–133
    spheres of, 2, 47–68
    of sun, perfumes, 263
    system of, 92, 200
    towering edifice of, 60
    of transcendence, perfumes, 263–265
    of water, 110
    of world, 113–138
Szakolczai, Árpád, 89
Száraz, György, 170

Tabernacle, 113, 120, 125, 130–131, 134–135

Taine, Hippolyte-Adolphe, 43
Talmudic literature, 50–53, 67, 149
Tao, 237
Tasso, Torquato, 110
Tawney, Richard H., 31
Teilhard de Chardin, 21
Teilhard de Chardin, Pierre, 50, 87
television, 218
   magic of, 125
temple
   imago mundi, 119–122
   symbol of the sacred, 119–122
Temple of Jerusalem, 130, 134,
   as *imago mundi*, 120
Terror Management Theory, 21–34
terror, 32–37, 39, 91, 245
   anomic, 61
   of death, 58–60, 57
   of history, 86
   and laughter, 257–259
   of sin, 159
terror, *see also* fear, and anxiety
Tertullian, 150, 154
Testament
   The New, 138, 142–143
   The Old, 138, 142–143, 149, 152
Thacker, Christopher, 110
Thanatos and Eros, 30, 45, 173–175
theodicy, 144–146
theomachia, 148
Thomas Aquinas, St., 51, 57, 146
Thompson, E. P., 42,
threats, external and internal, 39
Tice, D.M., 45
Tillich, Paul, 7, 21, 24, 31, 29, 59, 84–85, 162–165, 179–180, 201, 281
timor servilis, timor filialis (Augustine, St.), 29
Tooby, John, 30, 44
Torrance, Thomas, 202, 244
totalitarian regimes, 195
Toulouse-Lautrec, Henri de, 86, 208–209
Toynbee, Arnold, 43, 83, 190, 201
Trachtenberg, J., 156
tragedies,

Elizabethan, 7, 213–216
Greek, 86, 171, 179, 209–210, 213–216
Jacobean, 7, 213–216
modern, 213–316
Renaissance, 86, 213–216
Romantic, 213–216
tragedy
   essence of life, 13
   universal ... of man, 86
transcendence, horizontal, 126
transcendence, vertical, 126
transcendental carnival, 129–131
Tree of Life, 103, 106, 107
trivialities, 4, 261–276, 281
Tropp, Martin, 41
Tuan, Yi-fu, 37, 41, 108, 243
Turner, Victor, 41
Tylor, E. Burnett, 41, 43

Ulrici, Hermann, 218
ultimate concerns, 35–37, 49, 85,
ultimate equation, 198
uncertainty, 198–201, 225–227
   wisdom of, 202
Uncle Vanya (Anton Pavlovich Chekhov), 142
universe
   comprehensible, 186, 196
   harmony of, 227
   pointless, 186
   The Moral, 137–156
Updike, John, 201
Ur-Angst (Kern Horney), 29
utilitarianism, 180, 283
utopia, 129
Übermensch, 163

Vaihinger, Hans, 197, 277–279, 282
Vallacher, Robin R., 44–45
Valley of Death, 85
Van Gennep, Arnold, 41
VandenBos, G.R. 45
Vera Angi, 167–168
Vico, Giambattista, 22, 43
Virgil, 81, 135

Vischer, F.T., 218
Visit of the Old Lady, The (Friedrich Dürrenmatt), 214
vocabularies, 200
Voegelin, Eric, 2, 54, 89
Vogt, 43
Voltaire, Francois-Marie, Arouet, 42
Vulgate, 236
Vygotsky, L.S., 39

Waite, R.G.L., 180
Waiting for Godot (Samuel Beckett), 65–66
Walker, H., 135
Walsh, David, 83
Walt Disney, 260
Watson, John B., 44
Weber, Max, 10–12, 19, 35, 53–54, 68
Wechsler, Harlan J., 178
Wehrung, D.A., 45
Weinberg, Steven, 108, 186, 191, 202, 281

Wheel of Fortune, 243
White, Leslie A., 22, 242
Widmann, Wilhelm, 217
Wiener, Philip, P., 298
Wildavsky, Aaron, 39
Wilde, Oscar, 251–252
Willey, M., 41–42
Williams, Raymond, 4, 135
Williams, Rosalind, H, 135
Wills, Garry, 148
Wilson, Edward O., 5, 23, 25, 43
Wilson, F.P., 218
Wissler, Clark, 41–42
wit, *see* jokes
Witten, Edward, 196
world of "as if", 277–281

Závada, Pál, 166–167, 180
Zeidner, Moshe, 45
Zeus, 69
Zoroastrianism, 50–51, 95, 150, 155

CENTRAL EUROPEAN CLASSICS

Series Editor: Timothy Garton Ash, St Antony's College, Oxford

"Half a continent's worth of forgotten genius." **The Guardian**

The Sorrowful Eyes of Hannah Karajich
Ivan Olbracht

A lyrical, deeply moving story of love and the pain of emancipation, set in the now vanished world of rural East European Jewish village life. Olbracht's novella is both a great love story and a marvellous portrait of a world that modernity threatened and Hitler destroyed.

1999 194 pages, 963-9116-47-5 paperback $16.95 / £9.99

The Adventures of Sindbad
Gyula Krúdy

In these marvellously written tales, Sindbad, a voyager in the realms of memory and imagination, travels through the centuries in pursuit of an ideal of love that is directed as much at the feminine essence as at his individual lovers.
This deeply autumnal book, full of resonances and associations, is an erotic elegy to the dying Habsburg empire.

1998 206 pages, 963-9116-12-2 paperback $16.95 / £9.99

The Doll
Bolesław Prus

The Doll is the greatest Polish novel of the nineteenth century. The city of Warsaw, under Russian rule in the late 1870s, is the setting for this sweeping panorama of social conflict, political tensions and personal suffering. The middle-aged hero, Wokulski, bold and successful in business, is being destroyed by his obsessive love for the frigid, aristocratic society 'doll' Izabella.

1996 702 pages, 1-85866-065-3 paperback $19.95 / £12.50

Be Faithful Unto Death
Zsigmond Móricz

Be Faithful unto Death is the moving story of a bright and sensitive schoolboy growing up in an old-established boarding school in the city of Debrecen in Eastern Hungary. Misi, a dreamer and would-be writer, is falsely accused of stealing a winning lottery ticket.
The novel is brimming with vivid detail from the provincial life that Móricz knew so well and shot through with a sense of the tragic fate of a newly truncated Hungary.

1996 332 pages, 1-85866-060-2 paperback $16.95 / £9.99

Prague Tales
Jan Neruda

Prague Tales is a collection of Jan Neruda's intimate, wry, bitter-sweet stories of life among the inhabitants of the Little Quarter of nineteenth century Prague. These finely tuned and varied vignettes established Neruda as the quintessential Czech nineteenth century realist, the Charles Dickens of a Prague becoming ever more aware of itself as a Czech, rather than an Austrian city.

"How often is a reviewer privileged to make so marvellous a discovery?"
Michael Hulse, **The Spectator**

1993 368 pages 963-9116-23-8 or 1-85866-058-0 paperback $16.95 / £9.99

Skylark
Dezső Kosztolányi

An acknowledged masterpiece of twentieth century Hungarian fiction *Skylark* is a portrait of provincial life in the Austro–Hungarian monarchy at the turn of the century. Set in the autumn of 1899, it focuses on one extraordinary week in the otherwise uneventful lives of an elderly Hungarian couple. Their ugly spinster daughter, nicknamed Skylark, has left them for a holiday. At first the couple, is devastated by her absence, but they rediscover the delights of small-town society life, reaching the shocking conclusion that their daughter is a burden to them.

1993 240 pages, 963-9116-66-1 or 1-85866-059-9 paperback $16.95 / £9.99

Coming Winter 2000

National Cultures at the Grass-Root Level

Antonina Kłoskowska, Head of the Research Unit of Culture and Politics of the Polish Academy of Sciences

The major dilemma this volume addresses is the function of national identity in a modern society, for despite the trend towards globalization, the world continues to be riddled with national conflict.

Kłoskowska looks at the controversy between two competing concepts of the origin of the nation—political and ethnic. She examines the central issues of the argument, and in particular, the characteristics and effects of ethnic differences on personal identity and the appropriation of national culture. Her theories are based upon autobiographies by individuals belonging to various national minorities in Poland and other areas where ethnic borders are blurred. In her conclusion, Kłoskowska takes the view that national cultures are either 'open' or 'closed' and stresses the importance of participating in more than one cultural medium.

National Cultures at the Grass-Root Level is rich in information on contemporary theories of the nation, on its origin, character and future, and offers a deep insight into the complex and often ambiguous reality of national attitudes.

450 pages
963-9116-83-1 cloth $49.95 / £31.00

AVAILABLE TO ORDER AT ALL GOOD BOOKSHOPS OR CHECK OUT OUR WEBSITE WWW.CEUPRESS.COM FOR FULL ORDERING DETAILS.